ETHICAL AND ENVIRONMENTAL CHALLENGES TO ENGINEERING

ETHICAL AND ENVIRONMENTAL CHALLENGES TO ENGINEERING

Michael E. Gorman, Matthew M. Mehalik,
Patricia H. Werhane

University of Virginia

Prentice Hall
Englewood Cliffs, New Jersey 07458

Library of Congress Cataloging-in-Publication Data

Gorman, Michael E. [date]
    Ethical and environmental challenges to engineering / MICHAEL E. GORMAN,
MATTHEW M. MEHALIK, and PATRICIA H. WERHANE
        p.   cm.
    Includes bibiliographical references.
    ISBN 0-13-011328-X
    1. Engineering ethics Case studies.   2. Environmental ethics Case
studies.   3. Engineering design—Environmental aspects Case studies.
I. Mehalik, Matthew M.   II. Werhane, Patricia Hogue.   III. Title.
TA157.G7117   2000
174'.962—dc21   99-39256

Editorial director: *Charlyce Jones Owen*
Acquisitions editor: *Karita France*
Editorial/production supervision: *Edie Riker*
Buyer: *Tricia Kenny*
Cover director: *Jayne Conte*
Marketing manager: *Ilse Wolfe*
Editorial assistant: *Jennifer Ackerman*

This book was set in 10/12 Times by East End Publishing Services, Inc.,
and was printed and bound by RR Donnelly & Sons, Inc. The cover was
printed by Phoenix Color Corp.

Printed in the United States of America

10   9   8   7   6   5   4   3   2   1

ISBN   0-13-011328-X

Prentice-Hall International (UK) Limited, *London*
Prentice-Hall of Australia Pty. Limited, *Sydney*
Prentice-Hall Canada Inc., *Toronto*
Prentice-Hall Hispanoamericana, S.A., *Mexico*
Prentice-Hall of India Private Limited, *New Delhi*
Prentice-Hall of Japan, Inc., *Tokyo*
Pearson Education Asia Pte. Ltd., *Singapore*
Editora Prentice-Hall do Brasil, Ltda., *Rio de Janeiro*

CONTENTS

Part II: Environmental Challenges for Engineers

Part III: Engineering and Environmental Challenges in Developing Countries

Preface

This is a casebook for engineers, managers, and students interested in design and managerial dilemmas in a variety of settings. The book grew out of our growing conviction that case method teaching is the best pedagogy to teach design, environmental engineering, managerial, and engineering ethics. The cases we include are real-life events, not hypothetical situations, that mirror situations that students will actually face. Our approach involves extended, fine-grained case studies with multiple dilemmas that encourage students to engage in moral imagination. Many of the cases present a cultural dimension that is especially important as global diversity becomes an essential part of design, management, and engineering.

All the cases in this collection have been taught at least once, some of them several times, to undergraduates or graduate students in engineering and management programs. They have been taught in courses in business ethics, engineering ethics, managerial ethics, engineering management, design, and environmental ethics. The Unilever cases have also been used in entrepreneurship and corporate venturing courses.

This book can be used as a main text or it can compliment other texts as a casebook to accompany any engineering ethics, environmental ethics, applied ethics, social studies of science, entrepreneurship, sustainable business, or business ethics course.

Work on this book and many of the cases in it were supported by the Societal Dimensions of Ethics Science and Technology Program of the National Science Foundation (grant numbers SBR-9618851 and SBR-9743172). Support was also provided by the Darden Foundation, the Olsson Center for Applied Ethics, and the Batten Center for Entrepreneurial Leadership at the Darden Graduate School of Business Administration, and the School of Engineering and Applied Design at the University of Virginia. Further support was supplied by the Geraldine R. Dodge Foundation. Our thanks go to Prentice Hall's reviewers, Richard Wilson at Towson State University and Ronald Glass at University of Wisconsin–La Cross, for their helpful comments. We also wish to thank Wendell Dunn, R. Edward Freeman, and Ingrid Soudek for their encouragement and support. The editors and managers at Darden Educational Materials Services, Margaret Gorman, and Karen Musselman were invaluable in preparing the manuscript.

ETHICAL
AND
ENVIRONMENTAL
CHALLENGES
TO ENGINEERING

1

INTRODUCTION

Michael E. Gorman
Professor of Technology, Culture,
and Communications and Systems Engineering

Matthew M. Mehalik
Ph.D. candidate, Systems Engineering

Patricia H. Werhane
Ruffin Professor of Business Ethics, Senior Fellow,
Olsson Center, Colgate Darden School of Business

This book presents a series of full-length case studies accompanied by background readings that illustrate how one can integrate ethical and environmental challenges into engineering decisions, especially ones early in the design process. These cases will be useful for engineers in a variety of disciplines, including systems engineering, and they should also be useful to those who manage engineers and to those who wish to know more about how technology can address global problems.

We begin with the thesis that the best pedagogical method to teach design, environmental engineering, and engineering ethics is through the case study approach. This approach is used widely in law, medicine, and business (Lynch, 1997; Self & Ellison, 1998). Case studies are also being used increasingly to teach engineering design (Richards et al., 1994). There is growing evidence that experts acquire much of their knowledge through cases and examples (Kolodner, 1993; Kolodner, 1991).

James Rest's extensive research (Rest, 1988) concludes that moral reasoning skills (and by analogy, engineering and environmental considerations) can be taught to adults. Such skills are best taught, Rest and his colleagues argue, through the case method. Students are exposed to real-life situations that illustrate some particular set of issues. Students then are asked to develop criteria for reasoning through these dilemmas that take into account ethical and environmental concerns. In this book we focus on real-life cases, typically with more than one decision point. Hypothetical cases have a place in engineering education, but in our experience, students need to see multiple examples of how ethical dilemmas are handled in the real world. They also need to see the kind of detailed information available to actual decision makers. Real-life events pose multiple dilemmas for which there is no one simple right answer. These cases are useful not only as illustrations but also as ways to encourage the imagination of engineering students to think more creatively about their work. The idea is to challenge readers to think broadly about ethical issues, environmental issues, and the practicality of their creative inventions. Accompanying these cases are a set of short theoretical articles that serve as background foundational considerations to which readers can appeal to justify their case analyses.

A case study approach to engineering ethics produces at least three positive outcomes:

1. Through practice, students internalize these reasoning processes so that such processes become habitual ways of dealing with new engineering dilemmas. Lecturing about ethics and testing students on ethical theories and principles is useful, but it is hard for students to translate this kind of knowledge into practice. Cases constitute a kind of virtual apprenticeship, in which students can apply ethical principles to actual situations and discuss the outcomes with each other and with a faculty mentor.
2. By exposing engineering students to a variety of situations where the design criteria, environmental issues, and thus resolutions of the cases, are not simple, students are encouraged to think imaginatively about design. This thinking is amplified by considering issues such as the impact of technological systems on the environment and on those groups traditionally underserved by technology. Moral imagination involves recognizing the role, scheme, or mental model that one is adopting, disengaging from it, and evaluating alternative perspectives and courses of action. Engineers need to engage in moral imagination in the earliest stages of the design process—this allows them to see how an apparent technological improvement looks from other perspectives. This kind of imagination is similar to thinking about the needs of a user when designing a product (Norman, 1993) but has an additional ethical component. For example, even if the product fits a user's mental model and needs, will it harm the environment or have a negative impact on a particular group or culture?
3. Case studies can encourage engineers to think about how they will assume leadership roles. Most graduates from schools of engineering at universities will eventually find themselves in managerial positions; those who do not will still end up serving as team leaders. In the cases we develop students are placed in managerial as well as engineering decision roles. This dimension of these cases further stimulates students to think about design from a number of differing perspectives.

With these outcomes in mind, the cases in this book:

1. Give illustrations of designs that are environmentally friendly and economically viable.
2. Demonstrate that design always involves ethical considerations.
3. Help to develop the moral imagination of engineering students in order to face ethical challenges in their professions.
4. Increase student skills in making ethical design decisions via a case-based approach, involving multiple dilemmas that stem from a detailed description of a real-world problem.
5. Present stories that will inspire engineering students. Along with the inspirational tales, there are some cases of engineering heroes who try to make a better world. Accompanying these success stories are examples of what to avoid; for instance,
   a. Designs that fail because they do not meet standards of commonsense morality or the challenges of preserving the environment.

b. Designs that are created with good ethical motives but fail either because they are impossible to produce or because the inventor cannot create a market for them.

c. Designs that are created with sound engineering, ethical, and/or environmental criteria but run into difficulties because of unforeseen background social, cultural, religious, or emotional conditions.

As you read and analyze the cases, consider the following:

1. Evaluate the decision at issue, based on the evidence at the time, using moral reasoning skills.
2. Evaluate and challenge the assumptions and framework of the decision from perspectives that appear to introduce points of view that seem irrelevant to the issues at hand but that will turn out to be central to the outcome of the case.
3. For cases dealing with design: Consider the importance of a product, its viability, its marketability, and its substitutability from a managerial as well as from an engineering perspective. Ask questions such as: Is this product essential? Is designing, manufacturing, or marketing this product this way the only option? What are the environmental side effects of this product? What are its ethical side effects? What are its social side effects? Is there another viable approach to this design and this product that would better take into account a wider variety of perspectives or points of view?
4. For cases dealing with engineering disasters: Evaluate the design, the process, and the social and cultural context in which the events preceding the disaster are embedded. What are the elements that made this event possible? Could it have been prevented? What is the role of moral imagination in preempting such occurrences or preventing them from reoccurring?
5. For cases that involve engineering and environmental challenges in less developed countries, consider the cultural, social, and economic setting of the case. Given those conditions, how might your approach to this case be different than, say, if this challenge were situated in the United States or in another industrial country? How can one create a win-win situation that respects cultural and indigenous differences, that enhances the well being of the particular population, and that respects concerns for protecting and preserving the environment, all concerns facing the world today?

References Cited

Kolodner, J. (1993). *Case-Based Reasoning.* San Mateo, CA: Morgan Kaufmann Publishers, Inc.

Kolodner, J. L. (1991). Improving Human Decision Making Through Case-Based Decision Aiding. *AI Magazine* (Summer), 52-68.

Lynch, W. T. (1997). Teaching Engineering Ethics in the United States. *IEEE Technology & Society Magazine* (Winter), 27-36.

Norman, D. A. (1993). *Things That Make Us Smart: Defending Human Attributes in the Age of the Machine.* New York: Addison-Wesley.

Pritchard, M., and Holtzapple, M. (1997). Responsible Engineering: Gilbane Gold Revisited. *Science and Engineering Ethics*, 3(2), 217-230.

Rest, J. (1988). Can Ethics Be Taught to Adults? *Taking Sides*. 12:22-26.

Richards, L. G., Gorman, M. E., Kagiwada, J. K., Scherer, W. T., Pet-Edwards, J., Carlson, W. B., & Cline, A. C. (1994). Teaching Invention & Design. Paper presented at the 1994 ASEE Conference Proceedings.

Self, D. J., and Ellison, E. M. (1998). Teaching Engineering Ethics: Assessment of Its Influence on Moral Reasoning Skills. *Journal of Engineering Education*, 87(1), 29-34.

2

Moral Reasoning, Mental Models, and Moral Imagination

The study of ethics and the analysis of moral decision making are ancient traditions in the history of human life. Procedures for ethical decision making and reasonable standards for behavior are part of every society, and the description of values, moral beliefs, and mores is part of the way we define and describe people, institutions, cultures, and nations. Still, the task of justifying moral beliefs and integrating them into all parts of our daily lives, and the process of applying moral standards to all aspects of decision making is incomplete. In practice, these processes are difficult, because social, technological, and economic goals and demands of one's profession often appear to override moral considerations.

These difficulties are most obvious in engineering. Gusterson (1996) discusses the way in which nuclear weapons designers thought about ethical issues in private but thought it inappropriate to carry on much public discussion about them. Typical participants in weapons laboratories and in defense-related work are trained to compartmentalize; they cannot even talk about their work to others who do not have their security clearance. Engineers working on confidential projects for companies also have to compartmentalize. Some of this compartmentalization is necessary, but with it can come a similar bracketing of moral concerns and can lead to an unthinking compliance with the demands of a role.

This phenomenon, of compartmentalizing one's decision making, is illustrated by the famous obedience studies conducted by Stanley Milgram. Milgram wanted an empirical answer to a question raised by the Nazi holocaust: Could that kind of mass obedience happen here, in the United States? He was particularly disturbed by Nazis such as

Adolph Eichmann who contended that their behavior was excusable because they were "just following orders."

Milgram asked for volunteers to be paid participants in a study of the effects of punishment on learning. Each of these participants was assigned the role of a teacher, who had to administer an electric shock to a learner every time the learner got a wrong answer. The learner also appeared to be a volunteer participant, but in fact he was a confederate of Milgram's. Voltage of the shocks increased with each error, and the confederate's protests became more and more vehement, until he refused to participate in the experiment any further.

In the initial version of the experiment, the teacher heard the learner's protests through a wall: Milgram had tape-recorded them. The experimenter, in a white lab coat, responded to teachers' concerns by reminding them that the experiment required them to continue to administer shocks. To Milgram's surprise and dismay, a majority of participants continued to the highest level of shock, 450 volts (Milgram, 1974). In a later version of the experiment, Milgram arranged for the teacher to see the confederate as he shouted in pain, protested, and finally slumped over. When obedience remained high, Milgram added a permutation in which the teacher had to force the learner's hand onto the shock plate. Even in this condition, over one-third of the participants went to the highest level of shock, and many others went to high levels before quitting.

One possible explanation for this result is that participants bracketed or compartmentalized their ordinary responses in assuming a role subservient to the experimenter. Milgram demonstrated this with a clever permutation of the experiment, in which the experimenter was forced to volunteer to receive shocks while the confederate who would have been the victim ordered the participant to continue them. As soon as the experimenter, now strapped in the chair, objected, participants overruled the confederate and released him (Milgram, 1974).

Philip Zimbardo did a similar study in which he assigned volunteers at random to be prisoners or guards in a prison simulation. After six days, he had to cancel it because everyone had fallen too deeply into their roles . Zimbardo himself recalled preparing for a prison break by moving all the prisoners to another site, then sitting in the empty prison and listening with annoyance while a colleague asked him intellectual questions about the experiment. Zimbardo later wondered why he didn't treat the potential prison break as an opportunity to study rumor transmission. Instead, he fell victim to the rumor himself. Zimbardo became so absorbed in his role as prison director that he forgot his primary goal was to study the environment he had created. In the same way, engineers and managers can become so absorbed in their roles that they are unable to step out of them and see what they are doing from another perspective (Zimbardo, 1972).

We see, then, that integrating moral standards into practical decision making is not easy nor without risk. Yet, not to take into account normative considerations in practical affairs such as engineering and management decision making itself is a normative decision that ignores some elementary facts.

1. Most decisions, even those of science and technology, are choices. Sometimes there is a limited range of alternatives, even, sometimes, one acceptable choice. Still, not every engineer makes the acceptable decision in every instance.

2. Such decisions affect people, and an alternate decision (or inaction) would affect them differently.
3. Every decision or set of decisions is embedded in a belief system and culture that presupposes some basic values. For example, Union Carbide's decision to join the Indian government in building the Bhopal pesticide plant illustrates how what appeared to be technological and economic decisions have had enormous moral consequences for the company and for Bhopal residents living near the plant.

The term *ethics* or *ethical* is often used to refer to good behavior, and the term *morals* sometimes refers to the mores or norms of a particular community. In what follows we shall use these terms interchangeably. What is ethics? *Ethics* will be used as a generic word referring to the analysis, processes, and normative elements of decision making, including what is right or wrong, good or bad, how we should or should not act, and standards for judging conduct. An ethical judgment includes evaluating bad as well as good decisions, actions, motives, and behavior. Philosophical ethics is the study of moral discourse, the analysis of the nature of moral principles, and the study of the nature and justification of moral terms. In applied and professional ethics, including engineering ethics, part of its task is the study of the appropriateness of moral discourse in practice, for example, in the practice of engineering. Ethics is also more explicitly normative, and ethicians study, develop, and critique moral standards, moral rules, and procedures for ethical decision making. In engineering ethics the viability of these standards and procedures makes sense only when there is a possibility of their practical application in particular contexts. Ethics is also empirical or descriptive. The collection of information on professions, professional codes, or the belief structure of a particular institution or culture, or descriptive data analysis of actual decision-making habits of researchers, engineers, or managers are all part of such empirical work (Werhane, 1999). The development of the Dow Corning breast implant illustrates such an empirical study, and one cannot understand Dow Corning's recent predicament surrounding the breast implant controversy unless one carefully examines the development of the product.

The distinction between normative and descriptive ethics, although not clear-cut, allows us to distinguish what, in fact, is an accepted practice in a particular situation, and what someone or some culture deems to be acceptable or valuable as a standard for judging practices. The Eskom cases illustrates this distinction. In rural South Africa today many inhabitants of small villages tap into electric power without paying for it. This practice was developed during the apartheid era as a protest against the white Afrikaans government. Today this habit persists, and it is still an accepted practice in some of these communities to tap into the power lines. The task for a company such as Eskom, the South African national power company, is to change this behavior to what, under Mandela's leadership, is a more acceptable practice—paying for the use of electricity.

What is accepted practice, of course, is not always immoral, and this distinction leads to another: that between what is legal and what is ethical. What is enacted into law is often, but not always, grounded on moral principles; for example, on the basis of human rights or principles of justice. But no legal system covers all ethical considerations, and we often appeal to moral principles to judge laws or even legal systems. The Neemix cases exemplify these difficulties. Under Indian law it is permissible to patent products such as pesticides made from the neem tree. But the neem tree has been part of ancient religious and healing traditions in India for several thousand years. Do Indian patent laws defy ancient customs or indigenous property claims? What is acceptable in this circumstance?

SOME TRADITIONAL THEORIES OF MORAL REASONING

Let us turn to a brief discussion of some important components of a few prominent ethical theories. This discussion, although not inclusive or complete, will help us to develop a framework for moral reasoning and decision making that takes into account these theories and will have practical applications in engineering decision making as well.

Utilitarianism

When faced with an ethical issue in practice, one of the first questions concerns harms or costs versus benefits or gains. For example, as the large multinational company, Unilever, faces decisions concerning the design and development of environmentally sustainable processes and products, costs and benefits are part of its decision equation. Although this approach appears to be primarily economic, it is buttressed by a well-known ethical theory: utilitarianism. Utilitarianism traces its roots to two British thinkers, Jeremy Bentham and John Stuart Mill. Linking what is universally desired with what is desirable, a utilitarian argues, in brief, that what is most important and universally valued by almost everyone is the satisfaction of desires or interests, human pleasure or happiness, or the reduction of pain or suffering. According to utilitarians, whatever one's motives or intentions are, we tend to judge human action in terms of its outcomes, not merely on what an action was meant to achieve. A utilitarian measures harms and benefits in terms of their qualitative and quantitative merit, long-term versus short-term satisfaction, and also in terms of human interests, for example, freedom, health, autonomy, as well as well-being. The best sort of decision, the most useful, is one that maximizes human interests, best satisfies desires or pleasures, or minimizes costs or harms. According to Bentham, the principle of utility should be applied impartially over the range of persons affected by the decision or its outcomes, weighing each person and his or her interests equally. The best outcome is that which maximizes the interests or contributes to the well-being of the greatest number, or, minimally, costs least or reduces the most harms, all things considered (Bentham, 1789; 1948).

Utilitarianism raises some important considerations that should be factored into any decision-making process. These include:

- Any decision should be impartial, taking into account the broadest range of interests, treating each person equally, but only as an equal partner.
- An ideal decision is one that maximizes interests, pleasures, or well-being for the greatest number of people.
- Ordinarily, a decision is not acceptable if it results in a net increase of harms of any sort, even to a small number of people. However,
- In measuring utility it may be justifiable, in some cases, to sacrifice the well-being of a very few in order to prevent harms to or increase the well-being of a far greater number of people.

Making choices on the basis of utility is a very basic normative decision-making practice. This is standard fare in engineering and business, and utilitarianism is sometimes thought of as merely economic cost-benefit analysis. Cost-benefit analysis is clearly an utilitarian exercise, but we also measure the utility of maximizing other interests ranging from the utility of human freedom to the benefits of the intellectual enjoyment of an invention or the beauty of a design. Still, utilitarianism cannot always account for all that is at issue in a moral decision, even a very practical decision. As the DesignTex cases illustrate, it is difficult, on the basis of choosing the most efficient value-added design, to invest in the development of fabric that is compostable. Yet without companies that take on designing environmentally "green" products, the world will be faced with ecological disaster. How does one encourage companies to "do the right thing" environmentally when it is not to their benefit to do so?

Rule-Based Morality

In raising questions about utilitarianism we are appealing to a second set of traditional ethical theories, sometimes called *deontology* or rule-based morality. The father of this point of view is the eighteenth-century German philosopher, Immanuel Kant. Kant's theory is based on four premises. First, we do not hold animals or machines morally responsible. So ethics and moral decision making concern what is uniquely and universally human: our ability to make rational free choices independent of our circumstances. Second, although we cannot always predict or control outcomes, we can be self-regulatory in our decisions. So moral judgments focus on motives and actions, not consequences. Third, because moral choices involve or affect others, a correct moral choice is one that you would want others to do, without making yourself an exception, and it is a choice that respects all others as persons. Fourth, morality is not idiosyncratic or subjective, but rule-based, because moral judgments are judgments that have universal applicability. Therefore, a moral act is an act reasonable people would agree is right, that you would expect others to do, that could be formulated into a rule or law, and that respects people and respects everyone equally.

Kant's analysis introduces us to a criterion for moral assessment that is not simply an evaluation of utility or foreseeable consequences (Kant, 1785; 1956). Some actions are judged to be wrong not merely because of their positive or negative outcomes, but because they violate standards for acceptable behavior or moral rules. For example, most of us would agree that we should avoid deception, keep promises, respect basic rights, treat people fairly, as well as avoid causing harm. These rules set the criteria for acceptable behavior by specifying how we expect ourselves and others to act.

Some commonly held moral rules include the following

- Avoid gratuitous harm
- Avoid deception or lying
- Keep one's promises and contracts
- Respect people and their basic rights to life, freedom, and equal opportunity
- Respect professional codes
- Respect the law

- Administer mutual aid for those in need
- Respect property (however defined)

One often adds to these the mandate to respect diversity and in particular, gender, religious, ethnic, and cultural diversity. Whether or not this mandate overrides others is illustrated in the Neemix and Eskom cases, where cultural practices come into conflict with what is perceived to be ways to provide jobs, improve living conditions, enhance economic development, and foster "progress."

From a rule-based perspective the following should be factored into decision making:

- Does the decision or action set positive or negative precedents? That is, could you formulate a rule from this action that would recommend or prescribe this as acceptable practice?
- Is the action acceptable to other reasonable people?
- Does this action meet the criteria of professional excellence?
- Does it respect, or at least not denigrate, human dignity?

A Rights Approach

Rule-based morality is closely related to a rights approach to morality. Utilitarians such as John Stuart Mill defend human rights by arguing that freedom is a unique and primary interest of human beings, and that other human interests including economic welfare are subsidiary to freedom. This allows Mill to conclude that benefits are not utility maximizing if basic freedoms are violated or not realized. However, most rights theorists develop a notion of human rights from Kant's mandate that no act can be morally good if it does not respect human dignity. Rights theorists argue that human beings have certain moral rights simply in virtue of being *human*, independently of culture, historical context, or social institutions in which they find themselves. Rights to life, freedom, equal opportunity and the right not to be harmed are claims, without which living as a human being is impossible, because choice and control of one's own life would not be options. These are called *moral* rights, because in fact, they are not universally recognized, and they form the grounds for critiquing societies that do not honor these rights.

Utilitarian theories, rule-based morality, and a rights approach each entail a theory of moral obligation. If human happiness or the minimization of human suffering is desirable, then one has obligations built into one's decision making to achieve those ends. Interestingly, engineering professional codes of ethics all proscribe causing harm, and safety is of premier importance. From a rule-based perspective, professional codes specify rules that are allegedly obligatory for all members. From a rights perspective, if certain rights are basic to the human condition, then one has obligations to respect the rights of others.

But what is the extent of these obligations? Are one's duties as an engineer merely negative, that is, not to contribute in violations of rights or causing harms? Or does one have positive duties as well to be proactive in creating safe products, in protecting interests, or respecting rights? Companies such as Unilever that have taken proactive involvement in environmental sustainability initiatives demonstrate positive commitments to environmental sustainability. Are they *obligated* to do so? How far should they extend these commitments?

Often obligations conflict, and it is not always clear, even if one takes a positive stance, which should prevail. W. R. Grace has been committed to the manufacture of a much-needed pesticide in India from an indigenous plant—the neem tree. Such manufacture also provides jobs to Indians. However, does this commitment clash with the obligation to respect diverse cultural and religious practices? Dow Corning tried to design the safest breast implant, yet it is accused of causing harm to thousands of women who have implants and have become ill. What are Dow Corning's obligations and the obligations of its engineers who designed the implants to these women, when the scientific data overwhelmingly show that implants do not cause disease? Rohner Textil, a Swiss textile mill, has obligations to its parent company, to the village in which it is located, and to strict Swiss environmental regulations. Trying to honor the latter two and at the same time remain profitable may create conflicting and insurmountable obligations for Rohner and its director, Albin Kälin. Which should take precedence?

The debate over the extent of one's positive obligations cannot be resolved absolutely. Conflicts of commitment are inevitable in complex technological situations. But one can set some minimum guidelines:

1. Engineering and managerial decision making must question any design, decision, set of actions, or corporate goals that, on balance, contribute negatively to human well-being or harm human rights or dignity. So a prudent decision is one that at least recognizes minimum obligations not to worsen the status or viability of human options.
2. Concerning rights directly, ordinarily any action that, on balance, weakens human rights or contributes to worsening the human condition in some way, is not acceptable, even where economic or technological benefits are a result. Thus morality requires acting with self-restraint even when what appear to be important benefits are at stake.

A particular set of ethical issues that has come to be prominent in the late twentieth century—questions concerning environmental sustainability—illustrate how utilitarian and rule-based perspectives provide differing but overlapping tools for moral evaluation. Sustaining the environment has obvious benefits for present and future generations. Sometimes environmental issues are cast in terms of rights or rules; that is, that every person has a right to a livable environment. The essay, "Environmental Sustainability" included in this collection discusses various definitions and options. As you will see in the cases to follow what environmental sustainability means, what the consequences are of environmental degradation, and how "rules" for promoting sustainability can be operationalized in particular contexts remain difficult questions. The American Solar Network case focuses on an inventor who wants to make millions while benefiting the environment. The principle behind his design is that solar energy is recyclable, inexpensive, and does not harm the environment. But Albert Rich has to struggle with marketing. Should designers adopt a rule-based perspective and work for regulations or incentives that will encourage people to buy sustainable products because they do "least harm" to the environment? Or should they adopt a more utilitarian perspective and emphasize cost, aesthetics, and other criteria that are important to most people? The case involves a struggle to come up with a set of rules or principles that will lead to a new generation of sustainable products that can compete with existing products on cost and aesthetics.

Virtues and Virtuous Character

The qualities of self-restraint and prudence introduce the notion of professional virtue. Engineering (or various engineering disciplines, for example, systems, chemical, mechanical, civil) is a profession. Like other professions, there are independent professional engineering associations that have developed codes of ethics that spell out acceptable engineering behavior. That is, they spell out what it means to be a virtuous engineer. Underlying these codes is a model (derived from Aristotle rather than Kant) that proposes that the cultivation of excellence in moral character and moral behavior is characteristic as an ideal for all professions.

In a contemporary Aristotelian analysis, Robert Solomon cites six Aristotelian virtues central for managerial, and by analogy, professional practice:

- Excellence in the "craft" of engineering
- Membership and loyalty to the profession
- Integrity
- Good judgment
- Integration of wholeness
- Community or social responsibility

Solomon maps these professional virtues against civic virtues of loyalty, honor, truth telling, and a sense of shame, virtues that are extolled by most communities. The aim of Solomon's model is the common good, the well-being of society of which professions and institutions are integral participants, and the strength of this analysis is its focus on personal and professional character as part of moral excellence and civic responsibility (Solomon, 1992). Companies, too, can be classified according to whether or not they exhibit and encourage virtuous practices.

Virtue theory suggests that professional, managerial, and corporate excellence are virtues to be emulated. Any framework for ethical decision making would want to include the minimum requirement that one should avoid interacting with individuals or institutions who consistently exhibit or practice negative virtues. Indeed, some professional associations bar members for exactly that: malpractice.

But is virtue, alone, enough? Union Carbide is known as a very reputable company. Its former CEO, Warren Anderson, was a self-effacing, virtuous, deeply religious person of the highest moral character. Previous to 1984 Union Carbide's safety record with all its chemical plants worldwide was exemplary. Yet despite its expertise in safety, a plant it built in Bhopal, India did not follow many of Union Carbide's own safety standards and eventually leaked a deadly chemical that killed over 2500 people (Shrivastava, 1987). Similarly, Dow Corning was widely cited as an example of an ethical corporation, until women with breast implants started taking the company to court. Scientists at Dow Corning thought they had conducted adequate tests of their silicone implant, and these scientists and the company's management were surprised by the reports of problems and the eventual lawsuits.

It would appear that rule-based and utilitarian forms of reasoning are needed to help with preventive ethics. Yet, something more is at stake in these two cases. Ethical theories provide us with reasonable criteria for making moral judgments and evaluating decisions and actions. However, there is one difficulty with approaching moral reasoning strictly from a "moral theories" approach. The difficulty is that although most of us can learn about *theories,* we are less skilled at applying them in all practical contexts. Even intelligent, reasonable people, despite their knowledge of ethical theories or their personal value system, make moral mistakes. These mistakes cannot be solely attributed to ignorance or insensitivity, nor even to weakness of character, but rather, we will suggest, to a paucity of moral imagination.

Mental Models and Moral Imagination

Mental Models   To understand how incidents such as Bhopal could occur, let us focus our attention on the notion of a mental model. "Mental model" connotes the idea that human beings have mental representations, cognitive frames, mental pictures, or verbal representations of their experiences—representations that are models of the stimuli or data with which they are interacting. These are frameworks that set up parameters through which experience or a certain set of experiences is organized or filtered (Gentner & Whitley, 1997, 210-11). Peter Senge argues that mental models are "deeply held internal images of how the world works, images that limit us to familiar ways of thinking and acting" (Senge, 1990, 174). Mental models constitute the basis for our assumptions and points of view. They are created by theories, myths, stories, and images that frame, focus, or revise the ways each of us experiences.

Mental models are sometimes referred to as "frames." According to Hamel and Prahalad,

> Every manager carries around in his or her head a set of biases, assumptions and presuppositions about the structure of the relevant industry, about who the competition is and isn't, about who the customers are and aren't, about what customers want or don't want, about which technologies are viable and which aren't, and so on. This [network of mental models] encompasses beliefs, values, and norms about how best to motivate people; the right balance of internal cooperation and competition; the relative ranking of shareholder, customer, and employee interests; and what behaviors to encourage and discourage. These beliefs are, at least in part, the product of a particular industry environment. . . . Managerial frames . . . limit management's perception to a particular slice of reality. Managers live inside their frames and, to a very great extent, don't know what lies outside (Hamel and Prahalad, 1994, 53-54).

Senge and Hamel and Prahalad each focus on the negative side of mental models or frames—the ways in which they inhibit consideration of alternatives. But mental models can also facilitate creativity. Alexander Graham Bell, for example, had a unique mental model for a device that could transmit and receive speech or music or telegraph signals. He based it on the human ear. Competitors like Elisha Gray and Thomas Edison had different mental models, based on their experiences with telegraphy. According to Rouse and Morris, "[m]ental models are the mechanisms whereby humans are able to generate descriptions of system purpose and form, explanations of system functioning and observed system states, and predictions of future system states" (Rouse & Morris, 1986, 351). Mental models might be hypothetical constructs of the experience in question, or scientific theories; they might frame the experience through which individuals process information, conduct experiments, and formulate theories; or mental models may simply refer to human knowledge about a particular set of events or a system. Mental models account for our ability to describe, explain, and predict. They may function as protocols to account for human expectations, which are often formulated in accordance with these models (Rouse and Morris, 1986; Gorman, 1992, 192-235). Bell's mental model allowed him to generate a patent application that explained a system for translating any combination of sounds—including speech—into an undulating electric current. As a result, Bell obtained a patent of staggering breadth (Gorman, 1998, ch. 3).

In framing our experiences, mental models also function as focusing projectors. Often this process revises the meaning of the event, reinterprets or even leaves out data, and reframes its significance. This phenomenon is described by a former employee at Ford Motor Company, Dennis Gioia, now professor of organizational behavior at Pennsylvania State University. Gioia had always thought of himself as an extremely moral and socially responsible person. Yet he relates that, while functioning as recall coordinator, he was exposed to reports of Pintos "lighting up," "cars simply . . . consumed by fire after apparently very low speed accidents" (Gioia, 1991, 381). Although there were actually few reports of Pinto explosions, some contained detailed photographs including, in at least one incident, a report and photos of a number of people who were killed by the fire. After viewing one actual burned-out Pinto, Gioia brought up the Pinto model for departmental review as a possible recall. But after considering the case, neither Gioia nor anyone else at that meeting recommended recalling the model. Gioia was convinced by his own reasoning process and by other seemingly thoughtful managers not to recall those cars because, the managers argued, the evidence was not conclusive that the Pinto was more defective than its competitors, many subcompact autos had been subject to similar dreadful accidents, and the Pinto was a popular, best-selling auto.

Gioia left Ford in 1975 to work on a Ph.D. Later, when asked by his students why he did not order a recall, Gioia reports how he had learned to view his job through a "Ford-trained" perspective. Looking back on this scenario Gioia concludes:

> My own schematized knowledge influenced me to perceive recall issues in terms of the prevailing decision environment and to unconsciously overlook key features of the Pinto case, mainly because they did not fit an existing script. Although the outcomes of the [Pinto] case carry retrospectively obvious ethical overtones, the [mental models] driving my perceptions and actions precluded consideration of the issues in ethical terms because the [models] did not include ethical dimensions (Gioia, 1991, 385).

As this example illustrates, mental models function as specific frames. For example, one can have a mental model of what constitutes criteria for a recall, which then triggers the appropriate behavior. While Gioia was at Ford, he had learned to deal with his job-related work through a "Ford-trained" perspective, because he and others at Ford had developed shared mental models. Or the reverse can happen: One can be in the middle of a standard operating procedure and fit all events into the mental model that lies behind the procedure. Diane Vaughan has showed how these kinds of scripts contributed to an overall pattern of "normalized deviance" in the *Challenger* case, contributing to the disaster.

> Although all work groups probably evolve shared mental models of some kind, such models are more likely to be created (and to affect group processes and outcomes) under some conditions than others. Thus, we would expect shared mental models to form more quickly, to contain more information, and to exhibit greater coherence and integration when (a) the same people work together over a long period of time, (b) the group task is complex and requires a high degree of response coordination, and (c) important outcomes, such as money or status, are contingent on group performance (Levine & Moreland, In Press, p. 2).

Part of entering the work culture like NASA or Ford is acquiring the shared mental models that make coordinated efforts possible. However, these shared mental models can also blind one to potential ethical dilemmas. Hamel and Prahalad warn that "There is a fine line between socialization and brainwashing" (Hamel & Prahalad, 1994, 63). Gioia appeared to be unable to step out of his role as recall coordinator to explore the ramifications of the Pinto situation. At the time, he was not aware of the gap between his personal moral beliefs and his professional behavior, and it was only after he left Ford that he was able to see what mental models were at work in his thinking. For experts working in a familiar domain, mental models are tacit, or implicit—experts only become aware of them when there is a problem. It was only in retrospect that Gioia saw the mental models he had implicitly adopted. At the time he was at Ford, Gioia lacked moral imagination—the ability to step out of his corporate role, to take a fresh point of view, and to reevaluate what was going on with the Pinto fires.

Moral Imagination   Moral imagination is "an ability to imaginatively discern various possibilities for acting within a given situation and to envision the potential help and harm that are likely to result from a given action" (Johnson, 1993, 202). Being morally imaginative includes

1. Disengaging from and becoming aware of one's situation, understanding the mental model or script dominating that situation, and envisioning possible moral conflicts or dilemmas that might arise in that context or as outcomes of the dominating scheme.
2. The ability to imagine new possibilities. These possibilities include those that are not context-dependent and that might involve another mental model.
3. Evaluating from a moral point of view both the original context and its dominating mental models, and the new possibilities one has envisioned (Werhane, 1999).

But how do we do all of that while at the same time taking into account situational peculiarities, social context, and the precepts of moral theory? How do we act in a morally reasonable manner and trigger moral imagination? A good example of this process in practice is the work of Eskom. It was an all-white-managed company that thrived during apartheid in South Africa, while providing little power service to the non-white community or in the rural homeland areas. Yet even before the end of apartheid, the company began to evaluate itself and its practices. It became aware of itself as an all-white company with a narrow view of what its service commitments were to a country made up of a largely nonwhite population. That is, it stepped back from its traditions and practices, it reevaluated itself and its mission, and it began to develop a new mental model of what it *should be* as a national power company in a country where the majority of the population was nonwhite and poor. Eskom began training nonwhites for supervisory positions (an activity that was against the law at that time), it experimented with various ways to begin providing electricity throughout the whole country, and it explored ways to make power economically available to the rural poor and to those who had no conception of the value of electricity. As a result, Eskom today is the fifth largest electric utility in the world; it has made itself economically successful so that it can further experiment with ways to provide service to rural South African communities and develop the expansion of power in other even poorer African nations as well.

In a different context, Susan Lyons at DesignTex is trying to shake the company out of its traditional model for fabric manufacture and to explore new ways to create economically viable fabrics that are environmentally friendly. This process would involve changing a whole way of thinking about fabrics, fabric dyes and manufacture—a new mental model that required the elimination of the term *waste* (McDonough, 1998). To do that, she has to convince Rohner Textil, the potential manufacturer of this new fabric, to change its thinking as well.

Developing Decision Models One of the ways to develop moral reasoning skills and trigger moral imagination is to ask a series of questions. First, in disengaging oneself and self-evaluating one's present set of mental models, one might wonder,

1. What sorts of mental models are presupposed in the ways we as professionals, as a company, as managers do things?
2. How might a stranger evaluate our activities?
3. Can we explain what we do to other reasonable engineers or managers?
4. Can we defend our activities professionally? In public?
5. Could we recommend that others' follow our practices as well?
6. What would inverting our practices look like? For example, should we require all Ford engineers to drive Pintos? Should we ask all Eskom managers and their families to spend a week in rural areas without electricity?

Second, it is important to evaluate the kinds of schema we employ, the activities and decisions we engage in, the outcomes of these activities and decisions, and various new possibilities we envision by appealing to principles we derived from moral theory. These include

1. The utilitarian principle of maximizing interests or benefits or minimizing costs and harms: a principle that is part of one's professional obligation as an engineer.
2. Rule-based criteria of precedence, acceptability, publicity, and legislatibility.
3. Rules and rights-based criteria of respect for persons and their rights.
4. Commonly shared moral rules of truth telling; promise keeping; respect for professional codes, property, and laws; and mutual aid.
5. Criteria of excellence in virtue or moral character of oneself, of others, of one's company, and of the profession.

Third, to trigger creativity in revising one's mental models, one might ask:

1. How might we revolutionize what we do?
2. What kinds of new technology, design, or products can we develop?
3. What would be the costs and benefits of such a revolution? How could we mitigate the costs?
4. How could these changes be institutionalized both professionally and in companies?

Alexander Graham Bell, for example, did not respond to a perceived market need when he developed the telephone. "Everyone" knew that fame and fortune awaited the inventor of a device that could send multiple messages down a single wire. Bell, in contrast, had background in speech and audition; he knew the power of oral communication and gave demonstrations of his crude telephone to create a market for it (Gorman, 1998, Ch. 3). Akio Morita of Sony made a similar point:

> Our plan is to lead the public with new products rather than asking them what kind of product they want. The public does not know what is possible, but we do. So instead of doing a lot of market research, we refine our thinking on a product and its use and try to create a market for it by educating and communicating with the public (Hamel & Prahalad, 1994, 108-9).

In facing obvious moral dilemmas one should ask the following:

1. Is this dilemma solvable given the parameters of the context, and extant "scripts"?
2. What are the possibilities that are not context-dependent?
3. Might we have to revamp the operative script to take into account new possibilities that are not within the scope of one's particular situation or within one's role in that situation?

The notion of moral imagination is meant to challenge our embedded mental models and traditions with creative principled thinking. This sort of thinking perceives the nuances of a situation, challenges the scheme or mental models in which the situation, profession, or company is embedded, and imagines how it might be different *and* morally more acceptable. Developing this process is, at best, difficult, as cases in this collection will illustrate. But not to do so, as you will see in the cases to follow, risks moral and technological bankruptcy, threatens ecological sustainability in some cases, and prevents engineers from exercising their talents in ways that will benefit all of us.

References Cited

Bentham, J. (1789; 1948), *An Introduction to the Principles of Morals and Legislation.* New York: Hafner Publishing Co.

Gentner, D. and Whitley, E.W. (1997). Mental Models of Population Growth. In *Environment, Ethics, and Behavior,* eds. M.H. Bazerman, D.M. Messick, A.E. Tenbrunsel, and K.A. Wade-Benzoni. San Francisco, CA: New Lexington Press.

Gioia, D.A. (1991). Pinto Fires and Personal Ethics. *Journal of Business Ethics,* 11, 379-389.

Gorman, M. E. (1992). *Simulating Science.* Bloomington, IN: Indiana University Press.

Gorman, M.E. (1998). *Transforming Nature: Ethics, Invention and Design.* Boston: Kluwer Academic Publishers.

Gusterson, H. (1996). *Nuclear Rites.* Berkeley: University of California Press.

Hamel, G., and Prahalad, C.K. (1994). *Competing for the Future.* Cambridge, MA: Harvard Business School Press.

Harris, C.E., Pritchard, M.S., and Rabins, M.J. (1995). *Engineering Ethics: Concepts and Cases.* Belmont, CA: Wadsworth.

Johnson, M. (1993). *Moral Imagination.* Chicago: University of Chicago Press.

Kant, I. (1785; 1956). *Groundwork for the Metaphysic of Morals,* trans. H.J. Paton. New York: Harper & Row.

Levine, J.M., and Moreland, R.L. (In press). Knowledge transmission in work groups: Helping newcomers to succeed. In *Shared Knowledge in Organizations,* eds. L. Thompson, D. Messick, and J. Levine. Hillsdale, NJ: Lawrence Erlbaum Associates.

Milgram, S. (1974). *Obedience to Authority.* New York: Harper & Row.

Mill, J.S. (1861; 1968). *Utilitarianism.* New York: Meridian Books.

Rouse, W.B., and Morris, N.M. (1986). On Looking Into the Black Box: Prospects and Limits in the Search for Mental Models. *Psychological Bulletin,* 100, 349-363.

Schank, R., and Abelson, R. (1977). *Scripts, Plans, Goals and Understanding: An Inquiry into Human Knowledge Structures.* Hillsdale, NJ: Lawrence Erlbaum Associates.

Senge, P. (1990). *The Fifth Discipline.* New York: Doubleday & Co.

Shrivastava, P. (1987). *Bhopal: Anatomy of a Crisis.* Cambridge, MA: Ballinger Publishing Co.

Solomon, R. (1992). *Ethics and Excellence.* New York: Oxford University Press.

Vaughan, D. (1996)). *The Challenger Launch Decision.* Chicago: University of Chicago Press.

Werhane, P. (1999). *Moral Imagination and Management Decision-Making.* New York: Oxford University Press.

Zimbardo, P.G. (1972). *The Stanford Prison Experiment.* [Slide/tape presentation]. Philip G. Zimbardo, Inc., P.O. Box 4395, Stanford, CA 94305.

3

WHO INVENTED THE TELEPHONE?

If Gray had filed an application for a patent and Bell for a caveat, we should in all probability have today the Gray Telephone company in place of the Bell Telephone Company.[1]

On the day Alexander Graham Bell submitted a patent application for a device that could, among other things, transmit speech, Elisha Gray submitted a caveat for a device that would serve the same function. (A caveat was a statement of intention to perfect and eventually patent an invention—it was filed with the patent office and could be used to establish an inventor's priority.)

Did Gray and Bell arrive independently at the idea for what we now call the telephone, in which case Gray deserves equal billing as inventor? Does only one of the two deserves credit for the invention? Or is it that hindsight makes it appear that Gray and Bell were inventing the same thing?

COMPETITION OVER THE HARMONIC MULTIPLE TELEGRAPH

Initially, both Bell and Gray focused on harmonic telegraphy: the idea of using multiple tones, singly or in combination, to send multiple messages down the same wire. Bell's family was very involved with teaching the deaf. His father, Alexander Melville, developed a special "visual speech" alphabet which deaf people could use to read how to make

This case is adapted from a more detailed account in Chapter 3 of M.E. Gorman, *Transforming Nature: Ethics, Invention and Design* (Kluwer Academic Publishers, Boston, 1998). The author gratefully acknowledges the assistance of Sarah Diersen.

specific sounds. As a boy, Bell would participate in demonstrations in which he was placed out of earshot; his father would ask a member of the audience to make a sound, then he would write it in visible speech; Bell would enter, read what his father had written, and make the sound. So Bell inherited a family theme, or mission, having to do with teaching the deaf and making speech visible to the deaf.

Gray's background is harder to reconstruct than Bell's, because Gray left less in the way of written records and the only biography, by Lloyd Taylor, is an unpublished work of uneven quality (Taylor Unpublished Manuscript). The death of his father and his mother's precarious health made Elisha the primary breadwinner in the family at the age of 12. He took up carpentry, but the laying of the first transatlantic telegraph cable inspired him to read about telegraphy. Here the themes of hard work and telegraph invention seem to join, though we know very little about this period in Gray's life.

Like Bell, Gray often overworked to the point of illness—he managed to put himself through five years of Oberlin but paid with five years of convalescence (Hounshell, 1975). He gained much of his knowledge through his hands: "My habit of actually constructing everything which I saw or read of so far as my facilities would allow, was the best possible method of fixing the principles of its operation firmly in my mind" (Gray, 1977, p. 8).

His electrical researches paid off in 1867, when he developed a new form of telegraph relay. He formed a partnership with Enos Barton in 1869; they founded the Western Electric Company, which became the major manufacturer of telegraph equipment for Western Union. Bell's father introduced his son to the scientific community; Gray's hard struggle for survival inclined him more to the world of business.

Each inventor suspected the other of stealing his ideas at various points. Gray submitted a patent application for a multiple harmonic telegraph on February 23, 1875; two days later Bell submitted one for his.[2] so the famous controversy between Bell and Gray over the speaking telegraph, or what we now call the telephone,[3] was really one episode in a continuing controversy over multiple telegraphy.

ELISHA GRAY'S MULTIPLE HARMONIC TELEGRAPH

Gray claimed he got the first idea for using musical tones to send telegraph messages in 1867, when he was using a vibrating metal reed, or rheotome, in a circuit with an electromagnet and a telegraph key. When he closed the key, he "noticed a singing sound in the electromagnet, and by working the [telegraph] key as if transmitting a Morse message, the signals were audibly produced on the magnet by long and short sounds, representing the dots and dashes of the Morse alphabet" (Gray, 1977, p. 20). In this way, multiple messages could be encoded by multiple tuning forks, sent over the same wire, and decoded by a similar set of tuning forks on the receiving end.

Gray's next model for a harmonic telegraph came from observing his nephew touching a zinc-lined bathtub with one hand while in the other he held a coil connected to a vibrating rheotome, an electromagnetic device which produced a tone. When his nephew/s hand glided along the zinc, Gray heard the bathtub emit the same tone as the rheotome. When Gray put himself in his nephew's position, he found he could alter the pitch and volume by changing the speed and pressure with which he rubbed the zinc. A single telegraph receiver could potentially reproduce multiple tones. Gray was so excited by the potential of this discovery that he resigned as superintendent of Western Electric to pursue his inventions full time.

In April of 1874 Gray attempted to patent a musical telegraph, which consisted of a two-tone transmitter, consisting of two single-pole electromagnets, each with a vibrating armature. Each armature made and broke contact with a platinum point which switched the current on and off to the coil. Because each electromagnet had a different electrical resistance, each electromagnet exerted a different magnetic pull on its armature and thus caused each armature to vibrate at a different frequency. Each coil and armature combination was controlled by its own telegraph key, so that each frequency could be sent separately or simultaneously. These electromagnets were connected to an induction coil which functioned like a modern transformer and stepped up the current before it was sent out onto the telegraph line. For the zinc bathtub, Gray substituted a grounded piece of galvanized tin. In his patent application, Gray showed a man completing the circuit by holding the wire from the coil in one hand and touching the tin with the other.

The patent office initially rejected this application, on the grounds that one could not patent a circuit which included a person. So Gray substituted a variety of animal tissues, ranging from oyster shell to leather.[4] He was eventually granted a patent in February of 1876.

By then, Gray had expanded his two-tone transmitter to a two-octave device that could send twenty-four different pitches (two octaves) over one telegraphic circuit. Each tone was generated by a single tone transmitter turned to a different pitch. Gray often used several single tone transmitters inside more complex devices capable of sending multiple tones, such as his two-octave transmitter and printing telegraph.

Gray also developed several receivers to take the place of the awkward animal tissue combination. He based them on a receiver developed by an inventor named Philip Reis in Germany in 1854. According to Gray, the principle of the Reis receiver was that "when a coil of wire surrounding a bar of iron or the core of an electromagnet is traversed by an electric current, the said bar will be slightly elongated, and if these currents succeed each other with sufficient rapidity, a vibratory motion will be given said bar, and it will give forth a musical tone.[5]

All of Gray's receivers embodied this principle and hence were capable of reproducing several tones simultaneously. Gray used a variety of resonant cavities to amplify the sound. He got the idea of using a tin drum from a combination of the tin he used in his animal tissue patents and experiments with a violin with a metal plate on the back. His previous experience with using a bathtub as a receiver led him to try a wash basin.

Gray systematically tested every type of receiver with his two-octave transmitter. With these instruments Gray gave several impressive demonstrations in New York and Washington in May and June of 1874, after which he returned home to Chicago where he worked on the problem of creating a reliable harmonic telegraph transmitter. His two-octave transmitter could theoretically have been used for such a purpose, but Gray apparently thought it more suited to sending composite tones than isolated individual messages. His solution to the transmitter problem was to use "an ordinary electromagnet and a reed made of a piece of watch-spring, one end of which is fixed to one pole of the magnet while the other free end projects over the other pole, a short distance from it, so as to form an armature" (Gray, 1977, pp. 21-22). Each of these springs could be tuned to a particular frequency. These springs produced an excellent tone for a short time, "but the slightest change in the adjustment, even a jar of the table, causes it to break into nodes, and give a note a chord or an octave away from its fundamental" (Gray, 1977, p. 23).

ALEXANDER GRAHAM BELL'S PATH TO A MULTIPLE HARMONIC TELEGRAPH

When Elisha Gray began his multiple telegraph work, he was already an accomplished electrical inventor. Bell's area of expertise, by contrast, was speech and audition. Like Elisha Gray, much of Bell's knowledge came through building and tinkering. Bell discovered that he could hold a vibrating tuning fork in front of his mouth and while moving his tongue through the positions of the vowels, one of the vowel positions would cause the fork to resonate. He experimented with combinations of tuning forks and vowels, making what he thought were important discoveries. But when he sent a letter to Alexander Ellis, the great phonetician, he learned that he had been replicating experiments conducted by Hermann von Helmholtz. He derived some comfort from the fact that he had followed in the footsteps of one of the world's greatest scientists.

Bell's first idea for a multiple telegraph came from a conversation with Ellis about Helmholtz's apparatus for artificially producing vowel tones by means of combinations of tuning forks and resonant chambers. Ellis had to do some translating from the German for Bell, and as a result, Bell got the false impression that the device transmitted vowel sounds, when in fact it created them. If vowels could be transmitted, why not consonants and, eventually, speech?

Bell's initial focus was not on speech but on telegraphy. Why not take two forks that produced exactly the same tone and turn one into a telegraph transmitter and the other into a receiver? If one could do this with one pair of forks, why not do it with four, eight, or even sixteen distinct tones, all carrying information down the same wire?

Bell read everything he could get his hands on that was related to his invention ideas. From J. Baille's *The Wonders of Electricity*[6] Bell got the idea of substituting a steel plate for a tuning fork. Books like Baille's served almost as catalogues of possible electro-mechanical variations for inventors. The result was a steel reed device whose pitch could be precisely tuned simply by adjusting the length of it that was allowed to hang over the electromagnet. Bell's device is a "transceiver" because Bell intended to use the same as both transmitter and receiver.

Bell had great difficulty putting these reeds into an effective multiple telegraph circuit, which led him to develop a new theme, or goal, for himself in November of 1873, when he wrote, "It became evident to me, that with my own crude workmanship, and with the limited time and means at my disposal, I could not hope to construct any better models. I therefore from this time devoted less time to practical experiment than to the theoretical development of the details of the invention" (Bell, 1908, p. 8).

Gray, in contrast, worked to develop families of different transmitters and receivers. Gray was a master at constructing complex circuits. In order to make his reed assemblage better able to transmit single tones, Gray made the spring into a heavier metal reed, filed the end of the reed to tune it, and added a small spring to dampen its vibrations. For a single-tone or analyzing receiver, he first tried a tuning fork attached to one pole of an electromagnet. Then he substituted a spring or lever for the fork. Next, he tried a steel ribbon clamped on both ends: "The length and size of the ribbon depending upon the note we wish to receive upon it. If it is a high note, we make it thinner and shorter, if it is a low note, we make it thicker and longer. If this ribbon is tuned so that it will give a certain note when made to vibrate mechanically, and the note which corresponds to its fundamental is then transmitted through its magnet, it will respond and vibrate in unison with its transmitted note; but if another note be sent which varies at all from its fundamental, it will not respond. If a composite tone is sent, the ribbon will respond when its own note is being sent as part of the composite tone, but as soon as its own tone is left out it will immediately stop. This I am able to select out and indicate when any note is being sent, in fact, to *analyze* the tones which are passing over the line" (Ashley, October 21, 1876, p. 253).

THE ERROR THAT LED TO THE FIRST SPEAKING TELEGRAPH

Bell's first model for a speaking telegraph came from a variation on this reed mechanical representation and also from experiments he had conducted with piano strings. In the summer of 1874, he put reeds on either pole of a horseshoe magnet, and experimented with sending the sound of either reed, separately or in combination. Bell's goal was to magnetize the reed itself and therefore avoid distortions that occurred when he used a non-magnetic reed in combination with an electromagnet—exactly the sorts of distortions that Gray was able to avoid through clever use of dampers and electromagnets of different resistances.

Bell's horseshoe magnet experiment was partly successful, enough to lead him to imagine a device he called the "harp apparatus" with perhaps dozens of reeds on each pole of an electromagnet. Such a device might function like the strings on a piano and vibrate in response to any tone made near them; these vibrations would then induce a current which could be carried to a receiving harp. The problem with the harp apparatus was that it required too many reeds and the induced current would not be sufficiently strong to transmit speech. So Bell suspended the goal of speaking telegraphy, hoping a solution would emerge.

In June of 1875, Bell and his new assistant Thomas Watson were working on the problem of multiple telegraphy. Bell had obtained support from Gardiner Hubbard, father of one of his pupils, Mabel. Hubbard wanted to break Western Union's virtual monopoly on what we would now call information services. He proposed a plan that would put such services in the post office, under contract to a corporation that Hubbard himself would found and head. When the Congress did not pass his scheme, Hubbard looked for other ways of ending Western Union's dominance (Carlson, 1994). One way was through the development of new technologies like the multiple harmonic telegraph system proposed by his daughter's teacher.

To complicate matters, Bell was courting Mabel. Therefore, out of deference to Gardiner Hubbard, telephonic researches had to take a back seat to telegraphy. On May 2, 1875, Bell wrote to "Papa and Mama: I think that the transmission of the human voice is much more nearly at hand than I had supposed. However, this is kept in the background just now—as every effort is made to complete the Autograph arrangement so as to have it used on some line." The autograph was a device that would send printed or written letters over a wire, and Bell had just obtained an important patent for this kind of technology, barely beating Elisha Gray.

On June 2, 1875, Bell had set up three multiple telegraph stations, A, B, and C, each with three of his tuned reed mechanical representations. He wanted to be able to pluck the first reed in A and have the first reeds in B and C vibrate. When Bell depressed the telegraph key corresponding to first reed at A, the corresponding reed at B vibrated well, but Watson, who was in another room with C, noticed it was stuck. To release it, Watson plucked it; Bell noticed that this caused the corresponding reed at B to vibrate powerfully. Bell then listened to each of the reeds at B in succession, placing his ear right against them, and heard both the pitch and the overtones of the tuned reed.

Seen from the standpoint of multiple telegraphy, this result was an error—one stuck reed caused three reeds at the other station to vibrate, and one could hear the overtones of each reed, whereas what one really wanted was to hear a single, pure tone. But given Bell's harp model, this error suggested a route to the transmission of speech. "These experiments at once removed the doubt that had been in my mind since the summer of 1874, that magneto-electric currents generated by the vibration of an armature in front of an electro-magnet would be too feeble to produce audible effects that could be practically utilized for the purposes of multiple telegraphy and of speech transmission" (Bell, 1908, p. 59).

Bell immediately asked Watson to build a working telephone in which a reed relay was attached to a diaphragm or membrane with a speaking cavity over it. As one spoke into the cavity, the membrane would vibrate; these vibrations would be translated into an electrical current by the dampened reed, which would send them to a similar device on the other end. Unfortunately, this device did not produce intelligible speech, though Bell and Watson heard a kind of mumbling that suggested they were on the right track. Bell then wrote an application for a patent that included the transmission of speech; he used his reed relays to illustrate how this was to be done. The patent was submitted on February 14, 1876.

GRAY'S CAVEAT FOR A SPEAKING TELEGRAPH

A few hours later on the same day, Elisha Gray submitted his caveat for a speaking telegraph. His model for the transmission of speech was based on a device called "the lover's telegraph," or what we would now call a "string telephone." According to Gray, this device "proved to my mind that all the conditions necessary for the transmission of an articulate word were contained in any single vibrating point. . . . I saw that if I could reproduce electrically the same motions that were made mechanically at the center of the diaphragm . . . such electrical vibrations would be reproduced on a common receiver in the same manner that musical tones were" (Telephone Suits, Part II,1880, pp. 124-125).

In his caveat, Gray designed a speaking telegraph that looked like a lover's telegraph with a cylinder of water between transmitter and receiver. Gray intended to use water as a medium of high resistance. Hanging from the bottom of the speaking tube and diaphragm into which one spoke was a thin wire of rod. When one spoke into the resonant cavity, the diaphragm vibrated, causing the wire hanging from it to get alternately closer to, and farther away from, a contact on the bottom of the water; this motion caused a fluctuation in the current passing to the receiver that mirrored the movement of the diaphragm. The idea of using liquid variable resistance, Gray claimed, was "old in the art at the time" (Telephone Suits, Part I, 1880, p. 125).

Gray used familiar mechanical representations in constructing his speaking telegraph. For example, his receiver consisted of a resonant cavity he had used to receive single tones and a double pole electromagnet he had used in an analyzing receiver.[7]

Because he did not have a working device, Gray filed a caveat or preliminary disclosure instead of a full application, and he was not especially concerned if some details of the apparatus were left somewhat vague. For example, in his caveat, Gray raised the possibility of employing multiple diaphragms just as he had used multiple transmitters in his harmonic telegraphs: "I contemplate, however, the use of a series of diaphragms in a common vocalizing chamber, each diaphragm carrying an independent rod, and responding to a vibration of different rapidity and intensity, in which case contact points mounted on other diaphragms may be employed" (Gray, 1977, p. 79).

In his technical history of the telephone, J. E. Kingsbury cited Gray's preference for multiple chambers to argue that in 1876 Gray was only at the level of understanding that Bell reached with his harp apparatus in 1874, in that each of these diaphragms would function like one of Bell's reeds and it would take a large number of them to reproduce the human voice (Kingsbury, 1915).[8] But as we have seen, Gray's model was the lover's telegraph, which did not require multiple diaphragms.

In 1875 Gray had developed a mechanical transmitter with which "we obtained a great variety of sounds on the receiver, not unlike the human voice, imitations of vowel sounds, and also imitations of a groan as if in distress. . . . This experiment with the mechanical transmitter confirmed what my previous experiments had led me to believe: that not only could the receivers that had been named be used as receivers of articulate speech transmitted electrically, but that such speech could be transmitted through a single point. I mean by single point, without the intervention of a series of reeds or points differently tuned, and one that would be a common or universal transmitter, in the same sense that the receivers were universal or common" (Telephone Suits, Part I,1880, p. 124).

BELL'S EAR ANALOGY

On June 30, 1875, Bell wrote a triumphant letter to Hubbard: "I shall have ready tomorrow afternoon an instrument modeled after the human ear—by means of which I hope . . . to transmit a vocal sound. . . . I am like a man in a fog who is sure of his latitude and longitude. I know I am close to the land for which I am bound and when the fog lifts I shall see it right before me." The instrument was a second version of the Gallows telephone, constructed by Watson; it worked little better than the first, but Bell wrote his patent anyway. His reference to "an instrument modeled after the human ear" can be understood only by looking closely at another line of research in Bell's network of enterprises.

Bell's interest in teaching the deaf kindled his interest in devices used to visualize sound. At the Institute of Technology, he had experimented with the manometric flame capsule, a device that had a speaking tube and membrane on the other side of which was a chamber through which gas was fed to a small flame. As one spoke, the gas was alternately compressed and decompressed by the vibration of the membrane, resulting in higher and lower flames, respectively. Four mirrors were typically rotated as a unit to show the wave shapes; "when we speak to the apparatus, an undulatory band of light makes its appearance in the mirror. The upper edge of the luminous band appears to be carved into beautiful waves of various shapes and sizes, and when we sing different vowel sounds into the mouth-piece of the instrument, retaining the voice on a uniform level, the form or shape of the undulations visible in the mirror changes with every vowel. I thought that if I could discover the shape or form of vibration that was characteristic of the elements of English speech, I could depict these upon paper by photographic means for the information of my deaf pupils" (Bell, 1908, pp. 24-25).

Since Bell could not physically record the manometric flame patterns using photography and since the patterns were difficult to discern, he concentrated on another device, the phonautograph, which he also saw at the Institute of Technology. It consisted of a cone and membrane with a lever attached to the membrane; when one spoke into the cone, the lever vibrated. At the end of the lever was a bristle brush which traced the shape of the sound wave on a piece of glass covered with lampblack; the glass was moved horizontally in a direction perpendicular to the motion of the lever. "I proposed to use these glass plates as negatives, and by photographic means, print off copies of the tracings for the use of my pupils" (Bell, 1908, p. 26).

However, a comparison of phonautograph tracings and manometric flame shapes suggested to Bell that the phonautograph device needed extensive modification so that the tracings would match the flame shapes of the manometric capsule. Considering the phonautograph's geometry—with its thin, light membrane and the relatively heavy wooden lever and style—Bell was struck by the resemblance between the device and the structure of the human ear. The ear analogy suggested the sorts of modifications he might undertake to successfully replicate the flame shapes in the tracings of this device. The modifications aimed to make the analogy between technology and nature more literal. Bell sought to duplicate "the shape of the membrane of the human ear, the shapes of the bones attached to it, the mode of connection between the two, etc." (Bell, 1908, p. 29).

Following a suggestion from his colleague Dr. Clarence Blake, an expert on the ear, Bell built an ear phonautograph in the summer of 1874, roughly the same time as he was conceiving his harp apparatus. This grisly device included the actual bones from a human ear that were set into vibration when one spoke into a cone and diaphragm to which they were attached; these vibrations were traced on smoked glass by a bristle brush attached to the end of the bones.

From the phonautograph, Bell gained a tactile, "hands-on" understanding of how speech was translated into an undulating wave by the vibrations of the bones of the ear. From his multiple telegraph experiments, Bell gained a similar understanding of how the vibrations of a reed or a combination of reeds could be translated into what he called an undulating electric current that would reproduce the sinusoidal pattern of the sounds.

In his experimental notebook on February 18, 1876, Bell drew an ear with two different mechanical representations next to the bones.[9] On the left was an electromagnet, suggesting that the bones would serve a function similar to the steel reed he had so often placed over an electromagnet to transmit and receive complex tones. On the right was an iron cylinder attached to the bones and this vibrated in the center of a magnetized helix with an iron core. Bell had conducted experiments with such an arrangement, verifying that it could produce an undulatory current; he would later develop this mechanical representation into a telephone receiver (Bell, 1908). Beside the sketch, Bell wrote, "Make transmitting instrument after the model of the human ear. Make armature after the shape of the ossicles. Follow out the analogy of nature" (Bell, 1876, p. 13).

The ear analogy provided Bell with a model that suggested possibilities and problem areas. Consider Bell's ear diagram. It shows two possible arrangements of electromagnets that could be used to translate the vibrations of the ossicles into an electric current, one of which he had already used in building his Gallows telephone. . . . Bell knew he could not include the ossicles in an actual speaking telegraph. Therefore, [his] sketch served as a reminder of the model he had been working with at least since June 30, 1875, and possibly before.

As of February 1876, Bell had a patent, but not a device which actually transmitted speech. For Bell, the patent was not the end-point of a long process; it was the beginning of a new stage of research, of going from a patentable idea to a marketable product.

BELL'S PATENT AND GRAY'S CAVEAT COMPARED

Bell's patent and Gray's caveat were declared in interference with each other, a formal proceeding at the patent office in which the examiner has to determine whether, in the light of the interference, a patent should be granted to either party.

In fact, the two documents were very different. Gray's caveat covered a method for transmitting speech. The central claim of Bell's patent was that this undulating current was the best method to transmit sound, as opposed to the intermittent, or on-off, current commonly used in telegraphy. The undulatory current preserved the gradual changes in intensity produced by speech or musical tones; the intermittent current reduced these often subtle variations to an on-off code.

Gray's patent heuristic was to cover speaking and harmonic telegraphy by patenting as many variations as possible. Bell's heuristic was to try to claim the whole landscape in a single patent. In the first claim at the end of his patent 174,465, Bell claimed "a system of telegraphy in which the receiver is set in vibration by the employment of undulatory currents of electricity." (Bell, 1908, pp. 459-460); his main example of how to do this was his reed mechanical representation, which could send telegraph signals, musical notes, or even speech. Bell's patent was breathtakingly broad: anyone who used the undulating current to transmit information could potentially be in conflict with Bell's claims.

The interference was resolved in favor of Bell's patent because it had arrived in the Patent Office a few hours earlier than Gray's caveat, though technically Gray still had three months in which to submit a patent and could also have contested Bell's claim in court. Gray's backers felt the speaking telegraph was a "toy" that might be of occasional use over private lines, but would play no significant role in the transmission of multiple messages over long distances (Taylor, Unpublished Manuscript). Therefore, Gray did not contest Bell's patent until the commercial potential of the telephone became apparent.

After the interference had been voided, Bell learned from the patent examiner that the critical point of contention concerned a clause Bell had inserted at the last minute, in which he claimed the possibility of using variable resistance to create an undulating current. Gray's liquid transmitter depended on variable resistance. This conversation with the patent examiner became the source of endless debate during the years of litigation that followed, with some accusing Bell of outright theft of Gray's idea, in part because he eventually achieved the first transmission of speech with a device that looked similar to Gray's (Taylor, Unpublished Manuscript).

THE FIRST TRANSMISSION OF SPEECH

Bell received his patent on March 7, 1876. He had not yet successfuly transmitted speech. From March 7 to 10, 1876, Bell did a series of experiments which culminated in the first transmission of speech (Gorman 1995; Gorman 1997)—with a device that resembled the transmitter in Gray's caveat. It is likely that the patent examiner drew Bell's attention to this possibility.

Gray's liquid transmitter depended on immersing a needle deeply in a vessel of water. Bell's liquid transmitter, in contrast, worked poorly if the needle or tuning fork went too deeply in water; he wanted to minimize the surface area of the vibrating contact and maximizing the area of the other contact (Bruce, 1973). Furthermore, Gray thought the transmission of speech might have required multiple speaking chambers, whereas Bell demonstrated that only one would be necessary.

The differences in the transmitters were mirrored by differences in the two receivers. Bell used his familiar steel reed, which could reproduce any tone. Gray used one of the receivers he had designed to discriminate and enhance single tones. In other words, Gray's receiver design would have been best suited to enhance a particular range of vocal tones, whereas Bell's was intended to reproduce any spoken sound. In other words, Gray's receivers would have worked best with multiple speaking chambers, each tuned to a different frequency. In this way, Gray's device might have reproduced the composite tones of the human voice.

AFTER THE FIRST TRANSMISSION OF SPEECH

After his caveat, Elisha Gray all but abandoned speaking telegraphy until June, after a major Centennial exhibition in Philadelphia, when he heard the human voice through one of Bell's telephones. Had Bell used a liquid transmitter on this occasion, Gray's surprise might have turned to suspicion. But despite his early success with the liquid transmitter, at the Centennial Bell demonstrated magnetic induction designs that looked more like the ones in his first patent. Improvements on this magneto design formed the basis of his second speaking telegraph patent in 1877 (Bell, 1908). Why did Bell abandon the approach that led to the first transmission of speech?

Barney Finn tested the Bell apparatus housed at the Smithsonian and concluded that, "Bell apparently abandoned the variable-resistance transmitter in favor of the magneto transmitter for the simple reason that the latter worked better and with greater consistency than the variable-resistance liquid transmitter he had designed, and this decision came after an impressively large number of experiments. My recent experiments confirm the validity of Bell's judgment" (Finn, 1966, p. 15).

Finn tested Bell's devices with an oscilliscope; Bell used his ear, and compared current results with what he had written about previous ones in his notebooks. Therefore, a fairer judge of Bell's successes may be his notebook record, which suggests that he continued to obtain positive results with the liquid transmitter long after March 10th, results at least as positive as any he had achieved with magneto designs.

Another possibility is that Bell wanted to keep his liquid experiments a secret, knowing that Gray was working on something similar. This implies some clever guesswork on Bell's part, or a spy at the patent office. All Bell ever admitted knowing was that his patent and Gray's caveat were in conflict over the matter of variable resistance.

There is a third possibility: that Bell saw the liquid transmitter primarily as a way of testing his model for the transmission of speech, not as a practical device. The liquid would need to be kept at just the right level. One can imagine running to "top off the transmitter" every time the phone rang!

On May 5th, Bell returned to his classic magneto devices, relying primarily on transceivers that resembled his steel reed. From this point forward, the liquid transmitter virtually disappears from his notebook. Bell was preparing for a May 10, 1876, presentation to the American Academy of Arts and Sciences; the pressure of a deadline forced Bell to confirm that a magneto device could serve as both transmitter and receiver. In the talk, he placed much greater emphasis on his work with magneto devices, despite the fact that his notebooks suggested their performance was not consistently superior to that of liquid variable resistance devices: he could get either type to produce vowels, musical tones, and even occasional phrases, but neither would permit consistent discrimination of consonants.

Bell was hastily added to the program at the Philadelphia Centennial by Gardiner Hubbard, his backer and future father-in-law who also submitted Bell's patent. Bell did not want to take time from his teaching to go to the Centennial; his fiancée Mabel took him to the station and all but shoved him on the train.

Elisha Gray, in contrast, had an elaborate, carefully choreographed set of demonstrations ready, supported by Western Union. On June 25, the judges, accompanied by Dom Pedro, the Emperor of Brazil, listened to a long lecture by Gray and watched him demonstrate both musical and multiple telegraphy, but not speaking telegraphy.

The clever Hubbard had put Bell in the same hotel with three of the judges, so by the time they saw Gray's exhibit, they had already heard Bell's account of the scientific principles underlying his speaking telegraph. The judges then trudged off to see Bell's exhibit. It included multiple harmonic telegraph equipment, but also Bell's latest speaking telegraph—a magneto design that included a new receiver, which he had created by scavenging parts in Charles Williams' shop. Bell had found an iron cylinder with a rod running up the middle; when wire was wrapped around the rod, the whole apparatus became an electromagnet, with one pole represented by the pole of the cylinder and the other pole by the top of the rod. Bell added a lid of sheet iron, which vibrated in response to the undulating current from the transmitter.

Wires from this receiver ran to the corresponding transmitter in another part of the exhibit hall. Bell sang and shouted into his transmitter while Sir William Thomson, one of the judges, listened at the receiving end. He heard the words, "Do you understand what I say?", and shouted, "I must see Mr. Bell!" Thomson ran to find Bell, reported the success, and went back to hear more. Dom Pedro was next, heard part of Hamlet's soliloquy, and also rushed off to congratulate Bell. Even Elisha Gray heard "Aye, there's the rub" faintly when he took his turn at the receiver (Bruce, 1973, p. 197). Bell's use of a familiar passage was a clever way of insuring that listeners could fill in the gaps in the faint and unsteady transmission.

The delighted and surprised reaction of his listeners would be echoed time and time again when Bell, Watson, and others took their invention "on the road" and did live demonstrations. For a professional telegrapher like Gray, this invention had always been subsidiary to the telegraph. As he said in a letter to his attorney, A. L. Hayes, in October of 1875:

> Bell seems to be spending all his energies on [sic] talking telegraph. While this is very interesting scientifically it has no commercial value at present, for they can do much more business over a line by methods already in use than by that system. I don't want at present to spend my time and money for that which will bring no return.[10]

He also publicly conceded all priority in matters related to speaking telegraphy in a letter to Bell on March 5, 1877, in which he said,

> Of course you had no means of knowing what I had done in the matter of transmitting vocal sounds. When, however, you see the specification, you will see that the fundamental principles are contained therein. I do not, however, claim even the credit of inventing it, as I do not believe a mere description of an idea that has never been *reduced to practice*—in the *strict* sense of that phrase—should be dignified with the name invention.

In later years Gray regretted this concession, especially given the fact that Bell got a patent without achieving a reduction to practice. But Gray also had to admit that Bell was the first to achieve spoken transmission, and that his electromagnetic induction design was original: "I thought it would be impossible to make a practical working speaking telephone on the principle shown by Professor Bell, to wit: generating electric currents with the power of the voice, as it semed to me then that the vibrations were so slight in amplitude and the inductor necessarily so light that the currents thus generated would be too feeble for practical purposes" (Telephone Suits, Part I, 1880, 142-43). Eventually, Gray obtained design patents for several variations in speaking telegraphy, using familiar combinations like the washbasin and electromagnet design receiver in combination with other devices like the liquid transmitter featured in his caveat (Gorman, Mehalik et al, 1993). (These design patents did not circumvent Bell's utility patent; the former protects only the appearance of a device, whereas the latter protects its funciton).

In January 1877, Bell submitted a second patent that emphasized speaking telegraphy. The membrane was now gone altogether; in its place was a heavy plate of iron or steel, whose position with respect to an electromagnet or permanent magnet could be adjusted to produce the best transmission or reception. Bell and Watson's first production telephones were built along these lines, but were quickly superseded by better transmitters using carbon as a medium of variable resistance. Bell and Watson also put together an effective "road show" in which Bell would place a receiver in front of an audience and Watson would sing to them from a remote location (Bruce, 1973). Just as at the Centennial, these shows had a magical effect on audiences. Never mind that much of the effect depended on the way Watson bellowed into the transmitter.

Bell's telephone transmitter was quickly superseded by better devices, including a transmitter developed and patented by Thomas Edison that relied on carbon as a medium of variable resistance (Carlson and Gorman, 1989). The fledgling Bell Corporation was able to buy a similar patent by a German inventor, and used it to throw Edison's patent into an interference that lasted for 15 years. By the time Edison won, it was too late—the Bell Corporation dominated the telephone market.

Elisha Gray had correctly recognized that successful transmission of speech would depend on using a medium of variable resistance. Alexander Graham Bell mentioned this possibility only briefly in his first telephone patent, although he used it in his first successful transmission of speech. Gray did not follow up on his caveat until Bell's telephone began to achieve a measure of success.

Which one of these men deserves to be called the inventor of the telephone? Or should the telephone be counted as a simultaneous invention?

Notes

1. Lloyd Taylor, Unpublished Manuscript #270, Chap. IV, p. 6.
2. We have been unable to locate either of these applications, though their substance is described in other places: see Bell, 1908; Gray, 1877.
3. The word telephone was originally used to describe a device created by Philip Reis in 1860 to transmit musical tones: see Gorman and Carlson, 1990.
4. Elisha Gray, "Electric Telegraph for Transmitting Musical Tones," U.S. Patent 166,095 (filed Jan. 19, 1875, granted July 27, 1875).
5. Gray, "Magnet Receiver Application," in Telephone Suits, Part II, 1880, 583-587.
6. J. Baille, *The Wonders of Electricity* (New York: Charles Scribner, 1872), pp. 140-143.
7. The globe-shaped resonant cavity of the caveat receiver comes from a device that Gray constructed in December 1874. This device was tuned to respond to a single pitch so that it could be used as a receiver for a specific tone and its cavity was made out of glass. Gray, E. (1877). Experimental Researches in Electro-Harmonic Telegraphy and Telephony: 1867-1878. In G. Shiers (ed.), *The Telephone: An Historical Anthology*, New York: Arno Press, 54-55.
8. On April 9, 1878, Gray submitted a patent for an "Improvement in the Art of Transmitting Rhythmical Vibrations in an Electric Circuit," eventually granted as No. 205,378. In it, Gray outlined a system that would have functioned like the harp apparatus, using multiple transmitters tuned to different parts of a complex sound and battery cells that could be shunted in or out to reinforce these transmitters.
9. Gardiner Hubbard, Bell's future father-in-law and principle backer, told him, "Whenever you recall any fact connected with your invention, jot it down on paper, as time will be essential to us, and the more things you actually performed by you at an earlier date, the better for our case." Gardiner G. Hubbard to Alexander Graham Bell, November 19, 1874, Bell Family Papers, Library of Congress, Box 80.
10. Gray Papers, National Museum of American History, Box 2, Folder 1.

References

Ashley, J.N. (October 21, 1876). "Transmission of Musical Tones by Electricity. Article II—Application to Telegraphy." *The Telegrapher* 12: 253-54

Bell, A.G. (1908). *The Bell Telephone: Deposition of Alexander Graham Bell*. Boston: American Bell Telephone Co.

Bruce, R.V. (1973). *Bell: Alexander Graham Bell and the Conquest of Solitude*. Boston: Little, Brown.

Carlson, W.B. (1994). "Entrepreneurship in the Early Development of the Telephone: How Did William Orton and Gardiner Hubbard Conceptualize this New Technology?" *Business and Economic History* 23(2): 161-192.

Carlson, W.B. and M.E. Gorman (1989). "Thinking and Doing at Menlo Park: Edison's Development of the Telephone, 1876-1878." In *Thomas Edison's Menlo Park Laboratory*. (ed.) W. Pretzer. Detroit: Wayne State University Press.

Finn, B.S. (1966). "Alexander Graham Bell's Experiments with the Variable Resistance Transmitter." *Smithsonian Journal of History* 1(Winter): 1-16.

Gorman, M.E. (1995). "Confirmation, Disconfirmation and Invention: The Case of Alexander Graham Bell and the Telephone." *Thinking and Reasoning*, I(1): 31-53.

Gorman, M.E. (1997). "Mind in the World: Cognition and Practice in the Invention of the Telephone." *Social Studies of Science* 27(4): 583-624.

Gorman, M.E. and W.B. Carlson (1990). "Interpreting Invention as a Cognitive Process: The Case of Alexander Graham Bell, Thomas Edison and the Telephone." *Science, Technology and Human Values* 15: 131-164.

Gorman, M.E., M.M. Mehalik, et al. (1993). "Alexander Graham Bell, Elisha Gray and the Speaking Telegraph: A Cognitive Comparison." *History of Technology* 15:1-56.

Gray, E. (1977) "Experimental Researches in Electro-Harmonic Telegraphy and Telephony: 1867-1878." *The Telephone: An Historical Anthology*. (ed.) G. Shiers. New York: Arno Press. 10:15-96.

Hounshell, D. (1975). "Elisha Gray and the Telephone: On the Disadvantages of Being an Expert." *Technology and Culture* 16: 133-161.

Kingsbury, J.E. (1915). *The Telephone and Telephone Exchanges: Their Invention and Development.* New York: Longmans, Green. Reprinted Arno, 1972.

Taylor, L. (Unpublished Manuscript). The Untold Story of the Telephone.

The Telephone Suits: Bell Telephone Company et al. v. Peter A. Dowd, Part II: Exhibits of Complainants and Defendant. Boston: Alfred Judge & Son, Law Printers, 1880.

4

DOW CORNING CORPORATION (A)

June, 1975

Dow Corning Corporation (DCC) Chemist Kim Anderson[1] examined the situation. Some of her co-workers had expressed concern about the new, more fluid silicone gel for the breast implant. (A breast implant is a silicone sac filled with silicone gel that simulates natural breast tissue.) They worried that the new gel, with its thinner consistency and additional swelling agent, might be more likely to diffuse the swelling agent through the breast implant wall than the standard gel which had been used for ten years. Such an occurrence might lead to movement of the silicone in the woman's body. Although silicone was considered chemically inert, and therefore safe for use in the human body, such movement was undesirable since it would eventually become lodged in the lymph nodes.

Still, Anderson went over the new formulation in her mind. The new implant gel used a different ratio of basically the same ingredients as the old gel, materials already safety-tested and used in the human body. Moreover, since the new gel was a different

This case was written by Julie M. Stocker, under the supervision of Patricia H. Werhane and Michael E. Gorman. This case was written as a basis for class discussion rather than to illustrate effective or ineffective handling of an administrative situation. Copyright © 1997 by the University of Virginia Darden School Foundation, Charlottesville, VA. All rights reserved. *To order copies, send an e-mail to dardencases@virginia.edu. No part of this publication may be reproduced, stored in a retrieval system, used in a spreadsheet, or transmitted in any form or by any means—electronic, mechanical, photocopying, recording, or otherwise—without the permission of the Darden School Foundation. Rev. 5/97* formulation of these ingredients, Dow Corning had conducted more testing on it, along with some other experimental gels. The corporation had completed a two-week study focused on the reaction of rats and monkeys to the injected silicone gel,[2] and a similar three-month rabbit study.[3] The rabbit study found some localized reaction to the gels in the animals, but attributed it to the "trauma of implantation,"[4] not the gel itself. Anderson looked over some results of the other study including the statement: "None of the new gel formulations appear to be more susceptible to systemic migration than the standard formulation, which has been implanted with apparent safety in humans for the previous . . . [ten] . . . years."[5] Anderson's Product Management Group (PMG) leader had asked for her recommendation on going forward with production by four o'clock today. It was now two o'clock. What should she do?

Silicone???[6]

Silicon, silica, silicone—what's the difference? Silicon is a chemical element, one of the 109 known substances that constitute the universe's matter. Second only to carbon in its presence on earth, one-quarter of the earth's crust is silicon. Carbon is also the only element capable of producing more compounds than silicon; thus, silicon possesses immense potential for commercial application. One of the premier semi-conducting elements, silicon is used in many electronic devices, such as transistors and computers.

However, one does not find silicon alone in nature. It always exists as silica or silicates. Silica is silicon dioxide (SiO_2), commonly found in sand and quartz. A silicate is a compound made of silicon, oxygen, and at least one metal, sometimes with hydrogen, sometimes without it. Talc, all gemstones but diamond, and clays are natural silicates. The most widely recognized synthetic form is sodium silicate, or water glass, a combination of silica with sodium and hydrogen. Capable of ". . . combining chemically with most metallic oxides,"[7] silica is important in both the chemical and industrial realms. It appears in a wide range of products, from glass to cosmetics to the amorphous silica gel we find with our new shoes. (Materials lacking the molecular lattice structure of a solid state are amorphous, for example, all liquids. Thus, an amorphous form of a material possesses the same atomic makeup as the crystalline version, but without a "highly ordered geometry."[8])

Silicone is a synthetic polymer, or macro-molecule, whose backbone is a repeating chain of Si-O molecules, with various organic groups attached to the silicon. The most common silicone is PDMS, poly-dimethylsiloxane [$(CH_3)_2Si-O$), the foundation of all silicones. Silicones have been introduced into many products, from cosmetics to building materials to computers. Commercial silicones are separated into six groups according to the number of repeating units and the number of ties linking these units: ". . . fluids, emulsions, compounds, lubricants, resins, and elastomers."[9] A fluid is characterized by its uniform change in shape or direction when an outside force is applied, so that it includes all liquids. Typically, silicone fluids are straight chains of PDMS ending in trimethylsyl groups, ranging in viscosity from that of water to fluids that cannot be poured. An emulsion is a stable combination of at least two immiscible liquids, one present in the other as droplets, for example, oil in water. A compound in this context is a formulated or compounded mixture. Lubricants are "materials of low viscosity that separate moving solids, used to minimize friction and wear."[10] A silicone resin is a substance which is ". . . non-combustible, electrically nonconductive, hard and glassy when . . . cold, and soft and sticky . . . [above] . . . the glass transition point."[11] Finally, an elastomer describes a synthetic polymer which behaves much like natural rubber, i.e., can be stretched to several times its size and still snap back to its original length.

Silicone gels lie somewhere between a fluid and an elastomer. They are "lightly crosslinked" PDMS molecules, forming a three dimensional array "which . . . [is] . . . swollen with PDMS fluids to give a sticky, cohesive mass without form. . . "[12] and, thus, are more complex than a fluid; however, the gel's composition is less dense than that of the elastomer, which has only minute portions of its fluid not crosslinked. An elastomer surrounds the gel in silicone breast implants.

THE DOW CORNING CORPORATION[13]

Founded in 1943, the Dow Corning Corporation was created as a jointly owned business in commercial silicone technology by The Dow Chemical Company and Corning, Incorporated. Corning Glassworks had researched the commercial potential of silicone in the 1930's and early 1940's. What Corning needed, however, was an experienced chemical company to assist them in manufacturing this new ingredient, an organization like the chemical industry giant, The Dow Chemical Company. With Dow Chemical's experience and Corning's ideas, silicone would grow to be indispensable, finding applications in the aerospace, electronic, medical products, and construction industries, among others.

Dow Corning's first triumph was a sealant used to protect Allied fighter planes' ignitions from failure at high altitudes during the Second World War. When the war was over, Dow Corning explored non-defense applications of silicone, eventually creating more than 5,000 silicone products. Dow Corning continued to emphasize research and expansion throughout the 1950's and 1960's. During this time, the company ordered a substantial amount of testing on silicones' effects, both on organisms and the environment, though not required to do so by any Food & Drug Administration (FDA) regulations. Typically, silicone was found to be chemically inert, failing to cause harmful reactions in rats, monkeys, or even human embryonic cells. With such a characteristic, silicone seemed the perfect candidate for use in medical applications, for instance, in synthetic coverings for burn patients, in a coating on needles to ease insertion, and even in implantable devices like the heart pacemaker. To further encourage research in this area, Dow Corning opened the Center for Aid to Medical Research (CAMR) as a source of silicone for in-house and independent medical researchers. Thus, in the early 1960's, Dow Corning supplied Texas plastic surgeons Frank Gerow and Thomas Cronin with silicone for their medical implant device research. Gerow and Cronin, using Dow Corning silicone, invented the first silicone breast implant as a device to aid women who had undergone mastectomies or had congenital breast deformities. Although the FDA had no regulations governing implantable devices, the surgeons conducted two years of clinical trials on the implant prior to Dow Corning's product introduction in 1964. In the next several years, the implant grew popular for cosmetic surgery as well as reconstructive, and Dow Corning cornered both markets.

Not just an innovator in silicone technology, Dow Corning proved itself a leader in organizational management. In 1967, it adopted a matrix management structure, eventually called Dow Corning's "multidimensional management structure."[14] . . . Instead of the traditional divisions only along product lines, they organized themselves into a two-dimensional matrix with profit centers (i.e., business types) as the row headings and cost centers (departments) as the column headings. The resulting rows formed business boards according to product category, such as electronics, with one business manager and a representative from Marketing, Research, Manufacturing, Technical Service & Development, and Finance. (The multitude of countries across which this matrix was implemented was the third dimension, and time was the fourth. Hence its classification as multi-dimensional.) These business boards allowed for improved communication among different departments and decision making at lower levels. Within this structure, Dow Corning formed Product Management Groups, PMG's, similar in form to the business boards, except that PMG's focused on planning for a certain product and consisted of representatives from the lower rungs of department ladders. Even more focused were the ad/hoc task forces occasionally developed to speed a particular product to market. . . .

DCC's Contributions to Silicone in Medical Products[15]

Throughout the 1950's and 1960's, Dow Corning, as well as independent medical doctors and research scientists, performed scientific tests on silicones, evaluating it and sometimes using silicone material for medical applications. The Center's newsletter, *The Bulletin*, reported results of these tests from October, 1959 to July, 1972, including both Dow Corning and outside researchers' findings. Several of silicone's characteristics make it suitable for medical products. It is usually considered chemically inert, so that it will not react with the wide range of chemicals present in the body. It can endure extreme temperature fluctuations without changing consistency. This thermal stability is especially important to the medical world, since it can therefore be sterilized at high temperatures. Finally, silicone is water insoluble, and thus is a good candidate for use in water-based environments, such as a woman's breast.

Through their Center for Aid to Medical Research, CAMR, Dow Corning invented many important medical devices. For example, first introduced in the late 1950's, Dow Corning created the hydrocephalic shunt, a silicone drain implanted in a child's head to relieve the effects of hydrocephalus, "an excess of cerebrospinal fluid in the cranial cavity causing enlargement of the skull and mental retardation."[16] In 1952, Doctors F. E. Nulsen and E. B. Spitz originally developed the technique of treating hydrocephalus by inserting a valve into the skull, diverting the excess water from the ventricle to the jugular vein. Later, they used a shunt valve developed by Dow Corning and John Holter, with encouraging results.[17]

In the January, 1960 edition of *The Bulletin*, W. E. Wallace, MD, of the US Air Force Department of Neurosurgery in the Medical Corps, reported, "It has been my good fortune, however, to utilize the Spitz-Holter valve for hydrocephalus in 29 patients. Some of these patients came to re-operation, and it was possible to visualize the Silastic®[18] tubing used. In none of these cases was there any apparent tissue reaction to the silicone materials."[19]

Such medical breakthroughs were not introduced without testing. For example, the Dow Corning CAMR January, 1960 newsletter describes a scientific evaluation of silicones as organic tissue substitutes:

> Of the many synthetic materials we have investigated during the past nine years, including halogenated hydrocarbons and polyvinyl alcohol, silicones have proved most promising in clinical use. . . .[20]

—"Evaluation of silicones as tissue substitutes"

In the same newsletter, "An experimental study of silicone as a soft tissue substitute" stated:

> . . . seven healthy adult mongrel dogs were used . . . At time intervals varying between 3 months and 1 year the sponges were removed . . . Reaction at this stage is mostly one of fibrosis rather than exudation or foreign body reaction. Sponged Silastic® 250 and s=9711 (red and gray) implants observed in the gross showed almost no tissue reaction. There appeared to be more reaction to the 4-0 silk anchoring sutures than to the implant itself. . . . These studies indicate that clinical applications now served by silicones are justified.[21]

Other uses include silicone's presence in cardiac catheters, where, ". . . Neither oily nor greasy to the touch, such a silicone surface is said to reduce markedly the tendency of blood to clot in contact with the catheter."[22] Related to this, silicone has been successfully used to treat coronary air embolisms, where air bubbles lethally interfere in the blood flow of arteries to the brain or heart.

But what about long-term effects? How were the hydrocephalic patients doing, not just three months after surgery, but more than a year? In the October 1960 newsletter, we find R. H. Ames, MD, reporting on Silastic® tubing:

> Clinical experience indicates that Silastic® is extremely well tolerated. I now have patients in whom these materials have been implanted for upwards of three years without evidence of ill effects. Recently the opportunity presented itself to re-examine a ventriculocisternostomy performed in 1957. . . no adhesions were in evidence, and the silicone rubber tubing was unchanged by three years implantation in the tissues of the brain. . . .[23]

Furthermore, this October, 1960 newsletter also contains Part One of an article on the study of the toxicology of silicones by R. R. McGregor, Ph.D., of the Dow Corning CAMR. Indeed, 5 years prior to the commercial marketing of the breast implant, "With the exception of some very low molecular weight materials, silicone fluids were found by Rowe, et al. to cause little response in laboratory animals when injected subcutaneously, intramuscularly or intraperitoneally."[24] Subcutaneously means situated beneath the skin. Intraperitoneally is within the abdomen. Intramuscularly indicates something injected within the muscles. Such muscles include the heart, where the well known life-saving pacemaker, clothed in silicone, is placed. At that time, 30 such units had been tested: "Most recent publication describes the implantation of such devices in six patients. All were alive with results extremely gratifying in five of them. One completely disabled patient, in his middle thirties, was rehabilitated."[25]

Indeed, Dow Corning researchers were not the only scientists interested in the medical possibilities of silicone. Research on the potential uses of silicone in medicine, and reactions of animals to it, had been performed since the 1940's and 1950's. For example, in February, 1952, Windsor Cutting, MD published an article in the *Stanford Medical Bulletin* entitled "Toxicity of Silicones," studying the silicone used as a food additive to control foaming. Unlike previous studies which had found no lesion development due to the ingestion of silicone by rats, his study found such a reaction in rabbits fed silicone along with a high cholesterol diet.[26] In August, 1959, the article, "Tumors Associated With Embedded Polymers,"[27] appeared in the *Journal of the National Cancer Institute*. It found that only five rats out of the 299 that lived at least three hundred days with certain polymers, including various Silastics®, developed tumors, that is, only 1.7 percent. However, this percentage was lower than similar studies' results, so the authors suggested that more research was needed. In the July, 1961 edition of *The Bulletin* we find an abstract of Midland Silicones, Ltd.'s[28] work, "A Note on Bacteriological Toxicity Tests of Silicone Rubbers for Medical and Pharmaceutical Uses." (Written by I. H. Riley and H. I. Winner, it was published in the *Journal of Pharmacy and Pharmacology*.) It states: "In the great majority of cases. . . there was no inhibition at all. This complete lack of toxicity was true of the uncured rubber as well as pieces given all degrees of cure"[29]; and "the toxicity of suitably compounded rubbers which could be used in pharmacy, medicine and in contact with food stuffs . . . [was] . . . very low."[30] Other studies supporting the low toxicity and carcinogenesis of silicone followed.[31] By 1962, a study entitled "Tissue Reactions to Polymers" published in the British medical journal, *The Lancet*, stated:

> For clinical use a polymer must consistently prove innocuous. Of the polymers examined in the present series those which produced consistently good results were the silicones and the medium-density and low-density polyethylenes . . . None of the other types of plastic investigated produced completely consistent results."[32]

Thus, silicone's performance in medical applications was of interest to the global medical community, not just to suppliers like Dow Corning.

DEVELOPMENT OF THE CRONIN IMPLANT[33]

As mentioned previously, plastic surgeons Thomas Cronin and Frank Gerow of the University of Texas developed the first silicone breast implant in the early 1960's. As part of its CAMR efforts, DCC provided them silicone to use. As early as January, 1961, Cronin was corresponding with Dow Corning, informing them of his research and the background of the project. The original implant was developed for use by mastectomy patients to replace ones made of a sponge material, which tended to harden and appear less natural over time. This new mammary prosthesis was a breast-shaped silicone sac filled with silicone gel. The sac was in elastomer form, and the gel was a soft solid. The elastomer had a much more tightly woven molecular pattern, which kept the gel inside the sac. The gel was firm, yet pliable, so that it successfully simulated natural breast tissue. With over 10 years of research already completed on it, silicone was a natural candidate for use in breast reconstruction. In addition, it had already been utilized in other medical applications, such as the hydrocephalic shunt and life-saving pace-maker described earlier. These cases could provide information on the long-term effects of silicone on the host.

By the time of his correspondence with DCC, Cronin's protocol had already been approved by the Research Committee of the Houston Veteran's Administrative Hospital, as well as use of the laboratories and pathology facilities were approved. Cronin also reported that such devices would be tested in those laboratories before implantation in humans. For example, Cronin and Gerow's first implantable medical device, a fluid-filled cushion for the prevention of pressure sores in paraplegics, was implanted in dogs to explore an organism's reaction to it and the device's reaction to the host environment. In the 1960 issue of the Center for Aid to Medical Research's *The Bulletin*, Doctors Bassett and Campbell of Columbia University submitted an article affirming the performance of the Silastic® brand of silicone, i.e., what was later used in the breast implants: "Our experience indicates that clean Silastic® is one of the most inert materials available for implantation in the living organism. . ."[34] The January 1961 issue highlighted pacemakers clothed in Dow Corning silicone: "The entire assembly, including batteries . . . were potted in epoxy resin and then encapsulated in DC Silastic® RTV 502, which is better tolerated in the body."[35] Thus, a compendium of research supporting the use of silicone in medical devices had been compiled before Cronin and Gerow employed it in the mammary prosthesis.

1962 marked the first implanting of a mammary prototype. For the next two years, selected surgeons used the implants in clinical trials to obtain information on their performance, both long- and short-term, before Dow Corning took the Cronin implant fully to market in 1964. Additional support for the implants was found in the hydrocephalic shunt's performance results, since it used the same elastomer. By 1962, four thousand shunts had been placed in children's brains, treating their hydrocephalus without any apparent adverse effects.[36]

Also, in 1962, the National Institute of Health funded the Battelle Memorial Institute to conduct research[37] on the stability of silicone implants in animals. The Institute's two-year study focused on the effect of the body on the various polymers studied, which included Polyethylene, Teflon, Mylar, Nylon, and Silastic®. In particular, the study concentrated on the polymers' tensile strengths and elongations, along with the reaction of the implant site to the polymers. (Tensile strength is a measure of the polymer's ability to withstand elongation forces.) The studies used mongrel dogs as test sites, implanting samples of all five materials in each. The plastics were recovered after six, eleven, and seventeen month intervals. Their tensile strength was recorded before implantation and after each removal, to track any loss, along with any elongation due to implantation. After 17 months, Silastic® showed little decrease in tensile strength and slight elongation. According to the study:

> Changes [concerning tensile strength and elongation] in the Silastic® and Mylar are not believed significant. . . . In general, minimal local tissue reaction was observed grossly at nacropsy. There was no gross evidence of tumorigenesis either at the site of implant or in other organs and tissues. No irritation or inflammation was seen . . . [However, the Silastic® implant was observed to have] a poorly defined capsule which was accidentally incised. As in previous necropsies, a great deal of difficulty was encountered in locating the site of

the flank implant. The Silastic® strips were folded and wadded into a ball—no evidence of irritation or local tissue reaction other than the connective tissue encapsulation. . . .[38]

(Encapsulation is a common (and unharmful) foreign body reaction to any implanted device, where tissue walls the device off from the rest of the body.[39]) The study also provided a histological report on the 17-month findings. (Histology is the study of tissues.[40]) The histological findings on Silastic® showed "fibrous tissue segment without apparent inflammatory reaction."

Simultaneous to the introduction of the Cronin implant to market in 1964, Dow Corning contracted Food and Drug Research Laboratories, an independent research company, to complete more long-term testing on the implants, which had already been followed for two years in the clinical studies and seventeen months in the Battelle study. In the three-year Food and Drug Research Laboratories experiment, eleven polysiloxane compositions were implanted ". . . into intramuscular, subcutaneous, and intraperitoneal sites in sufficient numbers to permit samples and surrounding tissue to be removed at a number of periods prior to sacrifice of the animals. . . . The design of the study provided for replication of each treatment in three dogs, restricting one type of polysiloxane within each given dog, but permitting as many as four replications of each product and site combination in a given animal."[41] These silicones were implanted "over protracted periods" in five forms: "solid film, perforated film, sponge, amorphous forms, and miniature artificial breasts."[42] Microscopic examination of tissue reaction was completed at three, nine, twenty-four, and thirty-six months. The results of the study, published in 1968, proved encouraging for the use of silicone in medical implants, especially in mammary prostheses.[43]

Although implants were first targeted at mastectomy patients, even Cronin and Gerow would have been able to surmise the general population's desire to use the mammary prostheses for enhancement as well. Thus, other manufacturers developed similar implants, in response to a market which grew as women opted for cosmetic breast procedures. However, Dow Corning, where the implant originated, remained the industry leader. Dow Corning continued to look for improvements to the implant, developing a new outer lining in 1968. This elastomer envelope, while thinner, was also seamless. (At times, the line where the two halves of the original implant were joined was noticeable under the upper portion of the breast.) The seamless envelope was all one elastomer, a thinner covering that provided even more aesthetically pleasing results.

DOW CORNING PRODUCT STAGING SYSTEM[44]

Along with product improvements, Dow Corning considered improvements to its product development program. Prior to 1974, Dow Corning had product checkpoints in place. For example, the file on the original implant included a specification page, where the plant manager, research scientists, and bio-safety scientists from the PMG signed off that the product made was the product intended, verified a formulation page, and approved a recipe page which not only reiterated the formulation, but laid out the instructions for the manufacturing of the product.

(The table and figure that follow illustrate Dow Corning's Product staging system.[45])

Stage	I Conception	II Feasibility	III Product Development	IV Commercialization	V Market Expansion	VI Product Maturity	VII Product Obsolescence
Definition	Exploratory lab studies are conducted to define new science and technology or an external market need is conceptualized.	Lab work is done to translate basic science and technology into product concepts and prototype products.	Prototype products are defined with product specifications for specific applications.	Products are introduced that meet the requirements of the customer. A marketing strategy is implemented, price/value established and the first sales made.	That stage in a product life cycle characterized by market expansion and rapid growth.	That stage in a product life cycle characterized by product maturity and slow growth rate.	That stage in a product's life cycle when product profit and sales growth are topping off and product or market is becoming obsolete.
Objective	Develop new science and technology.	Define prototype solutions to well characterized market needs. Assess mfg. implications.	Develop a product that has a competitive advantage in satisfying a specified need.	Demonstrate commercial viability and begin market penetration.	Maximize rate of sales and distribution. Maintain balance in capacity and market demand.	Maintain business and maximize profit over as long a time span as possible.	Remove product from product line.

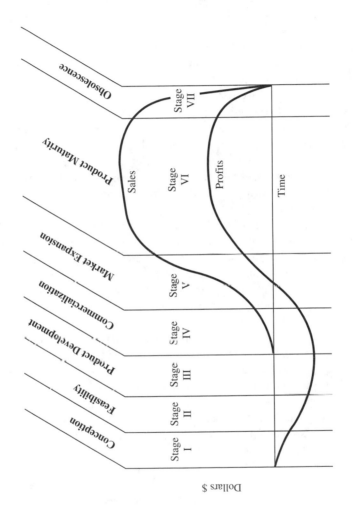

Conception — Stage I

Feasibility — Stage II

Product Development — Stage III

Commercialization — Stage IV

Market Expansion — Stage V

Product Maturity — Stage VI

Obsolescence — Stage VII

Sales

Profits

Time

Dollars $

Expanding upon this start, Dow Corning introduced a formal product staging system in 1974. Stage I, entitled "Conception," consisted of classic research in silicone technology, exploring various applications and demonstrating their profitability. Stage II, "Feasibility," was still focused on the Research and Development Department. Here, once the scientists had made a new material, they devised applications for it. They also performed preliminary toxicity tests. Before moving on to Stage III, the product's performance measures had to be well-defined, as well as its market specifications and long-range plans.

When all that was complete, a product moved on to Stage III, "Product Development." The Technical Service & Development Department held the main responsibility for Stage III, where product specifications and market applications were refined, more testing completed, and the legal environment researched. Manufacturing determined the quality controls along with the processing and packaging steps, and looked at environmental considerations concerning the product. Marketing organized literature about the product, establishing a potential sale price, a most-likely cost of production, and probable product terminology. The legal department determined applicable regulations and whether the product required a patent; and they wrote contracts on the new product. The Health and Environmental Science office reviewed the product's lab sheets and also conducted biocompatability tests.

Dow Corning's shift to matrix management in 1967, where decision making was pushed to the lowest level possible and the corporation was no longer solely organized along product lines, allowed the use of product management teams. These groups consisted of Marketing, Manufacturing, R & D, Technical Service & Development, Financial, and Legal employees who moved a product from idea to actualization, weighing all the departments' considerations at earlier Product Stages than previously, for example, at Stage II. A Product Action Form had to be approved by research, legal, and manufacturing staff before any devices could be moved to Stage III. At that stage, the team initiated interaction with the process engineer, who represented the people that would assemble the product day to day. A scale-up of the product was also made at this time, and the team reviewed the product and its market, making sure one more time that Dow Corning wanted to be involved with such a product and such a market. Not every product made it through these checkpoints, either. For instance, Dow Corning considered making a male contraceptive similar to the Dalkon Shield, but questioned its safety and decided against it. Similarly, Dow Corning rejected extremely large breast prostheses as an option, citing their inappropriateness.

At Stage IV, "Commercialization," Dow Corning began production of its new product—signifying a commitment to make the product conceivably forever. Responsibility, while still within the product management group, shifted mainly to the shoulders of the manufacturing members, who began production while Marketing continued work on the product campaign. At Stage V, "Market Expansion," Dow Corning made the full-blown product available. At this stage, Marketing assumed the main responsibility, which was to develop and maintain product demand. Stage VI, "Product Maturity," marked Manufacturing's maintenance of the product supply and viability. The goal was to maintain demand and profit for as long as feasible, until reaching Stage VII. Entitled "Product Obsolescence," this stage marked the demise of the product or its market, where demand leveled off. Here, Marketing directed the product's phase-out. Thus, Dow Corning developed a product staging system that encompassed the product's life-cycle and provided checkpoints before production.

(An interesting footnote to this explanation is that the breast implant never made it past stage four, since manufacturing did not want sole responsibility for the product, also desiring the freedom to call on TS & D when problems or questions arose.)

"New and Improved?"[46]

The official Product Staging System grew in combination with the Product Management Groups instituted in 1967. In 1968, Dow Corning started updating the breast implant, a process that would take approximately seven years. First, in 1968, they developed the seamless envelope, which provided a smoother finish and a more natural appearance. Now came the tough part. Doctors were requesting a softer, more natural gel formulation, so the breast implant product team went to work. Research scientist Jack Roberts worked on the new gel formulation the closest. By the first half of 1971, he had found one, and sent it for preliminary toxicity testing. Dow Corning employed a standard, widely used chemical test involving human embryonic cells. This test, commonly referred to as the CPE (CytoPathic Effect) test, was extremely sensitive, and was one of the few tests where cells would react to silicone contact. (However, such a reaction was rare even with this test.) The experimental gel was introduced to some of these embryonic cells, to investigate if any changed. As stated, although the cells rarely reacted adversely, they did so when introduced to this gel. However, such a reaction did not necessarily indicate that the gel was unsuitable for medical use. Dow Corning had two options: complete a large, expensive battery of tests to determine if this gel was suitable for implantation, or substitute a similar polymer into the original test.

Dow Corning chose the second option, since Roberts already had a gel similar to the first. Although Roberts' second gel overcame the embryonic cell hurdle, it also had to undergo a penetration test to measure its stiffness. (For example, the gelatin we eat is a fairly stiff gel.) Roberts and associates allowed a weighted probe to descend for a span of time into the gel. The farther into the gel the probe made it, the softer the gel. After tracking this characteristic in the second attempt gel, Roberts found that this gel was growing softer over time. This tendency was undesirable for an implant gel, since softer consistency could cause more diffusion through the envelope. Also, if the implant ruptured, more gel would migrate from the area of implantation. Thus, this gel, too, was rejected. All in all, by 1973, two ideas had made it to Stage II of the Product Development stages, where the PMG had to narrow application possibilities for the actual product, look into what the manufacturing system could handle, and perform preliminary toxicity tests, even though no FDA regulations required them to do so.

So, we arrive at June of 1974. Roberts had joined another product team, and Kim Anderson had joined the mammary prosthesis team in his place. She was a chemist by training and had been with Dow Corning since February of 1970. Taking over where Roberts left off, Anderson sought to understand the objectives of her mission clearly. As the team members explained to her, they had been trying to develop a more responsive implant gel, one that more closely simulated the behavior of actual breast tissue. (Although the Cronin had been quite an improvement medically and aesthetically over the sponge, it could still be better.) Meanwhile, during Dow Corning's progression toward this gel, its competitors had marketed new gels, softer and more responsive. An important restriction given to Anderson was to include only ingredients in her gel formulations that had previously been safety-tested, and/or had successful medical implant histories. This reduced the silicones from which Anderson could formulate the new gel, but seemed to ensure a safer implant for the customer.

Anderson set to work, manipulating and reformulating combinations of materials already used in medical implants, building upon Roberts' and the PMG's work. Although Anderson's gel utilized essentially the same ingredients as that in the Cronin (called the "firm gel" from now on), her more-responsive product had several important innovations. As stated previously, silicone gel consists of two parts: a cross-linked network which contains the liquid swelling agent. In the firm gel, the swelling agent constituted 50% of the gel, with 40% of that a vinyl polymer, and the last 10% PDMS.

In the new gel, Anderson was able to increase the cross-linked density of the network:

Firm   More Responsive

This increase provided more places for the swelling agent to reside, although the area of each location was smaller. Thus, Anderson was able to infuse a greater amount of the swelling agent (fluid) into the network of PDMS molecules. By increasing the amount of cross-linking, Anderson was enhancing the viscous component of the gel, allowing 30% more fluid (liquid swelling agent) to be infused. Thus, the new implant gel was 80% swelling agent, 75% of which was PDMS, and 5% of which was the vinyl polymer. This process resulted in a new gel that assumed the shape of its container more quickly than the prior firm gel, and recovered more quickly when depressed, hence, the reference to the new gel as "more responsive." With these characteristics, it behaved more like a natural breast. As a comparison, we look to the gelatin we eat for clarification. It is 99% water, with 1% cross-linked network. As we know, the gelatin, once formed, will retain the shape of its original container, and will not conform to a new container's outline.

With the added swelling agent, the task force was concerned about the diffusion rate of the swelling agent in the gel. Would more of it escape through the elastomer envelope? Anderson and colleagues compared the behavior of the new and old gel in identical seamless envelopes. Colleagues measured the strength of the envelope with the new gel and found it was comparable to its strength with the old gel. Anderson found the more responsive gel diffusion amount to be the same or slightly less than the diffusion of the old gel, which was only .78 grams over 10 years of implantation, that is less than 1/2 of a thimble.

Anderson's more responsive gel more closely copied the behavior of natural breast tissue, without any more diffusion than the old gel, while utilizing the same chemicals, albeit in a different ratio. By December of 1974, Anderson's formulation had achieved Stage III status. Anderson's formulation had passed the toxicity test of Stage II, and since she was focused on developing an implant gel, her formulation already had a marketable application. Also, the Legal and Health & Environmental Sciences departments had already stepped in, examining the researcher's lab sheets and results for patentability, and the product's biocompatability.

Other team members had invented new sterilized packaging. Thus, the Implant Development team (PMG) had created a product with three advances instead of one—

> The operating charter of the Task Force was to direct the design, testing, manufacturing scale-up, and product introduction of three changes to the existing line of breast implants:
>
> 1. Addition of Low Profile round and Low Profile Contour shapes in a variety of sizes.
> 2. Development and introduction of a more responsive gel material.
> 3. Design and introduction of a new sterile package.[47]

Meanwhile, with the arrival of new, more resilient prostheses, the implant market competition had grown very keen. Given Dow Corning's reputation as a pioneer of silicone products, doctors were requesting a new implant from the well-trusted name.

Dow Corning geared up to engineer a major effect on the breast implant market with this new, improved product. By introducing these three improvements together, Dow Corning would create a larger impact on the market. They created a special Mammary Task Force in January of 1975, to complete the final development of this new product for marketing by June. However, Dow Corning knew that two more issues had to be addressed before the new gel could go to market:

1. Can we manufacture the product?
2. We need further demonstration that the new product will be suitable for long-term implementation [in humans].[48]

While Anderson had been working on the new gel formulation, she had simultaneously addressed a manufacturing issue. Presently, the gel was divided into Parts A and B for production, with the ratio of ingredients needed A to B at 100:1. This incongruent ratio would not allow for true simultaneous production in Dow Corning's batch processing. (Since a batch of A required 100 times the number of ingredients as B, it took much more time.) In order to improve efficiency, DCC asked Kim Anderson to divide the batch ingredients for production more equitably. Her work ended in the masterbatching of the gel, with the ratio of ingredients needed A:B a much more equitable 3:1, allowing for improved efficiency in production. The new gel formula could essentially drop into this new process, and the question of whether Dow Corning could manufacture the new formulation was easily answered in the affirmative.

Anderson and the development team moved on to the second issue, concerning the safety of the product. In addition to Anderson, other scientists on the task force included a biocompatability expert along with Anderson's laboratory manager. With the second question, they found disagreement between the chemists and the biologists, since biologically inert and chemically inert do not mean the same thing. Chemists consider a material chemically inert if it is non-reactive and long-lasting. For example, silicone is considered chemically inert because it is difficult to break its Si-O backbone, requiring the introduction of a strong acid or base. From the biologists' vantage point, the body attempts to metabolize water insoluble materials such as silicone to make them water soluble (and thus excretable). Such materials, including silicone, are not biologically inert. Still, there was only one case where a silicone was biologically active on its own: the silicone found in phenyl-containing material, which is shaped the same as a steroid. Thus, this silicone acted like the steroid, much like a key that fits the same lock. This material was not used in breast implants.

In the chemists' opinion, no additional testing of the new gel was needed, since it utilized only components which had been previously tested and used in the original gel, already implanted without incident in humans for ten years. On the other side stood the biologists, arguing that since the new responsive gel was made from a new combination of those ingredients, it needed further testing. Since the new gel was much softer than that used in the Cronin implant, the biologists recommended to management a ninety-day rabbit study and a two to four week monkey study of the worst case scenario, the insertion of silicone gel without any elastomer envelope. Since the biologists were the experts in this area, their recommendations were taken. Dow Corning made the product introduction contingent on passing the tests recommended by the biologists. This was in addition to the typical manufacturing requirements.

In March/April 1975, the results of a Dow Corning two-week study on the effect of silicone gels injected subcutaneously into rats and monkeys were delivered. The current Cronin gel acted as the control gel, and the scientists at Dow Corning tried out three new gels, including the New Production gel, the one they tentatively planned on producing; an experimental High-fluid gel; and a Low-cross linker gel. Goals of this study included:

- finding the range of biologically acceptable gels for human implantation,
- determining if any of the gels displayed special characteristics, with marketable potential and future research expected,
- creating an acceptable means for ascertaining the behavior of such gels in biological systems/organisms.

Specifically, Dow Corning wanted to investigate any tissue reaction, tendency to systemic migration, or differences in general response to the gels among the monkeys and the rats. . . . The scientists found higher levels of silicon in the lymph nodes of two of the three monkeys than in the control monkey. However, such elevated levels of silicon were to be expected due to the gradual gel diffusion. The lymphatic system is designed to rid the body of foreign substances such as silicone. Thus, when any silicone escaped through the envelope, macrophages attached themselves to it and moved it away from the diffusion site, depositing it in the lymph nodes. Dow Corning scientists had both anticipated and predicted such occurrences, and noted that the levels in the lymph nodes were not significant in either animal. Also, while one iteration of the study produced an increase in the silicon in the axillary lymph node of the rats, this result could not be reproduced. No "grossly observable" tissue reaction in the monkeys was seen.[49] However, low cross-linker prosthetic formulation "E-2457-59, 3 (MG-4)" when implanted in the monkey did not encapsulate like the other formulations. Instead, the gel moved from its original implant site, along tissue surfaces. To further study this phenomena, another monkey was injected with the same formulation at multiple sites, and the final results were issued in December 1975. Again, the prosthetic gel moved from its original site along tissue planes.[50] Although this was an experimental gel and not the one tentatively scheduled for production, Dow Corning was concerned about the migration of the low cross-linked gel. Due to the systemic traveling, Dow Corning narrowed the window of safety-acceptable gels to ensure that gels with this degree of softness were excluded.

In addition, Dow Corning also contracted out the requested rabbit study to Biometric, an independent research laboratory in New Jersey. . . . Also, since the FDA did not regulate implantable devices until 1976, no proof of safety was legally required. Dow Corning performed such safety-testing as a matter of good manufacturing protocol. The experiment involved the four gels previously discussed, as well as 28 rabbits, certain of whom were to be sacrificed after 7, 14, 21, and 90 days to reveal what, if any, effects the injected silicone gels had on them. At the end of the first twenty-one days,

> . . . There were no significant gross pathological findings observed at autopsy. Histopathologic exam reveals the continued presence of a mild to moderately acute granulomatous inflammatory reaction occurring in almost all of the implantation sites. The only difference separating this group from the previous two [7 and 14 days] is that the reaction in this group of rabbits is lessened slightly. . . . Microscopic exam of the implant sites reveals a localized, mild to moderately acute granulomatous inflammatory reaction. This reaction lessened somewhat in the 21-day animals. Because this response was seen in almost every implant site and was unequally distributed around the circumference of the site, we feel that this reaction was due to the trauma of implantation and not due to the test gels.[51]

So far, the test results had indicated biocompatability. Eager to get its implants out, Dow Corning asked Biometric if the test could be shortened by 10 days without incident, and Biometric answered in the affirmative. After 80 days, the results were still promising:

> There have been no significant gross pathological findings. . . . At the 80 day period, this inflammatory region was observed in several instances, however, its severity was greatly reduced and was present in certain portions of the periphery of the implant site. The remainder of the site was normal. The majority of implant sites were entirely free of any reaction at all. These histopathologic changes observed during the 80 day course of this study were, in our opinion, due to the trauma of implantation and not due to the test gels.[52]

Thus, the extra studies were complete and could be added to the collection of independent and in-house research on silicone already available. Returning to Anderson in 1975, it was now near the end of April, and their target date was still June. Anderson knew that the product team had been working for upwards of four years on this project, and it seemed like the new gel's time had come. However, some people questioned the integrity of the implants, citing the combination of the more responsive gel with the elastomer envelope as more prone to diffusion than the old gel with the elastomer envelope. However, Anderson had tested this possibility, and she found that the implants with the new gel promoted a level of diffusion comparable to or slightly less than the Cronin, which had already been on the market without incident for ten years. The testing on the more responsive gel was complete, and the Mammary Task Force had to decide whether to produce this implant. They had asked Kim to make a preliminary recommendation. Kim thought: "Is there enough data? Is the testing we have done sufficient, since this product is going to be implanted in humans? Have I done everything I should have?" Anderson checked with the various scientists on the respective properties of the gel, who found it to be production-worthy according to the data already outlined. Given the explanation of silicone; the original implant and its testing; the scientific evidence available; and the explanation of the product staging system, should this new implant go to market?

Notes

1. Per agreement with Dow Corning Corporation, names have been changed.
2. Franklin, Benjamin H., Annelin, Ronald B., "Subcutaneous Implants of Developmental Prosthetic Gels in Monkeys and Rats: Examination of Tissue Deposition and Urinary, Fecal, and Respiratory Elimination Routes," Dow Corning Corporation File Number 2726-1, Dow Corning Corporation, December 12, 1975.
3. Carson, Steven, Ph.D., "Implantation Study in Rabbits with Four (4) Mammary Gels," Biometric Testing Inc., April 25, 1975.
4. Carson, Steven, Ph.D., "Implantation Study in Rabbits with Four (4) Mammary Gels," Biometric Testing Inc., April 25, 1975.
5. Franklin, Benjamin H., Annelin, Ronald B., "Subcutaneous Implants of Developmental Prosthetic Gels in Monkeys and Rats: Examination of Tissue Deposition and Urinary, Fecal, and Respiratory Elimination Routes," Dow Corning Corporation File Number 2726-1, Dow Corning Corporation, December 12, 1975, p.2.
6. This section is based upon information from: Eckroth, David; Graber, Eden; Klingsberg, Anna; Siegel, Paula M.; Editors, *Kirk Othmer Concise Encyclopedia of Chemical Technology*, John Wiley & Sons, New York: 1985. Lane, T. H., Ph.D., "Silica, Silicon, and Silicones . . . Unraveling the Mystery," Dow Corning Corporation: 1995. Rochow, Eugene G., *Silicon and Silicones: About Stone-age Tools, Antique Pottery, Modern Ceramics, Computers, Space Materials and How They All Got That Way*, Springer-Verlag, Berlin Heidelberg: 1987. Sax, N. Irving, & Lewis, Richard J., Sr., *Hawley's Condensed Chemical Dictionary*, Van Nostrand Reinhold Company, New York: 1987.
7. Sax, N. Irving, & Lewis, Richard J., Sr., *Hawley's Condensed Chemical Dictionary*, Van Nostrand Reinhold Company, New York: 1987, p. 1038.
8. Lane, T. H., Ph.D., "Silica, Silicon, and Silicones . . . Unraveling the Mystery," Dow Corning Corporation: 1995. Rochow, Eugene G., *Silicon and Silicones: About Stone-age Tools, Antique Pottery, Modern Ceramics, Computers, Space Materials and How They All Got That Way*, Springer-Verlag, Berlin Heidelberg: 1987. This quotation comes from p.1 of the World Wide Web extract of their works.
9. Lane, T. H., Ph.D., "Silica, Silicon, and Silicones . . . Unraveling the Mystery," Dow Corning Corporation: 1995. Rochow, Eugene G., *Silicon and Silicones: About Stone-age Tools, Antique Pottery, Modern Ceramics, Computers, Space Materials and How They All Got That Way*, Springer-Verlag Berlin, Heidelberg: 1987. This quotation comes from p.2 of the World Wide Web extract of their works.
10. *The New Lexicon Webster's Dictionary of the English Language*, Lexicon Publications, Inc., New York: 1988.
11. Sax, N. Irving, & Lewis, Richard J., Sr., *Hawley's Condensed Chemical Dictionary*, Van Nostrand Reinhold Company, New York: 1987, p.1004.
12. Lane, T. H., Ph.D., "Silica, Silicon, and Silicones . . . Unraveling the Mystery," Dow Corning Corporation: 1995. Rochow, Eugene G., *Silicon and Silicones: About Stone-age Tools, Antique Pottery, Modern Ceramics, Computers, Space Materials and How They All Got That Way*, Springer-Verlag, Berlin Heidelberg: 1987. This quotation comes from p.2 of the World Wide Web extract of their works.
13. This section uses general historical information about the Dow Corning Corporation obtained from corporate literature, numerous other case studies, and interviews with members of the Dow Corning Corporation.
14. Goggin, William C., "How the multidimensional structure works at Dow Corning," *Harvard Business Review*, 1976, pp. 54-65.
15. This section uses general historical information about the Dow Corning Corporation obtained from corporate literature, numerous other case studies, and interviews with members of the Dow Corning Corporation.
16. *The New Lexicon Webster's Dictionary of the English Language*, Lexicon Publications, Inc., New York: 1988, p. 475.

17. Carrington, K. W. "Progress in the treatment of hydrocephalus," *The Bulletin*, Dow Corning Center for Aid to Medical Research (CAMR) newsletter, Volume 1, Number 1, October, 1959, p. 1:

    For approximately, the last three years, Drs. Spitz and Nulsen have been successfully utilizing a valve designed by Mr. John Holter [a father of a hydrocephalus child in need of such a device]. Their results have not been published at this time, but certainly appear to be encouraging . . . Summary: 1. Fifty cases having ventriculo-venous shunts are reported. Follow-up periods ranged from two to eighteen months with 86 percent functioning well . . . 3. Sixty percent of the patients showed demonstrable physical or mental improvement following the shunt. In a paper delivered to the American Academy of Pediatrics meeting in New York City on October 9, 1956, Dr. E. B. Spitz reported on the first installations of the Silastic® tubes and valve designed by John Holter. During the 8 months following the first installation of this valve in February 1956, the same technique was employed in 68 cases. His procedure was successful in decompressing the brain in 57 cases, a feat he had previously achieved by other means in only 16 out of 122 cases . . . Holter valves are now being installed at a rate of more than 1200 a year. With about 4 million babies born per year in this country and an incidence of hydrocephalus in infants estimated at 1 in 500 per year among infants born in the United States.
18. "Silastic®" brand silicone is a trademark of the Dow Corning Corporation.
19. Wallace, W. E., MD, "Prosthesis for dual defects," *The Bulletin*, Dow Corning Center for Aid to Medical Research (CAMR) newsletter, Volume 2, Number 1, 1960, p. 1.
20. Brown, James Barrett, MD, & Ohwiler, David A., MD, "Evaluation of silicones as tissue substitutes," *The Bulletin*, Dow Corning Center for Aid to Medical Research (CAMR) newsletter, Volume 2, Number 1, 1960, p. 1.
21. Marzoni, F. A. Upchurch, S. E., and Lamvert, C. J., "An experimental study of silicone as a soft tissue substitute," *The Bulletin*, Dow Corning Center for Aid to Medical Research (CAMR) newsletter, Volume 2, Number 1, pp. 1-2. (Taken from Plastic and Reconstructive Surgery, 1959, 24(6), 600-608.)
22. Braley, S. A., "Materials and Methods: Silicone treatment for cardiac catheters," *The Bulletin*, Dow Corning Center for Aid to Medical Research (CAMR) newsletter, Volume 2, Number 2, 1960, p. 4.
23. Ames, R. H., MD, "Response to Silastic® Tubing," *The Bulletin*, Dow Corning Center for Aid to Medical Research (CAMR) newsletter, Volume 2, Number 4, 1960, p. 1.
24. McGregor, R. R., "Toxicology of the Silicones, Part I: Subcutaneous, intramuscular, and intraperitoneal injection and injection into the vitreous cavity," *The Bulletin*, Dow Corning Center for Aid to Medical Research (CAMR) newsletter, Volume 2, Number 4, 1960, p. 15.
25. Greatbatch, W., Chardack, W. M., & Gage, A. A., "Implantable pacemaker," *The Bulletin*, Dow Corning Center for Aid to Medical Research (CAMR) newsletter, Volume 3, Number 1, p. 1.
26. Cutting, Windsor C., MD, "Toxicity of Silicones," *Stanford Medical Bulletin*, Volume 10, Number 1, February 1952, pp. 25-26:

    1. DC 200 Silicone produces renal tubular damage in rabbits, but not in rats, when fed in concentrations of one per cent, for three or four months.
    2. DC Antifoam A Silicone produces widespread cellular infiltrations, particularly in the kidney and liver, when fed to rabbits in concentrations of .025 to one per cent for three or four months. Rats are spared these lesions.
    3. The lower of these concentrations is 25 times that customarily used as antifoaming agent in the preparation of foods and beverages.

    This study was partially funded by a grant from Broemmel's Pharmaceuticals in San Francisco.
27. Russell, F. E. Simmers, M. H., Hirst, A. E., and Pudenz, R. H., "Tumors Associated With Embedded Polymers," *Journal of the National Cancer Institute*, Volume 23, Number 2, August 1959, pp. 305-311. This study was funded by the Volker Grant #1 from The Council on Drugs of the American Medical Association, and by a Neurosurgical Research Fund from the Institute of Medical Research at Huntington Memorial Hospital in Pasadena.
28. Midland Silicones Ltd. was bought by Dow Corning in the early 1970's, several years after this study was published.
29. Riley, I. H. and Winner, H. I., "A note on bacteriological tests of silicone rubbers for medical and pharmaceutical uses," *The Bulletin*, Dow Corning Center for Aid to Medical Research (CAMR) newsletter, Volume 3, Number 3, 1961, p.11. (Taken from the *Journal of Pharmacy and Pharmacology*)
30. Riley, I. H., and Winner, H. I., "A Note on Bacteriological Toxicity Tests of Rubbers for Medical and Pharmaceutical Uses," *Journal of Pharmacy and Pharmacology*, Volume 13, 1961, pp. 111-114.
31. For more examples, see: Harris, Harold. I., MD, "Survey of Breast Implants from the Point of View of Carcinogenesis," *Plastic and Reconstructive Surgery*, Volume 28, 1961, pp. 81-83. This author mailed a questionnaire asking about the frequency of cancers seen in their implant patients to almost all U.S. certified plastics surgeons.

Conway, Herbert, MD, and Goulian, Dicran Jr., MD, D.D.S., "Experience with an Injectable Silastic® RTV as a Subcutaneous Prosthetic Material," *Plastic and Reconstructive Surgery*, Volume 32, Number 3, September, 1963, pp. 294-302. The authors were plastic surgeons from Cornell Medical Center in New York. They acknowledge "the interest and cooperation of the Dow Corning Center for Aid to Medical Research . . . in particular Mr. Silas Braley. . ."

Demergian, Vaughn, MD, "Experiences with the Newer Subcutaneous Implant Materials," *The Surgical Clinics of North America*, Volume 43, Number 5, October, 1963, pp. 1313-1321. Demergian was part of the Department of Plastic and Reconstructive Surgery at Jackson Clinic in Madison, Wisconsin, at the time.

32. Little, K. and Parkhouse, James, "Tissue Reactions to Polymers," *The Lancet*, October 27, 1962, pp. 857-861. A Professor J. Trueta provided facilities, and the chemical manufacturers supplied samples and information about their samples.

33. This section uses general historical information about the Dow Corning Corporation obtained from corporate literature, numerous other case studies, and interviews with members of the Dow Corning Corporation.

34. Bassett, C. Andrew L., MD, & Campbell, James B., MD, "Keeping Silastic sterile," *The Bulletin*, Dow Corning Center for Aid to Medical research (CAMR) newsletter, Volume 2, Number 2, 1960, p. 1.

35. Greatbatch, W., Chardack, W. M., & Gage, A. A., "Implantable pacemaker," *The Bulletin*, Dow Corning Center for Aid to Medical Research (CAMR) newsletter, Volume 3, Number 1, 1961, p.1.

36. Dow Corning Corporation's response to the University of St. Thomas Case Study series, 1995, p. 1.

37. Leninger, R. I., Mirkovitch, V., Peters, A. & Hawks, W.A., "Change in Properties of Plastics During Implantation," *Trans. Amer. Soc. Artif. Int. Organs*, Volume 10, 1964, pp. 320-321.

38. Leninger, R. I., Mirkovitch, V., Peters, A. & Hawks, W.A., "Change in Properties of Plastics During Implantation," *Trans. Amer. Soc. Artif. Int. Organs*, Volume 10, 1964, p.320.

39. Park, Joon B. and Lakes, Roderic S., "Tissue Response to Implants," *Biomaterials: An Introduction*, Second Edition, Plenum Press, New York, 1992, pp. 223-225.

With respect to breast implants, encapsulation of the implant can cause discomfort from the hardness and aesthetic displeasure, according to a Dow Corning scientist with experience in the medical implant area.

40. *The Random House College Dictionary*, Revised Edition, Random House, Inc., 1975, p. 628.

41. Carson, Steven, Ph.D., "Chronic Implantation Studies of Polysiloxanes in Dogs," November 29, 1968, p. 1.

42. Carson, Steven, Ph.D., "Chronic Implantation Studies of Polysiloxanes in Dogs," November 29, 1968, p. 1.

43. Carson, Steven, Ph.D., "Chronic Implantation Studies of Polysiloxanes in Dogs," November 29, 1968, p. 11:

In view of the large number of implants placed in some of these dogs, they all showed remarkable recoveries, and were singularly unaffected during the extended period when these foreign materials remained implanted. Behavior and appearance were normal in all. . . . Generally, no untoward chronic tissue reactions were noted with any of the implant materials. Systemic tissue responses were not observed at 24 or 36 months. There was no evidence of tumorigenesis, with any of the samples or at any of the sites of implantations over a 3-year period of testing in dogs. . . . The prosthetic breast samples [made of material numbered 372] . . . revealed no untoward tissue reactions.

44. This information is closely based on an interview with a Dow Corning employee, and *The Dow Corning Product Staging System: A Product Management Tool,* Dow Corning Corporation: 1974, pp. 3-7.

45. Taken from *The Dow Corning Product Staging System Introduction*, p. 3-4.

46. This section uses information obtained from members of the Dow Corning Corporation.

47. Dow Corning, "Position Statement on: Dow Corning Mammary Task Force," p. 2.

48. A Dow Corning employee.

49. Franklin, Benjamin H., Annelin, Ronald B., "Subcutaneous Implants of Developmental Prosthetic Gels in Monkeys and Rats: Examination of Tissue Deposition and Urinary, Fecal, and Respiratory Elimination Routes," Dow Corning Corporation File Number 2726-1, Dow Corning Corporation, December 12, 1975, in the summary section.

50. Franklin, Benjamin H., Annelin, Ronald B., "Subcutaneous Implants of Developmental Prosthetic Gels in Monkeys and Rats: Examination of Tissue Deposition and Urinary, Fecal, and Respiratory Elimination Routes," Dow Corning Corporation File Number 2726-1, Dow Corning Corporation, December 12, 1975, in the summary section.

51. Carson, Steven, Ph.D., "Implantation Study in Rabbits with Four (4) Mammary Gels," Biometric Testing Inc., April 25, 1975, pp. 4-5.

52. Carson, Steven, Ph.D., "Implantation Study in Rabbits with Four (4) Mammary Gels," Biometric Testing Inc., April 25, 1975, p. 4.

5

Dow Corning Corporation (B)

December, 1991[1]

Ellen sat at her lab table.[2] What was happening? A woman named Mariann Hopkins had just won a $7.3 million lawsuit against Dow Corning, against the breast implant Ellen's product management team had developed. How could this happen? It's not as if they produced the implant without testing and shipped it out, allowing an untested device to be placed in women. No—this implant, which had been on the mammary prosthesis market for 10 years with little incident, was a newer version of the original. The implant's gel was made of the same ingredients, just in a different ratio. Moreover, Dow Corning had ordered a two-week test with rats and monkeys and an 80-day test with rabbits on the redesigned implants, and had found no reason to keep them off the market.

In 1977, Dow Corning had settled for $170,000 with an implant recipient who claimed that her breast implants caused her "pain and suffering."[3] In 1984, Maria Stern,

This case was prepared by Julie M. Stocker and Brian D. Cunningham, under the direction of Patricia H. Werhane, Ph.D., Ruffin Professor of Business Ethics, Senior Fellow, Olsson Center, the Colgate Darden Graduate School of Business Administration, University of Virginia, and Michael E. Gorman, Associate Professor, Division of Technology, Culture, and Communication, School of Engineering and Applied Science, University of Virginia. This case was written as a basis for discussion rather than to illustrate effective or ineffective handling of an administrative situation. Copyright © 1997 by the University of Virginia Darden School Foundation, Charlottesville, VA. All rights reserved. *To order copies, send an e-mail to dardencases@virginia.edu. No part of this publication may be reproduced, stored in a retrieval system, used in a spreadsheet or transmitted in any form or by any means—electronic, mechanical, photocopying, recording, or otherwise—without the permission of the Darden School Foundation.*

claiming that her symptoms revealed an autoimmune disorder[4] and that it was caused by her Dow Corning breast implants, won $1.5 million in punitive damages against Dow Corning. Punitive damages meant that Dow Corning was being punished for alleged wrongdoing. Still, the lawyers at Dow Corning had assured Ellen that the Stern case was an anomaly—not the precursor to a flood of litigation. Dow Corning settled with Stern after appeals, the court records were sealed, and the corporation moved on to other business.

However, from 1989 until now, Stern's lawyer, Dan Bolton, had been representing Mariann Hopkins. It was hard for Ellen to understand the verdict that had just come down. Dow Corning was again accused of producing questionable mammary prostheses and allowing them to be placed in women's bodies. But the Dow Corning scientists had done testing. They monitored the medical literature throughout the 1970s and 1980s, keeping their product literature in line with complaints like build-up of scar tissue around the implant, which could lead to the contracture or hardening of this tissue, and the treatment of this capsular contracture sometimes caused rupture. [5] Why were these women suddenly contending that their implants caused an array of symptoms, from joint aches and pains to headaches and debilitating fatigue?

Mariann Hopkins claimed the implants gave her a mixed connective tissue disease. Such a disease is "Any of a group of diseases, . . . [such] as systemic lupus erythmetosus, polyarteritis, scleroderma, and rheumatoid arthritis, involving inflammation or degeneration of connective tissue and accompanied by deposition of fibrinous material."[6] But the symptoms were typical of many conditions, and, according to two doctors at the trial, Hopkins had displayed such symptoms before she received the implants![7] "How," Ellen thought, "could the jurors conclude that 'a preponderance of the evidence' showed the implants had caused Hopkins's problems? How could they have caused the problems, when the problems started before she even had the prostheses implanted? Didn't these people know anything about scientific evidence, and finding correlation and causation?"

Even before she joined the group in 1982, Ellen knew that her team had tested its products. Why were the courts suddenly after Dow Corning? Why were women who were not even sick worrying about terrible diseases they might contract based on two case verdicts in seven years? What about the rest of the scientific and medical community? What did they think? And the plaintiffs' lawyers—what were their motives?

The Hopkins decision the day before and the media attention given to breast implants had been the last straws. Suddenly, even Ellen's own company was questioning the situation, demanding an immediate explanation of how this could have happened. They not only wanted a summary of relevant tests, but an explanation of the void between the Dow Corning scientists' sanction of the implants as marketable, the women's alleged illnesses, and the lawyers' and courts' views of the devices. How could Ellen explain these differences? The science verifying the safety of the implants, in her and the rest of the team's opinion, was sound. Why wasn't that enough?

Notes

1. Some of the information in this section is taken from interviews with Dow Corning personnel. The facts about the litigation are available from many sources.
2. All names have been changed to protect Dow Corning personnel's privacy.
3. From http://www.pbs.org/wgbh/pages/frontline/implants.

4. An autoimmune disorder ". . . [o]ccurs when a specific adaptive immune response is mounted against the self." (http://www.pbs.org/wgbh/pages/frontline/implants/medical/glossary.html)
5. Carmichael, Barie. *Dow Corning's Disclosure of Gel-Breast Implant Complications 1960s-1985*, p. 4.
6. Definition from http://www.pbs.org/wgbh/pages/frontline/implants.
7. From interview with Dow Corning personnel and Xscribe Transcripts of Court Testimony from the Hopkins trial, Volume 9, pp. 1014-1200, 11/13/91, and Volume 10, pp. 1201-1379, 11/14/91. Gospe is the doctor in Volume 9 and Weisman in Volume 10.

ATTACHMENT A

Even though the first epidemiological studies[1] on implants and their potential risks, which were conducted between 1985 and 1989, found that there were no connections between breast implants and either cancer or scleroderma, Dow Corning and other companies had lost large lawsuits and access to breast implants was restricted in 1992.[2] In 1994 the Mayo Clinic conducted a retrospective cohort study, in which the researchers studied women from one particular county who had received implants between 1964 and 1991 and compared them to women from the same county who had not received implants. By choosing women from the same county, the researchers hoped to filter out other variables that could affect the cause of disease in women other than the implants, such as geographic location or type of medical care. In the study it was found that there were no discernable differences between the two groups of women and that the implants were not a risk factor in developing connective tissue disease. However, given that only 2,247 women participated in the study, some scientists argued that it was not a large enough sample to rule out some form of connection between implants and particular medical conditions.

A second epidemiological study was conducted, the Women's Health Cohort Study[3] and included about 400,000 women. This study did seem to find a slight increase in the reports of connective tissue disease among women with breast implants. However, the key word was "reports," for the researchers did not verify whether the reports were valid by examining the medical records of the women who were making the reports. On the other hand, a third epidemiological study was conducted, The Mayo Clinic and the Nurses' Health Study,[4] which included 90,000 women, also found no connection between implants and disease; both findings were validated by examining the medical records of the subjects who were making reports of possible disorders. This examination of the medical records allowed the researchers to discern what doctors and medical tests had determined about these women's reported disorders and allowed the researchers to see whether the reported disorders by the women were actually valid. Moreover, other studies[5] could not find any connection between breast implants and other reported associated disorders—scleroderma,[6] rheumatoid arthritis, and lupus.

As Marcia Angell writes in her book, *Science on Trial*, it is very difficult to prove that something is a risk factor, unless it is a very strong one.[7] For example, even though a woman who drinks alcohol has a bit of a higher chance of getting breast cancer, that does not mean that she will get breast cancer if she drinks. On the other hand, scientists and doctors are fairly justified in saying that cigarette smoking causes cancer, because it is extremely unlikely for people to develop lung cancer for any other reason. However, in order to determine whether something is correlated or causal to a particular ailment or disease, researchers are not simply able to expose people to the things that they want to study. Therefore, researchers obtain their data from what are called observational epidemiological studies. These are studies in which people who have already been exposed to a potential risk factor, for reasons other than researcher intervention, are compared for incidence of disease against others who are similar in many aspects other than having not been exposed to the potential risk factor in question. There are two types of observational studies, cohort (group) studies and case-control studies.

A cohort study for the possible risk factors involved with breast implants would involve a group of women with implants and a group without implants. If more of the women in the group that has implants develop a particular disease, then it could be said that the implants were a possible risk factor for the disease. However, the latter does not mean that it has been proven that the implants caused the disease, for there still could have been something else that was common to the implant group besides the implants themselves that caused the disease to occur. For example, what if all of the women who received the implants were all given the same sleeping agent at the time of surgery for their implants? Could it be that the agent they were all given is causing the disease and not the implants? In a case-control study, the researchers would study women who had a particular disease in question (cases) and women who did not (controls). Once studied, the researchers would then discern who had implants and who did not. If more women from the cases than the controls had the particular disease in question, then it could again be said that the breast implants were a possible risk factor for the disease. However, this also does not prove that the implants had caused the disease to occur.[8]

Notes

1. D. M. Deapen et al., "The Relationship Between Breast Cancer and Augmentation Mammaplasty: An Epidemiologic Study," *Plastic and Reconstructive Surgery* (1986): 361-67. Also see C. J. Burns et al., "The Epidemiology of Scleroderma Among Women: Assessment of Risk from Exposure to Silicone and Silica," *The Journal of Rheumatology* (1996): 1904-1911.
2. Implants could only be acquired for reconstruction purposes at this point.
3. C. H. Hennekens et al., "Self-Reported Breast Implants and Connective Tissue Diseases in Female Health Professionals," *Journal of the American Medical Association* 275 (1996): 616-21.
4. J. Sanchez Guerrero et al., "Silicone Breast implants and the Risk of Connective Tissue Diseases and Symptoms," *New England Journal of Medicine* 332 (1995): 1666-70.
5. H. J. Englert and P. Brooks, "Scleroderma and Augmentation Mammoplasty-A Causal Relationship?" *Australia and New Zealand Medical Journal* 24 (1994): 74-80; and M.C. Hochberg et al., "Frequency of Augmentation Mammoplasty in Patients with Systemic Sclerosis: Data from the Johns Hopkins-University of Maryland Scleroderma Center," *Journal of Clinical Epidemiology* 48 no. 4 (April 1995): 565-69.
6. A disease in which the skin, or an internal organ, hardens and scars.
7. Marcia Angell. *Science on Trial: The Clash of Medical Evidence and the Law in the Breast Implant Case.* New York: W. W. Norton, 1996. pgs. 98-99.
8. For more information: M. Angell, "The Interpretation of Epidemiologic Studies," *New England Journal of Medicine*, 323 (1990): 823-25.

6

CARTER RACING (A)

"What should we do?"

John Carter was not sure, but his brother and partner, Fred Carter, was on the phone and needed a decision. Should they run in the race or not? It had been a successful season so far, but the Pocono race was important because of the prize money and TV exposure it promised. This first year had been hard because the team was trying to make a name for itself. They had run a lot of small races to get this shot at the bigtime. A successful outing could mean more sponsors, a chance to start making some profits for a change, and the luxury of racing only the major events. But if they suffered another engine failure on national television. . . .

Just thinking about the team's engine problems made John wince. They had blown the engine seven times in twenty-four outings this season with various degrees of damage to the engine and car. No one could figure out why. It took a lot of sponsor money to replace a $20,000 racing engine, and the wasted entry fees were no small matter either. John and Fred had everything they owned riding on Carter Racing. This season had to be a success.

Paul Edwards, the engine mechanic, was guessing the engine problem was related to ambient air temperature. He argued that when it was cold the different expansion rates for the head and block were damaging the head gasket and causing the engine failures. It was below freezing last night, which meant a cold morning for starting the race.

Tom Burns, the chief mechanic, did not agree with Paul's "gut feeling" and had data to support his position (see Exhibit 1). He pointed out that gasket failures had occurred at all temperatures, which meant temperature was not the issue. Tom has been racing for twenty years and believed that luck was an important element in success. He had argued this view when he and John discussed the problem last week: "In racing, you are pushing the limits of what is known. You cannot expect to have everything under control. If you want to win, you have to take risks. Everybody in racing knows it. The drivers have their lives on the line, I have a career that hangs on every race, and you guys have got every dime tied up in the business. That's the thrill, beating the odds and winning." Last night over dinner he had added to this argument forcefully with what he called Burns' First Law of Racing: "Nobody ever won a race sitting in the pits."

John, Fred and Tom had discussed Carter Racing's situation the previous evening. This first season was a success from a racing standpoint, with the team's car finishing in the top five in 12 of the 15 races it completed. As a result, the sponsorship offers critical to the team's business success were starting to come in. A big break had come two weeks ago after the Dunham race, where the team scored its fourth first-place finish. Goodstone Tire had finally decided Carter Racing deserved its sponsorship at Pocono— worth a much needed $40,000—and was considering a full season contract for next year if the team's car finished in the top five in this race. The Goodstone sponsorship was for a million a year, plus incentives. John and Fred had gotten a favorable response from Goodstone's Racing Program Director last week when they presented their plans for next season, but it was clear that his support depended on the visibility they generated in this race.

"John, we only have another hour to decide," Fred said over the phone. "If we withdraw now, we can get back half the $15,000 entry and try to recoup some of our losses next season. We will lose Goodstone, they'll want $25,000 of their money back, and we end up the season $50,000 in the hole. If we run and finish in the top five, we have Goodstone in our pocket and can add another car next season. You know as well as I do, however, that if we run and lose another engine, we are back at square one next season. We will lose the tire sponsorship and a blown engine is going to lose us the oil contract. No oil company wants a national TV audience to see a smoker being dragged off the track with their name plastered all over it. The oil sponsorship is $500,000 that we cannot live without. Think about it—call Paul and Tom if you want—but I need a decision in an hour."

John hung up the phone and looked out the window at the crisp, fall sky. The temperature sign across the street flashed "40 DEGREES AT 9:23 AM."

EXHIBIT 1
NOTE FROM TOM BURNS

John,

I got the data on the gasket failures from Paul. We have run 24 races this season with temperatures at race time ranging from 53 to 82 degrees. Paul had a good idea in suggesting we look into this, but as you can see, this is not our problem. I tested the data for a correlation between temperature and gasket failures and found no relationship.

Relationship Between Temperature and Gasket Failures[1]

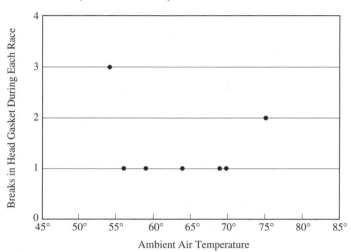

In comparison with some of the other teams, we have done extremely well this season. We have finished 62.5% of the races, and when we finished we were in the top five 80% of the time. I am not happy with the engine problems, but I will take the four first-place finishes and 50% rate of finishing in the money[2] over seven engines any day. If we continue to run like this, we will have our pick of sponsors.

Tom

1. Each point is for a single race. A gasket can have multiple breaks, any of which may produce an engine failure.
2. The top five finishers in a race are "in the money."

7

CARTER RACING (B)

"Get Paul Edwards for me." John was calling to get his engine mechanic's opinion on whether they should run. The data Tom put together indicated that temperature was not the problem, but John wanted to get Paul's direct assessment.

Paul Edwards was a classic "gas station mechanic." His fingernails were permanently blackened by grease and his coveralls never stayed clean for more than two minutes on Saturday mornings. He had been knocking around the professional circuit for ten years after dropping out of school at sixteen to follow drag racing. He lacked the sophisticated engineering training that was getting more common in racing, but he did know racing engines.

John had discussed the gasket problem with Paul two days ago. As he waited for Paul to come to the phone, he reflected on their previous conversation. Paul was a man of few words and was not given to overstatement. "The way I see it, the turbo-pressure during warm-up—in conjunction with the different expansion rates for the head and block—is doing a number on us," was about the extent of what he had to say on the problem. It was his personal opinion on the cause of the engine failures; he would never represent it as anything else.

It was the same story John had heard twenty times, but it did not match Tom's data. "Paul, we have chewed this over before. How do you know this is the problem?

Copyright © 1986 by Jack W. Brittain, College of Business and Public Administration, The University of Arizona, Tucson, Arizona 85721, (602) 621-1474, and Sim B. Sitkin, Department of Management, Graduate School of Business, University of Texas, Austin, Texas 78712, (512) 471-5277. Entered into the Stanford Case System by permission of the authors.

When we ran at Riverside the temperature was 75 degrees, and we still lost the gasket and engine."

"I am not sure what happened at Riverside," Paul had replied. "I am not sure that temperature is the problem, but it is the only thing I can figure out. It is definitely the gaskets that are blowing out and causing the engine to go."

Part of Carter Racing's success was due to a unique turbo-charging system that Tom and John had developed. They had come up with a new head design that allowed them to get more turbo pressure to the engine while maintaining fuel consumption at a fairly constant level. By casting the head and turbo bodies in a high-strength aircraft alloy, they had also saved almost fifty pounds of weight. The alloy they were using was not as temperature sensitive as the material in the engine block, but the head gasket should be able to handle the different expansion rates.

John could hear the sounds of race day in the background as Paul approached the phone. "Hello John," he said, obviously excited. "The Goodstone coveralls just got here. We are talking some fine threads. No sew-on patches from these guys. The logo on the back and our names are stitched right into the material. I guess this means we get to keep'em. Course, I got some grease on mine already, so they probably won't want 'em back anyway."

"I'm glad you like them," John said. "I need to get some information from you. What are we doing about the gasket failure business?"

"The car is set to go. We have been using a different seating procedure since Slippery Rock and had no problems for two races. Tom says the Goodstone deal is set as long as we finish in the money today. The guys in the shop want this bad. Goostone is a class act. They can make us the number one team on the circuit if they decide to take us on."

8

CARTER RACING (C)

John had only ten minutes to make up his mind when he called Tom. There was one last thing he wanted to know. "Give me the temperatures for the races where we did not have any gasket problems."

"What do you need them for?"

"Just call it idle curiosity. Do you have them?"

"Hold on." Tom was organized, which counted for a lot at a time like this. "Okay, here we are. I am going to give you the number of races at each temperature. Let's see, one race at 66 degrees; three races at 67; one each at 68 and 69 degrees; two at 70; one each at 72 and 75; two at 76; one each at 79, 80, and 82. That 82 was Tampa. What a scorcher that day turned out to be. And I do not have the last two races on my list. They were 78 and 73 degrees at race time."

John plotted the points as Tom read them off (see below). It was time to call Fred.

Ambient Temperature for Races Without Blown Gaskets

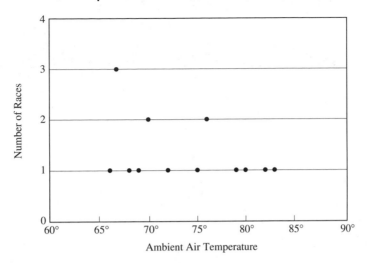

9

ENVIRONMENTAL SUSTAINABILITY

From very early civilizations we have inherited a vision of the planet as a virtually illimitable space where expansion, production, consumption, and unrestrained growth are positive paradigms for the progression of civilization. This view is in the process of revision. Since the end of the Second World War, perhaps beginning with the explosion of the first atomic bombs in 1945, there has been an increasing concern for maintaining, protecting, and improving, or, in a word, "sustaining" the environment. This concern has become pronounced in industrial countries such as the United States, Canada, nations in Western Europe, and in the Pacific Rim that use vast amounts of natural resources and whose industries and technologies have had lasting effects on the environment.

This interest in sustaining the environment arises from what is often called a "spaceship" analogy of planet earth. We have begun to think of the earth as a closed or finite system—a small globe with finite resources and limited possibilities to develop regeneration technologies. It is as if we are on a spaceship that has escaped the gravitational pull of our galaxy and is sent off to outer space with no chance of rescue or return. Under such conditions, those of us on the ship need to set into motion steps to preserve, recycle, and reuse what we have so that we and future generations may sustain the spaceship and survive on the planet.[1]

The term "environment" refers to one's surroundings, in the context of this note, to nature. Environmentalists use the term "ecology," to refer to the study of the relation-

---

This note was prepared by Patricia H. Werhane, Ruffin Professor of Business Ethics. Copyright ©1996 by the University of Virginia Darden School Foundation, Charlottesville, VA. All rights reserved.

ships between organisms and their environment. The term "ecosystem" refers to inter-relationships between particular kinds of organisms and the environment, to particular ecosystems, to the interrelationships between human beings and the environment, or more generally, to the whole of nature, including human beings.

"To sustain" something means to keep a phenomenon in existence, to prolong existence, to maintain, nourish, or encourage a phenomenon, and/or to strengthen or improve it. Environmental sustainability involves protecting the environment, preventing further harms to nature, cleaning up pollution and other harmful emissions, conserving and recycling, maintaining the ecosystem, improving the environment, and/or restoring the ecosystem to a former pristine, or prehuman condition.

There are a number of reasons why sustaining the environment is important, not the least of which is for the survival of our own and future generations. The first aim of environmental sustainability is to interact with the environment in such a way as to prevent further harm or degradation. This goal is important not merely to preserve what is left, but also to avoid further irreparable damage that decreases the ecosystem's ability to sustain life and to allow regeneration of life forms compromised by excessive pollution and use of natural resources. The second aim of most environmentalists is to clean up the environment. Thus most propose that, in addition to avoiding further harms to the environment we need to:

1. reduce waste emissions and pollution to the amounts that we can clean up,
2. reduce waste emissions and pollution to levels that are within the assimilative capacity of the environment,
3. reduce waste emissions and pollution levels at which these emissions do no further harm to the environment.

In addition, a number of environmentalists argue that we need to conserve and nurture the ecosystem through activities such as:

1. recycling,
2. using renewable resources only within their regeneration abilities,
3. using non-renewable resources only at the rate at which renewable substitutes can be developed,
4. maintaining the present "capital" of the ecosystem in at least three ways:
   a. maintaining present rain forest, wilderness areas, tundra, plains, and other uninhabited areas,
   b. protecting biodiverse species of plants and animals,
   c. maintaining the present level of natural resources.

The foregoing spell out principles underlying the promotion of "environmental health," an environment in which human beings may thrive for an extended period of time.[2]

Some environmentalists go further, however, and argue that the ecosystem is of value in its own right and thus is worth preserving and restoring for its own sake. We are members of that ecosystem, but we have no special claims as human beings. For centuries we have used the ecosystem for our own ends *as if* we had special rights to exploit the environment. Because we have exploited it, we now have duties to improve, reconstruct, and restore the ecosystem to its previous, pristine, less humanized state. To achieve these ends these environmentalists recommend the following:

  a. use only resources or materials that are recyclable,
  b. stop all uses of nonrenewable resources,
  c. halt all technologies, manufacturing, production, or services that pollute or produce waste emissions,
  d. restrict uses of renewable resources only to the present regeneration rates.

They also argue that we should not merely protect but actually restore more of the planet to its original state, and that, where possible, we should work to reintroduce virtually extinct animals and plants back into their original habitats.

ENVIRONMENTAL SUSTAINABILITY AND MORAL THEORY

Let us look at environmental sustainability from the point of view of moral theory. From a utilitarian perspective, environmental sustainability—at least in the sense of maintaining the present state and cleaning up pollution is necessary for the survival and well-being of present and future generations. It is not merely because of the obvious fact that we cannot survive for very long without clean water, clean air, and tillable soil. People in less developed countries (LDCs) also need opportunities to share in the development of natural resources so that they, too, can enjoy a better standard of living. Preserving biodiversity is critical not only for species survival but also because of the possibility of finding new uses for natural resources. Moreover, wilderness areas, rain forests, prairies, lakes, and oceans are part of our natural capital that needs to be preserved for future generations. It would be unfair if we left nothing of nature for the future.

What is more difficult to assess is how to achieve these utilitarian ends. It is tempting to argue that those in industrialized countries should simplify their lives, return to a less environmentally threatening way of life, so that resources can be shared more evenly by people throughout the world and saved for future generations.

Minimally, we must continue to seek ways to clean up pollution and emissions, recycle, and reuse, renew, or replace natural resources. These goals, the goals of environmental health, however, require technology we do not yet have: we have not yet perfected pollution and emission controls or found viable ways to clean up waste or replace used-up resources. Returning to an earlier, simpler lifestyle, cannot preclude the continued exploration of new technologies. That would be to our peril, because undoubtedly we have created some environmental hazards not yet recognized, whose clean-up will require new technologies. So the survival of present and future generations requires us *both* to preserve natural capital *and* to develop technology. Additionally, it is unconscionable from a utilitarian perspective to stop economic growth worldwide if that will preclude development in LDCs. A utilitarian would argue that we should rethink the notions of environmental sustainability so that it is compatible with advanced technology and economic growth.

From a human rights perspective, if each of us has certain inalienable rights, and if these rights include the rights to live and survive, it follows that each of us has a right to a livable, safe, and healthy environment. This much is obvious. What is less obvious is the extent of those rights. If we all have rights to survive, do we also have rights to access to resources that enable our survival? These rights have not been enjoyed equally, particularly in LDCs. Can we balance LDCs' rights to economic development against environmental sustainability and these against everyone's right to a livable environment?

Along with these rights claims, each of us has duties to respect the rights of each other. This is because we are all part of a world community and are dependent on one another for our very existence and well-being. Thus no one person has *more* in the way of rights than any other. Avoiding polluting, cleaning up, recycling, conserving, replacing, and restoring make sense because these activities enable us to replenish ecosystem capital that has been used more by some people than by others. The challenge is, How do we do that? Might it be possible to invent new technologies to achieve these ends, technologies that create economic growth as well?

Rights talk raises another issue. Do we have rights to enjoy nature as well, or only to be able to live in an environmentally nonthreatening world? Those with a more deontological perspective often argue that nature has value in itself. Human beings are part of nature, but they have no special claims as a species, so valuing the ecosystem and biodiversity is important in its own right. Indeed, restoring the ecosystem to its original condition, preserving and enhancing biodiversity, and appreciating nature are moral obligations, obligations, some argue, that are on a par with obligations to human beings.

But these arguments have their own difficulties. It is highly unlikely that we can restore the earth to its "original" or "pristine" condition or that we can even restore parts of it to that condition. Human beings have interfered with or "humanized" nature for our own ends to such an extent that we can neither restore nor resurrect its original condition. Humans has been interfering with nature since the first cave person scratched on the cave walls, cut down trees, picked berries, built fires, grew plants, and tamed, grazed, and bred animals. Indeed, terms such as "nature," "earth," "biodiversity," "ecosystem," and "natural or original condition" are humanized concepts. We conceive and think about the ecosystem through language and culture, and the meanings of terms we use to describe nature cannot be stripped of the humanized, even socio-political-economic, framework in which they evolved.

Rather than attempt to restore the ecosystem to its original prehuman state, perhaps we should think of how we can preserve and restore the ecosystem to long-term viability, given its present condition. That viable condition is defined by human interests, needs, and values. That enterprise involves prizing nature for its own sake, but that sort of valuing, is also an inescapably human phenomenon.

We might also think about environmental sustainability from the perspective of virtue. It is somehow thought not virtuous to be selfish, gluttonous, wasteful, messy, hurtful, or destructive, all adjectives that describe the environmental habits of some individuals, institutions, and industrial economies. The virtues of parsimony, thriftiness, cleanliness, respect for others, and fairness are demands of environmental sustainability. Notice, however, that they are demands of ordinary life as well. So it appears that practicing the virtues of environmental sustainability is not much different from being a generally virtuous person, an admirable institution, or a just political economy.

ENVIRONMENTAL VALUES AND DEVELOPING COUNTRIES

Different definitions of environmental sustainability raise different levels of demands. Almost all of these demands question whether we can continue technological development and economic growth, especially when these activities' natural resources (including the "capital" of fossil fuels) create a net increase in pollution and waste emissions, reduce biodiversity, and leave almost none of the earth in a wilderness or natural condition for future generations. Thus demands of environmental sustainability raise questions of fairness or justice. Some individuals and countries, particularly industrialized countries, have simply used up more of the world's natural resources than others, and have caused a great deal of the world's pollution. For example, it is estimated that one American uses the same energy as 531 Ethiopians. In addition, it is estimated that inhabitants of industrialized countries do approximately 7.5 times more damage to the environment than do inhabitants of LDCs.[3] By any measure of justice, these practices are unfair, unfair to those individuals and countries whose natural resources have been used up and who have not been able to participate equally in economic development, and unfair to future generations who will suffer as a result of depleted natural resources.

Again, however, we must ask: How is the best way to address these inequalities and resulting injustices? Even if it makes sense to demand restoring equity between developed and developing nations by measures of redistribution, yet political reality dictates otherwise. The industrialized nations have power and economic largess, and it is unlikely they are to relinquish either very soon.

However, this situation is not hopeless. Rather than continue to dwell on doomsday scenarios, we might think of the positive steps that can be taken to continue to improve environmental health without neglecting the economic plight of developing countries. The challenge is to encourage new technology appropriate to LDCs, technology that will permit them to develop economically within the guidelines of environmental health. This is a challenge for researchers, engineers, managers, and multinational corporations that offers opportunities for new discoveries and the exploration of new markets in LDCs. Such a challenge, if met, will allow us to turn to the serious task of ecosystem restoration, since it only makes sense to demand protection and restoration of wilderness, rain forests, prairies, and tundra, if we can provide minimally decent standards of living for all human beings.[4]

Notes

1. Boulding, Kenneth, "The Economics of the Coming Spaceship Earth," *Environmental Quality in a Growing Economy*, ed. Henry Jarrett. Baltimore: The Johns Hopkins Press, 1966.
2. Goodland, R. J. A. and Daly, Herman, "Universal Environmental Sustainability and the Principle of Integrity," *Perspectives on Implementing Ecological Integrity*, ed. John Lemons and Laura Westra. Dordrecht: Kluwer Academic Publishers, 1995, pp. 102-114.
3. Brown, Lester, *The State of the World 1984*. New York: W. W. Norton, 1984.
4. See also, Joel Reichart and Patricia H. Werhane, "Sustainable Development and Economic Growth," in Lemons and Westra, pp. 254-264.

10

AMERICAN SOLAR NETWORK

Albert C. Rich, an inventor and entrepreneur, had come up with a design for a new solar water heater. He argued:

> The average home electric water heater emits over 5.8 tons of carbon dioxide into the atmosphere each year (when the electricity is produced by coal), which is more than the average automobile emits! These systems also produce over 91 pounds of sulfur dioxide and 850 pounds of nitrogen oxides (which contributes to acid rain and smog). A solar water heater can prevent over 4,000 pounds of these pollutants from being emitted.

Rich also claimed, "If 50 percent of the homes in the United States had a solar collector, it would eliminate twelve large nuclear-, coal-, and oil-generating plants."

Rich was clearly committed to his invention and had sunk most of his own resources into it: "Henry Ford had a vision of an automobile for every family, and I have a vision of a solar water heater for every family." However, as of 1992, Rich was a long way from being able to accomplish this goal—so far, in fact, that he had to consider moving or going out of business.

This case was prepared by Michael E. Gorman and Patricia H. Werhane.©1997 by School of Engineering and Applied Science, University of Virginia, and University of Virginia Darden School Foundation. All rights reserved.

THE SOLAR WATER-HEATER INDUSTRY

People have tried to harness the power of the sun for centuries. As early as 1877, air blowing over a sun-heated iron was used to warm homes. In 1897, 30 percent of the homes in Pasadena, California were solar heated. One hundred thousand solar water heaters were installed in the United States in the 1930s and early 1940s.

In the 1940s, however, enhancements were made to the efficiency and productivity of gas and electric heaters. At the same time, improvements were made in oil and natural-gas extraction, and supplies of these natural resources and coal seemed virtually unlimited. Solar energy seemed far less practical. By the 1970s solar heating systems had fallen out of favor in the United States.

The 1973 energy crisis made the United States realize the extent of its dependence on natural resources, particularly fossil fuels. The Middle East oil embargo caused oil prices to quadruple; forcing Americans to reconsider their views of energy and conservation. In 1978, the U.S. government and many states decided to implement tax credits for anyone who installed a solar water heater prior to January 1, 1985. Federal income taxes allowed a credit of 40 percent off the entire solar domestic-water-heater expenditure, up to a maximum credit of $4,000.[1] This credit resulted in a significant reduction in cost to consumers. Due to energy awareness and the government tax credit, approximately 950,000 active solar systems and 200,000 passive solar systems were installed during this period, a remarkable growth in the solar industry.[2]

When the era of federal tax credits ended, American consumers became disenchanted with the high-priced, unattractive solar water heaters that were available. Despite the ability of solar water heaters to aid in energy conservation and improve a home's energy efficiency, the high-priced cost of these systems together with rapidly declining fuel prices spelled the demise of a vast majority of companies selling solar water heaters.[3] Fuel prices had dropped from mid-1970s levels and the country became apathetic about the conservation of natural resources.

THE BACKGROUND OF ALBERT C. RICH

When asked what motivated him to enter the field of solar power, Al Rich responded, "As a young boy, I was aware that what I was going to do when I grew up wasn't invented yet. But, I didn't know that I was going to invent it."

In July 1977, at the age of 27, Rich took a job at a summer camp in Colorado where he was asked to help install a solar water heater for the camp pool. He "lit up" at the thought of doing so. Inspired by the experience and driven by the desire to achieve, Rich attended Principia College in Illinois, and obtained a degree in political science. He also decided to focus on the solar-energy field because he saw it as one solution to problems like global warming. During his college years, he became active in the environmental movement by organizing and participating in senior seminars and conferences. His exposure to environmental issues at school, as well as the mid-1970s oil crisis, deepened his interest in solar power and the environment.

After graduation in 1979, Rich founded AC-Rich & Sun—a solar sales, installation, and service company. Rich also worked as a consultant and trainer for companies entering the solar market. His work included installing the first two solar systems for the United States Navy and holding professional solar sales and installation seminars.

In 1983, Rich became the district manager for the SEARS Solar Systems (a family retail outlet) in Herndon, Virginia. Over the next year, he succeeded in making the Herndon office the company's top-producing sales branch in the United States, selling a volume of $2.5 million annually. He was in charge of the management and training of 53 employees, ranging from sales to installation at the Herndon location. However, the market for solar hot water heaters at SEARS eventually ceased. As a result, Rich began to repair the systems he sold and researched innovative ways to market solar systems.

The work made him acutely aware of the problems with existing solar water heaters. He found that customers perceived them as being overpriced, unattractive, and cumbersome:

> Just from a marketing standpoint I had to decide how I could sell solar. Basically, solar energy had been built and designed by engineers. They had no concept of what the customers wanted, they just produced what worked. And they certainly did work. But the market wasn't that happy with how they looked or cost, so you had to come up with an artificial subsidy.

Due to the lack of available low-cost and attractive solar water heaters, Rich was challenged to design a system that would be inexpensive, attractive, easy to install, and dependable. So in 1987, Rich decided to design and market a new domestic solar water heater—one that would be less expensive and aesthetically pleasing to the eye. AC-Rich & Sun began work on the solar "Skylite"™ water heater in 1988. His second company, American Solar Network, Ltd. (ASN), was incorporated on February 2, 1989, in order to further develop and manufacture the new design.

THE SOLAR "SKYLITE" WATER HEATER SYSTEM

When Rich decided to design his own solar water heater, he asked himself: "Is there a need for it?" as well as, "What do people want?" In Rich's opinion, the answer to the first question was a resounding yes. One of his satisfied solar "Skylite" water heater system customers testified, "I had always liked the idea of solar water heaters because they could save my family a lot of money. My main objection to them is that, to me, they were ugly and far too expensive." This kind of customer feedback answered his second question. Rich knew that this opinion of current solar systems was widespread, so he decided to design and market an inexpensive, aesthetically pleasing solar water heater. As he worked on his design, it occurred to Rich that his ideas might be patentable. On June 16, 1989, he submitted a patent application. After almost a year of revisions and debates about the uniqueness of his designs, Rich was awarded his first patent, #4930492, on June 5, 1990. In 1993, Rich was awarded a second patent for improvements to his original design. . . .

The system worked in conjunction with a conventional water heater in order to supply hot water to the home. Water was heated by the solar system except when long stretches of cloudy days occurred or when a great deal of hot water was used. At these times, the conventional water heater would fire so that an adequate supply of hot water would be maintained.

The solar "Skylite" water heater did not directly heat the water a family used; it had its own separate water supply. This arrangement was known as a "closed-loop" system. The water was heated in plastic panel on the roof (1). When the water in the collectors on the roof was warmer than the water in the tank (4), a controller (2) triggered a pump (3), which circulated the heated water through a heat exchanger in the tank (4). Inside the tank was the water the household used to wash dishes, take showers, etc. This household water was drawn into the regular hot-water tank, where it could be heated to the desired household temperature if needed. Rich's system included a timer and a drainback tank (5) so that water would drain out of the system at night. Part of his patent included a floating valve manifold. The manifold allowed the water to fall into the drainback tank whenever the pump was not operating, thereby preventing the water from freezing in the exposed pipes during cold weather, which was a problem in many other active-solar designs. When the pump started up again, a floating ball rose and closed the L-shaped joint, which would have allowed the water to fall back into the drainback tank. Instead, the water was forced through the solar collectors absorber.[4] He also patented vents in the solar panel that released excess heat when the inside of the collector got too hot. (The above numbers refer to parts of the solar water heater diagram. See Exhibit 1.)

Rich had aimed to make the system cheap and easy to maintain, and he believed he had accomplished this goal. He used plastic instead of glass on the panels to make them easy to install and remove. He used EPDM rubber in his collectors because this material was light, flexible and could withstand freezing. He also designed the solar panels to look like skylights, so they would enhance the appearance of a house on which they were mounted.

Rich kept his company alive during the difficult period since 1985 by taking out a second mortgage on his home, scrambling for backers, and obtaining grants from states like New Hampshire, which provided him with a $14,900 grant under its Appropriate Technology Project in 1991. Although he was still based in Virginia, he installed his solar water-heating system in several homes in New Hampshire as part of a model project and documented that it reduced heating bills.

Rich had to evaluate his product and his situation. If he was to succeed, he had to demonstrate to customers that he had an environmentally sound and economical design. Was his design attractive? Did it produce any wastes that were not biodegradable? How long would it last, and what would happen to it after its effective life was over? Could he improve the design? He also had to decide whether to remain in Virginia.

Rich's goal was to manufacture 4,000 units a month in Virginia, as the large monthly manufacturing volume would decrease the manufacturing cost of each system to about $1,000. In 1992, he was actively pursuing the possibility of moving from Virginia to an area where subsidies (such as loans, fiscal incentives, tax deductions, etc. to induce the use of environmental technologies) could greatly reduce the cost of his system to consumers (see Exhibit 2). Otherwise, he feared he would have to give up his dream of putting his active solar technology on thousands of houses.

In addition to state incentives for solar-technology implementation, several utility companies resorted to Demand-Side Management Programs (DSM). Through DSM, utility companies can either buy and install or provide financing for the purchase and installation of solar systems (such as solar water heaters). Utility sponsored studies have revealed that the use of solar energy can reduce peak power demand, thus reducing the need to build new and costly power-generation facilities to adequately supply power to all customers in a specified area.

Several utility companies around the nation offered grant or rebate programs that gave consumers an incentive to invest in demand-reducing technology such as solar water heaters. Grant programs immediately reduced the purchase cost of the system, while rebate programs returned a percentage of the purchase cost to the consumer once a system had been purchased.

Atlantic Electric in Pleasantville, New Jersey, offered grants of up to $500. Northern States Power in Minneapolis, Minnesota, gave grants of up to 50 percent of the cost of the product. Eugene Water and Electric in Oregon gave performance-based rebates from $200 to $400. The City of Austin, Texas, offered rebates of up to $250. Madison Gas and Electric (in Wisconsin) had performance-based rebates from 10 percent to 50 percent of cost. Sacramento Municipal Utility District (in California) gave rebates of $1,000 as of 1991.[5]

Bibliography

Allred, Johnny, et al. *An Inexpensive Economical Solar Heating System for Homes.* Washington: US National Aeronautics and Space Administration, 1976.

Plante, Russell H. *Solar Domestic Hot Water. A Practical Guide to Installation and Understanding.* New York: John Wiley and Sons, 1983.

Shirley, Larry E. and Jodie D Sholar. "State and Utility Financial Incentives for Solar Applications." *Solar Today.* Volume 7, No. 4, pp. 11-14 (July/August 1993 issue).

Solar Energy Research Institute, *Engineering Principles and Concepts for Active Solar Systems,* New York: Hemisphere Publishing Corporation, 1988.

Notes

1. A tax credit is a reduction in the total amount of taxes owed to the IRS. It generally saves more than a deduction, which is applied only to the taxable income, not to the total amount owed.
2. An active system produces electricity from the sun, which then heats the water, while a passive system uses solar energy to heat the water directly.
3. For more information on solar water heaters and an overview of solar energy, contact the North Carolina Solar Center at North Carolina State University (1-800-33-NC-SUN). See also D. Beattie (ed), *History and Overview of Solar Heat Technologies*, Cambridge: MIT Press, 1997.
4. Details of this and other aspects of Rich's system are outlined in the copy of his patent on the World Wide Web, at URL http://cti.itc.Virginia.EDU/~meg3c/id/modules/asn/acrich_a_mod.html.
5. Details of other utility companies encouraging solar use can be found on the World Wide Web at URL http://www.crest.org:80/renewables/seia/sij/3Q95/pp-partner.html. More details on SMUD's program can also be found on the World Wide Web at URL http://www.smud.org.

EXHIBIT 1
The Technology: American Solar Network Patented Freeze-Proof Design

Solar "SKYLITE"™ Water Heater

Patented "Floating valve" manifold

2. Snap Switch
1. Solar Thermal Collector

5. Drainback Tank

110 Volt Timer

Cold Water Source

Heated Solar Water Out

Hot Water To Household

3. Pump

4. Solar Tank

Existing Water Heater

Superior strength glazing: Unbreakable 1/4" double walled, single extrusion, transparent polycarbonate glazing. Much stronger than glass and far superior to other non-glass glazings.

Low-profile, lightweight construction: Durable lightweight sheet aluminum construction for easy handling and installation.

High performance absorber: Long-lasting, freeze- and corrosion-proof EPDM rubber absorber with closely spaced flow channels for superior heat transfer.

Rigid insulation system: Closed cell insulation with protective backing provides structural rigidity and high heat retention.

How It Works:

1. The **Solar Thermal Collector** on the roof collects the sun's energy.

2. A thermal **Snap Switch** in the collector starts the pump when it senses temperatures above 110 degrees.

3. A **Pump** circulates five to seven gallons of ordinary tap water through the closed solar loop.

4. A **Solar Tank** incorporates a copper heat exchanger that heats water in the solar tank. Solar heated water is then transferred to your **Existing Water Heater**.

5. The **Drainback Tank** stores the water when the system is at rest.

The solar system water never comes into contact with domestic drinking water because the Cold Water Source never goes up to the collector.

Specifications:

Solar Thermal Collector:
Dimensions: 4 ft. x 8 ft., 4 ft. x 12 ft., 4 ft. x 16 ft.
Depth: all, 3 inches
Weight: 50 lbs., 70 lbs., 90 lbs.
Standard Color: dark bronze, custom available
Freeze protected system
Solar Tank with Internal Heat Exchanger:
50, 65, 80, 120 gallons; glass - foam insulated
Drainback Tank:
4-6 gallons
Options: choice of flush, tilt or lift mount; differential controllers; photovoltaic power and digital temperature display.

Technical Bulletin available for details on components.

Summary of Energy Use and Costs

On average it costs 8 cents per kilowatt hour for electricity in the United States. Shown below are four of the largest energy consumers in the average household, led by the electric water heater.

Kilowatt hours per year (2)

Electric range	800
Refrigerator	1500
Central air conditioner	3600
Electric water heater	4000

Rich estimates that the solar Skylite water heater will save between 55 percent and 80 percent of the energy used by a conventional electric water heater.

EXHIBIT 2
State and Utility Incentives in 1993

Since 1985, when the federal tax credit was dropped, and the early 1990s, the fledgling solar industry suffered heavy losses. Nevertheless, as environmental issues once again became prominent in the early 1990s, more and more states were taking the initiative and offering incentives for environmentally friendly solar technologies like Rich's water heater (see Exhibit 1).

State	Sales-Tax Exemp.	Property Tax Exemp.	Income Tax Credit	Income Tax Deduct.
Arizona	X			
California			10%	
Hawaii		X	35%	
Idaho				100%
Indiana		X		
Iowa		X		
Mass.	X	X	15%	
Minnesota	X	X		
Mississippi				
Montana		X		
Nevada	X	X		
N. Hamp.		X		
N. Jersey	X			
New York		X		
N. Carolina			25%	
N. Dakota		X	15%	
Ohio		X		
Oregon		X	35%	
Penn.				
Rhode Is.	X			
S. Dakota		X		
Tennessee				
Texas		X		
Utah			25%	
Virginia		X		
Wisconsin		X		
Wyoming				

Note: Tax exemptions are based on the cost of the system; therefore, a sales or property tax will not be levied on the cost of the system. A tax deduction is the percentage of the cost of the system that can be subtracted from your taxable income. As stated previously, a tax credit is a reduction in the total amount of taxes owed to the IRS.

11

ENVIRONMENTAL PROTECTION ENCOURAGEMENT AGENCY (EPEA)

Dr. Michael Braungart, a chemical engineer and professor, had good reason to feel a sense of accomplishment. He and his consulting company, the Environmental Protection Encouragement Agency (EPEA), had just been given a ringing endorsement at a major German environmental conference in June 1997. The conference, entitled "Economy and Environment," was hosted in Mainau by the high-profile, nonprofit German Environmental Aid Association (Deutsche Umwelthilfe) and was attended by some of the world's largest companies, such as Lufthansa and Unilever.[1]

Braungart was present in two official ways at the conference. First, he made a presentation about one of the key consulting tools that he and the EPEA had developed over several years. The tool, called a "Sustainability Index," was one part of a challenging methodology that Braungart was putting into practice at companies that hired the

This technical note was written by Matthew M. Mehalik under the direction of Michael E. Gorman and Patricia H. Werhane. Partial support for this project was supplied by grants from the Ethics and Values In Science program of the National Science Foundation (SBR-9319983), the Batten Center for Entrepreneurial Leadership at the Darden School, University of Virginia, and the Geraldine R. Dodge Foundation. The conclusions are the responsibilities of the authors, and do not reflect the views of the foundations. Copyright © by the University of Virginia Darden School Foundation, Charlottesville, VA. All rights reserved.

EPEA. Second, he was mentioned by Albin Kälin, Managing Director of Rohner Textil,[2] a company that had developed and was selling a compostable furniture fabric constructed from a nearly emission-free production process. Kälin had worked with the EPEA in order to optimize the fabric and his dye and weaving facility in terms of environmental sustainability criteria. Kälin was presenting some of the main outcomes from this endeavor.

The endorsement came at the very end of the conference, from the commentator, the Right Honorable John Gummer, England's secretary of state for the environment in former Prime Minister John Major's government. Gummer labeled the compostable fabric, Rohner Textil, and the EPEA as "the only existing example I have seen that embodies the spirit of Agenda 21." Gummer was referring to the international document developed at the 1992 Earth Summit at Rio de Janeiro, Brazil. Agenda 21 was on Gummer's mind, as he was headed the next week to New York for "Earth Summit II," on the five-year anniversary of the Rio conference. Gummer undoubtedly wanted to carry a strong message of European progress to the conference.

Braungart was not sure if his efforts would be mentioned in New York, but getting such an approval in front of Germany's press, financial institutions, and largest companies was reason enough to be pleased. Braungart had been fighting uphill battles to get his ideas accepted by a wide corporate community for over ten years. The difficulties formed part of the unique history of the EPEA, which Braungart originally founded to be a consultant for Greenpeace.

Braungart hoped for wider acceptance of the EPEA's methodology, which posed significant challenges to views advocated by the scientific community on analyzing a product in terms of environmental sustainability. The Society for Environmental Toxicology and Chemistry (SETAC) had standardized a set of such peer-reviewed procedures over the period of 1990-1994. At the time of the conference the procedures, called a product Life Cycle Assessment (LCA), were in the process of becoming an international document as part of the ISO 14000 series of environmental management documents. Specifically, it was in the process of being adopted as ISO 14040.

The EPEA had just published its own methodology, called Life Cycle Development (LCD) one week before the German conference as part of the proceedings for the Air and Waste Management Association's 90th Annual Meeting in Ontario, Canada. The endorsement of the methodology was a good sign, but Braungart was waiting to see if it would carry through to the international scientific community, or, more importantly, if it would be adopted by companies even though the SETAC standard existed.

FROM GREENPEACE TO CORPORATE CONSULTANTS

"Intellectually, I fell in love with my chemistry teacher," was how Braungart described the way he got involved in science. Science offered him what he thought to be a more rational means to make judgments and reach consensus about right and wrong. This possibility was different from the more fluid positions he learned from his family while he was growing up. His family had a background in philosophy, art and history, and from them he learned that morality is not something that is fixed or constant. As he described what he learned from them, "It is difficult to make arguments based on purely moral grounds, as it is impossible to judge matters from a morally fixed or level position." Because of the appeal of chemistry, Braungart attended seven different universities and obtained his Ph.D. in chemical engineering. [3]

Concurrent with his studies in the 1970's, Braungart was also inspired by the ideas put forth by the Club of Rome regarding waste and environmental problems. His concern existed at two different levels. At one level he was struck by the immense amount of damage being done to the land, air and water by the deposition of waste. At a second level, he was aware that the people often harmed the most by such pollution were the poorest, who lacked the political power to prevent the construction of waste dumps or incinerators near their homes. Braungart recognized that these people, lacking organization and resources to mount an opposition and facing powerful companies with close ties to government, stood little chance to prevent the mounting health problems of which Braungart and others were becoming aware.

By 1980, Braungart perceived that most people in Europe and Germany were aware that pollution was a problem, but public involvement in the issues was lacking. Braungart believed that some of the indifference was due to a lack of information. Nonetheless, the news was filled with dramatic protests taking place in Europe by environmental organizations, like Greenpeace, a branch of which was founded by Monika Griefahn in 1980.

Braungart decided to join Greenpeace to work to curtail pollution. He used his expertise in chemistry to come to the assistance of people who lacked information concerning the effects of waste incinerators and dumps near their homes. For one project Braungart calculated that the construction of a waste incinerator, combined with the emissions from the incinerator, actually generated more waste than the incinerator was capable of eliminating over a period of twelve years. By 1982 he had founded the Chemistry Division of Greenpeace, and he worked closely with Monika Griefahn as an activist in environmental concerns. The two married and worked together as protesters, with Braungart going the route of producing scientific evidence and Griefahn taking the cause into politics and government.

While at a Greenpeace protest in 1985, Braungart realized that products themselves could be a form of pollution. Braungart was active in a new Greenpeace campaign to stop a German paper company from dumping emissions of toxic chlorine compounds into a river by getting them to produce chlorine-free paper. Braungart looked across the river from the paper mill and saw a BASF chemical plant. Greenpeace was not protesting there because the water emissions from the BASF plant were not considered problematic. But Braungart realized that BASF was producing products like chromium audio tapes that could not be recycled and were themselves a form of hazardous waste. The BASF plant produced products at a high volume and thus was polluting at a high volume. Braungart saw that he needed to change from a strategy of pollution prevention by eliminating emissions to pollution prevention based on product redesign. Perhaps the whole production system needed to change, so that neither products nor emissions would pollute.

At the same time Braungart saw that Greenpeace protests were not as effective as hoped but were resulting in the stonewalling of support against the Greenpeace cause. Little positive change was taking place. Not only were the dramatic protests not uniting public support, but companies had mobilized to neutralize the Greenpeace movement.

Toward the latter 1980s Braungart decided to abandon his role as an opposition force and instead dedicate his time and energy to finding rational, scientifically-based solutions to the problems of waste management and disposal.

A breakthrough took place in 1987, when Braungart and other Greenpeace protesters were taking action against a Ciba Geigy chemical plant in Basel, Switzerland. Ciba Geigy's emissions permit had expired, so Braungart and the others were climbing down the chimney at night to ensure that Ciba Geigy had to stop production until they had their permits renewed. In the morning, Braungart was greeted by a security guard, who offered him breakfast because the guard thought what Braungart was doing was courageous. Alex Krauer, CEO of Ciba Geigy, also approached Braungart and offered an olive branch. He wanted to know not only what Braungart and Greenpeace wanted to be changed about the factory; he wanted Braungart to give him suggestions on how he could change the plant to make it less polluting but still profitable and functional. Krauer was tired of playing this cat-and-mouse game with Greenpeace. He was giving Braungart a chance for a rational solution and invited Braungart to act as a consultant.

Braungart founded the EPEA to fulfill this role. Originally, he called the organization the Environmental Protection *Enforcement* Agency, as he thought his consulting role was to make sure companies met pollution standards. Braungart and the EPEA continued to operate in the area of waste management and disposal for the first 5 years that the EPEA was in existence (1987-1992), mainly continuing to act as a consultant for Greenpeace.

As Braungart and the EPEA worked with Ciba Geigy through 1992, they were able to produce guidelines to help Ciba Geigy introduce innovation into their operations and improve their products. The EPEA team invented the "Intelligent Product System" from this project. The "intelligent" refers to their view that products should be redesigned so that their disposal does not conflict with natural processes, a situation that would eliminate waste management systems that "are impractical, too expensive, environmentally unsound, and have to be replaced." [4] The product classification system suggested that there should only be three types of products: consumption products, service products, and unmarketable products. Exhibit 1 contains additional information concerning the Intelligent Product System.

Braungart and the team developed additional criteria for sustainable production. The main, idealized standard for protection from pollution was: "Companies may no longer release chemicals into the environment which can be traced in mother's milk and which disturb ecological systems." [5] Braungart proposed five criteria to meet this standard:

1. Chemicals or products which are released into the environment must be biodegradable and must not accumulate in environmental media or food chains. They must not be teratogenic, mutagenic, or carcinogenic, and they must not be acutely toxic to human beings in the concentrations occurring under field conditions. These chemicals must not disturb ecological systems.
2. Companies must not produce organisms which disturb ecological systems. It is the responsibility of the company to prove that this criterion is being fulfilled.
3. The company must only use regenerative energy resources and must minimize energy consumption.

4. The company must establish the long-term goals worldwide with the help of international political activities.
5. The company must actively protect the existence of animals and plants in their natural habitats. [6]

Exhibit 2 contains 25 additional criteria and additional information pertaining to the EPEA's criteria for sustainable development of products and production.

Moving away from the role as "enforcers," the EPEA team found that by engagement and working together, their effectiveness at solving problems increased. Braungart changed the name to the Environmental Protection *Encouragement* Agency to reflect the new emphasis on acting as consultants over the role of protesters. For him, incremental change over time was better than expending lots of emotional and physical energy trying to demand a complete change all at once.

DESIGNING LIFE CYCLE ASSESSMENTS: SETAC's LCA

Having a set of criteria was one matter, but figuring out how to achieve implementation was an additional challenge. By 1990 Braungart was participating as a member of the Society for Environmental Toxicology and Chemistry (SETAC) in their workshops on producing a tool for redesigning products and systems to make them more environmentally sustainable. Originally founded in 1979 to provide a forum for individuals and institutions who studied environmental problems, the then-2,000 member organization held an August 1990 workshop in order to achieve consensus on a technical framework for a tool to assess the environmental aspects of a product and its production system. The workshop gave this tool the name "Life Cycle Assessment," or LCA.

Previous to the workshop, LCAs had been called Resource and Environmental Profile Assessments (REPAs). These earlier studies sought to determine which of several competing designs were "better" from an environmental point of view, by taking an inventory of all of the material and energy inputs into the product, comparing the means of disposal, and determining the impacts from this information. The first publicly available study was conducted in 1974, in which nine different beverage containers, such as glass bottles, steel cans, and aluminum cans, were analyzed. [7] Public interest in REPAs remained low between 1975 and 1988, when international government and public interest was preoccupied with the handling of hazardous and toxic waste issues and not product design. [8] By the 1990 workshop, international attention again returned to product redesign with Braungart acting as a leader based on his experiences with the EPEA. According to the report that emerged from this meeting,

> The charge given to workshop participants was to agree on a technical framework for key life-cycle components. Life-cycle assessments were still in their infancy: the methods for conducting life-cycle studies needed to be further developed and refined. The participants, therefore, were also charged with identifying the research needed to improve life-cycle assessment techniques. [9]

A major contribution from Braungart and the EPEA was the expansion of the REPA concept by adding two new components to the methodology: *an impact assess-*

ment, which attempted to describe the components' environmental burdens and an *improvement assessment*, which recommended on product changes for reducing the environmental impacts. Braungart's contribution reflected his desire to induce a positive reduction in the environmental effects of products. He suggested that all three steps be performed iteratively.

From this workshop and three others afterward through October 1992, SETAC established a series of guidelines for the technical, conceptual, and data quality issues for conducting LCAs. What also emerged was a definition of what an LCA was:

> Life-Cycle Assessment is a process to evaluate the environmental burdens associated with a product, process or activity by identifying the quantifying energy and materials used and wastes released to the environment; to assess the impact of those energy and material uses and releases to the environment; and to identify and evaluate opportunities to effect environmental improvements. The assessment includes the entire life-cycle of the product, process, or activity, encompassing extracting and processing raw materials; manufacturing; transportation and distribution; use, re-use, maintenance, recycling, and final disposal.
>
> LCA addresses environmental impacts of the system under study in the areas of ecological health, human health, and resource depletion . . . . Additionally, like all other scientific models, LCA is a simplification of the physical system and cannot claim to provide an absolute and complete representation of every environmental interaction. [10]

Exhibit 3 gives more details concerning the SETAC LCA methodology.

Although Braungart and the EPEA were able to get SETAC to accept the three modular components of a LCA, it became clear between 1990 and 1994 that most of the professionals conducting LCAs were not affecting product design as the EPEA had hoped. Because most practitioners were used to conducting an inventory only as part of the earlier REPAs, most consultants continued to focus heavily on the inventory step, not to consider the impact step enough, and to ignore the improvement step.

Second, most practitioners preferred to implement the three steps in a sequential fashion, a methodology that SETAC eventually incorporated as standard procedure at a Berlin conference in 1995. One reason for the linear bias was again the emphasis on the inventory step as carried over from the earlier REPA's. Another reason was that consultants were trying to be as comprehensive as possible by drawing the boundaries around the production processes very widely, so that the system being modeled was as encompassing as possible. Most consultants believed that if they were comprehensive, their decisions about impacts and about which product is better would be more informed. This was standard scientific protocol.

Finally, many consultants resisted doing the impact and improvement assessments altogether and instead focused on comparing one product with another. This again was standard scientific procedure: in an experiment, one compares an experimental item with a "control" to see how the two differ upon analysis. To make judgments on improvement without comparison to some reference was unprofessional. Such a move also carried great risk, since the consulting company would be assuming responsibility for deciding what constituted an improvement, instead of objectively providing information to a client who would assume the responsibility for deciding what was better or how to improve the product.

CLOSING THE LOOP: LIFE CYCLE DEVELOPMENT

Dr. Alain Rivière, a biologist, joined the EPEA in 1993. He had a different vision of how to do a product system analysis, one that fit the iterative model that Braungart originally proposed to SETAC. For Rivière interdependence and hierarchical arrangement of social systems in such things as product manufacturing systems worked much the way cells and organisms are built up and are interdependent. There are many feedback systems that exist.

The other analogy Rivière used was a fractal, as illustrated through the process by which a drop of water strikes and spreads through the napkin:

> Where you start [where the water first hits] determines a lot about what happens later. Thus it is important to start working on the most critical components of the system for optimization or it is important to work with the member of a network that has the greatest impact in a production chain. Later iterations of improvement to both the product or to the network occur in a manner that is linked in time and in a physical sense to the original. This is equivalent to the way water starts spreading through the napkin once the drop has struck. The water can spread out horizontally, corresponding to an expansion of the breadth of the product investigation or to including additional members in a network. The water can flow into the depth of the napkin, corresponding to an increase in the depth of the investigation of a particular part of the product's process, or in terms of refining the sophistication of what is accomplished at a particular node of the supply chain.

In other words, Rivière believed that it was unnecessary to draw the system boundaries as widely as possible at the beginning. What was important was to start with the parts of the system that needed the most improvement, and then to proceed through future iterations, changing the bounds of the investigation and improvement at each iteration. Following this procedure, the optimization stage (improvement assessment) is folded into every other stage and operates as a dynamic process of improvement. This is accomplished by including ecological criteria, such as those discussed in Exhibits 1 and 2, as goals of product and process design at the beginning and every subsequent stage of the LCA. The amount of data needed to be collected is reduced as choices are made from using materials that are known to have minimum impacts. The scope is not limited at the beginning of the study because, as the investigation progresses, the focus may shift from one area to another to achieve optimization. Setting priorities for optimization is accomplished by examining both the quantitative levels of material and energy flows and the qualitative aspects of the materials in terms of their possible irreversible environmental impacts at all times throughout the investigation, with the quantification as a subordinated goal to the qualitative one. [11]

Differing significantly with the consultants implementing the linear SETAC methodology, Rivière, Braungart, and other scientists at the EPEA were not hesitating to impose judgment on what constituted a "better" chemical over another. The EPEA crew believed that they were justified in following this strategy because they had accumulated experience and knowledge over their history. The EPEA had been screening substances and had categorized them over time using a simple scale: A, B, C, and X. The categories had the following meanings:

A represented a product [or product constituent] that is fully optimized concerning aspects of environmental and health soundness.

B corresponded to products [or product constituents] principally suitable but needing to be optimized along the life cycle.

C marked non-optimizable products [or product constituents] which are to be excluded as soon as alternatives are available.

X was a judgment leading to immediate exclusion since better alternatives are already available. [12]

The result of this classification was a series of what the EPEA called "positive lists." According to the EPEA *Profile and Scope of Work*,

> A positive list describes a pool of substances, that can be recommended from the ecological point of view. For a function to be fulfilled the applied substances and possible substitutes are screened and assessed in regard to their environmental and health impacts. Replacing a ban list, the result is a product recommendation that provides product safety. The use of positive lists leads to cost-reduced optimization of the ecological product features, as tests on hazardous substances in unspecified raw material are no longer necessary.[13]

When the EPEA encountered a new substance that they had not yet classified, they performed an impact evaluation and gave it an A,B,C,X categorization based on other available alternatives.

The EPEA personnel believed that as the result of using this methodology, the environmental sustainability of the product and processes would be improved as much as possible. Chemicals that could be replaced were done so with ones from the positive lists. Areas that could not be optimized were flagged as "weak points" documented by the chemical A,B,C, X classifications. The whole process thus became iterative and dynamic, and it required the company whose system was being optimized to participate in the improvement process over time. [14] The EPEA was acting as a catalyst by giving away some of its expertise to the company being helped. They hoped that the company would continue to look for ways to improve over time.

Braungart, Rivière, and others at the EPEA implemented this procedure with the Swiss textile company, Rohner Textil AG. The result of the project was the warm reception at the 1997 major German environmental conference. The EPEA was also working with some other companies to help redesign clothing, clothing dyes, pigments, and packaging wrap. They seemed to be making headway using their methodology, but the future lay uncertain as to whether their methods would gain wide acceptance.

Notes

1. Unless otherwise noted, the information used to write this case was obtained through interviews with EPEA personnel during the week of 24 June 1997 at the EPEA, Hamburg, Germany.
2. For more information on Rohner Textil's role in working with the EPEA, see Mehalik, M., M. Gorman and P. Werhane, *Rohner Textil AG. (A), (B), (C), (D), (E)* and *Teaching Note*, (Charlottesville, VA: Case Bibliography, University of Virginia. Mehalik, M., M. Gorman and P. Werhane (1996). *DesignTex, Inc. (A), (B)* and *Teaching Note*. Charlottesville, VA: Darden Case Bibliography, University of Virginia, both included in this book.

3. Personal interview with Michael Braungart, 29 August 1997 at the University of Virginia.

4. Michael Braungart and Justus Engelfried, "An 'Intelligent Product System' to Replace 'Waste Management,'" *Fresenius Environmental Bulletin* 1 (1992): 613-619.

5. Michael Braungart, Justus Engelfried, and Douglass Mulhall, "Criteria for Sustainable Development of Products and Production," *Fresenius Environmental Bulletin* 2 (1993): 72.

6. Braungart, Englefield and Mulhall, 72-73.

7. Robert G. Hunt and William E. Franklin, *Resource and Environmental Profile of Nine Beverage Container Alternatives*, EPA Report Number EPA/530/SW-91c (US Environmental Protection Agency, 1974).

8. Robert G. Hunt and William E. Franklin, "LCA—How it Came About," *The International Journal of Life Cycle Assessment* 1, No. 1 (1996): 6.

9. SETAC, *A Technical Framework for Life-Cycle Assessment* (Pensacola, FL: Society of Environmental Toxicology and Chemistry, 1991) xviii.

10. SETAC, *Guidelines for Life-Cycle Assessment: A "Code of Practice"* (Pensacola, FL: SETAC, 1993) 5.

11. Correspondence, Rivière to Mehalik, 16 January 1997.

12. Dr. Alain Rivière, "EPEA: Reducing the Threats of Textile Dyeing and Finishing to Human Health and the Environment," *Fashion News* (1996) 20.

13. Environmental Protection Encouragement Agency, Profile and Scope of Work (Hamburg: EPEA, March 1996) 4.

14. Alain Rivière, Jens Soth, Ralf Ketelhut, Joseph Rinkevich, and Michael Braungart, "From Life Cycle Assessment to Life Cycle Development," *Proceedings* of the Air & Waste Management Association's 90th Annual Meeting and Exhibition, June 8-13, 1997 Toronto.

EXHIBIT 1
Excerpts from "Intelligent Product System" to Replace Waste Management[1]

1. Consumption products

Consumption products are purchased to be consumed, i.e., converted by chemical reaction into energy or by-products, e.g., washing powder, food, etc. . . . These are usually used only once; then these products and/or their by-products become waste. They are normally put out into the natural environment after one use. In a system of "intelligent products," these products have to fulfill the following criteria and be:

- biodegradable (i.e., an accumulation in the food chain and in the environment does not occur),
- non-carcinogenic, non-teratogenic, non-mutagenic, and, in the used concentrations, non-toxic to human beings, and
- analyzed on a picogram-level, i.e., analytic methods have to be developed.

2. Service products

Service products are defined as goods which are used to provide services, such as automobiles, TV sets, washing machines, etc. . . . These products should only be used within a special "service concept": consumers with a demand for such a product can only lease the product from the producer who basically provides them with the product on a service basis. After the product has served its function and has to be renewed, the consumer returns it to the producer who is responsible for disassembly and recycling.

3. Unmarketable products

Unmarketable products cannot be consumed or used in an environmentally sound way. These are goods for which no safe recycling technology currently exists due to their dangerous effects and lack of demand or need.

In the long term, these products should not be manufactured and should be avoided completely.

---

1. Reproduced with permission from Michael Braungart and Justus Engelfried, "An 'Intelligent Product System' to Replace 'Waste Management,'" *Fresenius Environmental Bulletin* 1 (1992): 613-619.

EXHIBIT 2
Excerpts from Criteria for Sustainable Development of Products and Production[1]

The 25 criteria, encompassing goals for environmentally sustainable production, are presented in the following:

1. The company will apply the same environmental standards for products and production and provide enforcement possibilities by independent authorities globally.
2. The company will ensure that their production processes and facilities eliminate the possibility of any catastrophic accident.
3. The company will drastically reduce the number of chemicals produced and put only defined substances on the market.
4. The company will make complete declarations of all contents of its products publicly available.
5. The company will only produce analyzable chemicals, so that each substance can be traced even in concentrations of parts per billion.
6. The company will conduct life-cycle assessments for each of its products in this context; production processes for newly developed or persistent bio-accumulative and highly toxic substances are top priority.
7. The company will also conduct life-cycle assessments for production plants and waste/sewage treatment equipment. The basic elements to include in these analyses are energy, raw material and waste balances.
8. The company will drastically reduce its consumption of non-renewable energy and raw material resources, as well as the production of hazardous wastes.
9. The company will have full knowledge of the degradation processes of each of its products. The degradation should not produce any unknown and potentially harmful interim products.
10. The company will establish closed-loop systems for water used in cooling and production. The quality of the used resources—air, water, and soil will not be diminished during the production process.
11. The company will set a time limit and phase-out schedule for the use of environmentally unsustainable technologies which are currently used due to the lack of sound technologies.
12. The company will not contaminate groundwater either by production processes or by the use of products themselves.
13. The company will establish guidelines on the use of biotechnologies, especially genetic engineering, and translate them into action plans.
14. The company will promote environmental protection in order to encourage environmental activities in competing corporations.
15. The company will make all environmentally relevant data and information on the toxicological hazards induced by its products publicly available.
16. The company will ensure that individuals' or citizens' groups opposing specific technical processes or facilities will have the possibility of receiving technical advice similar to the project's proponents.
17. The company will acquire an appropriate plot of land to reduce the extinction of animal and plant species.
18. The company will strive to abolish animal tests and will set up a phase-out schedule for this purpose.
19. The company will not produce any biological or chemical weapons.

20. The company will accept responsibility for all chemical substances it has produced in the past.
21. The company will retain possession of all its unmarketable products until an environmentally sound utilization or elimination is possible.
22. The company will actively support international environmental groups and international committees in establishing standardized global environmental regulations and a qualified independent supervisory agency.
23. The company will be extensively liable for its products.
24. The company will take back products which cannot be disposed of in an environmentally sound manner (service concept). The company will provide clear instructions to consumers for this procedure, e.g., environmental passport, background information for the product.
25. The company will acknowledge long-term environmental goals as priorities. The company will make training and education available to the management and staff in order to translate long-term goals into reality.

1. Reproduced with permission from Michael Braungart, Justus Engelfried, and Douglass Mulhall, "Criteria for Sustainable Development of Products and Production," *Fresenius Environmental Bulletin* 2 (1993): 72

EXHIBIT 3
SETAC Life-Cycle Assessment Summary

There are four main parts of an LCA, which are implemented sequentially. The components are: goal definition and scoping, inventory analysis, impact assessment, and improvement assessment.

1. Goal Definition and Scoping: The goal definition and scoping component is the core of the four components. The purpose of the study is determined in this stage, addressing such questions as: Is the purpose to get a detailed inventory on a particular process or system? Is it to compare two products?

    Also, the bounds of the study are specified. This consists of agreeing on the limits of the system that will be studied. It may not be the client's wish to have a full, in-depth investigation into all of the components of the system, but instead he may want to limit the scope to certain areas and processes to a specified level of detail. An agreement is reached on what type of peer review process (if any) will be used in reviewing the study, as well as the means of communicating the results of the study.[1]

2. Inventory Analysis: In the inventory analysis stage, the system process elements are identified. For each process, the material and energy inputs and outputs are identified. Qualitative measures for material and data inputs and outputs are obtained by methods like direct measurement or databases. This stage evolved directly from the earlier REPA studies.[2]

3. Impact Assessment: For the impact assessment stage the inputs and outputs are assessed for their impacts in four categories: resource depletion, ecological degradation, human health effects, and other human welfare effects.[3]

4. Improvement Assessment: The final stage consists of an improvement assessment. This is an addition to the original REPA studies, because the earlier studies were not directed toward identifying and reducing impacts. The improvement assessment imbeds in the LCA methodology a goal to reduce such impacts.[4]

SETTING THE GOAL AND SCOPE OF THE PROJECT

Before any data collection or analysis can begin, the purpose of conducting the LCA should be established. The reason is that there is not just one way of conducting an LCA. It can be conducted at different degrees of breadth and depth; it may be limited by the type of data that are available for analysis; it may be used for different purposes according to which stakeholders will rely on the LCA for decision-making; it may be limited by time considerations; and it may be restricted according to budgetary requirements. There are several issues that should be addressed when deciding the goal and scope of the study.

System boundaries

One consideration is the boundaries of the system to be studied. It is imperative to choose the boundaries so that the results remain internally consistent throughout the inventory. The two issues are breadth and depth of analysis. Breadth refers to the extent of systems components that are included.

Basis for measuring performance

It is important to specify the unit or units on which the performance of the system can be judged. This is accomplished by first specifying the overall function of the system and then by examining the inputs and outputs and identifying how they can be quantified on a unit basis. An example of such a unit could be the amount of solid waste generated per meter of fabric produced.[5]

Time limits

It is important to consider whether or not the data requirements for the project can be met by the time restrictions on the project. Two such restrictions may include whether or not the process of collecting data can be accomplished in a time frame that makes it relevant to an adaptive or changing system and whether or not the database being used contains data that may be outdated and unsuitable for modeling the system.[6]

CONDUCTING THE INVENTORY ANALYSIS

There are many factors to be considered when conducting an inventory of the system inputs and outputs. The first stage is defining and identifying the inputs and outputs for the subsystems within the main system as described in the scope- and goal-setting stage above. For the purposes of an LCA, each subsystem consists of a single stage or operation for which material, energy, and product data are available. Single-stage process flow diagrams can be used to help this process. . . .

Each of the subsystems should be linked so that material, product, and energy flows are balanced through the entire system. A flow diagram of the interconnected subsystems can then be made to identify the general processing steps and the flow of materials, products and energy through the entire system [7]

After a map of the material, product, and energy flows of the system is completed, their use can be quantified at the single-stage process level. Energy and material inputs are measured and their concentrations noted. Outputs include products, co-products (which become inputs at a different processing stage), releases to air and water, and solid waste. These can be traced through the higher system levels and summed for the overall system.[8]

There are issues involved in deciding how inputs and outputs should be assigned because inputs and outputs often are distributed across multiple single process stages. Also, a single process can produce outputs which may not be considered all waste. In both of these instances, it is important to document the assumptions made in accounting for these distributions. It is also important to remain consistent throughout the inventory analysis.[9]

There are many issues to consider when gathering process data. One such issue is data availability. When process data cannot be obtained directly, other sources can be consulted, such as databases, persons experienced with the design of the process, and calculations. Other issues include data variability, uncertainty and sensitivity. SETAC recommends that a sensitivity analysis be conducted to test the effects of variability and uncertainty on the outcome. A final issue is the decision to omit some of the data in order to simplify the process. SETAC has published a volume[10] outlining detailed procedures for handling these issues, which are beyond the scope of the present discussion.[11]

The general procedures for conducting an LCA are being standardized as part of the ISO 14000 series of standards. ISO 14041 is the particular document that will standardize the inventory assessment portion of an LCA. The draft is being crafted from the guidelines proposed by SETAC. Final approval of ISO 14041 is not expected until 1998.[12]

IMPACT ASSESSMENT

SETAC defines an impact assessment as

> a technical, quantitative, and/or qualitative process to characterize and assess the effects of the environmental burdens identified in the inventory component. Impact Assessment is presently under development and has, as yet, no commonly agreed-to methodologies.[13]

Instead of attempting to find cause-and-effect relationships between the findings of the inventory stage (the resources that are depleted and the wastes that are generated) and environmental degradation, the impact assessment attempts to classify the findings into impact categories. This is because, as SETAC has found,

> It is unlikely that life-cycle impact assessment will prove that the product or process under study is responsible for a certain amount of loss of biodiversity. Such cause-and-effect relationships are usually difficult, if not impossible, to prove. Moreover, it was recognized that quantification of the actual specific impacts associated with any product or process is extremely difficult in the context of an LCA.[14]

The categories have been established through past research in hazard and risk assessment models. Some categories of environmental impacts are: resource depletion, ecological degradation, human health effects, and human welfare effects, like loss of recreational value or scenic beauty.[15] Once the analyst has classified the inventory data for a process into a chosen category, he can apply different models using the inventory data to capture a range of potential impacts. A complete description of all of the issues pertaining to the impact assessment stage are presented in SETAC's *A Conceptual Framework For Life-Cycle Impact Assessment*.[16] The ISO is working on a draft of standards for conducting an impact assessment under the series name ISO 14042. These standards are not expected to be approved for at least three or four years.[17]

IMPROVEMENT ASSESSMENT

The goal of the improvement assessment component of a life cycle assessment is to identify system components that can be changed to reduce the environmental burden of products or processes. Neither SETAC nor any other body has proposed consensus documents[18] on a methodology for conducting an improvement assessment. SETAC has identified the following as opportunities for reducing impacts:

- Minimization of energy and raw material consumption.
- Closed-loop systems for chemicals that are bioaccumulatives, persistent, etc.

- Minimization of activities resulting in species endangerment through habitat destruction.
- Minimization of waste releases.[19]

There are no current provisions for including standards for the improvement assessment as part of the ISO 14000 series.[20]

Notes

1. Gregory A. Keoleian and Dan Menerey, *Life Cycle Design Guidance Manual*, EPA Report Number EPA/600/R-92/226 (Cincinnati, OH: Risk Reduction Engineering Laboratory, US Environmental Protection Agency, January 1993) 100. Also, SETAC (1993) 10.
2. Keoleian and Menerey, 102.
3. Keoleian and Menerey, 109.
4. SETAC, *A Conceptual Framework for Life Cycle Impact Assessment.* (Pensacola FL: SETAC Foundation, 1993) 11.
5. SETAC (1993) 13-14; Keoleian and Menerey, 101-102.
6. Keoleian and Menerey, 102.
7. Adapted from SETAC, *A Conceptual Framework for Life Cycle Impact Assessment* (Pensacola FL: SETAC Foundation, 1993) 11.
8. Keoleian and Menerey, 105.
9. For details on handling these issues, see Keoleian and Menerey, 105, and SETAC (1991).
10. See SETAC (1993).
11. SETAC (1993) 18-21.
12. See the iso1400 infocenter homepage at http://www.iso1400.com
13. SETAC (1993) 24.
14. SETAC (1993a) 13.
15. Keoleian and Menerey, 109.
16. SETAC (1993a).
17. See the iso1400 infocenter homepage at http://www.iso1400.com
18. SETAC (1993) 28-29.
19. SETAC (1991) 123.
20. See the iso1400 infocenter homepage at http://www.iso1400.com

12

A CENTENNIAL SERMON: DESIGN, ECOLOGY, ETHICS, AND THE MAKING OF THINGS

It is humbling to be an architect in a cathedral because it is a magnificent representation of humankind's highest aspirations. Its dimension is illustrated by the small Christ figure in the western rose window, which is, in fact, human scale. A cathedral is a representation of both our longings and intentions. This morning, here at this important crossing in this great building, I am going to speak about the concept of design itself as the first signal of human intention and will focus on ecology, ethics, and the making of things. I would like to reconsider both our design and our intentions.

When Vincent Scully gave a eulogy for the great architect Louis Kahn, he described a day when both were crossing Red Square, whereupon Scully excitedly turned to Kahn and said, "Isn't it wonderful the way the domes of St. Basil's Cathedral reach up into the sky?" Kahn looked up and down thoughtfully for a moment and said, "Isn't it beautiful the way they come down to the ground?"

If we understand that design leads to the manifestation of human intention, and if what we make with our hands is to be sacred and honor the earth that gives us life, then the things we make must not only rise from the ground but return to it, soil to soil, water to water, so everything that is received from the earth can be freely given back without causing harm to any living system. This is ecology. This is good design. It is of this we must now speak.

If we use the study of architecture to inform this discourse, and we go back in history, we will see that architects are always working with two elements, mass and mem-

Sermon by William McDonough, The Cathedral of St. John the Divine, New York, February 7, 1993. Adapted by Paul Hawken and William McDonough. Copyright 1993 William McDonough Architects.

brane. We have the walls of Jericho, mass, and we have tents, membranes. Ancient peoples practiced the art and wisdom of building with mass, such as adobe-walled hut, to anticipate the scope and direction of sunshine. They knew how thick a wall needed to be to transfer the heat of the day into the winter night, and how thick it had to be to transfer the coolness into the interior in the summer. They worked well with what we call "capacity" in the walls in terms of storage and thermal lags.

They worked with resistance, straw, in the roof to protect from heat loss in the winter and to shield the heat gain in summer from the high sun. These were very sensible buildings within the climate in which they were located.

With respect to membrane, we only have to look at the Bedouin tent to find a design that accomplishes five things at once. In the desert, temperatures often exceed 120 degrees. There is no shade, no air movement. The black Bedouin tent when pitched, creates a deep shade that brings one's sensible temperature down to 95 degrees. The tent has a very coarse weave, which creates a beautifully illuminated interior, having a million light fixtures. Because of the coarse weave and the black surface, the air inside rises and is drawn through the membrane. So now you have a breeze coming in from outside, and that drops the sensible temperature even lower down to 90 degrees. You may wonder what happens when it rains, with those holes in the tent. The fibers swell up and the tent gets tight as a drum when wet. And of course, you can roll it up and take it with you. The modern tent pales by comparison to this astonishingly elegant construct.

Throughout history, you find constant experimentation between mass and membrane. This cathedral is a Gothic experiment integrating great light into massive membrane. The challenge has always been, on a certain level, how to combine light with mass and air. This experiment displayed itself powerfully in modern architecture, which arrived with the advent of inexpensive glass. It was unfortunate that at the same time the large sheet of glass showed up, the era of cheap energy was ushered in, too. And because of that, architects no longer rely upon the sun for heat or illumination. I have spoken to thousands of architects, and when I ask the question, "How many of you know how to find true South?" I rarely get a raised hand.

Our culture has adopted a design stratagem that essentially says that if brute force or massive amounts of energy don't work, you're not using enough of it. We made glass buildings that are more about buildings than they are about people. We've used the glass ironically. The hope that glass would connect us to the outdoors was completely stultified by making the buildings sealed. We have created stress in people because we are meant to be connected with the outdoors, but instead we are trapped. Indoor air quality issues are now becoming very serious. People are sensing how horrifying it can be to be trapped indoors, especially with the thousands upon thousands of chemicals that are being used to make things today.

Le Corbusier said in the early part of this century that a house is a machine for living in. He glorified the steamship, the airplane, the grain elevator. Think about it: A house is a machine for living in. An office is a machine for working in. A cathedral is a machine for praying in. This has become a terrifying prospect, because what has happened is that designers are now designing for the machine and not for people. People talk about solar heating a building, even about solar heating a cathedral. But it isn't the cathedral that is asking to be heated, it is the people. To solar heat a cathedral, one should heat people's feet, not the air 120 feet above them. We need to listen to biologist John Todd's idea that we need to work with living machines, not machines for living in. The focus should be on people's needs. And we need clean water, safe materials, and durability. And we need to work from current solar income.

There are certain fundamental laws that are inherent to the natural world that we can use as models and mentors for human designs. Ecology comes from the Greek roots *Oikos* and *Logos*, "household" and "logical discourse." Thus, it is appropriate, if not imperative, for architects to discourse about the logic of our earth household. To do so, we must first look at our planet and the very processes by which it manifests life, because therein lie the logical principles with which we must work. And we must also consider economy in the true sense of the word. Using the Greek words, *Oikos* and *Nomos*, we speak of natural law and how we measure and manage the relationships within this household, working with the principles our discourse has revealed to us.

And how do we measure our work under those laws? Does it make sense to measure it by the paper currency that you have in your wallet? Does it make sense to measure it by a grand summation called GNP? For if we do, we find that the foundering and rupture of the *Exxon Valdez* tanker was a prosperous event because so much money was spent in Prince William Sound during the clean-up. What then are we really measuring? If we have not put natural resources on the asset side of the ledger, then where are they? Does a forest really become more valuable when it is cut down? Do we really prosper when wild salmon are completely removed from a river?

There are three defining characteristics that we can learn from natural design. The first characteristic is that everything we have to work with is already here—the stones, the clay, the wood, the water, the air. All materials given to us by nature are constantly returned to the earth without even the concept of waste as we understand it. Everything is cycled constantly with all waste equally food for other living systems.

The second characteristic is that the one thing allowing nature to continually cycle itself through life is energy, and this energy comes from outside the system in the form of perpetual solar income. Not only does nature operate on "current income," it does not mine or extract energy from the past, it does not use its capital reserves, and it does not borrow from the future. It is an extraordinarily complex and efficient system for creating and cycling nutrients, so economical that modern methods of manufacturing pale in comparison to the elegance of natural systems of production.

Finally, the characteristic that sustains this complex and efficient system of metabolism and creation is bio-diversity. What prevents living systems from running down and veering into chaos is a miraculously intricate and symbiotic relationship between millions of organisms, no two of which are alike.

As a designer of buildings, things, and systems, I ask myself how to apply these three characteristics of living systems to my work. How do I employ the concept of waste equals food, of current solar income, of protecting bio-diversity in design? Before I can even apply these principles, though, we must understand the role of the designer in human affairs.

In thinking about this, I reflect upon a commentary of Emerson's. In the 1830s, when his wife died, he went to Europe on a sailboat and returned on a steamship. He remarked on a return voyage that he missed the "Aeolian connection." If we abstract this, he went over on a solar-powered recyclable vehicle operated by craftpersons, working in the open air, practicing ancient arts. He returned in a steel rust bucket, spilling oil on the water and smoke into the sky, operated by people in a black dungeon shoveling coal into the mouth of a boiler. Both ships are objects of design. Both are manifestations of our human intention.

Peter Senge, a professor at M.I.T.'s Sloan School of Management, works with a program called the Learning Laboratory where he studies and discusses how organizations learn. Within that he has a leadership laboratory, and one of the first questions he asks CEOs of companies that attend is "Who is the leader on a ship crossing the ocean?" He gets obvious answers, such as the captain, the navigator, or the helmsman. But the answer is none of the above. The leader is the designer of the ship because operations on a ship are a consequence of design, which is the result of human intentions. Today, we are still designing steamships. machines powered by fossil fuels that have deleterious effects. We need a new design.

I grew up in the Far East and when I came to this country I was taken aback when I realized that we were not people with lives in America, but consumers with lifestyles. I wanted to ask someone: "When did America stop having people with lives?" On television, we are referred to as consumers, not people. But we are people, with lives, and we must make and design things for people. And if I am a consumer, what can I consume? Shoe polish, food, juice, some toothpaste. But actually, very little that is sold to me can actually be consumed. Sooner or later, almost all of it has to be thrown away. I cannot consume a television set. Or a VCR. Or a car. If I presented you with a television set and covered it up and said, "I have this amazing item. What it will do as a service will astonish you. But before I tell you what it does, let me tell you what it is made of and you can tell me if you want it in your house. It contains 4,060 chemicals, many of which are toxic, 200 of which off-gas into the room when it is turned on. It also contains 18 grams of toxic methyl mercury, has an explosive glass tube, and I urge you to put it at eye-level with your children and encourage them to play with it." Would you want this in your home?

Michael Braungart, an ecological chemist from Hamburg, German, has pointed out that we should remove the word "waste" from our vocabulary and start using the word "product" instead, because if waste is going to equal food, it must also be a product. Braungart suggests we think about three distinct product types.

First, there are consumables and actually we should be producing more of them. These are products that when eaten or used, or thrown away, literally turn back into dirt, and therefore are food for other living organisms. Consumables should not be placed in landfills, but put on the ground so that they restore the life, health, and fertility of the soil. This means that shampoos should be in bottles made of beets that are biodegradable in your compost pile. It means carpets that break down into CO_2 and water. It means furniture made of potato peels and technical enzymes that looks just like your manufactured furniture of today except it can be safely returned to the earth. It means that all "consumable" goods should be capable of returning to the soil from where they came.

Second are products of service, also known as durables, such as cars and television sets. They are called products of service because what we want as customers is the service the product provides— food, entertainment, or transportation. To eliminate the concept of waste, products of service would not be sold, but licensed to the end-user.

Customers may use them as long as they wish, even sell the license to someone else, but when the end-user is finished with, say, a television, it goes back to Sony, Zenith, or Philips. It is "food" for their system, but not for natural systems. Right now, you can go down the street, dump a TV into the garbage can, and walk away. In the process, we deposit persistent toxins throughout the planet. Why do we give people that responsibility and stress? Products of service must continue beyond their initial product life, be owned by their manufacturers, and be designed for disassembly, re-manufacture, and continuous re-use.

The third type of product is called "unmarketables." The question is, why would anyone produce a product that no one would buy? Welcome to the world of nuclear waste, dioxins, and chromium-tanned leather. We are essentially making products or subcomponents of products that no one should buy, or in many cases, do not realize they are buying. These products must not only cease to be sold, but those already sold should be stored in warehouses when they are finished until we can figure out a safe and non-toxic way to dispose of them.

I will describe a few projects and how these issues are implicit in design directions. I remember when we were hired to design the office for an environmental group. The director said at the end of contract negotiations, "By the way, if anybody in our office gets sick from indoor air quality, we're going to sue you." After wondering if we should even take the job, we decided to go ahead, that it was our job to find the materials that wouldn't make people sick when placed inside a building. And what we found is that those materials weren't there. We had to work with manufacturers to find out what was in their products, and we discovered that the entire system of building construction is essentially toxic. We are still working on the materials side.

For a New York men's clothing store, we arranged for the planting of 1,000 oak trees to replace the two English oaks used to panel the store. We were inspired by a famous story told by Gregory Bateson about New College in Oxford, England. It went something like this: They had a main hall built in the early 1600s with beams forty feet long and two feet thick. A committee was formed to try to find replacement trees because the beams were suffering from dry rot. If you keep in mind that a veneer from an English oak can be worth seven dollars a square foot, the total replacement costs for the oaks were prohibitively expensive. And they didn't have straight forty foot English oaks from mature forests with which to replace the beams. A young faculty member joined the committee and said, "Why don't we ask the College Forester if some of the lands that had been given to Oxford might have enough trees to call upon?" And when they brought in the forester he said, "We've been wondering when you would ask this question. When the present building was constructed 350 years ago, the architects specified that a grove of trees be planted and maintained to replace the beams in the ceiling when they would suffer from dry rot." Bateson's remark was, "That's the way to run a culture." Our question and hope is, "Did they replant them?"

For Warsaw, Poland, we responded to a design competition for a high-rise building. When the client chose our design as the winner after seeing the model, we said, "We're not finished yet. We have to tell you all about the building. The base is made from concrete and includes bits of rubble from World War II. It looks like limestone, but the rubble's there for visceral reasons." And he said, "I understand, a phoenix rising." And we said the skin is recycled aluminum, and he said, "That's O.K., that's fine." And we said, "The floor heights are thirteen feet clear so that we can convert the building into housing in the future, when its utility as an office building is no longer. In this way, the building is given a chance to have a long, useful life." And he said, "That's O.K." And we told him that we would have opening windows and that no one would be further than twenty-five feet from a window, and he said that was O.K. too. And finally, we said, "By the way, you have to plant ten square miles of forest to offset the building's effect on climate change." We had calculated the energy costs to build the structure, and the energy cost to run and maintain it, and it worked out that 6,400 acres of new forest would be needed to offset the effects on climate change from the energy requirements. And he said he would get back to us. He called back two days later and said, "You still win." I checked out what it would cost to plant ten square miles of trees in Poland and it turns out it's equivalent to a small part of the advertising budget.

The architects representing a major retail chain called us a year ago and said, "Will you help us build a store in Lawrence, Kansas?" I said that I didn't know if we could work with them. I explained my thoughts on consumers with lifestyles, and we needed to be in the position to discuss their store's impact on small towns. Click. Three days later we were called back and were told, "We have a question for you that is coming from the top. Are you willing to discuss the fact that people with lives have the right to buy the finest-quality products, even under your own terms, at the lowest possible price?" We said, "Yes." "Then we can talk about the impact on small towns."

We worked with them on the store in Kansas. We converted the building from steel construction, which uses 300,000 BTUs per square foot, to wood construction, which uses 40,000 BTUs thereby saving thousands of gallons of oil just in the fabrication of the building. We used only wood that came from resources that were protecting bio-diversity. In our research we found that the forests of James Madison and Zachary Taylor in Virginia had been put into sustaining forestry and the wood for the beams came from there and other forests managed this way. We also arranged for no CFCs to be used in the store's construction and systems, and initiated significant research and a major new industry in daylighting. We have yet to fulfill our concerns about the bigger questions of products, their distribution and the chain's impact on small towns, with the exception that this store is designed to be converted into housing when its utility as a retail outlet has expired.

For the city of Frankfurt, we are designing a day-care center that can be operated by the children. It contains a greenhouse roof that has multiple functions: It illuminates, heats both air and water, cools, ventilates, and shelters from the rain, just like a Bedouin tent. One problem we were having during the design process was the engineers wanted to completely automate the building, like a machine. The engineers asked, "What happens if the children forget to close the shades and they get too hot?" We told them the children would open a window. "What if they don't open a window?" the engineers wanted to know. And we told them that in that case, the children would probably close the shade. And then they wanted to know what would happen if the children didn't close the shade. And finally we told them the children would open windows and close shades when they were hot because children are not dead but alive. Recognizing the importance for children to look at the day in the morning and see what the sun is going to do that day, and interact with it, we enlisted the help of teachers of Frankfurt to get this one across because the teachers had told us the most important thing was to find something for the children to do. Now the children have ten minutes of activity in the morning and ten minutes of activity when they leave the building, opening and closing the system, and both the children and teachers love the idea. Because of the solar hot-water collectors, we asked that a public laundry be added to the program so that parents could wash clothes while awaiting their children in school. Because of advances in glazing, we are able to create a day-care center that requires no fossil fuels for operating the heating or cooling. Fifty years from now, when fossil fuels will be scarce, there will be hot water for the community, a social center, and the building will have paid back the energy "borrowed" for its construction.

As we became aware of the ethical implications of design, not only with respect to buildings, but in every aspect of human endeavor, they reflect changes in the historical concept of who or what has rights. When you study the history of rights, you begin with the Magna Carta, which was about the rights of white, English, noble males. With the Declaration of Independence, rights were expanded to all landowning white males. Nearly a century later, we moved to the emancipation of slaves, and during the beginnings of this century, to suffrage, giving the right to women to vote. Then the pace picks up with the Civil Rights Act in 1964, and then in 1973, the Endangered Species Act. For the first time, the right of other species and organisms to exist was recognized. We have essentially "declared" that Homo Sapiens are part of the web of life. Thus, if Thomas Jefferson were with us today, he would be calling for a Declaration of Interdependence which recognizes that our ability to pursue wealth, health, and happiness is dependent on other forms of life, that the rights of one species are linked to the rights of others and none should suffer remote tyranny.

This Declaration of Interdependence comes hard on the heels of realizing that the world has become vastly complex, both in its workings and in our ability to perceive and comprehend those complexities. In this complicated world, prior modes of domination have essentially lost their ability to maintain control. The sovereign, whether in the form of a king or nation, no longer seems to reign. Nations have lost control of money to global, computerized trading systems. The sovereign is also losing the ability to deceive and manipulate, as in the case of Chernobyl. While the erstwhile Soviet Republic told the world that Chernobyl was nothing to be concerned about, satellites with ten-meter resolution showed the world that it was something to worry about. And what we saw at the Earth Summit was the sovereign has lost the ability to lead even on the most elementary level. When Maurice Strong, the chair of the United Nations Conference on the Environment and Development, was asked how many leaders were at the Earth Summit, he said there were over 100 heads of state. Unfortunately, we didn't have any leaders.

When Emerson came back from Europe, he wrote essays for Harvard on Nature. He was trying to understand that if human beings make things and human beings are natural, then are all the things that human beings make natural? He determined that Nature was all those things which were immutable. The oceans, the mountains, the sky. Well, we now know that they are mutable. We were operating as if Nature is the Great Mother who never has any problems, is always there for her children, and requires no love in return. When you think about Genesis and the concept of dominion over natural things we realize that even if we want to get into a discussion of stewardship versus dominion, in the end, the question is, if you have dominion, and perhaps we do have dominion, isn't it implicit that we have stewardship too, because how can you have dominion over something you've killed?

We must face the fact that what we are seeing across the world today is war, a war against life itself. Our present systems of design have created a world that grows far beyond the capacity of the environment to sustain life into the future. The industrial idiom of design, failing to honor the principles of nature, can only violate them, producing waste and harm, regardless of purported intention. If we destroy more forests, burn more garbage, drift-net more fish, burn more coal, bleach more paper, destroy more topsoil, poison more insects, build over more habitats, dam more rivers, produce more toxic and radioactive waste, we are creating a vast industrial machine, not for living in, but for dying in. It is a war, to be sure, a war that only a few more generations can surely survive.

When I was in Jordan, I worked for King Hussein on the master plan for the Jordan Valley. I was walking through a village that had been flattened by tanks and I saw a child skeleton squashed into the adobe block and was horrified. My Arab host turned to me and said, "Don't you know what war is?" And I said, "I guess I don't." And he said "War is when they kill your children." So I believe we're at war. But we must stop. To do this, we have to stop designing everyday things for killing, and we have to stop designing killing machines.

We have to recognize that every event and manifestation of nature is "design," that to live within the laws of nature means to express our human intention as an interdependent species, aware and grateful that we are at the mercy of sacred forces larger than ourselves, and that we obey these laws in order to honor the sacred in each other and in all things. We must come to peace with and accept our place in the natural world.

13

DesignTex, Incorporated

The contract-textile business is about offering choice, not volume.
—Susan Lyons

Susan Lyons, vice president of Design at DesignTex, a firm specializing in the design and manufacture of textiles for commercial interiors, knew the importance of looking ahead to the next design breakthrough. In February 1991, she had helped launch a new line of fabrics called the Portfolio Collection™, a design that evolved out of collaboration with very famous architects Aldo Rossi, Robert Venturi, Denise Scott Brown, and Richard Meier. This collection was provocative in its aesthetic sense, and it also demonstrated that well-designed fabrics could be marketed at reasonable prices.

Although Lyons was proud of the latest collection, she wanted the next design to focus on an issue, not be just a change in aesthetics. The issue of environmental responsibility seemed perfect. "Green" was popular in the trade literature and in the general media, and she had been receiving inquiries from DesignTex's customers about how

Prepared by Matthew M. Mehalik under the supervision of Michael E. Gorman, Andrea Larson, Assistant Professor of Business Administration at the Darden Graduate Business School, University of Virginia, and Patricia H. Werhane. Partial support for this project was supplied by grants from the Ethics and Values in Science program of the National Science Foundation and the Geraldine R. Dodge Foundation. The conclusions are the responsibilities of the authors, and do not reflect the views of the foundations. Copyright © 1996 by the School of Engineering and Applied Science of the University of Virginia and the University of Virginia Darden School Foundation. All rights reserved.

environmentally responsible DesignTex's products were. Her desire to pursue an environmental agenda was not, however, simply the result of customer demand. It sprang from deep personal beliefs about environmentalism that reflected her mother's influence. Lyons' mother had been "way ahead of her time": she had been recycling trash and other items and had been conservation minded back in the 1960s when Lyons was growing up. These childhood experiences had made Lyons sensitive to environmental concerns, and she had a strong impulse to act upon them.

Such a breakthrough, thought Lyons, would maintain DesignTex's leadership in the commercial-fabrics design market. DesignTex was vying to be the largest member of the Association of Contract Textiles (ACT), the industry trade organization. Located in New York, DesignTex worked with over 40 mills around the world, many of which manufactured the designs created by DesignTex.

DesignTex was also a member of the Steelcase Design Partnership, a collection of design industries purchased in 1989 by Steelcase, a giant corporation located in Grand Rapids, Michigan, that manufactured office furniture and supplies. Steelcase formed this partnership to capture a market that otherwise eluded the firm. Although the company was able to turn out huge amounts of products very profitably, it was not responsive to customers such as architects, who demanded specialty or custom designs. Small, nimble, and entrepreneurial companies were able to meet the demands of this growing market better than Steelcase, and DesignTex was such a company.

In order to maintain DesignTex's ability to respond to the rapidly changing, customer-design market, Steelcase permitted DesignTex's management to operate autonomously. In fact, as a fabric supplier, DesignTex sometimes competed against Steelcase for contracts. Steelcase typically brought in DesignTex as a consultant, however, in matters involving specialty-fabrics design. Susan Lyons summarized the relationship, "DesignTex is very profitable, and Steelcase receives a large amount of money from DesignTex's operation with no oversight, so Steelcase is happy to let DesignTex do its own thing. However, this situation could change if DesignTex's profitability began to decline." By taking the lead in the still volatile environmental market, Lyons hoped DesignTex would maintain its autonomy.

To launch her project, she began surveying the trade literature, contacted yarn spinners who claimed to be environmentally "correct," and paid attention to competitors who were also attempting to enter this market. The work was difficult because (1) she was also looking at approximately 40 other new designs and design improvements, (2) she wanted the design to look like others in the DesignTex line and (3) she wanted the design to be durable as well as environmentally viable.

Lyons continued her "research" for about two years, from 1991 through 1993. What she found was a jumble of information. As she pointed out, there were "conflicting claims about environmentally safe materials." Cottons were often heavily bleached, and most manufacturers were reluctant to talk about what was in their dyes. She considered using foxfiber with vegetable dyes, but the combination was available in only two colors. She considered using a yarn that was made from PET-recycled soda bottles. In fact, this appeared to be the most promising option, but the vendors were unreliable. These problems seemed difficult to reconcile with her belief that the "contract-textile business is about offering choice, not volume."[1]

THE CLIMATEX OPTION[2]

Because DesignTex also worked with over 40 contract mills around the world, Lyons contacted some of them to investigate their environmental efforts. In December 1992 she became interested in a sample of a fabric product line called Climatex. Albin Kälin, managing director of Rohner Textil, a mill located in Switzerland, sent Lyons a sample. He and Rohner Textil had been pursuing an environmental agenda of their own, and he was willing to team up with Lyons and DesignTex in developing a new product based on Climatex.

The fabric, a patented combination of wool, ramie, and polyester, was unique because it wicked away moisture from a person who was in contact with the material over long periods. It was intended to improve comfort in wheelchairs and trucks, since those applications involved extended periods of contact between people and fabrics.

Lyons also inquired about the possibility of recycling Climatex. Kälin informed her that recycling fabrics was possible only if the material was pure (e.g., 100 percent wool or cotton), but not if it was a combination of materials. Because Climatex was a blend of wool, ramie, and polyester, no recycling was possible. In addition, Kälin mentioned that recycling any commercial fabrics was questionable, because they were typically glued as upholstery, and the glue itself made recycling difficult. Nevertheless, he went on to add, "there is a far more important argument on the aspect of ecology to Climatex." Since the fabric was created without any chemical treatments, "the yarn in the fabric can be burnt [sic] without any damaging chemical reaction and are consisting [sic] of a good heating factor." By "good heating factor," Kälin meant that the fabric released a large amount of energy when burned, and he proposed using this energy in the operation of the mill. He also mentioned that Climatex was being tested in Germany by an independent institute, the International Association for Research and Testing in the Field of Textile Ecology (OEKO-Tex).[3]

Both Kälin and Lyons were pleased when Climatex passed the OEKO-Tex inspections in May 1993. The institute, concerned with human-ecology issues, tested for pH value, content of free and partially releasable formaldehyde, residues of heavy metals, residues of pesticides, pentachorophenole content, carcinogenic compounds, and color fastness. Having passed these tests, Climatex could bear the OEKO-Tex trademark and was certified to be allergy-free. Exhibit 1 contains the English translation of the OEKO-Tex Standard 110, which outlines in greater detail the criteria used in the certification process.[4]

By the middle of 1993, Lyons had several options to consider for an environmental design. The most promising one seemed to be the Climatex fabric from Rohner, which was certified to be manufactured within the OEKO-Tex specifications. But she was worried that because the fabric was not recyclable, and because it was difficult to make a grand environmental statement using the OEKO-Tex label, that option might not be as good as it seemed. In addition, the product was not cheap. It was priced competitively within the worsted-wool market niche, but that particular niche was on the expensive end of the overall market. She considered using yarn made from PET-recycled soda bottles, but she was not confident that the vendors could deliver reliably. Her research uncovered promising options, but each had difficulties and risks.

In July 1993, DesignTex owner Ralph Saltzman, president Tom Hamilton, consultant Steve Kroeter, and Lyons met to consider what the next generation of the Portfolio™ Collection would be. Launched in 1991, Portfolio™ had been a highly successful major product line. By mid-1993, however, the product's demand had peaked. At this meeting, the team agreed that the next Portfolio™ collection would have a major impact on the market if its design focused on the green issue.

During the meeting, Lyons brought up another factor that could not be neglected: aesthetics. In addition to being environmentally friendly the next Portfolio collection had to be as beautiful as the last. Lyons hoped to collaborate with a prestigious designer in producing beautiful fabrics for the new line, just as she had for the original Portfolio Collection™. At the meeting, Kroeter suggested that they contact Suzy Tompkins of the Esprit Clothing Company, which had just released a unique line of clothing based on organic cotton. Lyons suggested an architect who was well known for his environmental philosophy and his architectural-design accomplishments, William McDonough. The group agreed that they would contact both designers and invite them to participate in the next generation of Portfolio™. Tompkins declined to participate because as a clothing manufacturer, she rarely worked with commercial-fabric designers. Lyons did, however, receive a more enthusiastic response when she contacted McDonough.

WILLIAM McDONOUGH

During her environmental-literature search, Lyons had come across the name of William McDonough in two places. She had read the March 1993 issue of *Interiors* magazine, which was dedicated entirely to McDonough and his projects. She had also seen an article about him in the *Wall Street Journal*.[5] McDonough had just accepted a job as the dean of Architecture at the University of Virginia. After reading about him, Lyons viewed him as the most high-profile person working with environmental concerns in the design industry.

McDonough had no immediate plans to develop sustainable fabrics, but he responded quite enthusiastically when she made the suggestion to him. He was looking for opportunities to apply his design philosophy. The fabric-design project fit into his plans perfectly.

McDonough came to visit DesignTex in early October 1993. During their meeting, Lyons described the options she had turned up in her literature and marketplace searches and suggested the idea of the PET soda bottle fabric to him. In turn, McDonough presented his design philosophy (the elements of this philosophy are outlined in his article, "A Centennial Sermon").

"Two key principles hit home really hard," Lyons said, "the idea that waste equals food and the idea of a cradle-to-cradle design, not a cradle-to-grave design." McDonough stated that in order to meet the waste-equals-food and cradle-to-cradle design criteria, the product had to be able either (1) to compost completely with no negative environmental impact, thereby becoming food for other organisms (organic nutrients) or (2) to become raw material for another industrial product (technical nutrients). Furthermore, one should not mix the organic and the technical, or one would end up with a product that could be used neither as food for organisms nor as raw materials for technology. "The product should be manufactured without the release of carcinogens, bioacumulatives, persistent toxic chemicals, mutagens, heavy metals, or endocrine disruptors." McDonough discouraged the use of the term "environmentally friendly" and instead proposed "environmentally intelligent" to describe this method of design, because it involved having the foresight to know that poisoning the earth is not merely unfriendly, but unintelligent.[6]

"The key to the project," McDonough stated, would be "getting the fabric mills to open up their manufacturing processes to inspection to see where problems arise." In addition, the mills would have to examine the processes of the mill partners—the farmers, yarn spinners, twisters, dyers, and finishers—so that they could also meet the design protocol. McDonough suggested that his close colleague, Dr. Michael Braungart of the Environmental Protection Encouragement Agency (EPEA) in Germany, could help with this project. Braungart's profession was chemistry and he had led the chemistry department of Greenpeace. He had collaborated before with McDonough in implementing McDonough's design protocols.

In addition to the environmental criteria, McDonough's proposal addressed the aesthetic component of the fabrics. "The fabrics needed to be incredibly beautiful as well." He suggested that they use the mathematics of fractals to generate the patterns. Fractals were appealing to McDonough because "they are like natural systems . . . the smallest component is the same as the whole." He was interested in harmonic proportions throughout nature, and he felt that the new designs should reflect natural harmonies in the protocols and in the esthetics.[7]

FORMING THE NETWORK

The day following the McDonough meeting, Lyons contacted Rohner Textil to see if Kälin would be willing to participate in this project. He was encouraged by Lyon's report and looked forward to meeting McDonough, who traveled to Rohner a fortnight later. McDonough was encouraged by the Climatex project. Nevertheless the Climatex fabric was far from compostable, because the OEKO-Tex standards did not exclude all harmful chemicals that would be released during composting. In addition, McDonough was concerned about the use of polyester because it came from a fossil fuel. He explained to Kälin his design protocols, which, according to Lyons, was like asking Kälin to "reinvent his mill." Kälin responded enthusiastically to McDonough's ideas and eagerly awaited Braungart, who would help begin the assessment of the manufacturing processes.

Braungart traveled to the mill in December 1993. He examined it closely to determine the changes needed to meet McDonough's design protocol. Braungart was "pleasantly surprised" by Climatex and its OEKO-Tex approval. He was also impressed with the mill, which, he thought, had dealt with ecology issues in a manner far ahead of everything he had seen up to that point. Braungart's early suggestions were, as expected, in agreement with McDonough's: produce the Climatex product without using polyester so that all-natural materials would be used which would make the fabric compostable. The problem with Climatex, from McDonough's perspective, was that it mixed organic and technical nutrients, so the fabric could not be composted, yet the technical nutrients could not be recovered.

Braungart's evaluation required him to examine all stages of the fabric-construction process. Because the mill was involved with the fabric weaving, he also inspected the mill's suppliers: farmers, yarn spinners, yarn twisters, dyers, and finishers. Yarn spinners created a cord of yarn/thread from the pieces of individual material fibers, such as wool. Yarn twisters took two or more cords of thread/yarn and twisted them together, producing a much thicker, stronger piece of yarn. Dyers added the colors to the yarn. Finishers added chemicals to the finished weave to make it more durable, flame resistant, static resistant, and stain resistant, if these qualities were required.

Lyons was the main project coordinator and was responsible for creating the "construction," or generalized set of weaving patterns and color palette based on McDonough's designs. "Everyone on the project," she said, "knew that getting the mill contractors to open their books for Braungart's inspection would be difficult, and keeping track of the fabric's production would involve complex management well beyond the normal levels of supervision." Consequently, the team had concluded that the more they could do themselves, the easier it would be to produce the new fabrics. Acting on this philosophy, they intended to have the mill perform the role of dyer as well as of weaver. Kälin agreed: "We need as few members in the pool as possible."[8]

THE PROJECT UNDERWAY?

By the end of January 1994, Kälin had eliminated polyester from Climatex, producing a new blend of ramie and wool that preserved the fabric's moisture-wicking properties. He called this new fabric Climatex Lifecycle™. Using this fabric seemed easier than using material that reclaimed and reused polyester and other technical nutrients.

By the end of January, Kälin had sent Braungart all of the security data sheets and production details pertaining to the chemicals and dye substances used in the manufacturing of Climatex Lifecycle™. The team hoped that this information would be enough for Braungart to make recommendations on how to proceed by the end of February 1994. They wanted Braungart's examination to be totally complete by the end of March 1994.

At the beginning of March 1994, Braungart had some bad news. The chemicals used in the dye materials did not meet the design protocol. Furthermore, questions about the manufacture of the dye chemicals could not be answered by examining the security data sheets, even though they had passed the OEKO-Tex standards. DesignTex's next Portfolio Collection, McDonough's fractal patterns and design protocols, and Rohner's next generation of Climatex, depended on Braungart's ability to gain access to the manufacturing processes of the dye suppliers, which meant the dye suppliers had to open their books to Braungart. Kälin contacted Rohner's dye suppliers and asked them to cooperate with Braungart's inspection and answer his questions. By the end of March, however, it was clear that cooperation was not forthcoming. Braungart had contacted over 60 chemical companies worldwide, none of which had agreed to open their books for his inspection.

Another concern was the project's cost. Someone needed to pay Braungart and the EPEA as he studied the manufacturing processes. Kälin agreed to hire Braungart and the EPEA, because Rohner expected to acquire the patent rights for the next generation of Climatex. By the end of April, however, Braungart had already spent the funds

Rohner had provided and needed an extension. Rohner was willing to consider an additional payment, but only after the product had been introduced into the marketplace. None of the team were sure how much more money Braungart would require.

Lyons reflected on the situation. DesignTex had made a large commitment to this project, hoping it would propel the firm into the lead of the commercial-fabric market. It had already been three years since DesignTex had launched the first Portfolio Collection™, and she was aware of the pressure to get a product out the door. Waiting for Braungart to gain access to the dye process risked the whole project and would dramatically increase its cost, even if he succeeded. On the one hand, perhaps it would be better to relax McDonough's and Braungart's standards a little and test the results of the manufacturing process without inspecting the dye suppliers' dye-production processes. After all, Climatex Lifecycle was already a major improvement over currently available environmental designs. On the other hand, the whole project was about making a breakthrough in environmental design, and it was not clear that anything short of the McDonough/Braungart approach would represent a sufficient leap forward.

Notes

1. The information in this section was obtained during an interview with Susan Lyons on 31 July 1995.
2. Climatex is a registered trademark of Rohner Textil, AG.
3. Kälin quotes from correspondence from Kälin to Lyons, 3 December 1992, supplemented by the Lyons interview of 31 July 1995.
4. Correspondence, Kälin to Lyons, 28 May 1993.
5. *Wall Street Journal*, October 23, 1989.
6. The concepts "cradle-to-cradle," "waste equals food," "current solar income," "environmentally intelligent," and the design protocol discussed above are proprietary to William McDonough and are included in this document with his permission.
7. The material in this section was developed from interviews conducted with William McDonough on 29 June 1995, 16 August 1995, and 21 September 1995, and with Susan Lyons on 31 July 1995.
8. Interviews with Lyons on 21 July 1995.

EXHIBIT 1
ENGLISH TRANSLATION OF OEKO-TEX STANDARD 110

International Association for Research and Testing
in the Field of Textile Ecology (Öko-Tex)

Special conditions for the authorization to use
the Oeko-Tex mark for textile upholstry fabrics.

Contents

1. Purpose
2. Applicability
3. Terms and definitions
4. Conditions
5. Criteria for granting of authorization

1. PURPOSE

The Oeko-Tex Standard 100 specifies the general conditions for granting authorization to mark textiles with "Confidence in Textiles—Passed for harmful substances according Oeko-Tex Standard 100."

   This Oeko-Tex Standard 110 adds to Oeko-Tex Standard 100 laying down the special conditions for granting authorization for marking textile upholstery fabrics.

2. APPLICABILITY

This standard is to be applied to textile upholstery fabrics.

3. TERMS AND DEFINITIONS

The following terms add to those defined in Oeko-Tex Standard 100:

   Textile upholstery fabrics are those qualified for the purpose by the producer.

   Producer of textile upholstery fabrics refers to the company producing the ready-made product or having ordered the production of the ready-made product.

   Retailer of textile upholstery fabrics refers to the company selling the ready-made product as wholesale dealer or retailer (warehouses, mail-order houses, etc.).

4. CONDITIONS

The following conditions are added to those laid down in Oeko-Tex Standard 100:

4.1 Application

4.1.1 Applicant

The applicant may be either the producer or the retailer of the product.

4.1.2 Designation of the product

The designation of the product used by the producer or retailer is to be indicated.

4.1.3 Technical details

The following technical details are to be indicated as far as they are known or may be reliably ascertained from the deliverer or the pre-deliverer.

4.1.3.1 *Qualitative denomination of all types of fibres included in the textile upholstery fabrics:*

The fibre types are to be denominated according to DIN 60 001, part 1, and part 3. In case of fibres containing incorporated agents, e.g., delustrants, colour pigments (spun dyed fibres), antistatic agents, flame retardants, etc., the agents are to be indicated.

4.1.3.2 *Qualitative denomination of fibre and yarn preparations:*

All preparations, e.g., spinning avivages, softeners, sizing agents, etc., with which fibres or yarns have been treated during production and processings are to be indicated. The trade names of the products are to be given; product and safety data sheets are to be added.

4.1.3.3 *Denomination of finishing agents and dyestuffs:*

Dyestuffs are to be classified according to dyestuff classes. Their product denominations and trade names are to be indicated. The trade names of finishing agents are to be indicated. Product and safety data sheets are to be added.

4.1.3.4 *Denomination of special finishings:*

If special finishing procedures have been used (e.g., to obtain an improvement of handle, antistatic, antisoil, antimicrobial, mothproof, and other effects), the finishing agents and procedures used are to be indicated. Either the trade name and the producer or the chemical compositions of the finishing agents are to be denominated. Product and safety data sheets are to be added.

4.2 Sample material

For test purposes and for evidence samples the applicant shall provide at least two running meters per article.

The regulations of the packing instruction have to be met.

4.3 Issuing a commitment undertaking and a conformity declaration

4.3.1 Commitment undertaking

The commitment undertaking shall be given according to Oeko-Tex Standard 100.

4.3.2 Conformity declaration

The conformity declaration shall be issued according to Oeko-Tex Standard 100.

4.4 Testing

Test specimens having an odour extraneous to the product or an odour indicating an improper production technology will be rejected from testing.

Type and scope of testing depends on the type of the product and on the information about the product the applicant has given. They are determined by the respective institute of the International Association for Research and Testing in the Field of Textile Ecology (Öko-Tex).

Examples for tests are listed below. The respective testing procedures are laid down in Oeko-Tex Standard 200.

- Determination of the pH value.
- Determination of the content of free and released formaldehyde.
- Extraction with artificial acid sweat solution, testing of the extract for heavy metals.
- Testing for pesticides residues (only at textile fabrics containing natural fibres).
- Testing for pentachlorophenole (PCP) (only for textile fabrics containing natural fibres).
- Testing for dyestuffs unquestionably having or being suspected of having a cancerogenous potential either for themselves or after a reductive cracking to arylamines.
- Testing of color fastness.

5. CRITERIA FOR GRANTING THE AUTHORIZATION FOR MARKING

5.1 pH value

Testing procedure according to Oeko-Tex Standard 200 point 1.

Textile upholstery fabrics shall exhibit a pH value of the aqueous extract between pH 4.8 and pH 7.5. Only for articles made from wool a value of pH 4.0 may be accepted as the lower limit.

5.2 Content of free and partially releasable formaldehyde, referenced to the textile.

Testing procedure according to Oeko-Tex Standard 200, points 2.1 and 2.2, respectively.

less than 75 ppm

5.3 Residues of heavy metals, referenced to the textile

Testing procedure according to Oeko-Tex Standard 200, point 3.

- Mercury (Cotton Only)   less than 0.1 ppm
- Copper   less than 50 ppm
- Chromium   less than 20 ppm
- Chromium (VI)   not detectable
- Cobalt   less than 20 ppm
- Nickel   less than 10 ppm

5.4 Residues of pesticides, referenced to the textile

Testing procedure according to Oeko-Tex Standard 200, point 4.
        Total pesticide content less than 1 ppm

5.5 Pentachlorophenole (PCP) content, referenced to the textile

Testing procedure according to Oeko-Tex Standard 200, point 5.
        PCP content less than 0.5 ppm

5.6 Dyestuffs, that may reductively be cracked to aryl-amines of MAK group III A 1 (cancerogenous) and III A 2 (probably cancerogenous):

Testing procedure according to Oeko-Tex Standard 200, point 6.

- Benzidine
- 4-Chloro-o-toluidine
- 2-Naphtylamine
- 4-Aminodiphenyl
- o-Tolidine
- o-Dianisidine
- 4-Chloroaniline
- o-Toluidine
- 3,3-Dichlorobenzidine
- o-Aminoazotoluene
- 2-Amino-4-nitrotoluene
- 2.4-Toluylendiamine

The substances of the above list must not be detectable.

5.7 Colour Fastness

Testing procedure according to Oeko-Tex Standard 200, point 7.
        Minimum color fastness grade for staining:

Color fastness to water (heavy stress)	3
Color fastness to laundering (according to cleaning symbol)	3-4
Color fastness to perspiration, acid	3-4
Color fastness to perspiration, alkalic	3-4
Color fastness to rubbing, dry	4
Color fastness to rubbing, wet	2-3

If in the case of pigment or vat dyestuffs the above minimum grade is not achieved, a minimum colour fastness to rubbing grade of 3 (dry) and 2 (wet) may be accepted.

14

ROHNER TEXTIL AG (A)

It exists; therefore, it is possible.
—William McDonough

If you compare, you start to compromise.
—Albin Kälin

Albin Kälin[1] recalled making a special drive from Zürich airport, where he had just picked up the American architect William McDonough, to his workplace, Rohner Textil AG in Heerbrugg, Switzerland in October 1993. During their conversation on that hour-long trip McDonough said three words that Kälin had never forgotten: "Waste equals food."[2]

Kälin, managing director of Rohner Textil AG, had been systematically pursuing ecological issues in manufacturing since 1987 and had managed to position the company as a leader in industrial ecology. Until that moment with McDonough, however, he

Written by Matthew M. Mehalik and Michael E. Gorman, under the direction of Patricia H. Werhane. Partial support for this project was supplied by grants from the Ethics and Values in Science program of the National Science Foundation (SBR-9319983), the Batten Center for Entrepreneurial Leadership at the Darden School, University of Virginia, and the Geraldine R. Dodge Foundation. The conclusions are the responsibilities of the authors, and do not reflect the views of the foundations. Copyright © 1997 by the University of Virginia Darden School Foundation, Charlottesville, VA. All rights reserved.

had never been able to clarify his product design and manufacturing choices concerning the environmental profile of his weaving and dyeing mill to achieve perfection in eliminating waste emissions.

McDonough was a prominent designer of buildings and products using environmental criteria. Articles in the *Wall Street Journal* and *Interiors* magazine highlighted his accomplishments, such as the design of the Environmental Defense Fund's headquarters.[3] McDonough was bringing his expertise to Kälin to develop a fabric for commercial interiors that had minimum environmental impact.

This meeting came after one of Kälin's customers asked him to push the envelope in textile ecology. That customer was Susan Lyons, vice president of design at the New York company DesignTex, Inc., the second-largest textile design company in the United States. Lyons was aware of McDonough's accomplishments and had worked with Kälin in the past. Since 1991, she had been researching ways to define a new market in environmental textiles. By integrating her knowledge and skills with McDonough's and Kälin's, she hoped she would be able to sell a bold new product. She saw the meeting between Kälin and McDonough as a first step in achieving their mutual goal.

McDonough said that in order to meet the "waste equals food" criterion, the product either had to be able (1) to compost completely with no negative environmental impact, thereby becoming food for other organisms (organic nutrients), or (2) to become raw material for another industrial product without any reduction in material quality (technical nutrients). Furthermore, "The product should be manufactured without the release of carcinogens, bioaccumulatives, persistent toxic chemicals, mutagens, heavy metals, or endocrine disruptors."[4] One should not mix the organic and the technical, or one would end up with a product that could neither be used as food for organisms nor as raw materials for technology.

McDonough's statement "waste equals food" was exactly the inspiration Kälin hoped to get from the collaboration. The vision guided him and his network to create a fully compostable fabric. Kälin named the potential fabric Climatex Lifecycle.[5]

Eight months later, in late May 1994, the bold new product was in jeopardy. Kälin needed to find a twisting mill subsupplier who was able to experiment with his or her yarn-twisting procedures and who was willing to submit them for review so that they would pass the McDonough protocols, especially the "waste equals food" criterion.

ROHNER TEXTIL[6]

Kälin's previous efforts at ecological design and manufacturing began in 1987 with Kälin's decision that Rohner Textil remain a leader in the segment of high-quality upholstery fabrics. The mill was the smallest component of a much larger enterprise: Forster-Rohner, a company that employed more than 700 employees in five European textile mills with specialties that ranged from socks to jerseys to embroidery. Embroidery was the largest segment, comprising over fifty percent of Forster-Rohner's manufactures. In addition, the embroidery output was the largest in Europe.

Rohner Textil had 30 employees. In order for such a small company to remain useful to the larger enterprise and be competitive in general, it needed to remain at the cutting edge of providing the most creative and high-quality upholstery fabrics. Thus, the mill needed to customize quickly to the demands of customers who wanted small lots of unique upholstery designs. It also needed to remain price competitive and profitable, and wanted to increase production.

One of the first challenges in 1987 was to improve their looms to high-speed Jacquard looms. These new looms would have produced more noise and vibrations than the old looms. This was a major problem since the mill long had been part of a residential neighborhood in Heerbrugg. The building had been constructed in 1912, and the former parent company of Rohner Textil, Jacob Rohner AG, had occupied it since 1947. A kindergarten stood across the street to the east and houses surrounded the mill less than ten yards away on the other three sides. The vibrations from the new looms would disrupt the neighborhood and force regulators to eliminate the evening shift.

Moving the mill was immediately dismissed. The mill was already located in the "country." It was situated in the Rhine Valley and surrounded by mountains, just across the borders from both Germany and Austria. Land in the region was prohibitively expensive, and attempting to move the mill in that area or to another location would negate any benefit to the parent company for the mill's existence.

Kälin thus proposed to construct a special, independently suspended floor on which all of the weaving equipment would be mounted. The floor would be designed to dampen the noise and vibrations. This proposal was implemented reluctantly because it was expensive, but it achieved the desired result. The mill was quieter than before the new equipment was installed (one could barely hear the operation of the looms outside the mill), and the flexibility and quality of products increased dramatically, as well as the speed of production. There was no net reduction in profit from this ethical decision. With this new equipment, Rohner Textil was the first upholstery fabric weaver in the world to be able to produce fabrics with sixteen different colors in the weft, or crosswise, yarn. This ability permitted Rohner's designers to create fabrics with richer, more complex, and more beautiful color patterns.

This experience gave Kälin an important insight: Rohner Textil needed to consider a larger context when implementing design changes to improve quality. This larger context included a responsibility to people in the neighborhood and an environment that they shared in common. He also realized that policies were needed for handling such issues, so that future experiences could be handled more efficiently.

Kälin realized that merely updating his machinery was not sufficient to guarantee that his products' quality would improve over time. What was necessary was a system that committed every employee of Rohner Textil to look for ways to improve its products so that it remained on the cutting edge of its high-end product niche. Such a system co-evolved from 1987 to 1994 with the management system that was leading toward ISO 9001 certification. This process was part of the International Standards Organization (ISO) 9000 series management system. ISO 9001 required the development of a management plan that specified responsibility, authority, and operational procedures for employees so that an entire organization would be committed to improving the quality of its products and services. The certification process was taking place while Climatex Lifecycle was in progress, over 1993 and 1994. The ISO 9001 process was an important part of Rohner's commitment to quality.

An additional factor made Kälin sensitive to environmental issues: it was expensive to dispose of his waste selvages. The selvages consisted of the end-trimmings of the fabric. As the fabric came off of the loom, the edges were cut to a uniform length and were sewn to secure the edge. Additionally, some fabric at the beginning and end of the fabric needed trimming to the proper length. The selvages typically needed proper disposal, and this disposal cost was expensive. Some of the selvages were burned in the regional incinerator to generate electricity. The air pollutants were scrubbed before being released into the environment. Overall, the waste selvages consisted of about thirty percent of the total environmental costs at Rohner Textil.

This cost was an extra burden for a company such as Rohner Textil that processed smaller lots of fabrics. For instance, Rohner might process a sixty-meter order for a fabric from which one meter of waste and selvages was generated. A company which processed larger orders might generate 2.5 meters of waste selvage for a 240-meter order. Because of this disproportionality, it was easier to distribute the disposal cost of the selvages to customers who ordered a larger lot size than those who ordered the smaller size.

Rohner Textil was also conducting much of the fabric dyeing in its own dye house. This meant that it had to treat and dispose of its waste water. The cost of meeting strict Swiss regulatory requirements was high. If not properly treated, the waste water posed a potential threat to the largest drinking water reservoir in Europe: the Rhine River, just yards away, and the Lake of Constance, a few miles downstream.

Kälin realized in 1989 that the only way to decrease these disposal costs was to pursue a more environmentally sustainable agenda, since changing the process by which the fabrics were woven was not possible. In 1992, Kälin and the Rohner Textil crew debated an environmental policy while on a retreat in a cabin at the top of a small mountain in the Swiss countryside. The policy, entitled "Eco-Eco Conzept, 1993–2000," consisted of a plan of ecological and socially responsible goals as guiding principles for their entire product line. Kälin had also developed an environmental costing system in 1992. This system helped him identify ways of reducing the environmental costs of his products.

By late 1992 the mill had received certification by the German-based association, Eco-Tex, which tested and approved as ecologically safe for humans all of Rohner Textil's main products, such as Climatex.[7] According to Eco-Tex's standards, Climatex contained no chemicals that were found harmful to human beings. The process by which the material was manufactured was also free from harmful chemicals. Such an approval constituted one of the most stringent environmental tests that could be performed on textiles at the time. This approval was an important step for Kälin and Rohner Textil; however, they had only slightly reduced their disposal costs. The tests did not certify that the products were *completely* ecologically safe outside the human sphere. Plants, domestic animals, wildlife, and ecosystems could be harmed potentially by the chemicals used in Climatex.

It was at that same time that Susan Lyons of DesignTex asked him to push the envelope in textile ecology. Lyons first proposed the idea of going beyond the Eco-Tex ecologically-safe-for-humans fabric by creating an environmentally sustainable fabric. Rohner would supply the woven product to DesignTex, and DesignTex would then market the product to its commercial interior customers, such as Steelcase, a giant office furniture manufacturing company. Lyons wanted to work with Kälin because he had produced a high-quality product for her and DesignTex in the recent past, and because Rohner Textil had committed to an environmentally sustainable agenda.

Lyons's background research and networking brought together McDonough and Kälin in October 1993 to get the project underway. She wanted to work with McDonough because of his revolutionary design principles. As she had hoped, Kälin was stunned by McDonough's principle, "waste equals food." At that moment during the drive from Zürich, Kälin realized that his disposal problem could be eliminated if he pursued McDonough's philosophy of zero emissions. If what was coming out of his factory was suitable to be food for biological cycles, he would have no disposal costs. Climatex Lifecycle would thus be a compostable product.

INITIAL SUCCESS[8]

In order for Climatex Lifecycle to be a successful "environmentally intelligent" product, McDonough insisted that Climatex Lifecycle be designed according to his other ecology design principles in addition to "waste equals food." These were "work from current solar income and respect diversity," as well as his five design criteria, "cost, performance, aesthetics, environmental intelligence, and social justice." Every aspect of the fabric's development would be evaluated according to that framework.[9]

It was therefore necessary to inspect every chemical in every process of the fabric's design. McDonough's close friend and business associate, Dr. Michael Braungart, whose profession was chemistry, would handle the inspections. Braungart was the former head of the chemistry division of Greenpeace. At the time of the project, he directed the Environmental Protection Encouragement Agency (EPEA), an organization based in Hamburg, Germany. Braungart and the EPEA would evaluate the raw materials and all production processes.

Kälin and his Rohner staff committed completely to examining every aspect of Climatex Lifecycle's design. The review eventually led to a standoff with dye manufacturers. By the beginning of March 1994, Kälin contacted Rohner's dye suppliers and asked them to cooperate with Braungart's inspection and answer his questions. By the end of March, however, such cooperation was not forthcoming. Braungart contacted over 60 chemical companies worldwide, none of which had agreed to open their books for his inspection.

To the delight of everyone working on the project, however, by the end of April 1994 Braungart was able to convince Ciba Geigy that it was in their best interest to permit the inspections of their proprietary dye formulas. Among other reasons, Braungart argued that if the products coming out of their factories were nontoxic, there would be no need to worry about regulations or unforeseen litigation due to long-term toxicity.

By the end of May 1994, success with McDonough's protocols continued. Out of 1,600 dyestuff chemicals that Braungart and the EPEA screened from Ciba Geigy, they found sixteen that were safe for disposal in the environment, with a minimum of risk. Out of these sixteen they could make any color for their textiles except black.[10]

All members of the network—Kälin, McDonough, Braungart, and Lyons—were quite pleased that two major hurdles had been cleared. Kälin realized that this situation was highly unusual: a project at his small, 30-person textile mill in the Swiss countryside had resulted in one of the world's largest chemical companies, Ciba Geigy, agreeing to submit to highly unorthodox scrutiny for the sake of the environment. Such a breakthrough gave Kälin a sense that, with diligence, any remaining obstacles could be cleared. William McDonough had repeatedly stated that redesign for the environment constituted the "Second Industrial Revolution." The change at Ciba Geigy made Kälin realize that such a bold statement might indeed be accurate.

MANAGING THE SECOND INDUSTRIAL REVOLUTION: GETTING TO FOOD[11]

Because of their commitment to constantly improve the process by which the fabric would be made, celebrations did not last long. Kälin and the EPEA's Dr. Alain Rivière, who worked under Dr. Braungart, had many other aspects of the fabric's manufacture to investigate.

One such component of the manufacturing process was the twisting of the yarn. After the wool and ramie had been harvested, combed, blended, and spun into a single yarn onto cones, the two or more single yarns needed to be twisted about one another in order to make the yarns strong enough to be fed through the loom. If the yarns were not strong enough or nonuniform, they would break, forcing the weaver at Rohner Textil to stop and repair them. This process kept the loom down for some time, obviously reducing productivity and quality of the product.

The problem that Kälin faced was eliminating a coating chemical from the twisting process. It was a normal procedure to apply a chemical to the yarns as they were twisted. This process improved the strength of the twisted yarn. Rivière and the EPEA, however, rejected the chemical since it did not meet the design criteria. Thus, Kälin had to come up with a way to increase the strength of the twisted yarns without it.

This posed an additional problem: finding someone who was willing to experiment with their twisting procedures and submit them for review by Rivière at the EPEA. Kälin reconnoitered the local region in Switzerland, Germany, and Austria for such cooperation.[12] He evaluated companies based on the following criteria:

- Does the supplier possess the technology or machinery to handle the project?
- Is the company willing to open their books to reveal their manufacturing processes to Rohner Textil and the EPEA at any time?
- Will the company be willing to sign nondisclosure agreements in order to protect their joint project with Rohner Textil?
- Is the company open to change?
- Does the company have a past history of integrity and an image of credibility?
- Is the company aware of its own environmental issues? If so, is there some system in place to handle such issues?

Based on these criteria, Kälin and his team narrowed the field to two potential yarn-twisting companies, both of which offered possible solutions.

One option consisted of using the same German company that was doing the spinning of the yarn for this project. They had already agreed to submit to the EPEA all information on the spinning of the yarns, and they were willing to cooperate for the twisting as well. This company was medium sized, consisting of about 270 full-time employees. It had a good past history of reliability and technological capability. It was putting out its own line of environmental textiles; they were of the undyed variety, however, which made them limited in color range.

The EPEA had approved a procedure that could be implemented at this company. Instead of the original chemical used for twisting, this company could use a natural, oil-based chemical. The technological capability of this company was such that the process could be completed at a rapid pace. Having both the spinning and twisting done at the same place was an attractive situation since this agreed with Albin Kälin's philosophy of "keeping the number of players in the pool as small as possible."[13]

Another option consisted of a small, four-person operation in Switzerland, located halfway between Rohner Textil and the spinning factory. This factory also had worked previously with Kälin and Rohner. Its entire business consisted of twisting yarn. This mill used older machinery that operated at lower speeds than newer machines, such as those located at the spinning mill. Because the machinery was slower, the price of twisting here was higher than at the spinning mill; however, this slower speed afforded two advantages. First, the yarn could be twisted in such a way that it was strong enough for the loom without added chemicals that had to be washed out after weaving. Second, the slower winding on the cones made the yarn rest more uniformly on the cones. Since the cones were dipped at Rohner in the EPEA-approved dyes purchased from Ciba Geigy before proceeding to the looms, this uniformity could produce a dyed product with less waste than by the method at the spinning mill. The small company worked with natural yarns and used no chemicals in any of its twisting operations, except for lubricants for the machinery. The EPEA approved the twisting procedure of this company.

Both companies satisfied all of Kälin's screening criteria. They also satisfied McDonough's criteria that waste equals food, and the EPEA gave its approval to both processes. Even though the project could continue with either twisting methodology, one was the clear choice for Kälin.

Notes

1. Information in this section was obtained through interviews with Albin Kälin May 28 to June 1, 1996.
2. The concept "waste equals food" quoted in this paragraph and case is proprietary to William McDonough and is used here with his permission.
3. See *Interiors*, March 1993, and *Wall Street Journal*, Monday, October 23, 1989.
4. As quoted in Darden case "DesignTex, Inc. (A)" (UVA-E-0099). The maxims quoted in this paragraph are proprietary to William McDonough and are used here with his permission.
5. Climatex Lifecycle is a registered trademark of Rohner Textil AG.
6. Information in this section was obtained through interviews with Albin Kälin May 28 to June 1, 1996.
7. Climatex is a registered trademark of Rohner Textil AG.
8. Information on this section was obtained from interviews and correspondence with Susan Lyons, William McDonough, and Albin Kälin.
9. The maxims quoted in this paragraph are proprietary to William McDonough and are used here with his permission. See Darden cases "DesignTex, Inc. (A)" (UVA-E-0099) and "DesignTex, Inc. (B)" (UVA-E-1000) for more information about McDonough.
10. See "DesignTex, Inc. (A)" and "DesignTex, Inc. (B)" for a complete portrayal of the issues of this dye chemical dilemma. The current case, "Rohner Textil AG (A)" is designed to be used independent of or in a sequence immediately following "DesignTex, Inc. (A) and (B)."
11. Kälin interviews.
12. With assistance from his designers, Lothar Pfister and Fabiola Fornasier, and his production manager, Walter Fehle.
13. Kälin interview.

15

ROHNER TEXTIL AG (B)

Even though you have the product, the project is not finished.
—Albin Kälin

When you come to a fork in the road, take it.
—William McDonough

The McDonough design protocol was paying off for Albin Kälin. Back in March 1994, even before Ciba Geigy agreed to grant access to their dye formulas, an agreement between Susan Lyons of DesignTex, William McDonough, and Kälin gave Rohner Textil the patent rights for the manufacture of Climatex Lifecycle.[1] In exchange, Kälin agreed to pay the cost of having the Environmental Protection Encouragement Agency (EPEA) continue its inspections of other stages of the manufacturing process. Kälin also agreed to grant DesignTex exclusive use of the fabric in the United States until the

This case was written by Matthew M. Mehalik and Michael E. Gorman, under the direction of Patricia H. Werhane. Partial support for this project was supplied by grants from the Ethics and Values in Science program of the National Science Foundation (SBR-9319983), the Batten Center for Entrepreneurial Leadership at the Darden School, University of Virginia, and the Geraldine R. Dodge Foundation. The conclusions are the responsibilities of the authors, and do not reflect the views of the foundations. Copyright © 1997 by the University of Virginia Darden School Foundation, Charlottesville, VA. All rights reserved.

end of 1996, after its planned release in July 1995 under the trade name "The William McDonough Collection."[2] The product was not set for release in Europe until December 1995, so this arrangement gave DesignTex and McDonough a head start in the market. Possessing the patent and trademark, however, gave Rohner Textil a great deal of flexibility over the projected long-term product life of Climatex Lifecycle.[3]

Granting exclusive use to DesignTex also had potential additional benefits for Rohner: access to a very large customer. DesignTex existed in a partnership with Steelcase, at that time the world's largest manufacturer of office furniture. In 1994, Steelcase was a $2.3 billion company, employing 17,700 people worldwide.[4] Between 1986 and 1990, Steelcase averaged a dominant 21 percent of the U.S. office furniture industry, and in 1989 it purchased a series of design-oriented companies to bolster this level, which they feared was stagnating. DesignTex was one of the companies it purchased to create the Steelcase Design Partnership, and the office furniture giant desired creative products from the partnership members.[5] The William McDonough Collection could deliver what Steelcase wanted.

In the fall of 1994, Susan Lyons made arrangements to use the McDonough Collection fabric on Steelcase's award-winning Sensor chair. The chair was designed in 1986 using two radical ideas for furniture design at the time—ergonomics and simultaneous engineering. Steelcase's Business Management Group, a multidisciplinary team, put the Sensor through design, engineering, and marketing at the same time, resulting in a better quality product. They also made the chair adjustable to make it adaptable to the user. Proof of the success of these methodologies came when the Industrial Designers Society of America gave the Sensor chair its highest honors. Steelcase sold over one million chairs from 1986 to 1990.[6] The Sensor chair had become a benchmark for the industry by 1994, and it presented an opportunity for the McDonough Collection to reach a large customer base quickly.

In addition, Steelcase pursued environmental conservation. In 1993 the company implemented two different task forces that met every two weeks to evaluate products and processes in environmental terms. The company joined the Environmental Protection Agency's Green Lights program in 1992. This meant that they began converting their lighting to more energy-efficient technology. They also pursued a massive recycling and waste-reduction initiative. This initiative produced many instances of waste reduction, including the following achievements:

- selling 15,000 tons of scrap steel to mills for recycling
- selling 335 tons of scrap fabric to be used in automotive sound-damping material
- selling 96 tons of foam scrap for carpet backing
- recycling over 1,300 tons of corrugated cardboard
- recycling 6,750 gallons of used oil
- reclaiming 400,000 gallons of paint solvents[7]

The William McDonough Collection would be a benefit to Steelcase's efforts, and Kälin, Lyons, and McDonough may have been encouraged by the initiative. By mid-October 1994, Kälin had samples of the William McDonough Collection ready for the Sensor chair, and Susan Lyons passed them along to Steelcase in early November.[8]

MEETING STANDARDS

Before the fabric could be used, it needed to undergo rigorous testing to meet a number of different performance standards. Kälin desired that the fabric meet all International Standards Organization (ISO) and Swiss textile standards since he eventually wanted to sell Climatex Lifecycle in the European market after December 1995. Testing the fabric was the responsibility of Rohner's assistant production manager and quality and environmental manager, Alexandra Rumpf. Rumpf, a chemical engineer specializing in textile chemistry, ran several tests to check fabric peeling, colorfastness to perspiration, flame resistance, and abrasion resistance.[9] She strove to make Rohner's internal performance and environmental standards exceed those set by the outside organizations, a requirement that led to several incremental improvements in the fabric's design. By controlling the yarn's thickness, twisting process, mixture of fibers, and finishing procedure, she could control the quality of the fabric.[10]

More immediately, to sell the William McDonough Collection in the United States, Climatex Lifecycle had to pass the standards set by the Association of Contract Textiles (ACT), to which DesignTex belonged. In 1994, ACT consisted of over 36 members with a combined annual fabric sales volume of over 450 million yards, with woven upholstery consisting of about half the total volume.[11]

ACT standards were important because Steelcase was an associate member of the organization. Before the William McDonough Collection could be used on the Sensor chair, it needed to pass the ACT standards. As Susan Lyons wrote, "Needless to say that it is critical that we have a product that meets the ACT standards—otherwise it won't be taken seriously."[12] Testing to meet ACT standards continued through November 1994, again resulting in incremental changes and improvements to the fabric.

MOVING TARGET

By the middle of November, the efforts of Kälin, Rumpf, and Lyons were paying off. Each iteration of testing resulted in an improvement of the fabric, and it appeared that the performance goals were within reach. At that time, however, Steelcase introduced a new test required of all fabrics to be used on its furniture. The test was not the result of a new standard set by ACT, but in response to Steelcase's updating its manufacturing processes. As Kälin later reflected, "As this test was new at the time, we were not able to get sophisticated details. The only parameters we knew were that it was a test to ensure that the newly introduced robots could upholster the chairs easily, so that the fabric did not slip out of the grips of the robot."[13] During the upholstering process for molded seating, the robotic machinery gripped the fabric tightly and wrapped the fabric around the shells of chairs. The test ensured that the fabric would not slip out of the robotic machinery.

The new test was a disaster for the fabric project. The ramie content made the fabric unable to be stretched in order to pass the new test; the fabric was ripping instead of stretching. Lyons wrote to Kälin, "Well, this is an adventure—everything failed on Steelcase. . . . The reason for failure was cited as a lack of stretch in the filling direction. I am thinking that the ramie may be too rigid . . . I think it is . . . urgent to get the molded seating pass."

At Rohner, Kälin, Rumpf, and the other textile technicians proceeded to make the fabric less rigid so that it could pass the new test.[14] They tried a number of approaches, but the only ones that were successful involved adding chemicals to the fabric. The chemicals were applied during the finishing process, after the fabric had been dyed and woven. The chemicals made the fabric more stretchable. The team came up with four different finishing chemicals that permitted the fabric to pass the Steelcase robot test.

All four chemicals were from Ciba Geigy and were open to inspection by the EPEA. The EPEA approved only one of the four chemicals, and expressed its dissatisfaction with the addition of any chemicals to the fabric at all. It could pass the EPEA protocols, but only with the caveat that Rohner would have to commit to eliminating it. Moreover, the fabric would now have to be retested according to all of the ISO and ACT standards because of the new finishing chemical.[15]

Kälin needed to make a decision. Along with McDonough, Braungart, and Lyons, he had fought an uphill battle to make the product as environmentally intelligent as possible, and they had overcome overwhelming odds in the past. Now he was faced with having to compromise the "waste equals food" standard in order to please one major customer.

Notes

1. Climatex Lifecycle is a registered trademark of Rohner Textil AG.
2. The William McDonough Collection is a registered trademark of DesignTex, Inc.
3. Correspondence, Kälin to Lyons, April 7, 1994.
4. Robin Yale Bergstrom, "Probing the Softer," *Production* (November 1994): 52.
5. Margery B. Stein, "Teaching Steelcase to Dance," *The New York Times Magazine*, April 1, 1990.
6. Ibid., 52.
7. Patricia M. Fernberg, "No More Wasting Away: The New Face of Environmental Stewardship," *Managing Office Technology* (August 1993): 16, 19.
8. Correspondence, Kälin to Siblano, September 14, 1994, and Lyons to Kälin, November 7, 1994.
9. For example, *ISO/DIS 12947-1 Textiles:* "Determination of abrasion resistance of fabrics by the Martindale Method." *ISO/DIS 13934-1 Textiles:* "Tensile properties of fabrics—Part 1: Determination of maximum force and elongation at maximum force—strip method." *ISO/DIS 13934-2 Textiles:* "Tensile properties of fabrics—Part 2: Determination of maximum force—grab method" (Revision of ISO 5082:1982).
10. Interview with Alexandra Rumpf, May 30, 1996.
11. ACT financial survey, 1994.
12. Lyons to Kälin, November 7, 1994.
13. Facsimile correspondence with Albin Kälin, August 3, 1996.
14. Correspondence, Lyons to Kälin, November 30, 1994.
15. Interviews with Albin Kälin, May 28 to June 1, 1996, and correspondence, Kälin to Lyons, December 6, 1994.

16

ROHNER TEXTIL AG (C)

THE DYE-AUXILIARY SWITCH[1]

Paul Flückiger, dyemaster at Rohner Textil AG, had just finished speaking with a fabric-dye salesperson. Without hesitation, he decided to substitute one of the dye-auxiliary chemicals this salesperson offered for one that Rohner was currently using in its compostable fabric line, Climatex Lifecycle.[2] To him, the choice seemed clear. The salesperson argued that his dye auxiliary was much less expensive than the one they were currently using, was of equal quality, and contained no chemicals harmful to the environment. The fabric would still be compostable, and it would now be a little cheaper to make. He did not realize that his decision would alarm his supervisor, Albin Kälin, managing director of Rohner Textil.

Flückiger strongly believed that he acted within his authority to decide to substitute the dye-auxiliary chemical. Having this authority and flexibility was the reason

This case was written by Matthew M. Mehalik and Michael E. Gorman, under the direction of Patricia H. Werhane. Partial support for this project was supplied by grants from the Ethics and Values in Science program of the National Science Foundation (SBR-9319983), the Batten Center for Entrepreneurial Leadership at the Darden School, University of Virginia, and the Geraldine R. Dodge Foundation. The conclusions are the responsibilities of the authors, and do not reflect the views of the foundations. Copyright © 1997 by the University of Virginia Darden School Foundation, Charlottesville, VA. All rights reserved.

Flückiger decided 10 years ago to work for Rohner as its dyemaster. He was happy to be in a small company so that he could be responsible for everything in the dye department.

Flückiger had over 35 years of experience in several different textile mills, with expertise ranging from laboratories to the dyeing of stockings, from piece dyes to hank dyes and yarn dyes. Flückiger was awarded his master's certificate in textile dyeing and had worked in both large and small plants long before coming to Rohner. Kälin had great confidence in Flückiger's abilities, and gladly let him run the dyehouse.[3]

Flückiger's autonomy had been reinforced under Kälin's tenure since 1988. Kälin was a strong believer in continually increasing the quality of textile products that he and his team dyed and wove at Rohner.[4] At the heart of his beliefs was the recognition that employees with experience should be given responsibility, authority, and autonomy to take measures to improve quality in every process and product.[5] Kälin's management style was to act as a collaborator with his team of leaders. Kälin was ultimately responsible for all operations at Rohner, but he felt the best way to accomplish this was to work together with his team.

QUALITY MANAGEMENT

Kälin's emphasis on product and plant environmental quality was not merely ideology, but a serious, systematic approach to management: "You cannot produce environmental products without quality, and there must be a control system in place to direct it."[6] By control system, Kälin was referring to the International Standards Organization (ISO) 9000 series management system. Through Kälin's and his team's commitment, Rohner successfully passed its quality system audit in 1994 and received its certificate for quality management according to ISO 9001, the applicable standard for suppliers during "design, development, production, installation, and servicing."[7] The ISO 9001 standard included specifications for the purchasing of materials from subsuppliers: "[Rohner] shall establish and maintain documented procedures to ensure that [a] purchased product conforms to specified requirements."[8] In addition,

> [Rohner] shall . . . evaluate and select subcontractors on the basis of their ability to meet subcontract requirements including the quality system and any specific quality-assurance requirements . . . This shall be dependent upon the type of product, the impact of subproduct on the quality of final product, and, where applicable, on the quality audit reports and/or quality records of the previously demonstrated capability of performance of subcontractors.[9]

The ISO 9001 certification process also required the development of a management plan, which specified responsibility, authority, and operational procedures for employees. "Mr. Flückiger is responsible for the dyehouse, with all co-workers in the dyehouse responsible to him,"[10] read Rohner's management plan, "Eco-Eco Conzept, 1993–2000," which documented a process that had been in place nearly a decade before the ISO 9001 certification.

The management plan also contained a strong emphasis on improving the ecological aspects of Rohner's products as a natural extension of product quality. In early 1995 there was no approved "standard" of environmental quality. The International Standards

Organization had been moving towards creating such a standard, but there was still much debate over what such a standard should contain. A draft of ISO 14001, "Environmental Management Systems" existed, but nothing had been officially approved at the time. It was possible, however, to be certified against the draft of ISO 14001, and Kälin was already taking the steps to obtain that certification.

"But," Kälin stated, "these management systems do not work by themselves. With them, we still must maintain the commitment to McDonough's protocols and the EPEA approval process."[11] In other words, only all four things together—the ISO 9001 certification, Rohner's management plan, the McDonough protocols, and the EPEA approval process—would make Climatex Lifecycle a successful product and Rohner a competitive company over the long term. If you took away any one of these items, Kälin believed, Climatex Lifecycle and Rohner faced jeopardy.

JEOPARDY?

"What is this?" Kälin asked Paul Flückiger about a week after Flückiger's meeting with the salesman. Kälin noticed on the shelf a dye-auxiliary container bearing a label not from Ciba Geigy, the company whose chemicals had been approved by the EPEA for Climatex Lifecycle yarn. Flückiger explained his meeting with the salesperson and his subsequent decision to substitute the dye auxiliary.

Kälin thought that Flückiger's judgment was probably correct; however, if he was not, Rohner had just produced a week's worth of yarn that Kälin could not weave into his products and sell. He had to decide what steps he could take to resolve this potential immediate crisis. Kälin was most concerned about his decision to give his employees such freedom, especially when one of his major team players had fallen back into the "old" way of thinking, not taking into account McDonough's design criteria and the EPEA's inspections.

Notes

1. Information in this section was obtained through interviews with Albin Kälin May 28 to June 1, 1996, at Rohner Textil.
2. Climatex Lifecycle is a registered trademark of Rohner Textil AG.
3. Facsimile communication with Kälin, August 6, 1996.
4. Recall from "Rohner Textil (A)," "In order for such a small company to remain useful to the larger enterprise and be competitive in general, it needed to remain at the cutting edge of providing the most creative and high-quality upholstery fabrics. Thus, the mill needed to be able to customize quickly to the demands of customers who wanted small lots of unique upholstery designs. It also needed to remain price competitive and profitable, and wanted to increase production."
5. Lothar Pfister, designer and research and development director; Fabiola Fornasier, designer; Walter Fehle, production manager; Markus Diethelm, weaving master; Alexandra Rumpf, assistant production manager and quality and environmental manager; and, of course, Paul Flückiger.
6. Kälin interviews May 28 to June 1, 1996.
7. ANSI/ISO/ASQC 9001-1994, vii.
8. ANSI/ISO/ASQC 9001-1994, 4.
9. 9ANSI/ISQC 9001-1994, 4-5.
10. "Eco-Eco Conzept, 1993-2000," Rohner Textil AG, section 6.1.2.
11. Kälin interviews.

17

ROHNER TEXTIL AG (D)

This process never ends. If you never get this point, you never get to food.
—Albin Kälin

TOUGH TIMES[1]

Given the terrible state of the Swiss textile industry, Albin Kälin was not surprised when the ramie spinning mill closed its doors in early 1996. The textile industry worldwide was changing with the opening of markets in Eastern Europe and the continued expansion of production in Asia. The Swiss textile industry, with its tradition of stability and high standards for wages, was suffering from these structural changes. A recession in European and North American textiles since 1993 was not helping matters. Overall, Swiss textile industry sales were down 9.5 percent between 1994 and 1995, and the trend was continuing.

Written by Matthew M. Mehalik and Michael E. Gorman, under the direction of Patricia H. Werhane. Partial support for this project was supplied by grants from the Ethics and Values in Science program of the National Science Foundation (SBR-9319983), the Batten Center for Entrepreneurial Leadership at the Darden School, University of Virginia, and the Geraldine R. Dodge Foundation. The conclusions are the responsibilities of the authors, and do not reflect the views of the foundations. Copyright © 1997 by the University of Virginia Darden School Foundation, Charlottesville, VA. All rights reserved.

The spinning mill's closing could not have occurred at a worse time for Kälin and his team of 30 at Rohner. They could not afford to be cut off from their supply of ramie yarn when Climatex Lifecycle,which consisted of a blend of wool and ramie, was new to the marketplace.[2] Rohner Textil was weathering the recession rather well because Climatex Lifecycle had been well received in the United States through Rohner's large, important customer, DesignTex, Inc. DesignTex released the fabric to the public in a grand display at the Guggenheim Museum in New York City in late May 1995 under the design trade name the William McDonough Collection.[3] It won the Best of the Show award at the NEOCON convention in Chicago in June 1995, the largest annual gathering of textile design companies. The fabric became available to the DesignTex sales offices in late August 1995. The sales force was educated by watching a video presentation of William McDonough at the museum and by listening to an audio tape conversation with Susan Lyons, DesignTex's vice-president for design. Both presentations delineated the necessity of the design protocol to create "environmentally intelligent" products. DesignTex shipped a brochure with the fabric that discussed why the environmental design of the fabric was important. Customers were responding to the information.

Initial sales reports from DesignTex and Rohner were very positive. Swiss television dedicated seven minutes of the business news to the operations of the Rohner mill. The product was introduced to the European market in January of 1996, and because of all of the good publicity about the product, Kälin had little trouble attracting customers.

Kälin needed to act quickly since his team did not have a significant stockpile of ramie yarn. He needed to find another spinning mill capable of handling ramie fibers before he could drastically increase his customer base, or even fulfill the contracts he already had.

Unfortunately, the mill that was spinning the wool fibers for Climatex Lifecycle did not have the machinery for preparing the ramie for spinning. Not every spinning mill was capable of processing ramie fibers because it was a particularly difficult process. The fragile fibers were harvested from the ramie plant. When the raw ramie arrived at the spinning mill, the fibers were bunched together with an inconsistent texture. The raw ramie was then combed and stretched in a process called "worsting." Worsting and spinning ramie was identical to processing wool, except that wool fibers were only 10-15 cm (3-6 inches) long, whereas ramie fibers were up to 60 cm (24 inches) long. The length of the fibers was the source of the difficulty.

The stretching part of the worsting process used a series of rollers that pulled on the ramie in order to create the desired consistency of the ramie before spinning (see Figure 1). On typical stretching machinery, wool fibers were much shorter than the distance between the stretching rollers. As the material passed through the successive sets of rollers, which rotated at increasing speeds, the wool fibers were pulled apart from one another and the material was stretched. Ramie fibers, however, were longer than distance between rollers. If ramie fibers were fed through the series of rollers, the fibers would be snapped or broken as the rollers pulled on them. Instead of stretching the raw ramie material, the process would break and shred it.

What was needed was machinery that had the stretching rollers set farther apart than the length of ramie fibers. Kälin was aware of manufacturers worldwide that made all types of textile machines, such as looms, twisting machines, spinning machines, and

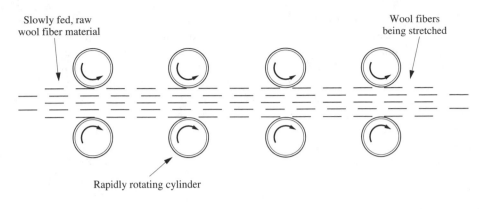

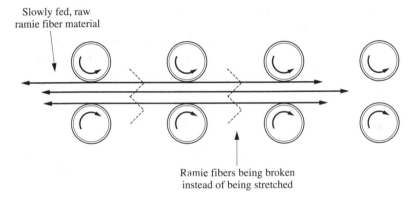

Figure 1: Stretching of Wool and Ramie Fibers

stretching machines. Because very few firms processed ramie fibers, not one manufacturer made machines suitable for stretching ramie. Kälin explained, "For most cases manufacturers can use linen and cotton as substitute materials for ramie, so ramie is not a popular fiber."[4] This was not an option for Kälin, since ramie and wool were the materials the EPEA approved for Climatex Lifecycle.

The spinning mill that had just closed overcame this problem when one of its machine operators was able to modify a wool worsting machine to handle ramie fibers. The operator moved the rollers farther apart and knew how to modify the speed of the machinery so that the ramie fibers would not break. The process was highly dependent on his skill at operating and maintaining the modified machinery, in contrast with wool spinning, which was highly automated.

Kälin and designer Lothar Pfister, also responsible for product development, canvassed Europe to see if there were other mills that might have modified their equipment accordingly. They found none, but they did find four spinning mills that were willing to purchase the equipment from the recently closed spinning mill and transfer the equipment to their location. Each mill said it would be willing to finance the cost of purchasing and transporting the machinery.

Knowing the state of the industry, Kälin and Pfister were not sure if the mills could afford to finance the machinery. They wanted to avoid repeating this process by choosing a spinning mill in danger of bankruptcy. They were not even sure if the machinery, once transported, could be reassembled to deliver high-quality ramie fibers. They gathered as much information about each alternative as they could.

The first mill that they considered was located less than 100 km (about 60 miles) from Rohner. It was a large company and possessed several other spinning mills in Europe. This company had the technological know-how and financing available to acquire the ramie equipment from the closed spinning mill. The management of this company seemed very committed and ethical, although it was difficult for Kälin and Pfister to judge because the company was large. The financial condition of the company seemed stable, and the risk of failure unlikely. The company had a clear and feasible market strategy: spin and sell a large volume of materials. They were willing to take risks to develop new products if the sales volume justified it. At the time, they had little experience with producing ecological projects, but the company met all environmental legal limits and indicated that it might be willing to cooperate with the EPEA for process evaluations. Since the company was large, it was unlikely that they would modify their processes to adopt Rohner's quality standards; however, Rohner had worked with them in the past without notable problems.

The second firm owned its yarn dyeing and spinning mills in Northern Europe, about 1,000 km (600 miles) from Rohner. This was a medium-sized company that was willing to purchase the equipment from the bankrupt spinning mill. Rohner had worked with this company in the past by using a few samples of their work in Rohner's products. The company had proven to be highly flexible at meeting Rohner's demands for producing these sample lots, showing that they valued Rohner's business. Because this company was located in Northern Europe, Kälin and Pfister were not sure if this company was meeting all environmental legal limits because they were not sure of the regulatory requirements in place there; however, the company indicated that it would likely cooperate with the EPEA inspections.

The third company under consideration possessed yarn dyeing and spinning facilities about 100 km (60 miles) from Rohner. Rohner had ten years of experience working with this small company, which was bought out by it managers two years earlier in an effort to save its probable closure. The company was producing one ecological line of products and was in compliance with local environmental legal limits. It was likely that the company would cooperate with the EPEA inspections and would be flexible about Rohner's quality demands. The firm had the technological expertise to operate the ramie spinning equipment, but purchasing the equipment seemed a sticking point. Money was not previously an issue for this mill, when it had been owned by a large European department-store conglomerate. After the buyout, however, the company's future was uncertain and depended on innovation to secure its long-term stability. Although the company was willing to purchase the equipment, Kälin and Pfister wondered whether the investment would be too great for this struggling mill.

The last mill under consideration was located 300 km (190 miles) from Rohner. It was a medium-sized company with experience in spinning for the fashion industry. This was a very old, family-owned company with highly committed family members managing the operations. Since the company worked for the fashion industry it was very flexible and adaptable to rapid changes in customer demands. Management was also willing to take risks in developing new products, a necessary condition for survival in the fashion industry. Rohner had worked with this company in the past, successfully producing a few sample trials. The mill did not have an ecological line of products, but it indicated possible cooperation with EPEA inspections. The company was willing to purchase the ramie spinning equipment from the closed mill, but because this was a family-owned company, Kälin and Pfister could not glean information about the financial condition, the environmental legal compliance, nor the technical expertise of the company.

After gathering this information over several months of research, Kälin and Pfister were hoping that one of their alternatives would outperform its rivals. The men needed to choose a course of action since moving and assembling the machinery and fine tuning the equipment to produce good quality would take several months. Their stockpile of ramie yarn was being depleted daily. The task of choosing a spinning mill would require detailed analysis, but that did not discourage them.

Notes

1. Information in this section was obtained through interviews with Albin Kälin, May 28 to June 1, 1996, at Rohner Textil.
2. Climatex Lifecycle is a registered trademark of Rohner Textil AG.
3. The William McDonough Collection is a registered trademark of DesignTex, Inc.
4. Kälin interview, November 23, 1996.

18

ROHNER TEXTIL (E)

Remember, my friend, while you live among your fellow creatures, to value your shadow more than your money.[1]

Albin Kälin,[2] managing director of the Swiss firm Rohner Textil AG, was completing his morning rounds. With breakfast roll and coffee cup in hand, he greeted the workers at the 30-person weaving and dyeing facility to ensure all systems were operating at peak efficiency. Kälin knew that this was a critical time for Rohner, since he was beginning to reap the rewards of an eight-year quest to reconcile issues of Rohner's competitiveness with issues of environmental sustainability. He was able to increase the total

This case was written by Matthew M. Mehalik, under the direction of Michael E. Gorman and Patricia H. Werhane. Partial support for this project was supplied by grants from the Ethics and Values in Science program of the National Science Foundation (SBR-9319983), the Batten Center for Entrepreneurial Leadership at the Darden School, University of Virginia, and the Geraldine R. Dodge Foundation. The conclusions are the responsibilities of the authors and do not reflect the views of the foundations. This case was written as a basis for discussion rather than to illustrate effective or ineffective handling of an administrative situation. Copyright © 1998 by the University of Virginia Darden School Foundation, Charlottesville, VA. All rights reserved.

output of the facility at the half-year mark by 30 percent over the entire previous year's output, extending a trend of an overall increase of 100 percent over a three and one-half year period between January 1993 and June 1997 without hiring additional personnel. Over the same period, he was able to make significant decreases in energy and water use and solid waste production (see Exhibit 1).

Kälin was looking over the facility with special care this morning. In the afternoon he would be hosting visitors from a major Swiss bank who were interested in Rohner as a model of reconciling issues of economy and ecology. The financiers were in the midst of gathering criteria for rating companies for an environmental-sustainability mutual fund. Since Rohner Textil was a privately held company, it would never be traded in such a fund; however, Kälin was genuinely interested in showing that supposed conflicts among economic and environmental issues could be resolved using creative means and that those means made his company much more competitive than it would be otherwise. Kälin had introduced changes into every aspect of his operation, including the accounting and financing procedures, which would be of great interest to the bankers. Becoming a corporate model for financiers would be the ultimate endorsement of Kälin's methods, which had proven to be controversial over his eight-year quest. He was not sure how the officials would react. But he had faced many such challenges over the years.

ROHNER'S SHADOW

The issue for Kälin was achieving both short-term competitiveness and long-term survival. In the early 1990s Rohner was in a condition where its production capacity was suppressed because of old looms, warping machines, dye equipment, and heating systems. Rohner was in danger of not being capable of generating the high-end quality and volume necessary to compete in the short term with this old equipment. Paying for the capital improvements was a problem, because the investments were substantial and Rohner's ability to pay them off was limited.

For Kälin the issue was not simply the scaling-up of the operation. Even if there were production increases, he projected that Rohner would be in bad position if the utility rates and disposal rates increased. As Kälin described his situation, "These costs were Rohner's shadow. The costs were always there, as a projection of Rohner's operational policies, but they were difficult to recognize, were often distorted by the accounting system, and were often ignored altogether in financial planning."

Kälin began worrying about Rohner's shadow in the late 1980s and early 1990s. Initially, he was influenced by the ideas put forth by the Club of Rome in the book *Limits to Growth*. Also, Kälin looked at the current state of public-utility infrastructures and thought about projected growth of requirements for utility use over the upcoming decades. This long-term thinking was important to Kälin because his product lifecycle lasted 10 to 15 years, so he had to figure out how he would not be locked into a system that would put the mill at the mercy of utility costs.[3]

The water supply and treatment plants were old in the Rhine valley above the Lake of Constance, where Rohner Textil is located. The plants had been built mostly in the 1960s and 1970s, and Kälin believed they would need replacement soon. The capacity of these plants would need to be expanded to account for growth in the region. The modest growth was spurred by more people and companies moving into the region. Companies that were there already would be placing heavier demands on the system as they expanded their operations. Kälin knew that companies traditionally paid lower utility rates than the general public. The total cost of providing service from the utility company was added up and the billing rates were determined by the rate structure set for the companies and the rate structure for the public. The public was subsidizing the industry in the region at the time with the current rate structures. This situation was true for both water and electrical-utility costs. Kälin knew that a rate structure change could endanger the mill.

In addition, Kälin perceived that electricity costs were due to increase after the nuclear power plants in operation were eventually closed. The Swiss had banned the construction of new nuclear power plants, so the replacement costs when these plants closed would make electricity more expensive.

There was also the issue of solid-waste disposal. Kälin knew that most of the solid wastes in the local communities were handled by the local communities themselves. The wastes were not shipped to regional areas for disposal. Kälin perceived that these disposal systems were in danger of running out of space in the next ten-year period. Rohner generated a large amount of solid waste in the form of waste selvages (trimmings of fabric from the loom edges). Disposal of these selvages was very expensive, and Kälin needed to find a way to reduce this cost over time.

Another important factor was that Rohner operated in an area that had very high operational costs. Labor, land, and capital were all obtained at a premium in the region and throughout Switzerland. In addition, the town of Heerbrugg did not really care if Rohner existed there or not. Rohner employed only 30 people, so the town did not depend very heavily on Rohner's existence in the area for revenues.

There was little room for problems in product development, a process that was taking longer and longer each year. In 1993, Rohner had just developed a fabric for a major chair manufacturer. The process took five years, and Kälin expected the product to have a lifetime of over fifteen years. Unforeseen changes in regulations could have a significant impact on this and other products' returns for Rohner.

In the early 1990s the Swiss textile industry was going through significant structural changes. Rohner was able to survive because it was part of a larger enterprise, Forster-Rohner, which consisted of over 700 people and seven mills worldwide and because it had succeeded, initially, in entering the high-end, custom textile-design market. Most of the mills that closed had tried to compete in the low-end, high-volume market.

Forster-Rohner's main business was embroidery, not commercial furniture textiles. The owners would close Rohner Textil rather than suffer significant losses. They made it clear that any capital investments would have to be earned by the mill itself. They also believed that ecological improvements were a good idea, but that investment in ecological improvements would provide little return. The return-on-investment factor and the profitability of the company were the bottom line. The owners would not yield on this policy. If matters became too difficult, they could close or sell the mill, but they were unwilling to sink money into the venture. The only reason they were hanging on to the firm was that it was still making money. Kälin needed to find a way to solve both his short-term and long-term issues.

Kälin knew that, as the mill was currently operating, he could not provide a return on the investment in both new equipment and changes in production to make the mill more ecological. He knew that in both the short and long term, he would need to do both. How could Kälin manage these monetary concerns? Kälin knew that he needed to find a way within this framework to solve this problem. If he did nothing, he and the mill would be closed within just a few years.

ECOLOGY AS A SOLUTION TO ECONOMY?

One of the first steps Kälin took to reduce waste-selvage disposal costs was to look into incineration. At the time, a local wood-chipping company was already implementing such an incinerator system. Disposal costs were high enough that Kälin actually proposed building an incinerator on site to burn the selvages. First, Kälin made sure that his product lines would not produce any toxic emissions when burned. His products passed an inspection by the International Association for Research and Testing in the Field of Textile Ecology, an independent institute in Germany. Concerned with human-ecology issues, the institute tested for pH value, the content of free and partially releasable formaldehyde, residues of heavy metals, residues of pesticides, Pentachorophenole (PCP) content, carcinogenic compounds, and color fastness.

The problem was that local laws prohibited Rohner from building such a system. The Swiss categorized wastes into two categories: wood-chip waste, which was permitted to be burned in an incinerator and "other waste," which was not. If Rohner had been located twenty miles to the north in Germany it could have constructed such an incinerator because German laws had three waste categories, and Rohner's selvages would have fit the criteria for the third. Kalin's initial plan was not leading to the solution Kälin had hoped.

Kälin consulted a tax adviser, who found a tax loophole allowing a high depreciation for environmental expenditures that improved the environmental performance of a business. Such laws were common in several regions of Switzerland. For instance, residents could take tax deductions for investments to improve their homes. Kälin was able to paint his house and invest in a new heating system and deduct these costs on his taxes. For the factory, improved efficiency looms could be tax depreciable because they used less electricity. Other possibilities of tax-deductible improvements included the greening of the Rohner factory roof, higher-efficiency heating systems, using rainwater for sanitary systems, low-water consumption dye equipment, and more extensive electricity-use measuring equipment. Kälin was able to get into the budget and produce calculations per line item for such expenditures, which were called "Calculated Environmental Cost" (see Exhibit 3). In effect, Kälin was charging his products their environmental costs, such as electricity costs, in their cost calculation system and budgeting for these costs in the annual budget. This made sense to the finance and accounting personnel. It reduced the amount of taxes they had to pay and also permitted capital

expenditures at lower rates. With most of these investments Kälin believed he could prepare for potential increased environmental regulations, lowering the risk of being caught
off guard should new regulatory laws be passed.

The other potential benefit from implementing these large improvements in environmental performance was decreasing his use of the utilities he foresaw as increasing
over time. The new dye equipment reduced water and electricity use dramatically
because of the recycling of hot water. Kälin's solutions permitted him to get a handle on
his problems of short-term competitiveness and long-term avoidance of increasing utility costs. His solution permitted him to increase his capacity and efficiency while positioning the mill on the safe side of environmental regulations.

The loophole would not, however, solve his waste-selvage disposal problem, and
Kälin viewed selvage disposal as his most serious environmental cost. These disposal
problems would not be solved by updating equipment; the content of the fabrics themselves were the source of the problem. Kälin's solution came in the form of hiring consultants William McDonough, an American architect renowned for his environmental
approach towards design, Michael Braungart, a German chemical engineer and former
founding member of Greenpeace Germany's Chemistry Division, and the Environmental Protection Encouragement Agency (EPEA), with a team of scientists. Kälin hired
this team to redesign his production line and to inspect his production processes and
suppliers so that his waste selvages were suitable for composting without any toxic
releases. The philosophy that the consultant team adopted was "waste equals food."[4]
The product line, dubbed Climatex Lifecycle, was released in June 1995 and had won
awards at the Neocon Convention in Chicago in 1995 and the Arge Alp award in Europe
in 1996.

Kälin paid the consultants out of the budget's R&D allocation. The funding was
awarded after competing with other funding requests for R&D. In other words, if the
Rohner designers wanted to develop a new fabric line, the money needed to accomplish
this project was in direct competition with the EPEA project.

Kälin decided which projects should be funded and what the allocations for each
funded R&D project should be. This was part of the glory and risk if his job—his vision
for the company determined what would be produced. If this vision was not in accordance with Rohner's survival, Kälin would be fired, and the company would be in danger of closing. Since Kälin decided that the long-term possibilities of environmental
costs presented the most important issues for new product development, he chose to
fund the EPEA instead of developing additional designs.

The result of this initiative was that Kälin converted his waste selvages into a sal-
able product. The selvages were sent to a felt manufacturer which shredded and combined the selvage fibers into felt blankets. The blankets were being sold in a local gar-
dening shop. They were useful in gardens because they kept weeds from growing, and
also served as fertilizer as they decomposed. Kälin succeeded in converting a high-cost
disposal item into a source of revenue.

Kälin also needed to get his employees involved in understanding the importance
of ecology with quality and cost concerns. "You cannot produce environmental products
without quality, and there must be a control system in place to direct it."[5] By control
system, Kälin was referring to the International Standards Organization (ISO) 9000

series management system. Through Kälin and his team's commitment, Rohner successfully passed its quality-system audit in 1994 and received its certificate for quality management according to ISO 9001, the applicable standard for suppliers during "design, development, production, installation, and servicing."[6] By 1996 Kälin had passed the inspection of an independent auditor against the ISO 14001 environmental standards. Rohner was one of the first companies in Europe to pass these standards. Rohner also passed an audit against the European standard, Environmental Management and Auditing System (EMAS). He continued to repeat and update these certifications yearly.[7]

Instead of being cynical about incorporating environmental concerns into the mill's operations, most of the employees took the matter to heart. Alexandra Rumpf, Environmental and Quality manager, summarized her views: "First of all, we need to sensitize one another to environmental issues. We have to work with one another so that we understand how important it is to live in a healthy environment while remaining profitable. We do this by building groups at Rohner and sharing our concerns openly and documenting changes."[8]

Walter Haug of the shipping department declared, "Whenever you produce or design a new product, you have to account for the environmental idea. And do not just say that it is impossible to do that. Our children should have the same living conditions as we have today. What we fail to do for the environment we cannot cancel."[9]

By the middle of 1997, Kälin had managed to build several interdependent systems around the idea of environmental sustainability. It was no longer just a matter of receiving tax benefits. He and the mill had appeared on both the German and Austrian news, and had won an award from Deutshe Umweltinstituit (German Environmental Aid) in July 1997. Kälin also received an endorsement at a German business conference in June 1997 from the Right Honorable John Gummer, former Secretary of State for the Environment of England in Prime Minister John Major's government. Gummer labeled the Climatex Lifecycle and Rohner Textil as "the only existing example I have seen that embodies the spirit of Agenda 21." Gummer was referring to the international document developed at the 1992 Earth Summit at Rio de Janeiro, Brazil. Agenda 21 was on Gummer's mind as he was headed from that conference to New York for "Earth Summit II" on the five-year anniversary of the Rio conference.

It was at that time that Rohner Textil came to the attention of the Swiss banking industry. Investors became increasingly interested in evaluating companies in terms of their environmental performance for the purposes of including them in a mutual fund of sustainable companies and for rating in terms of risk for granting loans. The team of Swiss bankers was coming to look at Kälin's systems. They were also interested in looking at how he managed to budget for the changes that he had implemented.

Kälin was prepared to show them some figures to illustrate how he made his changes. He had prepared a finance and accounting report for his visitors. (The report is reproduced as Exhibit 2. A sample budget is included as Exhibit 3.) Kälin had disguised the actual numbers of the company in this report to protect the privacy that the owners desired, but the figures that he used were not distorted from the original plans he proposed. In that way he could show them the ideas behind his system. He eagerly awaited their arrival and wondered whether his successes would continue.

Notes

1. Adalbert von Chamisso, *Peter Schlemihl* (Henly on Thames: Langtry Press, 1992), 78.
2. Unless otherwise stated, information for this case was obtained through interviews with Albin Kälin, 29 June through 5 July 1997 at Rohner Textil AG and on 6 June 1997 in New York.
3. For more information on Rohner Textil's background, see Darden case UVA-E-0107 and UVA-E-0108 *"Rohner Textil AG (A) and (B)."*
4. This story has been told in detail in Darden cases UVA-E-0099 *"DesignTex, Inc. (A)"* and UVA-E-0100 *"DesignTex, Inc. (B)."*
5. Kälin interviews 28 May-1 June 1996.
6. ANSI/ISO/ASQC 9001-1994, vii.
7. For more information on Rohner's approach to environmental management systems, see Darden case *"Rohner Textil AG (C),"* UVA-E-0109.
8. Interview with Alexandra Rumpf at Rohner, 2 July 1997.
9. Interview with Walter Haug, 1 July 1997.

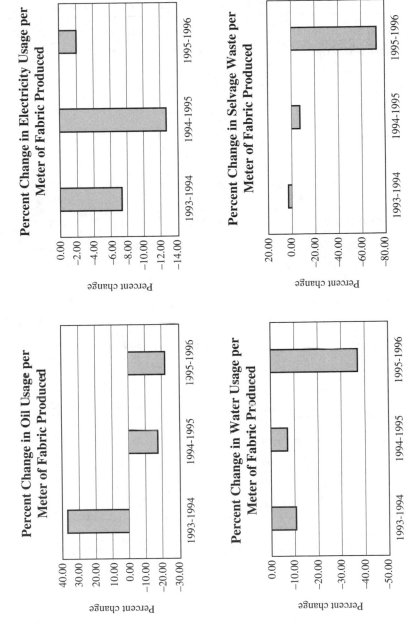

EXHIBIT 1

Graphs of Selected Categories of Percent Change in Environmental Data
Normalized Per Meter of Fabric Produced

Percent Change in Electricity Usage per
Meter of Fabric Produced

Percent Change in Selvage Waste per
Meter of Fabric Produced

Percent Change in Oil Usage per
Meter of Fabric Produced

Percent Change in Water Usage per
Meter of Fabric Produced

EXHIBIT 1 (Continued)

Percent Change in Environmental Data
Normalized per Meter of Fabric Produced

	1993–1994	1994–1995	1995–1996	1993–1996
Products sold (m)*	-0.84	34.47	13.61	51.48
Yarn usage (MT)	8.92	0.99	-4.78	4.75
Energy				
Oil (l)	36.15	-17.37	-22.25	-12.53
Electricity (kWh)	-7.14	-12.83	-1.85	-20.55
Water usage				
(million liters)	-10.35	-7.04	-38.38	-48.65
Water wastes				
Undissolved substances(mg/l)	-93.01	-19.13	608.23	-59.99
Conducting capacity (myS/cm)	-59.46	1.01	66.93	-31.65
Total phosphates (mg/l)	-76.47	-76.98	3894.86	116.39
Sulfates (mg/l)	-84.84	118.90	197.83	-1.17
Chlorides (mg/l)	-88.96	-59.44	1411.05	-32.34
Dissolved organic				
compounds (mg/l)	-83.42	30.14	25.75	-72.87
Air emissions: Heating system				
CO (ppm)	0.85	-100.00	n/a	
NO$_2$ (ppm)	n/a	n/a	1.97	n/a
Exhaust gas loss (% total)	0.85	-70.16	-13.33	-73.92
Air emissions: Hot water boiler				
CO (ppm)	n/a	n/a	n/a	n/a
NO$_2$ (ppm)	-13.23	-25.63	-27.19	-53.02
Exhaust gas loss (% total)	n/a	-25.63	-21.76	n/a
Solid waste				
Selvage waste (kg)	0.85	-7.04	-75.24	-76.79
Normal waste (kg)	0.85	-25.63	-22.16	-41.62
Cardboard recycled (kg)	0.85	31.38	-34.80	-13.61
Tubes recycled (kg)	0.85	-13.24	-39.81	-47.33
Metal recycled (kg)	51.28	-25.63	322.51	375.32
Toxic waste**				
Caustic substances (l)	0.85	-25.63	n/a	n/a
Toxicity class 3 (kg)	0.85	-25.63	-38.47	-53.85
Toxicity class 4 (kg)	0.85	-25.63	-25.68	-44.26
Flammable substances + oxidizers	0.85	-25.63	-22.98	-42.24

* This category is not normalized but represents actual values.
** This category refers to the amount of toxic materials on hand, not the amount used per year.
Sources: Rohner Textil AG, *Environmental Report 1995; Environmental Report 1996.*

EXHIBIT 2

Part 1:
Non-Environmental Item
Investment Forecast 1993-2000

Investment Item	Investment $US
Yarn dye house	2,000,000
Winding machinery	500,000
Warping machinery	1,000,000
Weaving equipment	4,000,000
Inspection system	500,000
Computer equipment	500,000
Computer administration	1,000,000
Building equipment	500,000
Total	10,000,000

8 years
1,250,000 $US/year investment

Source: Rohner Textil AG Investment Forecast 1993-2000.

EXHIBIT 2 (Continued)

Part 2:
Environmental Cost Projections for Operations
(see next page for comments)
(figures in thousands U. S. dollars)

Category/Item	1993 Inv.	1993 Exp.	1994 Inv.	1994 Exp.	1995 Inv.	1995 Exp.	1996 Inv.	1996 Exp.	1997 Inv.	1997 Exp.	1998 Inv.	1998 Exp.	1999 Inv.	1999 Exp.	2000 Inv.	2000 Exp.
AIR																
Heating System for Building					100											
Heating System for Yarn Dyeing													200			
CO_2 Taxes														10		10
WASTE WATER																
Reduction Water Consumption (Through water recycling system)				20		20		20		20		60		60		60
*savings through investment								*20		*20		*60		*60		*60
ENERGY																
Cost		200		200		200		200		200		200		200		200
Savings in reusing water/ reduction in temp.								*20		*20		*20		*20		*20
Reduction in Airflow with heating system								*1		*1		*1		*1		*1
Solar Energy							20								200	

* savings through investment

Category/Item	1993 Inv.	1993 Exp.	1994 Inv.	1994 Exp.	1995 Inv.	1995 Exp.	1996 Inv.	1996 Exp.	1997 Inv.	1997 Exp.	1998 Inv.	1998 Exp.	1999 Inv.	1999 Exp.	2000 Inv.	2000 Exp.
WASTE																
Selvages		400		400		400		400		400		400		400		400
* savings through improved products								*50		*50		*150		*150		*150
Other costs		420		420		420		420		420		420		420		420
HAZARDOUS SUBSTANCES																
Storage of Chemicals					2		3								5	
Oil tank Containment System							10									
ENVIRONMENTAL INVESTMENTS																
Grass Roof Installation	100											150				
ISO 9001					50		100									
ISO 14001					50		100									
Internet									100							
Total Investments/Expenditures	100	1020	0	1040	202	1040	233	949	100	949	150	849	200	859	355	859
Total Savings on Expenditures								91		91		231		231		231

Overall Investment Total (thousand $US)   1340 or 167.5 per year
Overall Expenditure Total (thousand $US)   7565 or 945 per year
Overall Savings on Expenditures (thousand $US)   875
Max expenditures: 1040
Min expenditures: 849
Difference   191

Source: Rohner Textil AG Cost Projections Forecast 1993-2000.

COMMENTS ON ENVIRONMENTAL COST PROJECTIONS FOR OPERATIONS

Investment Forecast

- The chart shows investments of $1,340,000 over a period of eight years. The investments are allocated to areas not belonging to the typical investments involving the building or machinery of Rohner. These investments were or will be financed through the inclusion of a corresponding percentage environmental cost figure included in the production cost of each product. This percentage figure is reflected in the annual budget and is tax depreciable.
- An average of $167,700 must be allocated each year for environmental investments. This is approximately 1.6 percent of the annual turnover. When factored into the non-environmental planned investments of 12.5% per year (as shown in Part 1 of this report), the overall investments are 14.1% per year.

Expenditure Forecast

- The environmental expenditures amount to $7,565,000 over a period of 8 years. The average is $945,000 per year. Through the various investments in machinery with improved environmental performance (such as improved yarn dyeing equipment) and through investments into environmentally improved nonproduction items gives a reduction of environmental costs from $1,040,00 to $849,000. The difference of $191,000 can be allocated to cover the cost of the above investments in environmental areas.

EXHIBIT 2 (Continued)

Part 3:
Design Costs for Product Development
(see next page for comments)
(figures in thousands of U.S. dollars)

Category/Item	1993 Inv.	1993 Exp.	1994 Inv.	1994 Exp.	1995 Inv.	1995 Exp.	1996 Inv.	1996 Exp.	1997 Inv.	1997 Exp.	1998 Inv.	1998 Exp.	1999 Inv.	1999 Exp.	2000 Inv.	2000 Exp.
RESEARCH AND DEVELOPMENT																
Total Cost		416		430		457		457		450		450		450		450
PERSONNEL COSTS (SALARIES)	210	215	220	240	250	250	260	270								
EXTERNAL COSTS (Includes designs from outside designers jacquard cards, and computer design patterns)		70		120		122		92		50		50		40		50
VARIOUS EXPENSES		20		20		20		20		20		20		20		20
ENVIRONMENTAL R&D COST	16	75	95	105	130	130	130	120								
Total Investments/Expenditures	0	732	0	860	0	914	0	914	0	900	0	900	0	900	0	910

Overall Investment Total (thousand $US)   0
Overall Expenditure Total (thousand $US)   7030
Overall Environmental Expenditures (thousand $US)   801

Forecasted improvement percentage of product environmental costs cue to environmental R&D expenditures:

year	% improve	year	% imprcve
1993	0	1997	0
1994	4	1998	2
1995	6	1999	2
1996	7	2000	0

Source: Rohner Textil AG R&D Projections 1993-2000.

COMMENTS ON ENVIRONMENTAL DESIGN COST PROJECTIONS

- The design cost budget includes environmental R&D costs. These expenditures are directed towards reducing the environmental costs associated with the products.
- The external cost line item is being reduced as a result of an offset with increases in the environmental R&D expenditures. The external costs are planned to be further reduced through an investment in improved computer aided design (CAD) equipment, reducing the dependence on externally-produced jacquard cards.
- The cost of hiring consultants, such as the Environmental Protection Encouragement Agency (EPEA) to do product environmental optimization is included in the environmental R&D cost line item.
- The figures show that a total of $801,000 has been budgeted for environmental R&D expenditures over a period of 8 years, or an average of $100,100 per year.
- The projections of the reductions in product environmental costs forecast reductions in cost over the period shown. The real benefits of the environmental R&D investment and corresponding environmental costs are forecasted to occur over a 15-year time span, when the products would normally require disposal in a landfill or incinerator, but through the R&D investment the products will instead qualify for composting without any disposal costs.
- The resulting savings from environmental R&D investment will become even more dramatic should the political climate change and require that products be returned to the manufacturers for disposal. This would normally result in very high product environmental costs, but the R&D investment reduced this cost because the products will be designed for composting locally.

EXHIBIT 2 (Continued)

Part 4:
Cost Savings through Environmental R&D Expenditures
(see next page for comments)
(figures in thousands of U. S. dollars)

	1993	94	95	96	97	98	99	0	01	02	03	04	05	06	07	08	09	10	11	12	13	14	15	16
DISPOSAL COSTS WITH NO ADDL ENVIRO. DISPOSAL COSTS	10	10	10	10	10	10	20	20	20	20	20	20	30	30	30	30	40	40	40	40	50	50	50	50
DISPOSAL COSTS WITH GOODS RETURN DISPOSAL COSTS																								
for product line without environmental R&D investments								250	250	250	250	250	250	250	250	250	250	250	250	250	300	300	400	400
for product line with only Oeko-Tex inspections								50	50	50	50	50	50	50	50	50	50	50	50	50	70	70	70	70
for enviro R&D investments to make compostable product line		0	0	0	0	0	0	0	0	40	40	40	30	30	30	30	30							
savings for this category		0						200	200	200	200	200	200	200	200	200	160	160	170	200	200	300	300	300

Source: Rohner Textil AG Cost Savings 1993-2016.

COST SAVINGS PROJECTIONS THROUGH ENVIRONMENTAL R&D IMPLEMENTATION

- The first item projections show that, if no changes in disposal policy occur, the overall environmental costs remain relatively small over the period under consideration.
- However, if regulations change and goods are returned to the manufacturer for disposal, the environmental disposal costs will be very high. The main cost for Rohner Textil will be transportation costs, assumed to be $200,000 per year along with a disposal cost of $50,000 per year. If the products required additional, special disposal procedures, the disposal cost could rise from $50,000 per year to $200,000 per year.
- As Rohner Textil has passed the Oeko-Tex standards for its entire product line, it is possible that our customers may not have to send the waste products back to us for disposal, since they will be able to dispose of them without restrictions. It is therefore assumed that transportation costs can be excluded from this category.
- The Climatex Lifecycle, compostable line of fabrics, will not require either transportation or disposal, as the customers will be able to compost the wastes. However, the projections include a disposal cost in the year 2009, assuming increases in restrictions even for composting.
- The environmental R&D expenditures will show their payback after the year 2000, assuming that the disposal regulations are implemented.
- The earnings associated with Rohner's pioneering steps in the areas of ecology are not reflected in these figures, such as better corporate image or reduced impacts on externalized costs. These benefits will be reflected in the general business success of the company.
- Rohner Textil will be able to reduce its future projected insurance costs, because insurance companies requiring an environmental audit and basing their premiums on environmental risk projections will be able to offer Rohner lower rates.
- Rohner's leading position in the area of industrial ecology will improve its position with financial banking institutions in the future. Such institutions will be more likely to lend Rohner assets for meeting its financial needs because the company presents an overall lower environmental risk at present and in the future.

EXHIBIT 3
PORTION OF SAMPLE ROHNER BUDGET*

Ecology-Economy Concept Category	Budget thousand $US	%
Gross Sales	**10,000**	**100.00**
Profit Reductions	586	5.86
Net Sales	**9,414**	**100.00**
Raw Material Supply	4,063	43.16
Custom Twisting/Finishing	537	5.70
Inventory Value Change	-175	-1.86
Total Cost of Materials	**4,425**	**47.00**
Subtotal 1	**4,989**	**53.00**
Custom Weaving	507	5.38
Internal Production Cost	1,490	15.82
Calculated Environmental Cost	96	1.02
Calculated Cost of Production	464	4.93
Subtotal 2	**2,432**	**25.84**
Research & Development	416	4.42
Cost for Product Samples	-	0.00
Sales Costs	425	4.51
Advertising	26	0.28
Packaging & Shipment	100	1.06
Administrative Costs	464	4.93
Administrative Cost from Headquarters	245	2.61
Total Expenditures Cost	**1,676**	**17.82**
Subtotal 3	**756**	**8.02**
+		
Additional Earnings	—	0.00
Additional Expenditures	66	-0.70
Additional Calculated Costs	240	-2.56
Total Earnings	**450**	**4.77**
Return on Equity		
Total Calculated Cash Flow	**750**	**7.97**

*Figures adapted from 1993 Rohner Textil Budget as supplied by Albin Kälin,
6 October 1996.

19

UNILEVER (A)

In 1994, Dr. Jan-Kees Vis was attending a social function for his new job with the Unilever Foods Executive Quality Assurance Group. At the reception, Vis was approached by his new boss, Mr. Jan Peelen, the Chairman of the Foods Executive. In the ensuing discussion, Peelen asked him about his plans for his new position.[1]

This was a moment of opportunity that Vis had been working towards for quite some time. He had sought his current position so that he could have an impact on the strategy decisions taking place at Unilever. His past experiences as a chemist and as a leader in developing software for conducting product environmental lifecycle assessments (LCAs) led him to believe that sustainable development presented an opportunity for competitive advantage for Unilever; however, his technical knowledge remained on the fringe of operations at Unilever, one of the world's largest packaged consumer goods companies.

This case was written by Myles Standish, graduate student, Systems Engineering and Division of Technology, Culture, and Communication at the University of Virginia, under the direction of Michael E. Gorman and Patricia H. Werhane. Partial support for this project was supplied by grants from the Ethics and Values in Science program of the National Science Foundation (SBR-9319983), the Batten Center for Entrepreneurial Leadership at the Darden School, University of Virginia, and the Geraldine R. Dodge Foundation. The conclusions are the responsibilities of the authors, and do not reflect the views of the foundations. This was written as a basis for class discussion rather than to illustrate effective or ineffective handling of an administrative situation. Copyright © 1998 by the University of Virginia Darden School Foundation, Charlottesville, VA. All rights reserved.

Based jointly in the Netherlands and the United Kingdom, Unilever made and marketed more than 1,000 brands of consumer goods in the industrial categories of foods, beverages, detergents, and personal products. At the time, Unilever employed about 300,000 people in companies operating in over 90 countries around the world; their products were sold through third parties in 70 additional countries. In the United States, some of Unilever's most recognizable brands were Lipton, Five Brothers pasta sauces, Chicken Tonight, "All" detergent, Calvin Klein perfume, Dove, Helene Curtis, Vaseline, and Q-tips.[2] Unilever's products were bought by more than half the families in the world.

Vis felt strongly that Unilever had an obligation to more carefully examine its environmental impacts. Furthermore, he believed that fulfilling environmental obligations was not inconsistent with sound business practice. If he could convince Peelen of his beliefs, perhaps he could have an impact on Unilever strategy. Confident that his ideas were beneficial to Unilever, Vis carefully expressed his opinion that Unilever was not doing enough work with sustainable development.

"What do you mean we aren't doing enough?" Peelen responded. "You are Unilever and I am Unilever. If you think more should be done, then do something about it." Recognizing this as an invitation to promote change, Vis considered a proposal to explore sustainable development in Unilever.

BACKGROUND ON UNILEVER'S PRODUCTS

Products marketed by Unilever Foods included frozen fish dinners, culinary products, bakery goods, margarine, pasta sauces, ice cream, tea, soups, and others. Additionally, Unilever's detergents and personal products groups marketed a variety of non-food goods ranging from detergents and household cleaning products to toothpaste, cosmetics, deodorants, perfumes, shampoos, skin care, and personal hygiene products.

In the United States Unilever marketed a variety of teas, soups, margarine, pasta sauces and frozen fish products. The brand names included: Lipton teas and soups; Country Crock, "I Can't Believe It's Not Butter!"; Wish-Bone salad dressings; Ragu pasta and pizza sauces; Gorton's frozen seafood products; Popsicle, Klondike and Breyers ice cream products. Major non-food products included laundry detergents, soaps, toothpaste, hair care products and fragrances. The brand names included: Surf, Wisk and "All" laundry detergents; Caress, Lever 2000, and Dove soap bars; Q-tips cotton products; Aim, Mentadent, Pepsodent and Close-up toothpaste; Finesse, Salon Selectives, and Rave hair care products; and Elizabeth Arden and Calvin Klein cosmetics and fragrances.[3]

BACKGROUND ON UNILEVER'S ORGANIZATIONAL STRUCTURE

Netherlands-based Unilever N.V. and U.K.-based Unilever PLC each owned half of Unilever, one of the world's largest packaged consumer goods companies. Unilever NV and Unilever PLC have the same board of directors and essentially operate as a single entity, although they list their stock separately.

In 1995, Unilever operations were managed by a Special Committee made up by the chairmen of Unilever (at the time, the chairman of Unilever PLC was Niall Fitzgerald, and the chairman of Unilever NV was Morris Tabaksblat), and a vice chairman who was a chairman-in-waiting. The special committee had responsibility for setting long-term strategy and monitoring company performance.

The Unilever Board, which reported directly to the Special Committee was formed by the Chairmen of executive committees representing each of Unilever's four product groups (foods, detergents, personal products, and specialty chemicals) and directors with various responsibilities including personnel, finance, and research and engineering. The directors had mixed global responsibility for product strategy and bottom-line responsibility for specific regions. This brought together a mixture of strategic and operational responsibility from many different operational categories.

Within each of the four product groups was a hierarchy that delegated performance responsibility to groups and individuals around the world. The actual production operations within Unilever were carried out by hundreds of operating companies around the world (each belonging to a product group). The chairmen of these operating companies reported performance through the hierarchy of the product group to their respective executive committee.

As chairman of the Foods Executive, Peelen was responsible for the performance of Unilever Foods in the United States and Europe. (Foods operations elsewhere were the responsibility of other directors with specific regional responsibilities.) He was responsible for determining the overall performance targets and strategies of Unilever Foods. This included, among other things, setting sales targets, brand strategies, and environmental performance goals with the various committees within the foods product group. Peelen was a member of the Unilever Board and reported directly to the Special Committee.

Within the Foods Executive were various groups and individuals whose goals were to support the strategies and initiatives set in place for Unilever Foods. One example of this was the Foods Environmental Quality Assurance Group, which Vis joined in 1994. This group reported to the Foods Executive. Their goal was to support the worldwide implementation of the Foods environmental policy by the product groups and their respective operating companies.

Unilever's leading environmental group, the Unilever Environmental Group (UEG) had responsibility for developing and communicating Unilever's environmental strategy and policy. This group discussed company environmental strategy with the Special Committee and the Unilever Board. There was a level of communication between the UEG and the Foods Executive; the Product Group environmental policies had to be consistent with Unilever environmental policy.

See Appendix A for a diagram of the operational structure of Unilever in 1995.

VIS'S BACKGROUND

Vis was not a newcomer to Unilever when he had his discussion with Peelen in 1994. He joined the company in 1986 as a researcher with a Ph.D. in chemistry. His specialty was heterogeneous catalysis, a background that related directly to his research job. After spending 6 years doing research, supporting laboratory management systems and research policy management, he decided to seek a position in an operating company where he could become involved in the implementation of his work.

The opportunity came when he happened to meet a colleague on a train in the Netherlands. The colleague encouraged Vis to post for a recent opening in a Unilever margarine factory, a position that would expose him to the implementation of his research. The job involved the analysis of the factory's products and the design of software to analyze the environmental impacts of the products and manufacturing processes. Vis posted for and landed the job, where he soon became an expert in life-cycle assessment (LCA).

Vis performed LCAs on several product systems (margarine, low-fat spreads, edible oils, packaging systems and others) during his stay at the margarine company. (Others in Unilever in the meantime had also taken up LCA, and over the years several dozen LCA studies of Unilever products would be done on detergents, personal care products, household cleaning products, etc.) In performing LCAs, Vis became familiar with the effect Unilever products were having on the environment at all stages along their life cycle. Soon he began to realize that much could be done to reduce the environmental impact of Unilever products. However, he did not have the authority to change policies or introduce new initiatives at his current job level. In 1994 he began seeking a position within Unilever where he could be more involved in determining strategy.

He finally got the chance when he landed a position working for the Foods Executive at Unilever's Head Office in Rotterdam, the Netherlands. The Foods Executive had responsibility for Unilever Food's multi-billion dollar business in the US and Europe. At his new post, Vis hoped to become more involved with developing environmental strategy and policy.

VIS'S PROPOSAL TO PEELEN

Vis had begun discussing sustainability with Ben de Vet, who had direct responsibility for the Foods environmental policy. This rekindled de Vet's interest in the subject, and they considered possible ways to address sustainable development for Unilever Foods. In the spirit of his conversation with Peelen at the reception, Vis saw an opportunity to build the Foods environmental policy around the theme of sustainable development. Shortly after his conversation with Peelen at the social function, Vis proposed that a new policy be written to include a commitment to pursue sustainable development. De Vet supported this initiative.

At this time, the Unilever Foods environmental policy did not mention sustainable development. The current policy, which had been adopted in May, 1990, outlined how Unilever Foods would address environmental concerns. Specific measures included accepting responsibility for environmental protection and demonstrating a reduction in environmental impact. The policy seems to have been most focused on anticipating and reacting to future environmental issues and consumer pressures. Listed as rationale were the belief that the "green consumer" movement would grow stronger and create demand for cleaner products, growing pressure from consumers and governments to address environmental issues, and the benefits of avoiding costly changes due to new legislation.[4]

There were factors that complicated rewriting the policy. It was unclear what sustainable development meant for Unilever's Foods business. The operating companies that ultimately implemented the Foods environment policy required guidelines and standards to set performance targets. It was unclear how sustainability related to the Foods business operations. Vis also found that sustainable development had been included in Unilever's environmental policy in 1994. However, he felt that no action had really been taken to appropriately address sustainable development in Unilever. This, he thought, was partially due to the vague nature of the policy:

> Unilever wishes to be part of a sustainable future, in which economic growth combines with sound environmental management to meet the needs and aspirations of people throughout the world.[5]

This statement was, perhaps, as unclear as the concept of sustainable development itself. Sustainability and sustainable development had ambiguous and disputed definitions that were just beginning to emerge from a worldwide debate over the environment and the global impact of human activities. The roots of most definitions of sustainability come from a 1987 report titled "Our Common Future," although the report was better known as the Brundtland Report. In the report the definition of sustainable development was to meet the needs of the present without compromising the ability of future generations to meet their own needs.[6]

A more recent and very well-known declaration was issued in 1992 at the Conference on Environment and Development in Rio de Janeiro. Called *Agenda 21*,[7] it declared sustainable development a top priority for all countries in the world. According to *Agenda 21*, sustainable development should fulfill economic, environmental and social responsibilities. *Agenda 21* outlined an approach for achieving sustainable development, where the basic needs of citizens are met through economically feasible and environmentally sound means.

On the one hand, the statement in Unilever's 1994 environment report seems to have reflected top management's growing concern about the environment and a recognition that sustainability was an important topic. The company's first sign of awareness came in 1993 when Unilever representatives signed the International Chamber of Commerce (ICC) Charter for Sustainable Development. The major focus of the ICC Business Charter was to make environmental management "among the highest corporate priorities" and to "establish policies, programs and practices for conducting operations in an environmentally sound manner." The details of the charter addressed developing measures aimed at process improvement, educating employees about environmental responsibility, reducing environmental impact of products and services, efficient use of energy, and other efficiency and safety improvements.[8]

On the other hand, it appears that the statement provided no guidance or plan of action for achieving sustainability. The ICC Charter for Sustainable Development offered little discussion of what sustainability actually meant for businesses or how it could be achieved.[9] The implications of signing the ICC Business Charter were limited, and no sustainable development initiatives in Unilever resulted from it. People within the company had been referring to "sustainability" during 1994-95 without knowing what the term meant in terms of corporate activities.[10] Although Unilever had stated in its formal environmental policy that it wished to be "part of a sustainable future," the lack of understanding of what this implied presented a huge obstacle to creating change. As a result, sustainable development remained a low-key priority in Unilever during this time period.

Vis saw rewriting the Foods environmental policy as an opportunity to clarify how Unilever Foods would begin implementing sustainable development concepts in its operations. He hoped the new policy would serve as a starting point for a broader investigation of sustainable development at Unilever. Vis and the other members of the Foods Executive working on the task decided to include in the new policy the following commitment, defining the first steps Unilever would take towards understanding sustainable development:

> We will aim for sustainable development. In the years to come, we will work towards a definition of sustainability that is meaningful to our business and acceptable to relevant stakeholders.[11]

This was adopted by Foods management and issued as part of the formal Foods Environmental Policy in 1995. The policy contained the following responsibilities for implementation:

- Directors are responsible for the coherent implementation of this policy. They will discuss relevant aspects with company chairmen and urge the marketing function to incorporate environmental considerations into their strategies. They will make resources available for central support, including research funds to develop necessary tools.
- Intermediate management bodies (Product Groups, Category Boards) are responsible for follow-up with companies. They will develop models and targets for specific products and processes.
- The Foods Executive will provide assistance in implementing this and will audit progress

Vis and his colleagues in the FEIG began contemplating how they might work to fulfill the commitments made in the new policy. They continued to report their progress to the Foods Executive.

Notes

1. Unless otherwise noted, information in this case was taken from correspondence and interviews with Unilever employees between October, 1997, and November, 1998.
2. Copyright © 1997-98 Hoover's, Inc. Taken from: *http://www.hoovers.com/capsules/93845.html.*
3. Company Press Release, "Unilever Board Changes," May 6, 1998.
4. Unilever Foods Executive Environmental Policy, May 11, 1990.
5. Information in this section was taken from correspondence between the authors and Jan-Kees Vis, dated March 3, 1998.
6. Information in this section was taken from: The World Commission on Environment and Development, *Our Common Future* (New York: Oxford University Press, 1987) 8.
7. For the entire text of *Agenda 21*, see United Nations document E.92-38352; A/CONF.151/26 (Volumes II and III).
8. Unilever Environment Group, "Unilever Environmental Report 1996: Our worldwide approach," Unilever Corporate Relations Office, April 1996, 46-47.

9. See Jan Bebbington and Rob Gray, "Incentives and Disincentives for the Adoption of Sustainability by Transnational Corporations" (presented at the United Nations Conference on Trade and Development, Geneva). Published in the 1995 Review, *Environmental Accounting* (New York: United Nations, 1996) 2.

10. Hans Broekhoff and Jan-Kees Vis, "Sustainable Development and Unilever: Putting the Corporate Purpose into Action" (unpublished).

11. Unilever Foods Environmental Policy, Foods Executive Committee, Rotterdam, May 1995.

APPENDIX A
UNILEVER ORGANIZATIONAL DIAGRAM (1995)

This diagram shows the general management chain existing for Unilever Foods prior to 1996 reorganization. Similar structures existed for Unilever Personal Products, Detergents, and Specialty Chemicals Product Groups.

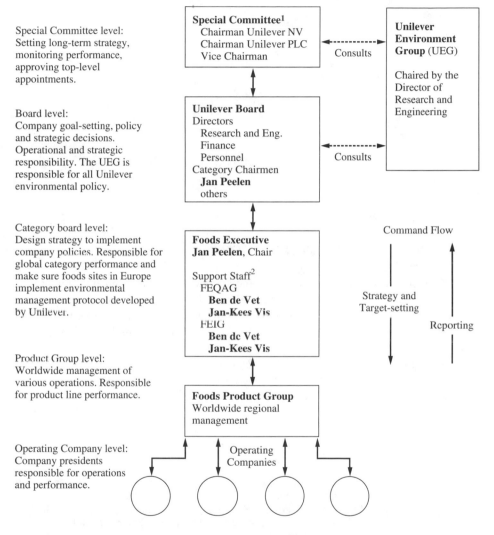

Special Committee level: Setting long-term strategy, monitoring performance, approving top-level appointments.

Special Committee[1]
Chairman Unilever NV
Chairman Unilever PLC
Vice Chairman
Consults

Unilever Environment Group (UEG)
Chaired by the Director of Research and Engineering

Board level: Company goal-setting, policy and strategic decisions. Operational and strategic responsibility. The UEG is responsible for all Unilever environmental policy.

Unilever Board
Directors
  Research and Eng.
  Finance
  Personnel
Category Chairmen
  Jan Peelen
  others
Consults

Category board level: Design strategy to implement company policies. Responsible for global category performance and make sure foods sites in Europe implement environmental management protocol developed by Unilever.

Foods Executive
Jan Peelen, Chair

Support Staff[2]
  FEQAG
    Ben de Vet
    Jan-Kees Vis
  FEIG
    Ben de Vet
    Jan-Kees Vis

Command Flow

Strategy and Target-setting

Reporting

Product Group level: Worldwide management of various operations. Responsible for product line performance.

Foods Product Group
Worldwide regional management

Operating Company level: Company presidents responsible for operations and performance.

Operating Companies

[1]The Special Committee is Unilever's highest level of management. The Unilever Board consists of the Special Committee, the Directors, and the Category Chairmen.

[2]Within the Foods Executive are various support functions, such as the Foods Executive Quality Assurance Group and the Foods Environmental Implementation Group (FEIG). These groups assist in the implementation of Unilever policy and strategy at the Foods category level.

20

UNILEVER (B)

1995: TOWARDS A DEFINITION OF SUSTAINABILITY

In 1995, the Unilever Foods Executive adopted a new Foods Environmental Policy that included a commitment to "aim for sustainable development" and "work towards a definition of sustainability that is meaningful to our business and acceptable to relevant stakeholders." Jan-Kees Vis, a researcher at the Unilever Foods Executive Quality Assurance Group, was a key player in the development of the new policy. He had urged the chairman of the Foods Executive, Jan Peelen, to address Unilever's role in sustainable development. The new policy represented the first commitment to investigate sustainable development in Unilever Foods. [1,2]

This case was written by Myles Standish, graduate student, Systems Engineering and Division of Technology, Culture, and Communication at the University of Virginia, under the direction of Michael E. Gorman and Patricia H. Werhane. Partial support for this project was supplied by grants from the Ethics and Values in Science program of the National Science Foundation (SBR-9319983), the Batten Center for Entrepreneurial Leadership at the Darden School, University of Virginia, and the Geraldine R. Dodge Foundation. The conclusions are the responsibilities of the authors, and do not reflect the views of the foundations. This was written as a basis for class discussion rather than to illustrate effective or ineffective handling of an administrative situation. Copyright © 1998 by the University of Virginia Darden School Foundation, Charlottesville, VA. All rights reserved.

That year, an advisory group was established to move forward with the commitments made in the new policy. The Foods Executive created the Foods Environmental Implementation Group (FEIG) to explore Unilever's role in sustainable development. Vis was appointed technical secretary of the group. The FEIG immediately began working to put into action the 1995 Foods Environmental Policy.

Implementing the policy presented several challenges to the FEIG. Foremost, there was a lack of understanding of what sustainable development meant and, more importantly, what Unilever's role in sustainable development should be. Bringing clarity to this issue was the first order of business for the FEIG.[3]

Vis and FEIG proposed a project to define Unilever Food's potential role in sustainable development. It was unclear how the Foods portion of Unilever's business should become involved with sustainable development. The first step toward implementing the policy, they reasoned, was to understand how Unilever could contribute to sustainable development.

The Foods Executive, under the direction of Jan Peelen, authorized a study to investigate this topic. In doing so the Foods Executive made certain requirements. Specifically, they asked that the FEIG work to relate sustainable development to Unilever's activities in business terms. The FEIG was also expected to develop a set of sustainability indicators suitable for determining how sustainable Unilever Foods operations were.[4]

The FEIG had to develop a plan to proceed with the initiative. After considering performing an internal study, they decided to begin an external investigation of Unilever Foods and sustainable development. The goal was to make progress towards the commitments in the 1995 Foods Environmental Policy and to meet the requirements made by the Foods Executive. The FEIG developed drafts for two studies to explore how sustainable development related to the Foods business. As the secretary of FEIG, Vis commissioned both studies in the fall of 1995.

Independent consultants were obtained for the two studies. Specifically, the goals of the studies were 1) to perform a review of external perspectives, focusing on the views and the needs of key stakeholder groups in Unilever's Foods business; and 2) to perform a review of existing theories, concepts, and definitions of sustainable agriculture, food production, food processing, sustainability indicators, and an interpretation of these in economic terms.

The first task was contracted to SustainAbility, an environmental consulting company based in the UK. SustainAbility sought the opinions of different stakeholders around the world, of a definition of sustainable development that was appropriate for Unilever's Foods business. They obtained opinions from leading players and opinion formers among the consumer, farmer, agribusiness, food industry, retail, and environmental- and sustainable-development, nongovernment organization (NGO) communities. They aimed to review stakeholders' perceptions and to make practical recommendations for Unilever's Foods business to start implementing sustainability.[5]

The Institute for Applied Environmental Economics (TME) in the Netherlands performed the second study to determine a set of indicators for measuring sustainable development in Unilever Foods operations. The "project aimed to translate the concept of sustainability into a set of operational indicators for use in Unilever practice. The outcome of the project was to be such that it [could] be used by Unilever to assess 'fitness for sustainability' of its products."[6] The FEIG and the Foods Executive were hoping to develop a way to quantify the level of sustainability in Unilever Foods operations.

It was unclear what sustainable development meant for Unilever Foods; the primary challenge the FEIG faced was to develop a definition that was relevant and meaningful to the Unilever Foods business. Furthermore, with the TME report on indicators of sustainability, Vis and the other members of the FEIG hoped their obligations to the Foods Executive would be fulfilled. They awaited the conclusion of the reports to determine how Unilever should proceed with sustainable development.

FEBRUARY 1996: UNILEVER'S FIRST ENVIRONMENT REPORT

In 1996, under the direction of the Unilever Environment Group (UEG), Unilever published its first Environment Report. The report was designed to present the environmental initiatives, priorities and accomplishments of each of Unilever's Product Groups. The UEG had been working to publish Unilever's first Environment Report for over a year.

In the report, Unilever Foods presented findings from its life-cycle assessment (LCA) research. Unilever used LCA as a method of quantifying the environmental impact of their products over the entire product life cycle. LCAs provided Unilever a supposedly quantifiable, objective, and scientific method of determining the environmental impact of a product in the raw material production, manufacturing, and consumption phases of its life. The intent was to use LCAs to identify opportunities to lessen Unilever Foods's environmental impact and to help guide their research and development efforts.[7]

The Foods section of the report focused on how LCAs were helping the Foods Executive prioritize initiatives and identify areas where improvements were most needed. In the report they provided an example LCA for margarine (see Appendix A for the margarine LCA).

The margarine life cycle had been broken into the four stages: raw material acquisition, manufacture, distribution, and use/disposal. At each stage environmental impacts from six sources are presented: use of natural resources, energy use, emissions to land, emissions to air, emissions to water, and solid waste. As the margarine LCA shows, Unilever found that the major environmental impacts occur during the raw materials acquisition stage of its life cycle. For margarine and many other Foods products the majority of the environmental impact was not occurring in the manufacturing, distribution and use/disposal stages of the life cycle.

Unilever Foods published the following statements that reflected the work Vis and the FEIG were doing to define sustainable development for Foods, and made loose commitments for the future direction of their initiatives:

> We are now exploring the implications of "sustainability" in a way that is both meaningful to our business and acceptable to our stakeholders. Since agriculture products form the bulk of our raw materials, the development of sustainable agricultural practices is particularly important.[8]

The LCA method helped Unilever Foods recognize that the largest environmental impact from their operations occurred during raw material acquisition. The statement above, taken from the 1996 Environment Report, indicates that reducing the impact from this stage in the product life-cycle was particularly important to Unilever Foods. Furthermore, as the report states, sustainable agriculture was understood as a means of decreasing environmental impact.

The statement made explicit the importance of sustainable agriculture, a conclusion that was also emerging from the SustainAbility report on stakeholders' opinions of sustainable development in Unilever Foods. This reflected the type of business Unilever Foods was. The majority of their raw materials came from agricultural produce, and as the LCA indicated, this was where the largest impact on the environment occurred.

Unilever had known this for some time and had developed agricultural best practice principles that addressed some of the environmental impacts of its operations. Unilever defined agricultural best practice for contract farmers who produced the raw materials for Unilever Foods. Unilever experts would choose crop varieties, and offer expert advice on fertilizing, irrigation, soil preparation, harvesting, and other issues. This process had allowed Unilever to influence agricultural operations, develop relationships with farmers, and reduce environmental impact. In some cases, Unilever had worked with farmers for nearly 20 years to develop agricultural best practice guidelines.

SEPTEMBER 1996: UNILEVER REORGANIZES, VIS GETS MOVED

While Vis and the FEIG were involved with the two studies to define sustainable development for Unilever Foods, Unilever was undergoing a major reorganization of its senior management. As a result of the reorganization, Unilever's worldwide operations were divided into two categories: Foods, and Home and Personal Care (HPC). Additionally, a new seven-member Executive Committee was formed. Sitting on this Committee were the two Unilever chairmen, category directors (one for Foods, one for HPC), a science and technology director, finance director, and personnel director. See Appendix B for a diagram of Unilever's organization after these changes.

The Foods Executive was replaced by the Foods Category. Jan Peelen was moved to the position of personnel director on the Unilever Executive Committee. Lex Kemner became the Foods Category director, assuming the responsibilities of the former chairman of the Foods Executive.

As a result of the reorganization, Vis and the other members of the Foods Executive Quality Assurance Group were moved to the Safety and Environmental Assurance Center (SEAC). SEAC was a central Unilever research organization comprised of over 300 employees working in five research facilities. SEAC was Unilever's central group of experts on safety and environment. SEAC supported Unilever Categories (Foods and HPC) and Business Groups by maintaining the skill base in terms of ensuring safety of products, employees and operations.

As part of SEAC, Vis essentially became an internal Unilever consultant, making sure Unilever management, employees, and operating companies could cope with health, safety, and environmental quality matters within the company. Mainly, he would concentrate on providing scientific support for the development and implementation of new environmental initiatives and policies in the areas of toxicology and human safety, LCAs, environmental management systems, and raw material and product quality.[9] His function as a member of SEAC was to provide support to many levels of management and operations within Unilever.

Vis's role changed slightly when he moved to SEAC. Since this position required him to support the implementation of new systems and initiatives, he would find it much more difficult to be involved in developing strategy. Investigating new environmental policies was not part of his new job description.

Upon reorganization the FEIG became the Foods Environment Group Europe (FEGE). The function remained unchanged: dealing with the implementation of the environmental policy and looking after long-term implications of the Unilever environmental policy for the Foods part of the business. Vis remained secretary of this group after he was moved to SEAC. The FEGE reported to Lex Kemner, the Foods Category director.

When Vis joined SEAC in 1996, he met Hans Broekhoff, SEAC deputy head of the Environment.[10] Broekhoff shared many of Vis's opinions about the potential role for sustainable development in Unilever and was also very passionate about the environmental responsibilities the company faced. Broekhoff had recently left his position as director of Detergents Research with HPC (the non-Foods half of Unilever). HPC did not have a focused sustainable development effort, so Broekhoff soon joined the FEGE (formerly FEIG) project on their behalf. He worked closely with TME on the development of sustainability indicators. The TME study soon became an initiative involving Unilever Foods and HPC operations around the world.[11] What had begun as an investigation of sustainable development for Unilever Foods had grown to a study of Unilever's worldwide operations.

The reorganization had company-wide implications. When the new seven-member Executive Committee took over in October of 1996, an internal initiative called "Shaping for Outstanding Performance" was adopted. Its purpose was to communicate the responsibilities and obligations Unilever decision-makers could expect under the new organization. It described the reorganization in terms of how it would affect Unilever's operations and the company goals. As part of this initiative, the new Executive Committee developed a mission statement that defined Unilever's highest-level strategy and objectives. The Executive Committee's main responsibility was to fulfill the obligations set forth in the document called "Unilever's Corporate Purpose." Furthermore, Unilever operations and initiatives at all levels of the company would be expected to reflect the ideology of the Corporate Purpose:

> Our purpose in Unilever is to meet the everyday needs of people everywhere—to anticipate the aspirations of our consumers and customers and to respond creatively and competitively with branded products and services that raise the quality of life.
>
> Our deep roots in local cultures and markets around the world are our unparalleled inheritance and the foundation for our future growth. We will bring our wealth of knowledge and international expertise to the service of local consumers—a truly multi-local multinational.
>
> Our long-term success requires a total commitment to exceptional standards of performance and productivity, to working together effectively, and to a willingness to embrace new ideas and learn continuously.
>
> We believe that to succeed requires the highest standards of corporate behavior towards our employees, consumers and the societies and world in which we live.
>
> This is Unilever's road to sustainable, profitable growth for our business and long-term value creation for our shareholders and employees. [12]

The sustainable development work being done by the FEGE would ultimately have to support the tenets of the newly-adopted Corporate Purpose. Although it was not immediately clear how sustainable development would help Unilever fulfill its new obligations, Vis and Broekhoff believed there was a potential connection, and they began to discuss the possibilities. In their minds, sustainable development had a place in Unilever's operations and company strategy. However, the challenges for Unilever would not be entirely clear until the two reports were concluded. Unilever Foods would require a definition of sustainable development that was not only meaningful to their everyday business but also supported the new Corporate Purpose.

FEBRUARY 1997: THE STUDIES ARE COMPLETE

In early 1997, the studies commissioned in 1995 were completed and the reports were submitted to Unilever. Both studies were successful in fulfilling their objectives. SustainAbility was able to interview stakeholders, mainly in Europe and North America, about the perceived role of sustainable development in Unilever Foods business. Additionally, through a review of literature, TME developed a set of sustainability indicators for Unilever.

Stakeholders' Perspectives

The study by SustainAbility revealed that stakeholders around the world viewed sustainable agriculture as central to the discussion of sustainable development in Unilever Foods. The focus of the report centered more on the raw material production and supply than on the food processing operations at Unilever Foods. Stakeholders understood sustainable agriculture to be a subset of sustainable development. The perception was that sustainable agriculture required concern for not only the physical aspects of agriculture but also for the social and economic aspects. Similar to definitions of sustainable development that describe social, economic, and environmental responsibilities, the report by SustainAbility indicated that stakeholders believed sustainable development in Unilever Foods embodied the same concerns.

Of the three issues central to sustainable development—social, physical, and economic—the discussion in the report tended to concentrate on the physical and social aspects of sustainable agriculture. Stakeholders clearly identified the need for Unilever Foods to address the environmental impacts of agriculture by examining the potential harm caused by intensive, chemical-based farming. Furthermore, the social dimensions of sustainable agriculture were a top concern. The preservation of farming and rural communities was fingered, by stakeholders, as a dominant issue in sustainable agriculture.[13]

The report did not include a discussion of how Unilever Foods should address the economic aspects of sustainable development or sustainable agriculture. It was reported that sustainability in Unilever Foods needed to account for economic issues; however, there was no indication of the relationship between sustainability and Unilever Foods' economic or business obligations.

Fitness for Sustainability

The report by TME aimed to "translate the concept of sustainability into a set of operational indicators for use in Unilever practice."[14] The objective was to develop a set of indicators for use in Unilever's Foods and HPC. The indicators were designed to cover a range of Unilever products and to be relevant to a variety of definitions of sustainable development. The delivered report covered Unilever's worldwide operations.

TME was able to generate, from a review of literature, a list of over 200 indicators of sustainability. In the final report, however, this list was reduced to contain only fifteen measurable sustainability indicators.

Similar to the report on stakeholders' perspectives, the TME report identified three dimensions of sustainability: social, economic, and environmental. In each area, TME had identified indicators that could be used to measure Unilever's level of sustainability. The list of fifteen indicators consisted of two relating to economics, six relating to social aspects, and seven with environmental relevance. Table 1 contains the indicators reported by TME.

Table 1   Indicators of Sustainability

Indicator	Comment
Economics	
1 Total life-cycle value to total life-cycle cost	Total life-cycle costs includes cost to natural systems currently unaccounted for.
2 Ratio of local investments to local profit	This encompasses investment in distribution systems and infrastructure.
Social	
3 Compliance with legislation or internal guidelines	Understood through auditing
4 Number of consultations with stakeholders	Frequency of consultations is in itself a measure for meaningfulness of relationship.
5 Hours vocational training to working hours	
6 Frequency of product safety incidents	Incident management
7 Working hours lost due to incidents	Working hours lost due to occupation-related illnesses
8 Periodic assessment of product functionality in a regional setting	Foods: contribution to dietary requirements HPC: contribution to hygiene and well-being
Nature	
9 Material use per functional unit of product	
10 Product miles	Distance product travels to consumer
11 Energy use per functional unit of product	
12 Water use per functional unit of product	
13 Percentage supplies from preferred suppliers	Supplier rating on basis of environmental considerations
14 Foods: amount of (H)CFC consumption per unit of product	
15 HPC: amount of Volatile Organics per functional unit of product	Already determined by life-cycle assessments

Vis and Broekhoff spent many hours reviewing the reports and discussing the information contained within. The studies focused much more on sustainable agriculture than on the general topic of sustainable development in Unilever Foods. This was a result of the worldwide opinion, by stakeholders, that sustainable agriculture represented the biggest challenge and obligation for Unilever's multinational Foods business. Since Broekhoff had joined the initiative, the project had grown to include all Unilever operations. Therefore, the original task of investigating sustainable development specifically for Unilever Foods had changed somewhat. Broekhoff and Vis needed to reach some conclusion about the role of sustainable development in all of Unilever's business, not just Foods.

Neither Vis nor Broekhoff felt that a discussion specific to sustainable agriculture would be successful without a more general understanding of what sustainable development meant for all of Unilever. It would be useful, they believed, to first develop an understanding of the relationship between sustainable development and Unilever's mission and responsibilities. Once they had articulated how Unilever could view sustainable development, they hoped to propose the first steps Unilever Foods could take towards sustainability.

Although the two studies provided necessary information, they lacked simple economic concepts like shareholder value and value creation. Without supplementation, Vis saw them as having limited value to Unilever business. Broekhoff and Vis spent the spring and summer of 1997 translating the wealth of information in the studies into terms that were meaningful to Unilever's everyday activities.

Their goal was to link sustainable development to Unilever's business obligations identified in the recently adopted Corporate Purpose.[15] In doing this, the major question that Vis and Broekhoff faced, and one that neither study answered, was whether or not the pursuit of sustainability would support Unilever's business obligations. If sustainable development were to be adopted as a corporate initiative—as Vis and Broekhoff hoped it would—they would have to articulate a vision that sustainability supported Unilever's overall business mission. It was clear that Unilever executives would not back sustainable development without a proper explanation of how it supported their objectives.

Convinced that sustainable development had an important role in Unilever's operations, Vis and Broekhoff began to seek corporate endorsement to make it a Unilever strategic goal. Furthermore, since the project had originated as an investigation of sustainable development for Unilever Foods, Vis felt that it was necessary to address this. In addition to his work with Broekhoff, Vis began shaping a proposal specifically for Unilever Foods. In it he planned to describe how Unilever Foods could proceed with sustainable development.

Notes

1. Unless otherwise noted, information in this case was taken from correspondence and interviews with Unilever employees from the Unilever Head Office in Rotterdam, the Netherlands, between October, 1997, and November, 1998.
2. Information in this section was taken from: Unilever Foods Environmental Policy, the Foods Executive Committee, Rotterdam, May 1995.

3. Information in this section is from correspondence between the authors and Jan-Kees Vis, March 4, 1998.

4. Information in this section was taken from a discussion with Jan-Kees Vis at Unilever Head Office, Rotterdam, the Netherlands, July 20, 1998.

5. Dr. Vernon Jennings, "Sustainable Agriculture and Food: A Summary of Stakeholder Perspectives," SustainAbility, February 12, 1997 (confidential).

6. J. Krozer and K. E. H. Maa, "Fitness for Sustainability," Institute for Applied Environmental Economics (TME), February 1997.

7. "Unilever Environmental Report 1996: Our Worldwide Approach."

8. Ibid.

9. Ibid.

10. Information in this section is from correspondence between the authors and Jan-Kees Vis, June 11, 1998.

11. Jan-Kees Vis, "Sustainable Development and Unilever: Putting the Corporate Purpose into Action" (unpublished).

12. Information in this section was taken from: Unilever Environment Group, "Environmental Report 1998: Making progress," Unilever corporate relations department, April 1998.

13. Jennings.

14. Krozer and Maa.

15. Vis.

APPENDIX A
MARGARINE LIFE-CYCLE ASSESSMENT (1996)

The following LCA was taken from the Unilever 1996 Environment Report.[1] It shows the environmental impacts from margarine throughout its life cycle. Unilever used LCAs to understand and manage the environmental impacts of their products.

Margarine Life Cycle. The chart shows the important stages in the life cycle of a table margarine and indicates the relative inputs of energy required at each stage and the type of emissions resulting.

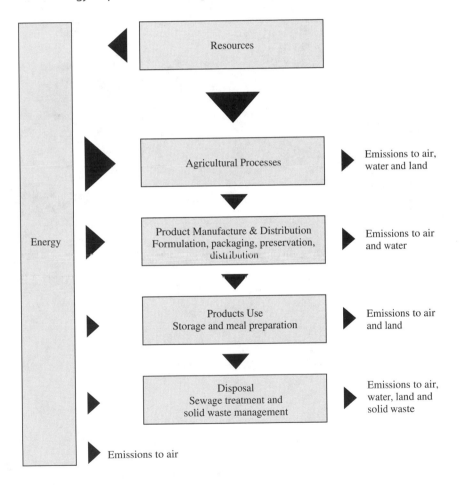

1. Diagrams on this page taken from "Environment Report: Our Worldwide Approach," Unilever Environment Group, April 1996, 17.

APPENDIX A (Continued)

Margarine Relative Impacts. The table indicates the relative size and type of environmental impact arising at each stage in the life cycle of a table margarine.

Life Cycle Stages Environmental Impact	Raw Materials	Manufacture	Distribution	Use/Disposal
Use of Natural Resources	■	□	□	□
Energy Use	■■■	■	■	□
Emissions to Land	■■■	□	□	■
Emissions to Air	■■	■	■	■
Emissions to Water	■	■	□	■
Solid Waste	□	■	□	■■

□   Negligible
■   Small relative impact
■■   Medium relative impact
■■■ Large relative impact

APPENDIX B
UNILEVER ORGANIZATIONAL STRUCTURE
AFTER COMPANY REORGANIZATION (1996)

This diagram shows the general management chain existing for Unilever Foods after the 1996 reorganization.

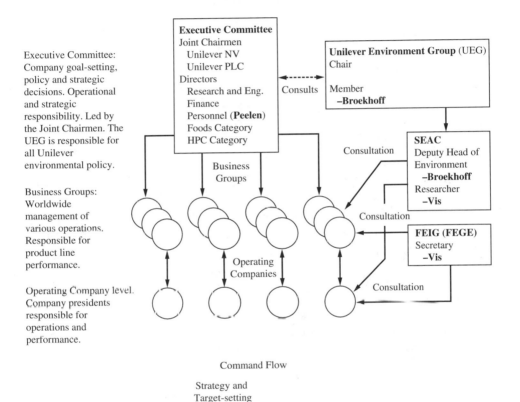

Executive Committee: Company goal-setting, policy and strategic decisions. Operational and strategic responsibility. Led by the Joint Chairmen. The UEG is responsible for all Unilever environmental policy.

Business Groups: Worldwide management of various operations. Responsible for product line performance.

Operating Company level. Company presidents responsible for operations and performance.

Executive Committee
Joint Chairmen
   Unilever NV
   Unilever PLC
Directors
   Research and Eng.
   Finance
   Personnel (**Peelen**)
   Foods Category
   HPC Category

Consults

Unilever Environment Group (UEG)
Chair

Member
   –Broekhoff

Business Groups

SEAC
Deputy Head of Environment
   –Broekhoff
Researcher
   –Vis

Consultation

Consultation

FEIG (FEGE)
Secretary
   –Vis

Operating Companies

Consultation

Command Flow

Strategy and Target-setting

Reporting

21

UNILEVER (C)

In 1997, Jan-Kees Vis and Hans Broekhoff were working to translate sustainable development into terms that related to Unilever's business. Their goal was to have sustainable development adopted, by Unilever management, as a strategic, company-wide initiative. Broekhoff and Vis wanted to start the discussion of sustainable development at the Unilever Environment Group (UEG) level. The UEG was Unilever's leading body on environmental issues—their main purpose was to develop and review corporate environmental policies, strategies and targets. The UEG reported directly to the Unilever Executive Committee. UEG support was needed in order to attain Unilever corporate commitment and have sustainability secured as a strategic goal company-wide.[1]

The challenge for Vis and Broekhoff was to develop a definition of sustainable development that was meaningful to Unilever's business activities. Two studies, which aimed to define sustainable development for Unilever and develop measurable indica-

This case was written by Myles Standish, graduate student, Systems Engineering and Division of Technology, Culture, and Communication at the University of Virginia, under the direction of Michael E. Gorman and Patricia H. Werhane. Partial support for this project was supplied by grants from the Ethics and Values in Science program of the National Science Foundation (SBR-9319983), the Batten Center for Entrepreneurial Leadership at the Darden School, University of Virginia, and the Geraldine R. Dodge Foundation. The conclusions are the responsibilities of the authors, and do not reflect the views of the foundations. This was written as a basis for class discussion rather than to illustrate effective or ineffective handling of an administrative situation. Copyright © 1998 by the University of Virginia Darden School Foundation, Charlottesville, VA. All rights reserved.

tors of sustainability, had failed to identify a link between Unilever's general business interests and sustainable development. It was not clear how, or if, sustainable development would help Unilever management achieve its goals of profit generation and long-term growth of the company.

Broekhoff and Vis wanted to write a paper on which the UEG could base a discussion of sustainable development as a potential corporate environmental initiative.[2] They wrote a document titled, "Sustainable Development and Unilever: Putting the Corporate Purpose into Action." In it they aimed to create a link between sustainable development and Unilever's Corporate Purpose (see Unilever (B) for the Corporate Purpose).

DEFINING SUSTAINABILITY IN TERMS OF UNILEVER'S BUSINESS

External studies performed for the company revealed that sustainable development in Unilever would require an understanding of the importance of the social, environmental and ecological concerns central to most definitions of the term. However, without linking these three dimensions to the preservation and growth of financial assets, sustainable development did not seem to support the overall direction and guidelines of behavior established in the Unilever Corporate Purpose. The decision-makers in Unilever would certainly want to understand the motivation for pursuing sustainable development. How would Unilever shareholders realize value from such an initiative? Unilever, after all, had operated as a profitable and successful business for nearly a hundred years. Why change?

Vis and Broekhoff attempted to describe sustainability as being central to Unilever's business operations. Their paper contained the following argument:

> So how do we start to tap the large reservoir of value locked up in sustainable development and translate it into shareholder value? One practical approach extends the idea of the stewardship of company assets from the traditional focus on financial assets to stewardship of the ecological and social assets, which Unilever employs to generate value in the business. The "Triple Bottom Line" principle addresses these three categories of assets as crucial to the value of the Company. It shows us how, by preserving and growing the value of all three types of asset, we can embed sustainable development throughout Unilever's operations and use it to give life to the Corporate Purpose.

The value of Unilever to those invested in the company, they reasoned, depended on certain assets over which Unilever had control. In most traditional frameworks, financial assets were considered to hold all the value in a company. However, most definitions of sustainability include the concept of social, environmental *and* financial assets. Vis and Broekhoff sought to develop a link between growth of all three assets and the value of Unilever.

THE "TRIPLE BOTTOM LINE"

The "Triple Bottom Line" was a framework that Broekhoff and Vis used to illustrate their belief that Unilever's business depended on financial (economic), ecological (environmental) and societal (human) assets. Using this framework, they planned to explain how each asset impacted Unilever's business, and why it was necessary for Unilever to change company operations to preserve these assets. To fulfill the corporate obligation of providing "sustainable, profitable growth for our business and long-term value creation for our shareholders and employees," Vis and Broekhoff argued that the value of Unilever would have to grow over the long term. Furthermore,

> Each type of asset represents a source of value to the company and its shareholders. The sustained development of each of these sources of value ensures that the overall value accruing to shareholders is built up sustainably over the long term. This is in essence the significance of sustainable development to a company that aims at sustainable profit growth and long-term value creation for its shareholders and employees.

They next had to describe Unilever's dependence on these assets and how stewardship of the assets could be assessed in terms of value creation for Unilever. The basic challenge was to describe why Unilever's long-term profitability depended on more than just financial assets, and then to communicate a strategy for creating value through increasing the worth of these assets. Vis provided the following summary of the fundamental argument he and Broekhoff presented in the paper:

> [The paper] builds around the concept of value creation, and defines Sustainable Development as any development that increases capital: be it financial, or social, or environmental. This is basically picking up on the idea that a society (or a business or an individual) cannot live off its capital, but should live off the interest of the capital while preferably increasing it. This allows us to align our way of valuing the business (on the basis of the potential for creating Total Business Return, which should be aligned with Total Shareholder Return) with our view on sustainable development.[3]

It was still not clear what each category of assets embodied. In the paper they sought to make explicit the relationship between each type of asset and Unilever's business performance. Furthermore, they wished to discuss the level of control and influence Unilever had over these assets.

STEWARDSHIP OF FINANCIAL, SOCIAL AND ECOLOGICAL ASSETS

In their paper, Broekhoff and Vis discussed Unilever's stewardship responsibility for: a range of financial assets which are mostly internal to the company; a range of physical, or ecological, assets mostly external to the company; and, a range of human resource, or social, assets partly internal and partly external to the company. Each asset represented a source of value for Unilever, they reasoned. Sustainable profit growth in Unilever implied sustained growth of each source of value to the company.

Through the summer of 1997, Vis and Broekhoff struggled to conceptualize and communicate the concepts of ecological and social assets. The paper they were writing had to define what these assets were, and it had to describe how they contributed to shareholder value and profit generation. Financial assets alone were not enough to create Unilever products. Along the entire life cycle of its goods, Unilever relied on natural resources to ensure the availability of raw materials, and human resources to shape the raw materials into Unilever products.

Financial Assets

The role of financial assets in Unilever's operations was very well understood. Quarterly earnings, earnings per share, stock prices, shareholder dividends, total sales, and many other indicators, were traditional measures of a company's financial performance. Shareholder value meant a steady, long-term cash return on financial assets and accounting for discounted costs of capital. Growing shareholder value required sustained profit growth over the long term, not just the short term. Hence, preserving and growing financial assets was not a foreign concept to Unilever business leaders—it was their primary task.

Environmental Assets

In 1997 the Unilever External Environmental Advisory Group was established to provide independent views and to advise Unilever on emerging and complex environmental issues. The group had four members that met with the UEG twice a year, and individually with senior management, to discuss Unilever's relationship with the environment.[4] That year, with the input of the Unilever External Environmental Advisory Group, it was determined that Unilever depended most heavily on three resources: agricultural produce, fish, and water. Fish and agricultural products were required for Unilever Food's products, and water was necessary for both Unilever Food's and Unilever Home and Personal Care (HPC) products. Production, distribution, and use of Unilever products were extremely dependent on all three assets.

The fact that senior-level management understood that these three resources were extremely valuable to Unilever helped Broekhoff and Vis explain the value of environmental assets to Unilever operations. They used agriculture and clean water as examples to illustrate the concept that environmental assets are a source of value.

They believed Unilever could monitor and control the value of environmental assets just as they did with their financial assets. The concept was to control all inputs that add cost, and to seek continuous improvement in the productivity of the asset in the short-, medium-, and long-term.

In agriculture, the natural resource upon which Unilever Foods most heavily relied was mainly healthy, fertile and productive soil. Long term, sustainable business operations required soil that was capable of producing the raw materials Unilever products required (a variety of vegetables, tea, oils and fats, fruits, etc). A sustainable Foods business, they came to believe, relied on sustaining the productivity of the land Unilever used to grow agricultural raw materials. In this way, the land and soil could be viewed as ecological assets; preserving and growing their value permitted the sustained growth of shareholder value. The summary from the paper states:

> The value of a piece of land is simply represented by the cash flow generated by its produce over the years to come, discounted for the cost of capital. Sustainable development requires us to assure that on the whole the value of agricultural land is preserved or increased over the years. The productivity of the land should be maintained without systematic increases in input costs in terms of labor, energy, fertilizers or pesticides and without systematic, persistent damages to the surrounding ecosystem.

Measures aimed at reducing inputs such as

- Irrigation volumes per ton of net produce,
- Fertilizer input per ton of net produce,
- Pesticide and herbicide input per ton of net produce,
- Fossil fuel consumption per ton of net produce,

as well as maintaining mean productivity and quality, could make a significant contribution to value growth of our ecological assets. Monitoring and bench marking the suppliers of agricultural raw materials "at the cradle" on these five parameters, resulting in target setting for improvement to mutual benefit, would be a practical way forward and a significant contribution towards sustainable development.

In the case of water, it had been agreed that Unilever was utterly dependent on the availability of clean, potable water in all of its markets. Without ample amounts of clean water, consumers would be unable to use many of Unilever's products. Furthermore, producing Unilever products required large amounts of water along the entire chain. Unilever's reliance on clean water was understood throughout the company, partly as a result of the work done earlier that year by the Unilever External Environmental Advisory Group. However, Vis and Broekhoff aimed to discuss how Unilever could approach valuation of water.

In the paper, they argued that any detrimental input into the water system essentially threatens the supply of clean, potable water, and increases the costs of purification. This included the output of pollutants from Unilever operations into the water system. Additionally, using more water than was available through natural production stood to increase the amount of purification necessary. Therefore, limiting the amount of water used, and reducing the amount of harmful outputs into the water system were described as methods of value preservation.

Social Assets

The role of social and human assets in Unilever's business was more abstract than that of ecological assets. Did Unilever truly depend on social and human assets? Literature on sustainable development and a study on stakeholders' opinions identified social factors as a fundamental element of sustainability in Unilever's operations. It was employees, after all, that grew the raw materials, processed the goods and sold the Unilever products. Furthermore, it was members of society that purchased Unilever goods. Unilever's social assets could be seen as its employees and customers. Without employees and their knowledge, Unilever products could not be produced. And without customers that were willing and capable of buying Unilever products, there would be no business to sustain.

In terms of Unilever employees,

As the professional development of each person progresses, his or her job market value will increase. A sound corporate reputation with respect to opportunities for personal development will in turn make the company more attractive for recruitment. It is recommended that Unilever monitor the development of the job market value. An indirect but valuable measure of company stewardship of personal development is the number of hours of vocational training. Other measures relate to the preservation of physical health and well being rather than earning potential.

Sustainable development extends the human resources stewardship concept in principle to those benefiting from or affected by the total supply chain of products marketed by the company.

They also discussed the importance of viable markets to Unilever's continued success. They noted that Unilever should measure and monitor its contribution to the development of the economic viability of the markets in which it operates.

VIS AND BROEKHOFF MAKE A PROPOSAL

In 1997, Jeroen Bordewijk became the Senior Vice President of Unilever's Manufacturing and Supply Chain Technology division (SVP MAST). The MAST division is responsible for generating competitive advantage in the Foods supply chain. This is done by developing and capitalizing on supply chain opportunities in the areas of manufacturing, sourcing, and delivery. As the SVP MAST, Bordewijk assumed direct responsibility for generating advantage in all supply chains in Unilever's Foods business.

Shortly after he assumed his new position, Bordewijk was offered a seat on the UEG. At one of his first meetings with the UEG, it was decided that he would be placed in charge of the FEIG project.[5] Bordewijk soon became aware of the work that Vis, Broekhoff and others had been doing over the past two years. In September of 1997, Bordewijk presented the Broekhoff/Vis paper to the UEG and to Lex Kemner, the Foods Category Director.

Proposing Sustainable Development as a Unilever Strategic Initiative

The paper Broekhoff and Vis wrote sought endorsement for sustainable development as a strategic Unilever goal. In it, Vis and Broekhoff described the value of the triple bottom line to Unilever's continued business performance. They hoped the paper successfully linked sustainable development to the Corporate Purpose.

They were proposing large-scale changes to a business that had operated successfully and profitably for nearly a hundred years. Ultimately, they had suggested adoption of a new strategic initiative by the highest level of decision-makers in Unilever.

In their paper, Broekhoff and Vis proposed Unilever begin to address sustainable development through specific, practical initiatives in agriculture, marine fisheries and water. A summary of the proposal taken from the paper follows:

Overall, our strategies for sustainable development should address each issue from three different perspectives where each perspective operates on a different time scale. We must also be prepared to address these questions from a position of openness, realism and pragmatism while avoiding the trap of problem denial:

1. Clean up product and process emissions, introduce management systems:
   current status—in progress
   time-scale—ongoing

2. Design and implementation of clean processes and much cleaner and less resource intensive products, on the basis of rational environmental product strategies:
   current status—partly in place
   time-scale —to be emphasized over the next five years

3. Radical redesign of systems and services, so as deliver outstanding consumer benefits within the limits of global carrying capacity; development of the necessary business restructuring scenarios.
   current status—strategic investments in intellectual capital are underway.
   time-scale—25 years, but starting now: exploration of opportunities and prospects for business adaptations.

Notes

1. Unless otherwise noted, information in this case was taken from correspondence and interviews with Unilever employees from the Unilever Head Office in Rotterdam, the Netherlands, between October, 1997, and November, 1998; and from Hans Broekhoff and Jan-Kees Vis, "Sustainable Development and Unilever: Putting the Corporate Purpose into Action" (unpublished).
2. Information in this section taken from correspondence between the authors and Jan-Kees Vis, dated June 11, 1998.
3. Information in this section taken from correspondence between the authors and Jan-Kees Vis, dated February 27, 1998.
4. Unilever Environment Group, "Unilever Environmental Report 1998: Making Progress," Unilever Corporate Relations Office, April 1998.
5. From an interview with Jeroen Bordewijk, at Unilever Head Office, Rotterdam, the Netherlands, on July 22, 1998.

22

UNILEVER (D)

INTRODUCTION

In 1995, the Foods Environmental Implementation Group (FEI) had set out to implement a recently adopted policy calling for an investigation of sustainable development
for Unilever Foods. In the policy was a commitment to "aim for sustainable develop
ment." However, there was no agreed-upon definition of sustainable development, and
certainly no concrete understanding of what it meant for Unilever's Foods business.[1]

The FEIG began their investigation of sustainable development at Unilever Foods
by commissioning two studies on the topic. External consultants were obtained for the
two studies. Specifically, the goals of the studies were 1) to perform a review of external perspectives, focusing on the views and the needs of key stakeholder groups in
Unilever's Foods business; and, 2) to perform a review of existing theories, concepts,

This case was written by Myles Standish, graduate student, Systems Engineering and Division of
Technology, Culture, and Communication at the University of Virginia, under the direction of
Michael E. Gorman and Patricia H. Werhane. Partial support for this project was supplied by
grants from the Ethics and Values in Science program of the National Science Foundation (SBR-
9319983), the Batten Center for Entrepreneurial Leadership at the Darden School, University of
Virginia, and the Geraldine R. Dodge Foundation. The conclusions are the responsibilities of the
authors, and do not reflect the views of the foundations. This was written as a basis for class discussion rather than to illustrate effective or ineffective handling of an administrative situation.
Copyright © 1998 by the University of Virginia Darden School Foundation, Charlottesville, VA.
All rights reserved.

and definitions of sustainable agriculture and food production and processing, and sustainability indicators, and an interpretation of these in economic terms. A company called SustainAbility was contracted to perform the first study, and Applied Environmental Economics (TME) performed the second study.

What started as a general investigation of sustainable development for Unilever Foods had turned more towards a debate over sustainable agriculture. According to the study performed by SustainAbility, stakeholders held the opinion that agriculture posed the largest challenge to sustainable development for Unilever Foods. Also evidence from Unilever's life cycle analysis (LCA) work indicated agriculture was a major source of dependency and environmental impact for Unilever Foods.

In the spring of 1997, Jan-Kees Vis and Hans Broekhoff were engaged in work to promote sustainable development at Unilever. Their work progressed along two separate, yet related, paths. Together they worked on a document to discuss the role of sustainable development in increasing Unilever's shareholder value. Their objective was to argue that continued growth of value in Unilever's business would benefit from sustainable development (see Unilever (C) for more information).

Vis decided to write a paper specific to sustainable agriculture. His goal was to use the report by SustainAbility as a basis for suggesting initiatives Unilever Foods could implement in its agricultural operations. There was considerable debate over the future of agriculture, the definition of sustainable agriculture, and how Unilever should prepare for an uncertain future in the agriculture business. As the study revealed, there were a variety of differing opinions of the role of technology, the use of biotechnology and the importance of social factors in farming.

Vis began to shape a definition of sustainable agriculture that he felt would best benefit Unilever in the years to come. He aimed to propose specific initiatives to implement a new form of agriculture in the coming year.

Stakeholders' Opinions on the Future of Agriculture

Stakeholders around the world have very different opinions about the future of agriculture. As a result, there are different perceptions about how Unilever Foods should meet the future challenges it will face in agriculture. The range of viewpoints was reflected in the SustainAbility study performed for Unilever Foods. Jules Pretty,[2] an author of several books on sustainable agriculture, provided input to the SustainAbility study. He provided useful descriptions of the popular opinions on the future of agriculture, which were included in the report submitted to Vis:

Environmental Pessimists

The *environmental pessimists* believe that there are limits to the growth the earth can sustain. Furthermore, they contend that these limits are being approached and have already been met in some areas.[3] As populations grow rapidly, the world will be met with falling agricultural yields. The growth of ecological output, they argue, is constrained by factors such as deforestation, loss of topsoil, overuse of pesticides and fertilizers, and increased consumption of livestock products. Technology will not be capable of meeting the ecological demands of a growing world population. Therefore, population control is the major priority of environmental pessimists. Lester Brown of the Worldwatch Institute in Washington represents this point of view: "I don't see any prospect of the world's fishermen and farmers being able to keep up with the growth in world population."[4]

Business-as-Usual Optimists

This is a mainly market-driven viewpoint. The *business-as-usual optimists* believe that supply will always meet increasing demand. Thus, they expect a growth in world food production.[5] The fact that food prices are falling is an indication that there is no lack in demand. For example, the price of most commodities has fallen by over 50% in the last decade. Additionally, research in biotechnology and plant technology will continue to boost food production in industrialized countries. They foresee a growth in exports of foods from industrialized countries to underdeveloped parts of the world. If food production is left to respond to market conditions, they argue, world food demand will be met. There is limited use in implementing lower yield technologies. Referring to arable farming in East Anglia, Sir Derek Barber famously put it this way in the 1991 Royal Agricultural Society of England study on agriculture and the environment: "Why clutter up such landscapes with thin green threads of new hedges? Why not let this type of highly efficient grain country get on with its job of producing a tonne of wheat at the very lowest cost?"[6]

Industrialized-World-to-the-Rescue

The *industrialized world to the rescue* viewpoint is that the poorer countries will never be able to meet their own food production demands. These demands will be met by increased production in industrialized countries.[7] Proponents of this viewpoint believe that the key to saving wildlife and ecosystems is through the implementation of highly mechanized and technological agricultural techniques that require less land than low-input farming. Smaller farmers will go out of business as larger, high-output operations become very efficient. This, they argue, will relieve pressures on the environment by allowing massive food production on less land. The threats of using large amounts of pesticides, fertilizers, and chemicals are minor when compared to the danger of committing large amounts of land to low-output agriculture. One of the best known advocates of these techniques is Dennis Avery of The Hudson Institute, and author of *Saving the Planet with Pesticides and Plastic*. In an edition of *Farmer's Weekly* the view was summarized: "The biggest threat to bio-diversity is the ploughing down of much of the world's remaining forests to produce low yielding crops and livestock."[8]

The New Modernists

The *new modernist* view is a combination of those already presented. They believe that through the use of modern technology, yield increases are possible on existing farmland in poorer nations.[9] Their argument is that farmers in the underdeveloped parts of the world are not using enough pesticides and fertilizers. By implementing more scientific approaches to agriculture, pressure will be kept off natural habitats. They fully support the high-input approach. This is exemplified by Norman Borlaug, Nobel laureate for his contribution to international agricultural development. In 1992, he said that agriculturalists "must not be duped into believing that future food requirements can be met through continuing reliance on . . . the new complicated and sophisticated 'low-input, low-output' technologies that are impractical for the farmers to adopt." In 1995, he then said, "Over the last decade, extremists in the environmentalist movement in the affluent nations have created consumer anxiety about the safety of food produced using agricultural chemicals."

Sustainable Intensifiers

The *sustainable intensifiers* contend that high productivity is possible with low-input techniques. This group does not support no-input farming; rather they feel that higher reliance on human ingenuity, and a lower reliance on chemical inputs, will increase yields and decrease damage to the environment.[10] This form of agriculture seeks to develop better pest, nutrient, soil, and water management technologies. Specific aims are waste reduction and an increase in the use of natural processes on farms to replace high levels of external inputs. They argue that this can result in high-yield farming that is less environmentally damaging and even restorative.

The debate over agriculture was characterized by these viewpoints. Stakeholders held very different opinions of the future of agriculture, depending on their affiliations. The opinions of large, chemical-based agribusinesses were different from those of non-governmental organizations (NGOs). Viewpoints also differed regionally.

Stakeholders Identify Issues and Define "Sustainable Agriculture"

A wide range of issues was raised in the report. The two major issues were:

1. Intensive, chemical-based farming
2. Preservation of farming and rural communities.

These issues were represented through the viewpoints discussed previously. At one extreme, the predominant view was that the future of agriculture would be one of high-technology; at the other extreme was support for the organic movement. These polar opinions were generally held by industrialists and NGOs, respectively.

Nearly all stakeholders agreed that meeting the food needs of between eight and ten billion people in the next century would be a central challenge. There was much less agreement on the methods of meeting this need. Again, the two ends of the debate were characterized by high-input technology-intense agriculture and organic approaches.

Despite the extreme differences in opinion regarding how Unilever should proceed with agriculture, stakeholders generally agreed that sustainable agriculture should aim for the goals listed in Table 1.

Sustainable agriculture is a subset of sustainable development, and therefore it must account for not only environmental issues, but also social and economic consider-

Table 1 Goals for Sustainable Agriculture[11,12]

1 Maximize the incorporation of natural processes such as nutrient recycling, nitrogen fixing, and pest-predator relationships

2 Minimize the use of external and nonrenewable inputs that damage the environment or harm the health of farmers or consumers

3 The full participation of farmers and rural communities in all processes of problem analysis, and technology development, adaptation, and extension

4 A more equitable access to productive resources and opportunities

5 The greater productive use of local knowledge, practices and resources

6 An increase in self-reliance among farmers and rural communities

7 An emphasis on building strong rural social organizations and dynamic rural economies

---

ations. Most stakeholders agreed that social issues, although the most difficult to address, were central to the debate.

Further complicating the discussion of sustainable agriculture was the fact that viewpoints differed regionally; Unilever operates in over 90 countries around the world. The agricultural and food production issues of most concern varied by region. Some of the major issues and viewpoints as identified by regional stakeholders were:

North America (United States mainly)

- Preservation of wilderness and the physical environment.
- Soil erosion.
- Maintaining the number of farms (not losing farms).
- Support of biotechnology as a useful component of sustainable agriculture. Stakeholders believe that the benefits are greater than the risks. Support at the consumer and government level.
- Support for the labeling of foodstuffs containing genetically modified organisms (GMOs).

Europe

- Maintaining biodiversity.
- Distribution of government food subsidies.
- Producing high-quality and enjoyable food products.
- Transportation issues.
- Fear of contaminated food (partially a result of "mad cow" disease).
- Labeling all foodstuffs containing GMOs to give consumers a choice.
- Skepticism over the consumer benefit of foodstuffs using GMOs.
- Food industry should be held responsible for problems with new technologies.

The Developing World

- Land tenure.
- Farmers' rights.
- Women's rights.
- Ownership of genetic resources and equitable distribution of profit derived from the commercial use of genes from these countries.
- Introduction of fat- and meat-rich diets.

The report by TME aimed to "translate the concept of sustainability into a set of operational indicators for use in Unilever practice."[13] The objective was to develop a set of indicators for use in Unilever's Foods and HPC Categories. The indicators were intended to cover a range of Unilever products and to be relevant to a variety of definitions of sustainable development. The delivered report covered Unilever's worldwide operations.

Similar to the report on stakeholders' perspectives, TME identified three dimensions of sustainability: social, economic, and environmental. Provided in the report were indicators that could be used to measure Unilever's level of sustainability. The list of fifteen indicators consisted of two relating to economics, six relating to social aspects, and seven with environmental relevance. Table 2 contains the fifteen indicators developed by TME.

Table 2   Sustainability Indicators

Economic
 1 Total life cycle value to total life cycle cost
 2 Ratio of local investments to local profit

Social
 3 Compliance with legislation or internal guidelines
 4 Number of consultations with stakeholders
 5 Hours vocational training to working hours
 6 Frequency of product safety incidents
 7 Working hours lost due to incidents
   Working hours lost due to occupation-related illnesses
 8 Periodic assessment of product functionality in a regional setting

Environmental
 9 Material use per functional unit of product
10 Product miles
11 Energy use per functional unit of product
12 Water use per functional unit of product
13 Percentage supplies from preferred suppliers
14 Foods: amount of (H)CFC consumption per unit of product
15 HPC: amount of volatile organics per functional unit of product

Internal and External Issues Affecting Agriculture

The discussion of sustainable agriculture for Unilever Foods was influenced by a range of issues internal and external to the company. As Vis shaped his proposal for new agricultural initiatives, he had to consider the relevance of issues such as biotechnology, consumer confidence, and supply chain management. Embedded in each issue were arguments for and against introduction of new agricultural policies. Addressing these issues was necessary to fully understand the implications of sustainable agriculture for Unilever. Following are three sections describing events that directly affected agriculture at Unilever.

UNILEVER SELLS OUT OF THE BIOTECH BUSINESS

In the 1990s Unilever began to sell companies that did not contribute to its core strengths. This was part of an effort within the company to concentrate on its core strengths. These core strengths, or core concentrations, were determined to be in product areas such as margarine, tea, ice cream, frozen foods, culinary products, yellow fats and a range of areas in the non-foods portion of the business. As part of this sell-off strategy, Unilever disposed of its specialty chemicals business in 1997. Other businesses that were not contributing to these core areas were candidates for disposal.

During the same time Vis was doing work with sustainable agriculture, Unilever executives were making strategic decisions relating to the company's biotechnology interests. Unilever owned Plant Breeding International (PBI), a British-based company that was a leader in the development of genetically modified strains of wheat and other cereal crops. PBI represented the large majority of Unilever's scientific plant knowledge, and their only commercial interest in biotechnology.

Unilever disposed of PBI in a sale to Monsanto, the US-based biotechnology giant. Unilever officials stated that the sale was based on an effort to further concentrate all Unilever operations around their core strengths (see above). Biotechnology and plant science, they stated, were not areas where Unilever intended to develop strong business interests.

It remained unclear to some within Unilever how sustainable agriculture would support Unilever's core strengths any more than biotechnology did. Given the debate over the future of agricultural production, it seemed possible that Unilever management would not support sustainable agriculture on the grounds that it was not in line with their commitment to build around their core concentrations.

ISSUES OF SUPPLY CHAIN MANAGEMENT

Adopting new agricultural practices would require Unilever to influence the operations involved in agriculture. This raises the issue of ownership of supply chains. Unilever does not own all of the operations that grow (agricultural produce), raise (livestock and poultry), or catch (fish) its raw materials. In fact, Unilever owns only a small percentage of its supply chain-roughly 25 percent in the case of agriculture. The remaining quantities are bought from farmers under contract to Unilever or as commodities on the open market.

In the case of fish, Unilever does not own a single fishing business, and therefore purchases 100 percent of its fish from independent fisheries. Since Unilever does not actually own any fishing businesses, it cannot directly influence the operations of its suppliers. However, Unilever is one of the world's largest purchasers of fish. Therefore, many of their suppliers depend heavily on Unilever's business. In 1996 Unilever decided to use its economic clout to encourage changes in the supply chain of its fish products. Unilever was concerned that declining fish stocks would threaten its business and decided to take measures to address this issue.

The Marine Stewardship Council (MSC) was established by Unilever and the World Wide Fund for Nature (WWF) to develop a method to certify fisheries that were being sustainably operated. Unilever pledged that by 2005 it would purchase its fish exclusively from fisheries that complied with MSC certification criteria. The hope was that this would provide an economic incentive for fisheries to adopt sustainable practices and attain MSC-certification. Fisheries that complied with MSC standards would be allowed to carry an MSC logo on their products.

The supply of Unilever's agricultural raw materials was much more complicated. Agricultural raw materials generally came from three sources: from operations that Unilever owned, from farmers under contract with Unilever, or through commodity trading on the open market. Unilever-owned operations accounted for only a small percentage of the yearly agricultural raw material requirements (less than 25 percent in most cases). The majority of Unilever's agricultural raw materials were grown by contract farmers or bought on the open market. Therefore, the level of control Unilever could exert over operations it did not own was limited.

Unilever made efforts to build relationships with the farmers under contract with them. They would work to establish guidelines and regulations for "agricultural best practice." Unilever would dictate the types and amounts of fertilizers, pesticides and herbicides the farmers could use. Furthermore, Unilever agricultural officers would make the decisions about when and how to irrigate, and ultimately when to harvest the crops. The farmers were obligated to follow these practices after signing a contract; however they were not obligated to sign contracts with Unilever.

Introduction of sustainable agriculture guidelines would represent a significant change from the practices used by most of Unilever's suppliers. Considering its limited influence over its supply chain, an area of major concern for Vis was how Unilever could expect to implement any practices that were consistent with the definition of sustainable agriculture in the study.

ISSUES OF CONSUMER CONFIDENCE

Unilever's Foods business was fundamentally dependent on consumers' confidence in their branded goods. Vis, in an interview, summed up the importance by stating that "maintaining consumer confidence in the quality and safety of our goods is absolutely necessary. What do you think would happen if tomorrow people lost confidence in our product? It would be disastrous."

There were several incidents, relating to agriculture, that eroded consumers' confidence in Unilever's Foods products. Two that were particularly damaging were the bovine spongiform encephalopathy (BSE or "mad cow disease") contamination, and the introduction of GMOs into Unilever products. These two incidents were highly publicized and somewhat damaging to Unilever's business, especially in Europe.

In March of 1996, Britain released a report suggesting that mad cow disease could be passed on to humans. As a result, demand for beef throughout Europe slumped dramatically as consumers reacted to the news. For Unilever, who sells beef products, this was a major problem. Unilever was forced to report losses of over £21 million (around $34 million) to remove beef from its stocks. A Unilever spokesman commented that "consumer confidence is still being unnerved by the continuing debate over the BSE issue. We have seen some recovery in meats in the UK but not back up to pre-BSE levels."[14]

A result of BSE was that the demand for organic beef increased. The two potential causes of BSE, feeding bonemeal to cattle and the use of organophosphorus compounds for parasite control, were not allowed in organic farming.[15] Therefore, there was more consumer confidence in organic beef. Suppliers of organic beef were seeing drastic increases in demand. Butchers in Ireland experiencing bad sales began to react to consumers' desires and offer organic beef.[16] In 1996, sales of organic food in England rose by 40 percent, driven in part by consumers' concerns over BSE.[17]

One product that is widely used in Unilever's food goods is soya. As with most of its fats and oils, Unilever purchases a vast majority of its soya as a commodity on the open market. The soya that Unilever purchases is grown around the world by thousands of farmers. By the time Unilever receives the goods it is very difficult, or impossible, to determine their original source. The nature of the commodities market is such that tracing products to the original producer is impossible.

In 1996 and 1997, Unilever faced a problem with the supply of soya. Monsanto, a life sciences company based in the US, had developed soya containing genetically modified organisms (GMOs). The strain was "designed" to resist damage to an herbicide that they also sold. The genetically modified seeds and the herbicide had been sold throughout the US, and in 1996 an estimated 2 percent of the US output of soya was genetically modified. There were no efforts made to segregate genetically modified and non-genetically modified soya. On the commodities market, where the majority of soya is purchased, there was no means of determining the origin of the product, and consequently no way for Unilever to segregate the supply.[18]

The end result was that Unilever could not guarantee its consumers that its products were GMO-free. The introduction of GMO soya in Europe was met by consumer protests. Greenpeace protested at Unilever headquarters in London,[19] and other activists held demonstrations at the homes of Unilever management elsewhere in Britain.[20] Customers were demanding that Unilever label its products that contained GMOs. Unilever claimed it could not separate the soya and was therefore unable to guarantee GMO-free products containing soya. The *London Financial Times* reported that a spokesman said that Unilever had found it was "just not practicable" to buy GMO-free soya "because of the quantities of soya required for its products."[21] However, some companies were able to offer GMO-free goods to consumers. Sainsbury, a giant supermarket chain in Europe, was the first to offer GMO-free goods.

According to Vis, these two incidents related to the discussion of agriculture at Unilever. In both cases, Unilever had suffered from practices used in its supply chain. Consumer confidence had been eroded by BSE, yet Unilever was not in direct control of the farmers raising the beef they sold. Additionally, consumers were protesting the use of GMOs and the lack of alternative, GMO-free products. According to Vis, Unilever was very concerned over the "mixing" of GMO soya with non-GMO soya. However, Monsanto was refusing to make efforts to segregate the supply.

Vis's Proposal

In 1997, Jeroen Bordewijk became the Senior Vice President of Unilever's Manufacturing and Supply Chain Technology division (SVP MAST). The MAST division is responsible for generating competitive advantage in the Foods supply chain. This is done by developing and capitalizing on supply-chain opportunities in the areas of manufacturing, sourcing, and delivery. As the SVP MAST, Bordewijk assumed direct responsibility for generating advantage in all supply chains in Unilever's Foods business.

Shortly after he assumed his new position, Bordewijk was offered a seat on the UEG. At one of his first meetings with the UEG, it was decided that he would be placed in charge of the work Vis had done with the FEIG, and with sustainable agriculture.[22] Bordewijk reported directly to the Foods Category Director, Lex Kemner, and had regular interaction with the UEG. In September of 1997, Bordewijk presented Vis's work to Kemner, who would decide whether or not Foods would support implementation of sustainable agriculture.

In his proposal, Vis drew on work he had done with Broekhoff (see Unilever and Sustainable Development (C)) to make the argument that sustainable agriculture was beneficial to Unilever's business.

> It is conceptually simple to define sustainable agriculture in terms of shareholder value. In our definition of sustainable agriculture, the land is managed so as to guarantee ongoing high yields of organic produce over time, while minimizing inputs and costs in terms of fossil energy, fertilizers, pesticides, herbicides, or other auxiliaries. It is in our definition not sustainable to keep yields high by continuously increasing inputs into the process, while eroding the intrinsic productivity of the soil.

Vis outlined an approach Unilever Foods could take to implement sustainable agriculture. The plan included setting up a number of pilot projects around strategic crops, using internal and external agronomic knowledge to provide the required expertise, and working with local NGOs and other groups to create the network necessary to facilitate sustainable agriculture.[23]

In order for sustainable agriculture to be successful, Vis proposed setting up projects that would work towards achieving the goals identified by stakeholders (see Table 1). He argued for projects that would address the environmental, social, and economic challenges of sustainable agriculture. To achieve this, Vis proposed that the pilot projects ensure that:

- Output was high enough
- Negative environmental impacts were reduced
- Product quality and safety were guaranteed
- Changing consumer demands were met
- Profitability remained competitive with other industry sectors
- Agriculture offered an attractive livelihood to workers.[24]

Vis proposed formation of a Sustainable Agriculture Steering Group to design and implement pilot projects. One of the priorities of the pilot projects would be to set up the systems required to measure Unilever's level of sustainability. Implementing the list of indicators developed by TME (see Table 2) served as a good starting point. Regarding the indicators, Vis noted,

> The indicators now need to be tested in practical situations. They have been chosen on the grounds that they can be measured at site level or product level as well as at category or market level. While this represents a useful starting point, it is the product of an external review of Unilever, and is not yet driven by a clear Unilever strategy on how to pursue Sustainable Development. The indicators will therefore need further pruning and selection as our strategy develops.
>
> Sustainable agriculture poses the greatest challenge to Unilever. The company currently lacks a broad strategic initiative [in sustainable agriculture]. There is now an urgent need to initiate [a] strategic investigation covering Unilever Foods world-wide and any other Unilever raw materials sourced from agriculture.[25]

Vis's proposal called for immediate action. He was arguing for a world-wide investigation of sustainable agriculture in all of Unilever Foods operations. If his proposal were accepted, funds would be allocated to create the Sustainable Agriculture Steering Group and to coordinate the creation of pilot projects as part of the 1998 work schedule.

Notes

1. Unless otherwise noted, information in this case was taken from correspondence and interviews with Unilever employees from the Unilever Head Office in Rotterdam, the Netherlands, between October, 1997, and November, 1998.
2. Information in this section on the viewpoints of the future of agriculture were provided by Jules N. Pretty, director, Centre for Environment and Society, John Tabor Labs, University of Essex, Wivenhoe Park, Colchester CO4 3SQ, email: Jpretty@esses.ac.uk. More information is available in Jules N. Pretty, *The Living Land: Agriculture, Food, and Community Regeneration in Rural Europe* (London: Earthscan Publications, 1998) 128-132; and Pretty, *Regeneration in Agriculture: Policies and Practices for Sustainability and Self Reliance* (Washington, D.C.: Joseph Henry Press, 1995).
3. L. R. Brown,. "The World Food Prospect: Entering a New Era," in *Assisting Sustainable Food Production: Apathy or Action?* (Arlington, VA. Winrock International, 1994); L. R Brown. and H. Kane,. *Full House: Reassessing the Earth's Population Carrying Capacity* (New York: W.W. Norton and Co., 1994); P. Ehrlich, *The Population Bomb* (New York: Ballantine Books, 1968).
4. Brown, 1994.
5. See M. W. Rosegrant and M. Agcaolli, *Global and Regional Food Demand, Supply and Trade Prospects to 2010.* (Washington, D.C.: IFPRI, 1994); D. O. Mitchell and M. D. Ingco, *The World Food Outlook.* (Washington, D.C.: International Economics Department, World Bank, 1993); FAO, *Strategies for Sustainable Agriculture and Rural Development (SARD): The Role of Agriculture, Forestry and Fisheries* (Rome: UN, FAO, 1993).
6. D. Barber, *State of Agriculture in the UK,* Report to RASE prepared by a study group under the chairmanship of Sir Derek Barber, RASE, Stoneleigh, 1991.
7. D. Avery, *Saving the Planet with Pesticides and Plastic* (Indianapolis: The Hudson Institute, 1995); I. Carruthers, "Going, Going, Gone! Tropical Agriculture as We Knew It," *Tropical Agriculture Association Newsletter* 13 (3): 1993, 1-5; R. D. Knutson, J. B. Taylor, J. B. Penson, and E. G. Smith, *Economic Impacts of Reduced Chemical Use* (College Station: Texas A&M University, 1990).
8. C. Abel, "Big Threat from Low Input Farms," *Farmers Weekly,* (November 21, 1997): 8.
9. N. Borlaug, "Small-scale Agriculture in Africa: The Myths and Realities," *Feeding the Future* (Newsletter of the Sasakawa Africa Association, Tokyo, 1992): 42; N. Borlaug, "Agricultural Research for Sustainable Development," Testimony before U.S. House of Representatives Committee on Agriculture, March 1, 1994; N. Borlaug, "Chemical Fertilizer 'Essential,'" in letter to *International Agricultural Development* (Nov.-Dec., 1994) 23; Sasakawa Global 2000, *Annual Reports, 1993-1995* (Tokyo:

Sasakawa Africa Association); World Bank, *Agricultural Sector Review*. (Washington, D.C.: Agriculture and Natural Resources Department, 1993).

10. Pretty, A. McCalla, "Agriculture and Food Needs to 2025: Why We Should Be Concerned," Sir John Crawford Memorial Lecture, CGIAR Secretariat, The World Bank, Washington, D.C., October 27, 1994; NAF, *A Better Row to Hoe, The Economic, Environmental and Social Impact of Sustainable Agriculture* (Minnesota: Northwest Area Foundation, 1994); T. I. Hewitt and K. R. Smith, *Intensive Agriculture and Environmental Quality: Examining the Newest Agricultural Myth* (Greenbelt, MD: Henry Wallace Institute for Alternative Agriculture, 1995).

11. Pretty, *Regeneration in Agriculture*.

12. Vernon Jennings, "Sustainable Agriculture and Food: A Summary of Stakeholder Perspectives," *SustainAbility*, February 12, 1997 (confidential).

13. J. Krozer and K.E.H. Maa, "Fitness for Sustainability," Institute for Applied Environmental Economics (TME), February 1997.

14. Christopher Sims, "Birds Eye Hamburgers Suffer Losses as Consumer Confidence is Dented by Mad Cow Disease: Unilever Counts Cost of BSE," *The Herald*, Glasgow, August 10, 1996, 17.

15. Josef Finke, "Organic Beef," in Letters to the Editor, *The Irish Times*, December 8, 1996, 17.

16. Audrey Magee, "BSE Threat Shows the Consumer is Boss," *The Irish Times*, April 13, 1996, 7.

17. "Organic Sector Reaps Benefits of Food Awareness," *London Financial Times*, November 7, 1998, 5.

18. Joe Rogaly, "Beans and Genes: Genetically Altered Soyabeans Are in Our Food—Like It or Not," *London Financial Times*, December 7, 1996, 1.

19. *The London Independent*, October 17, 1996, 2.

20. Peter Beaumont, "Greens Target Crop Designers' Homes and Research Stations," *The Observer*, December 15, 1996, 14.

21. Peggy Hollinger and Maggie Urry, "Sainsbury Claims Modified Soya 'First,'" *London Financial Times*, May 2, 1998.

22. From an interview with Jeroen Bordewijk, at Unilever Head Office, Rotterdam, the Netherlands, July 22, 1998.

23. Information in this section was taken from correspondence between the authors and Jan-Kees Vis, dated November 5, 1997.

24. Jan-Kees Vis, Unilever and Sustainable Agriculture: discussion paper and preliminary project proposal (unpublished).

25. Information in this section taken from: Hans Broekhoff and Jan-Kees Vis, Sustainable Development and Unilever: putting the Corporate Purpose into action. (unpublished.)

23

THE NATURAL STEP

INTRODUCTION

The Natural Step (TNS) is a framework for understanding ecological principles and environmental problems. TNS is also a Swedish nonprofit institution (spreading worldwide) that offers training and education. The TNS framework evolved from a lengthy process of scientific debate from which consensus was reached on a set of principles to explain our current situation and help guide future action. Based on the framework, and inherent scientific principles on which there is widespread agreement, four system conditions were identified as necessary for a sustainable society. The framework, principles, and system conditions are offered as a vehicle for education and conversation. They are also being used as a compass to guide organizations on environmental issues. The TNS approach is not set in concrete. It has evolved through a process of consensus building in scientific communities and has spread outward, and its original architects welcome constructive criticism and revision if more useful or powerful methods can be suggested. The compass is broadly applicable to corporations, communities, governments, academic institutions and other nonprofits. In the private sector TNS has been used by many companies to examine current strategy and practices.

From a corporate standpoint, TNS is seen by some as a logical extension of quality management and strategic systems thinking which extends out to networks of suppliers and customers. Companies, such as Electrolux and IKEA, that have trained employees in the TNS framework have found it a stimulus to product design and process innovation. Other adoptees, for example Interface and Monsanto, are using the framework to educate the workforce, change strategic direction and achieve long term competitive advantage.

DR. ROBÈRT AND THE DEVELOPMENT OF THE NATURAL STEP FRAMEWORK

The Natural Step was founded in 1989 by Dr. Karl-Henrik Robèrt, a leading pediatric oncologist at Sweden's top cancer institute. Dr. Robèrt had long been focused on cell mutation and was active in cell science research as well as patient procedures. He studied cancer cell systems, asking how they differed from normal systems, with the goal of devising new strategies for treating cancer patients. Noticing an increase in rare types of cancers in children too young to have been damaged through lifestyle exposure, he sought answers to questions regarding environmental causes. As a cell researcher he knew that there were non-negotiable conditions necessary for the health and survival of the cell. For example, you cannot ask the cell to process heavy metals (lead, mercury) and he wondered if similar non-negotiable conditions could be derived for the larger system of the natural environment. He described the dilemma faced by doctors like himself in the cancer hospital,

> One cell changed and a few years later the child died. In the meantime, the doctors gathered around to save the child in the hospital, but often there was little that could be done. Yet outside we were destroying our habitat and this seemed to account in large part for the changes to that original cell in the child.

Furthermore, Dr. Robèrt pointed out that the cell of a human being, when compared to those of other living organisms including plants, was not as different as is usually assumed and, in fact, that only at the molecular level can you perceive the differences. According to Dr. Robèrt the basic structures and functions of our bodies are nearly identical to those of other living organisms.

Dr. Robèrt reached out and asked environmental scientists to explain to him in simple terms what was happening with environmental degradation. He found the environmental debate often was characterized by conflict and strongly held and highly divergent views. Debates were heated with each person seeing a piece of the picture and arguing over details rather than finding common ground for agreement. The first Natural Step consensus paper developed as a result of Dr. Robèrt's frustration that people were unable to have productive conversations about environmental issues. He saw there was no way to define environmental problems that enabled the diverse stakeholders in the discussion to come together and forge solutions. Key to Dr. Robèrt's approach was his observation that environmental progress was bogged down in disagreements over details. He noted that many commonly asked questions ignored the broader more important issues of the environment. For example: are chloroflourocarbons the main causes of ozone depletion? Is it possible that natural processes such as volcanic eruptions are equally responsible for ozone depletion? How many people can the earth's natural resources sustain? In reality, it is impossible to reach a definitive answer to these and many other environmental questions. Dr. Robèrt compared these questions to focusing on the "leaves" of the environment while ignoring the more important "branches" and "trunk." The leaves symbolize crucial environmental concerns that are often controversial or isolated. The trunk and branches symbolize scientific consensus regarding core problems. In Robèrt's view, ". . . Scientists are like monkeys arguing about withering leaves in a dying tree, instead of paying attention to facts on which there is agreement, i.e. that the tree is dying." This analogy brought the problem into focus. A different diagnostic approach was needed and participants in the environmental debate needed new language and a different way to converse.

His goal was to see if the scientists could agree on something. For example, there was consensus among scientists that there are only very small differences on a genetic and molecular level between people and plants, making human beings nature itself (as opposed to something apart from nature). Could other areas of agreement be found? Dr. Robèrt began by articulating his views and then sent out his draft to academic scientists who reviewed, commented, and returned it to him for revision. A steady flow of ideas and revised drafts flowed between Dr. Robèrt and the growing number of scientists. The process encouraged participants to withdraw from the details of disagreement that might separate them on environmental issues to overall principles on which there was agreement, principles that were solid in terms of scientific legitimacy yet without reductionism. "Simplicity without reductionism" became a guiding theme throughout. The goal was to identify an irrefutable foundation—what is non-negotiable about the subject—around which the scientific community could agree so that a productive debate could follow. He listened carefully to feedback, acknowledged it in subsequent drafts, and continued to build his conceptual paper as an organic and ongoing educational tool.

Next Dr. Robèrt enlisted the support of government officials and a group of leading Swedish media figures and subsequently was able to take his ideas to the public through television. A royal family is an important part of Swedish history and culture; he gained the support of the King of Sweden and asked if he would be a patron for these ideas. In this incremental way, through developing the ideas on paper and cultivating the support of groups and influential leaders, by the mid-1990s, step by step Dr. Robèrt had built what amounted to a social movement within Sweden. With the public support of diverse groups of Swedish society, he was able to raise the equivalent of $7 million from a variety of sources including a growing number of corporate sponsors. These were enlisted through Dr. Robèrt's resourceful and persistent discussion with CEOs, bringing groups of them together to encourage their collaboration in the effort. By 1995 Dr. Robèrt estimated there were over 10,000 people in the support network for The Natural Step, including individuals from every arena and sector of Swedish society.

While resources were important, the key was reaching agreement on a conceptual model or overall principles that did not change. The *process* led by Dr. Robèrt was critical in that enough time was spent on the fundamentals, so that once the principles were identified and agreed upon, no one could criticize the outcome as shallow and unsubstantiated. This process was long and included setbacks. It required a positive outlook and a refusal to see obstacles. Yet it also demanded that critics be brought in close around the process to ensure the integrity of the outcome.

Eventually this careful process of consensus-building was recognized by outsiders. In 1991, Britain's Institute for Social Inventions awarded Dr. Robèrt its prize for best social invention. This note emphasizes the process dimension of TNS because it enabled a breakthrough in thinking in the Swedish context and it mirrors processes being followed today in the United States and other countries as organizations form to develop their own Natural Step framework. The first meeting of American scientists was held in late 1996. According to the Institute for Social Inventions,

> Dr. Robèrt's most significant social invention is his method for achieving consensus on tricky, complicated, often highly scientific matters in a way that does not reduce agreement to the lowest common denominator but that actually produces rather radical [far-reaching] position statements.[1]

THE SCIENCE WITHIN THE PROCESS

From the perspective of molecular scientists and oncologists the cell is concerned only with the conditions necessary to sustain and propagate life. At a macro level, the history of the planet earth is one of a closed material system slowly evolving the cyclical processes which have allowed life to flourish. The earth receives light from the sun and in turn emits infrared radiation. The difference in thermodynamic potential (energy) between the two flows provides the conditions for biospheric self-organization. Individual plant cells through photosynthesis use the energy to break down waste material which is then used to prolong and propagate the life of the plant. The cell is the foundation of life's natural cycle of birth, growth, death, decay and rebirth. While all living processes deplete the quality of natural resources, the sun and green cells act as a "quality machine" that cyclically rebuilds and reorganizes dead matter. Thus the process of healthy cell life depends upon a cyclical process of regeneration within the large, closed system of the planet's biosphere.

Understanding cyclical systems is key. Cyclical processes continuously regenerate themselves while linear processes eventually must end. The scientific consensus embodied in The Natural Step asserts that humankind has disrupted natural cyclical processes by using resources in a linear fashion. For example, material (mined, extracted from the earth) and unnatural compounds (synthetics) are produced and processed, and in growing volumes added to the biosphere. A five-fold increase in the world's economic output in the last fifty years has created an unprecedented increase in material that cannot be re-assimilated into ecological systems. As a consequence, as resources are used in industrial society they become vast stockpiles of garbage, most of which are invisible to us in the form of microbial air, water and soil pollution. Most of this pollution is unable to be assimilated within natural or societal cycles. Natural cycles cannot breakdown and re-use much of the material, such as toxic metals and stable compounds produced synthetically in chemical laboratories, particularly since it is not returned to nature in a usable form and industry for the most part does not fully recycle waste matter back into productive processes. The result is increasing quantities of waste with a corresponding decrease in the natural resources available to cleanse and regenerate the system overall. In addition, it is impossible to predict the consequences of this process because we cannot know the tolerance level of ecosystems for assimilating molecular garbage due to their complexity, delay mechanisms and interactions between cyclical processes. According to TNS it should be self-evident that to continue along this linear path is not compatible with wealth creation as currently pursued, nor human and ecosystemic health.

For Dr. Robèrt the message of TNS is this:

> No matter what our values, we should still be able to join forces to defend the interests of the living cell. In all essential respects, down to the tiniest molecule, we humans have the same structure as endangered birds of prey, seals, and otters. In a biological sense we are neither the masters of nature nor its stewards, but a piece of nature ourselves, just like seals and otters. And if these species have become threatened with extinction in the space of a few decades because of our environmental pollution, we too are threatened. We have enough knowledge to say that the only way of reversing this process is to avoid introducing substances into nature that it cannot process and to learn to live cyclically—just like cells in nature.[2]

THE SCIENTIFIC PRINCIPLES

TNS uses a systems approach to explain the links between ecology and the economy. It offers a way to move from an unsustainable, linear model (resource wasting) to a sustainable, cyclical model (resource preserving). The principles of TNS are built on the following reasoning and premises.[3] While scientists did not agree on details they did agree on some basic and well-known laws.

- Matter and energy cannot be created or destroyed (according to the conservation laws, the Law of Conservation of Matter and the Law of Conservation of Energy).

    E.g. Gasoline does not disappear when burned but is converted into invisible gas.

- Matter and energy tend to disperse (according to the 2nd Law of Thermodynamics). This means that sooner or later, all matter that is introduced by human activity is released into natural systems.

    Matter and energy spontaneously disperse. Containment only delays this process. In the process matter and energy lose order (for example, a car rusts) as a consequence of increasing entropy. This order loss is described as a loss of concentration and structure. Consequently the consumption of resources converts those resources into less order and less economic value as resources convert ultimately to waste. We do not consume a resource (matter or energy) but instead extract its quality and structure (the degree of order within energy and matter).

If matter and energy do not disappear and everything disperses, what generates order in the larger system? Earth is a closed system with respect to matter but open with respect to energy. Light energy from the sun is received by the earth and heat energy is emitted into space. This dynamic of energy flows creates the physical conditions for creating order within the biosphere. Plant cells are the primary producers of order.

Through photosynthesis they use solar radiation directly to concentrate and structure dispersed matter and energy (including creating oxygen). Humans and other animals lack the ability to directly convert solar energy to matter, but we indirectly use solar power through food consumption and other natural resource use, hence are totally dependent on the continued health and vitality of natural systems. In natural cycles of converting solar energy to plant matter, consumed in turn by animals, in turn converted to waste that is pulled up once more into plant cells, there is no "waste" as we commonly use the term. Everything is food for the next step in the cycle, driven by the larger solar cycle.

The implication of these cyclical realities is that waste must not systematically accumulate in nature, and that reconstitution of material quality must be at least as large as its dissipation. In other words, restoring the quality of material is necessary to offset the activities that break it down. Nature has a metabolism that circulates energy in a continuous breakdown and restorative processes. The activities of humans, the societal metabolism, must be integrated into the cycles of nature consistent with its non-negotiable rules. Understanding this necessity avoids a systematic shift in adverse environmental parameters.

TNS SYSTEM CONDITIONS

Up to this point we have reviewed the origins of The Natural Step ideas, their basis in well-known scientific principles, and their roots in a systems and cyclical view of human activity within a biosphere that obeys certain non-negotiable rules. From this flow of logic, four conditions for the maintenance of quality in the whole system were deduced[4] (as shown in the table on page 191).

These system conditions offer a guide for organizations to evaluate their current practices. To what degree does a company's activities violate the system conditions? Are there ways to incrementally move a firm's behavior away from these violations? "The Natural Step" does not refer to nature alone; it suggests that organizations can take small steps that are natural and comfortable given financial and strategic constraints. When firms examine their activities in light of the system conditions, many obvious small steps can be taken at low expense and often involving immediate returns. These steps can be seen as logical extensions of firm's existing activities in total quality that include environmental considerations. Firms that have already taken initiative, as opposed to passivity or simple compliance, in the face of environmental concerns will see the logic of applying the system conditions as a next step in becoming more resource efficient. Companies farther along the learning curve with TNS principles have already introduced product designs that meet the system conditions and will be used to replace existing products. The pressures to shift knowledge and design expertise in this direction will only increase over the next few decades.

Pressures on firms can be illustrated by the use of a funnel. The funnel walls, closing off options for companies, are represented by *decreased resource availability* (decreasing amounts, declining quality, and reduced assimilative capacity of natural systems) and *increased resource demand* (driven by rising population and increased consumption of goods).

System Condition	This means:	Reason:	Question to ask:
1. Substances from the Earth's crust must not systematically increase in the ecosphere	Fossil fuels, metals and other minerals must not be extracted at a faster pace than their slow redeposit and reintegration into the Earth's crust	Otherwise the concentration of substances in the ecosphere will increase and eventually reach limits—often unknown—beyond which irreversible changes occur	Does your organization systematically decrease its economic dependence on underground metals, fuels and other minerals?
2. Substances produced by society must not systematically increase in the ecosphere	Substances must not be produced at a faster pace than they can be broken down and integrated into the cycles of nature or deposited into the Earth's crust	Otherwise the concentration of substances in the ecosphere will increase and eventually reach limits—often unknown—beyond which irreversible changes occur	Does your organization systematically decrease its economic dependence on persistent unnatural substances?
3. The physical basis for productivity and diversity of nature must not be systematically diminished	We cannot harvest or manipulate ecosystems in such a way that productive capacity and diversity systematically diminish	Our health and prosperity depend on the capacity of nature to reconcentrate and restructure wastes into new resources	Does your organization systematically decrease its economic dependence on activities which encroach on productive parts of nature, e.g., overfishing?
4. Fair and efficient use of resources with respect to meeting human needs	Basic human needs must be met with the most resource-efficient methods possible, and their satisfaction must take precedence over provision of luxuries	Humanity must prosper with a resource metabolism meeting system conditions 1-3. This is necessary in order to get the social stability and cooperation for achieving the changes in time	Does your organization systematically decrease its economic dependence on using an unnecessarily large amount of resources in relation to added human value?

THE NATURAL STEP ORGANIZATION

TNS headquarters are located in Stockholm, Sweden. The organization is an educational foundation with a strategy of education and active support of "ecocyclical development" in households, companies, and local governments. TNS has spread rapidly from Sweden to other countries including Australia, Belgium, Great Britain, France, the Netherlands, Taiwan, United States, Canada, and New Zealand.

The Natural Step, Sweden

In 1997, The Natural Step in Sweden was made up of 16 professional groups comprised of approximately 10,000 individuals and a series of supporting networks. With only six full time employees, TNS's professional networks had produced consensus papers anchored in Dr. Robèrt's original consensus document and four system conditions. The resulting papers were then used to guide decision making and inform professionals and the general public. TNS networks produced consensus papers in such areas as: energy, metal flows, transport, political/economic measures, agriculture, forestry, plastics, culture and ethics, and strategy for economic/ecological planning. Since its founding, over 50 companies and 50 municipalities throughout Sweden use TNS principles. Members of TNS include banks and insurance companies, major corporations, the State railways, the Church of Sweden, big trade unions and the Country's most important retailers of convenience goods. As word has spread of TNS ideas and their practical application, Dr. Robèrt has received increasing international attention and has spoken at leading universities and with corporate executives.

The Natural Step, United States

The Natural Step vision is taking shape in the United States. The successful application of TNS principles by corporations and municipalities throughout Sweden brought a demand for training in the U.S. about this environmental awareness program. In December 1994, a group of environmental and educational thinkers met with Dr. Robèrt in Newburyport, MA, to discuss the possibility of bringing the work of TNS to the U.S. A steering committee was formed to create a non-profit organization in the U.S. In March 1995, the group met again in Charlottesville, Virginia, and further planning ensued. In April 1995, TNS office opened in Cambridge, Massachusetts and in 1996 moved to be permanently located in Sausalito, California. TNS/US is replicating the consensus building process as originally pioneered in Sweden, however the process and outcome will have a distinctly American stamp due to the differences between the Swedish and American cultures. By using the consensus process in the United States, TNS/US will help to ensure that "the principles of sustainability and their practical consequences are expressed in ways that are specifically relevant to American communities and institutions" (*Compass*, Fall 1996, see attached Appendix A). Within the next five years goals for TNS/US include:

- Train one million people in the principles of TNS.
- Introduce TNS principles to 250 colleges, universities, business school and other institutions of higher learning.
- Train 500 of the Wilshire 5,000 companies, including 100 of the Fortune 1,000.[5]

CORPORATE APPLICATIONS OF TNS FRAMEWORK

The Natural Step framework was developed out of recognition that environmental problems are a societal problem, to be tackled at all levels by all members of society. Consequently it does not judge whether a company is good or bad. Nor does it demand immediate and radical change. The system conditions and educational framework are used as a vehicle for firms to evaluate their current product designs and operations and to change their activities to be incrementally more closely aligned with the systems conditions. Firms that have integrated TNS ideas see such movement positioning them at a strategic advantage relative to their competitors.

This section provides a look at how various Swedish and U.S. companies are using TNS as a framework for making changes and developing ecological strategies.

A.B. Electrolux:

We appreciate the four system conditions and find the framework useful . . . TNS has some specific advantages, including its ability to provide a scientific basis for environmental issues. . . . The scientific basis of TNS enabled us to create [company-wide] consensus about the direction we want to go. TNS [also] emphasizes the logic of integrating environmental issues into business strategies.

—Per Grunewald, A.B. Electrolux Environmental Affairs Manager[6]

A.B. Electrolux is developing life-cycle assessments within its major product groups, as approximately 90% of the products' environmental impacts are related to product use. TNS is valued as a practical tool and is aligned with the company's approach by considering the whole chain when developing and manufacturing products. Professional customers and everyday consumers are becoming more environmentally conscious regarding product purchases and how these products impact the environment. This thought was reflected quantitatively in the 1995 annual report for A.B. Electrolux. The demand for environment-friendly products grew steadily. The result was ". . . more efficient products, manufactured with more environment-friendly materials and production processes."[7] Examples of products produced include washing machines and dishwashers with lower water consumption, and refrigeration alternatives.

Monsanto:

Before you can discuss Monsanto's involvement with TNS, you have to start with our involvement in the area of sustainability. . . . Our focus in the late 80s and early 90s was on pollution prevention. . . . Monsanto is now looking at how it can play a role in addressing global conditions that are threatening the health of the ecosystem we rely on for personal and business survival.

—Diane Herndon, Manager of Environmental Communications[8]

In January, 1996 TNS held the first training workshops at Monsanto. A delegation of Monsanto employees has visited Swedish companies using the TNS framework. The company is developing sustainable guiding principles to help evaluate if they are moving in sustainable directions, identify sustainable products and services, and educate their employees on sustainable issues and how they can play a role. TNS is used because the four system conditions are easy to understand. "They are directional—any business can use them as a compass" to determine whether or not they are moving in the right direction—a sustainable direction. For Monsanto, TNS principles are a useful tool in assisting with the development of their Monsanto Sustainability program. ". . . [T]hey are a building block which, along with a few other blocks, will form the framework from which we build our program."[9]

Interface, Inc.:

Interface, the first name in industrial ecology worldwide through substance, not words.[10]

—Ray C. Anderson, Chairman, President & CEO, Interface, Inc.

On June 5, 1996, Interface, Inc. became the first corporation in the United States to make a formal commitment to TNS. On that day, Ray Anderson declared his intent to redesign Interface's business practices to conform to TNS principles. He stated:

> We have become convinced as a company that The Natural Step is a way to create environmental awareness throughout a company and set in motion the life-change among our people that is necessary if we are to achieve our goal of sustainability. That is the way to make "thousands of little changes" that collectively are just as important as the few big ones.[11]

Dr. Robèrt accepted a partnership with Ray Anderson to help lead the company— a leader in worldwide commercial interiors selling floor coverings, interior fabrics, upholstery products, specialty chemicals, and interior architectural products—to industrial sustainability. To reach his goal, Anderson envisions a closed-loop recycling system for carpet. This means that carpet or carpet tiles would be leased instead of sold to consumers. As the pieces wear out, they are recycled into new products—thus reducing not only the amount of natural resources taken from the earth, but also reducing the amount of waste that enters landfills, and our air and water when new carpet is manufactured. TNS will be used as a training and awareness program that will help to emphasize ". . . Interface's perspective on business as a biological cycle like the earth." Perhaps Ray Anderson's words summarize best Interface Inc.'s commitment and collaboration with TNS: "We have committed to this framework as our compass in our search for the path to sustainability. This is hard stuff. These are unrelenting principles. Today, we are violating every one of the system conditions in ways that must not go on."[12]

Notes

1. Eronn, R. "The Natural Step—A Social Invention for the Environment," *Current Sweden*, No. 401, 1993.
2. "That Was When I Became a Slave," Interview with KHR.
3. TNS NEWS, No. 1, Winter 1996.
4. TNS NEWS, No. 1, Winter 1996.
5. TNS NEWS, No. 1, Winter 1996.
6. "Perspectives: Using The Natural Step Framework," *Business and the Environment,* Reprint, p. 5. Originally appeared in *Business and the Environment*, Vol. 7, No. 7 (1996), Cutter Information Corporation.
7. *Ibid.*
8. *Ibid*, p. 6.
9. "Perspectives: Using The Natural Step Framework," *Business and the Environment*, Reprint, p. 6.
10. *EcoSense NetLetter*, August 25, 1996, Interface Corporation.
11. *Compass*, TNS Newsletter, Fall 1996.
12. *EcoSense NetLetter*, June 5, 1996.

APPENDIX A
TOP SCIENTISTS BEGIN A CONSENSUS PROCESS IN THE UNITED STATES

In 1989, Karl-Henrik Robèrt patiently began a process of working with 50 of Sweden's most prominent scientists to outline the basic conditions necessary for a sustainable society. Twenty-one iterations later, Dr. Robèrt and the scientists completed a consensus document that later served as the scientific basis for a simple set of "System Conditions" that could be used as a "compass" to guide society toward a sustainable future.

These scientists, representing a broad range of disciplines, agreed that the laws of thermodynamics and other fundamental physical and natural laws imposed "nonnegotiable" limits upon human activities. Ultimately, the scientific consensus became the basis for many of the achievements of TNS/Sweden, the heart of which was an educational campaign that reached a majority of Swedish citizens and profoundly influenced the behavior of major Swedish corporations and municipalities. This scientific consensus process remains the core from which TNS's influence emanates.

The Swedish consensus process is now being replicated by The Natural Step/U.S. Dr. Peter Raven, Director of The Missouri Botanical Garden, a noted life scientist, has agreed to lead this effort with our Director of Science, Donald W. Aiken, Ph.D., a respected physicist.

In September this year, 132 letters were mailed to U.S. leaders in the scientific community from many disciplines. The recipient list included 22 Nobel Laureates and 50 winners of other prestigious awards, such as the National Medal of Science.

Even though the Swedish consensus document continues to lend credibility on an international level, TNS/US will benefit substantially from its own effort. Replicating the consensus process in this country will help us ensure that the principles of sustainability and their practical consequences are expressed in ways that are specifically relevant to American communities and institutions. It will also help us define responsible and effective follow-up actions that can be facilitated by The Natural Step/US.

In the U.S., The Natural Step will seek consensus on the underlying scientific principles that form the foundation of the Natural Step model. In addition, we are vitally interested in the scientists' views on the four system conditions and the way in which they are presented, especially if a revised approach would enhance the effectiveness of The Natural Step in the U.S.

In addition to the Swedish consensus documents, TNS/US is also building upon a consensus document created under the auspices of the Union of Concerned Scientists, which published its "World Scientists Warning to Humanity" in 1991. There were more than 1,670 signatories from around the world including 129 Nobel Laureates. This precedent is important because many of the world's finest scientists demonstrated their comprehension of the gravity of the deteriorating ecological situation and pledged themselves to be participants in the solution.

The next step in the U.S. consensus process will be a two-day meeting in early 1997. At this time, the scientists will be asked to discuss, refine, and validate The Natural Step core scientific principles as they are interpreted for U.S. audiences, to prioritize topics for subsequent research and publications, and to identify effective follow-up actions, particularly those that can be led by TNS/US.

Source: *Compass*, The Newsletter of the United States Natural Step, Number 2 (Fall 1996).

APPENDIX B
AN INTRODUCTION TO THE NATURAL STEP

The mission of The Natural Step is to create and promote a shared framework for understanding and solving environmental problems. The Natural Step was founded in Sweden in 1989 by Swedish oncologist Dr. Karl-Henrik Robèrt. As a scientist at Sweden's leading cancer research institute, he became convinced that effective action in response to environmental problems was being constrained by endless disagreements over details, preventing society from addressing the issue as a whole. To remedy this, he asked fifty fellow scientists to assist him in drafting a paper outlining the fundamental principles that could define a sustainable society. Twenty-one-working drafts later, the consensus document was endorsed by all participants.

From the consensus document, four fundamental "system conditions" necessary for a sustainable society were developed and the model was adapted into a one-day training program. Thousands of people including managers from some of Sweden's largest companies and municipalities have taken the training and, as a result, have begun the process of completely redesigning their processes and activities according to the system conditions, shown below.

The Natural Step/US is bringing this framework to interested communities, educational institutions and corporations in the United States. Other countries in which The Natural Step is active or forming include the United Kingdom, New Zealand, Australia, France, Brazil, the Netherlands, and Canada.

System Conditions

1. Substances from the Earth's crust cannot systematically increase in the biosphere.
This means that fossil fuels, metals, and other minerals cannot be extracted at a faster rate than their re-deposit back into the Earth's crust.

2. Substances produced by society cannot systematically increase in the biosphere.
This means that substances must not be produced at a faster rate than they can be broken down in nature. This requires a greatly decreased production of naturally occurring substances that are systematically accumulating beyond the natural levels, and a phase-out of persistent human-made substances not found in nature.

3. The physical basis for the productivity and diversity of nature must not be systematically deteriorated.
This means that we cannot harvest or manipulate ecosystems in such a way as to diminish their productive capacity, or threaten the natural diversity of life forms (biodiversity). This requires that we critically examine how we harvest renewable resources, and adjust our consumption and land use practices to fall well within the regenerative capacities of ecosystems.

4. In order to meet the previous three conditions, there must be a fair and efficient use of resources to meet human needs.
This means that basic human needs must be met with the most resource-efficient methods possible, including a just resource distribution.

Source: *Compass*, The Newsletter of the United States Natural Step, Number 2 (Fall 1996).

24

W. R. Grace & Co.
and the Neemix Patent
(A)

[Neem] seems to be one of the most promising of all plants and may eventually benefit every person on the planet.
—National Research Council report on Neem, 1992

Derived from the seeds of the Indian neem tree and touted as a safe, natural biopesticide, Neemix seemed to be a benevolent product that promised W. R. Grace & Company (WRG) profits and farmers a sustainable means of fighting pests. However, in 1995 controversy erupted around Neemix. Three years earlier, Grace researchers had been granted a patent on the pesticide, and since that time Neemix had become far more than just another product in the company's line. Grace, the world's largest manufacturer of specialty chemicals, had never expected Neemix to be a major source of income for the company, but steady sales since its introduction to market supported the prediction that consumers were interested in purchasing completely natural, environmentally friendly pesticides, rather than chemical ones. The active ingredient in Neemix, azadirachtin, is a compound that occurs naturally in neem seeds and possesses the ideal characteristic of

This case was prepared by Kristi Severance and revised by Lisa Spiro under the supervision of Patricia H. Werhane. This case was written as a basis for discussion rather than to illustrate effective or ineffective handling of an administrative situation. Copyright ©1997 by the University of Virginia Darden School Foundation, Charlottesville, VA. All rights reserved. To order copies, send an e-mail to dardencases@virginia.edu. No part of this publication may be reproduced, stored in a retrieval system, used in a spreadsheet or transmitted in any form or by any means— electronic, mechanical, photocopying, recording or otherwise—without the permission of the Darden School Foundation. Rev. 12/98.

being fatally harmful to more than 200 species of insect pests, while remaining non-toxic to other plants and beneficial animals. By early 1995, sales of Neemix brought in about $60 million annually out of Grace's total of $5 billion in annual sales, and references in the press to the effectiveness of Neemix were becoming frequent.[1]

By late summer of 1995, however, the product's success became clouded by a growing controversy over the patent held to protect it. Protests against Grace had been gaining momentum in India in the preceding months. Farmers in India had been using neem "teas," the emulsion resulting from crushing neem seeds and soaking them in water, as pesticides for thousands of years, and for that reason many Indians believed that Grace had no right to a patent on a neem-based pesticide. There were voices of protest in the United States as well, most notably that of the Foundation on Economic Trends (FET), a biotechnology industry watchdog agency. On September 14, 1995, the FET, together with more than 200 supporting organizations from the United States, India, and other countries, filed a petition with the U.S. Patent and Trademark Office to reexamine the Neemix patent in hopes of having it revoked. They charged Grace with committing what they called "biopiracy," saying that the company had appropriated and profited from knowledge of natural resources that rightfully belonged to the indigenous peoples of India.

W. R. GRACE—COMPANY BACKGROUND[2]

From its inception Grace was a company defined by its interests in natural resource products. In 1854 William Russell Grace traveled from Ireland to Callao, Peru, hoping to rebuild the family fortune, which had been depleted by the potato famine. He first became a clerk and later a partner in a trading firm that specialized in shipping guano (bird dung) and nitrate of soda (sodium nitrate), both used as fertilizers. Under William's direction, the company grew to be the largest of its kind in the country. In 1865, William moved to New York City, where he established W. R. Grace & Company (WRG). The company established three-way shipping routes from South America to North America and to Europe for trading fertilizer, agricultural products, and U.S.-manufactured goods, and remained connected with the Peruvian government as its agent for the sale of nitrate of soda. After William died in 1904, his brother Michael took control of the company and was succeeded in 1909 by William's son Joseph. With Joseph at the helm, the company underwent a period of rapid growth. He purchased cotton mills, sugar plantations, sugar refineries in Peru, and nitrate production facilities in Chile. During this time the company expanded its shipping interests, and in 1914 Grace Lines sent the first ship through the Panama Canal. Grace also moved into the banking industry with the establishment of Grace National Bank. Another new area of interest for Grace was aviation, and together with Pan American Airways, they established Panagra airlines, which offered the first international air service down the west coast of South America.

In 1945, after his father's retirement, Joseph R. Grace's son, J. Peter Grace, was elected president of the company at age 32. At the time, W. R. Grace had $93 million in assets and J. Peter wanted to both protect and increase them. The company's primary interests were in Grace Lines, Grace National Bank, Panagra, and agricultural products.

Concerned with political and economic instability in South America, J. Peter began to look for ways to make the future of Grace more secure. He was impressed with the success of chemical companies in the United States, and under his direction the company began its foray into the chemical industry. He initiated a plan to reduce South American investments from 100 percent to 5 percent, by expanding into the U.S. chemical industry, and, in order to raise the money to do so, the company went public in 1953. In 1952, Grace purchased its first U.S. chemical manufacturing plant in Memphis, Tennessee. In 1954 they purchased Davison Chemical and then Dewey and Almy Chemical, which provided the foundation from which Grace grew to be the world's largest specialty chemical company. The transfer to primarily chemical interests became more pronounced in the mid- to late-1960s, when Grace sold Grace National Bank, Panagra, and the Grace Line. During the next 11 years, Grace acquired 23 additional chemical companies for 4 million shares of stock.

In the 1960s and 70s Grace expanded into the food and sporting goods industries, a diversification that lasted only until the mid-80s. Later Grace expanded into the water treatment, food-service packaging, and health-care products industries. By 1988, Grace was prepared to begin research and development of a natural pesticide. Although soft pesticides would probably not knock synthetic insecticides out of the market, Grace nonetheless realized that a neem-based pesticide had the potential to provide the company with some of the profits from a natural pesticide market that was, according to a National Research Council survey, expected to increase from $450 million in 1993 to $813 million annually in 1998.[3] After investigating several avenues, Grace joined a growing number of Western scientists and companies who saw neem as the source with the most potential.

NEEM

The neem tree (*Azadirachta indica*) is a member of the mahogany family and is native to numerous countries with subtropical climates. It is particularly prevalent in India, where an estimated 18 million trees flourish.[4] Resembling an oak in stature, it is tall, with wide spreading branches bearing masses of white honey-scented flowers and bitter fruit similar in appearance to olives. The neem is a rapidly growing tree that only loses its leaves in cases of extreme drought and in general thrives in hot, arid conditions. Its extensive root system allows it to extract nutrients from even the poorest soils. The combination of these characteristics makes it ideal for growing in the areas most in need of its benefits. In many villages in the hottest parts of India, the only available relief from the heat is the substantial shade that the neem tree provides. Pilgrims to the holy Islamic site of the Plains of Arafat in Saudi Arabia are protected from the sun by 50 thousand neem trees planted by a Saudi philanthropist.[5] In Ghana and several other African countries where a need for fuel has led to problems with deforestation, a campaign to introduce the neem, which requires little maintenance and is non-invasive, helped counter the effects of massive soil erosion. The neem tree has provided a double benefit in these countries: in addition to stabilizing the soil, the tree provided an invaluable, renewable source of timber because it could mature in only 5-7 years.

NEEM'S ROLE IN INDIA

Neem has played an integral role in Indian culture for thousands of years. In a culture where the alliance between human beings and the natural environment is of great importance, the tree is one of the five "essentials" traditionally prescribed for planting in Indian gardens, and its properties are a focal point of daily Indian medicinal and agricultural life.[6]

Revered by Hindus, neem has always been an important part of annual New Year celebrations, when its leaves are eaten to ensure good health throughout the year. Accounts of its usefulness for medicinal purposes date back thousands of years. Ayurvedic doctors, who practice medicine based on the idea of harmony between humans and their environment, have continued to prescribe neem cures, and neem has been among the most frequently found items in Indian apothecary shops. In fact, neem has been so widely used throughout India to prevent and treat a variety of illnesses that it is commonly referred to as "the village pharmacy." Despite being too poor to afford either toothbrushes or toothpaste, millions of Indians have had good dental health because they chewed daily on neem twigs, fraying the ends and using them to clean teeth and gums. Compounds within the twigs have an antiseptic effect and appear to prevent tooth and gum disease. As a result, neem can now be found in numerous commercially available dentifrices. Neem is also used to treat skin ailments. Ground neem leaves are made into creams and poultices for application to skin disorders from acne to leprosy, and neem oil is a common ingredient in soaps valued for their antiseptic qualities. Neem has traditionally been believed to be effective against viruses like chicken pox. Various neem components have been used as contraceptives, and tests have indicated that the oil is a strong spermicide. It has been considered a promising avenue for development of new birth-control methods, and researchers in several countries have been working to develop this aspect of neem. In New Delhi scientists at the Defense Institute of Physiology and Allied Sciences isolated a substance from neem oil that kills sperm on contact. They were particularly optimistic about the possibility of a viable neem contraceptive because neem's status as an important part of India's folklore may make it a more socially acceptable form of contraception than commercial birth control methods.[7] Some scientists both in the United States and India have also cited neem as a potential weapon against the human immunodeficiency virus (HIV).

In addition to its medicinal uses, neem is one of the primary means of controlling insect pests in India. Planting neem trees in village centers is common practice because they help ward off biting insects. Neem leaves scattered in closets and food and grain bins keep pests away for up to several months. Farmers soak neem seeds overnight in water and apply the resulting emulsion to crops to keep pests away, and neem cake, the residue left once the oil has been removed from the seeds, is used to combat soil-borne pests. Neem cake also assists plants with nitrogen take-up. Use of neem products is not restricted to only those farmers too poor to have access to commercially produced insecticides: many wealthy growers of cardamom, an Indian spice and valuable export, use neem cake to protect their crops against invasion by pests in the soil. It was these numerous pesticidal qualities of neem that first attracted the attention of the West.

NEEM DEVELOPMENT

In addition to the substantial body of traditional knowledge, formal scientific study of neem's pesticidal properties began in India in the 1920s. At that time two Indian scientists conducted tests and found that a dilute suspension of ground neem seeds in water repelled the desert locust when it was applied to plants. Neem continued to be a topic of scientific study in India, but formal recognition of this work was scarce, despite important findings that emerged from it. In 1962, N. Pradhan conducted field tests in New Delhi that demonstrated the effectiveness of spraying a neem seed and water suspension on several crops to prevent insects from feeding on them, and in 1965 a chemist at the National Chemical Laboratory in Pune identified the structure of nimbin, a compound in neem with anti-viral properties.[8] Despite the results of research conducted in India, neem's attributes remained largely unrecognized in the West until German entymologist Heinrich Schmutterer observed its natural pesticidal properties in the Sudan in 1959. During a locust invasion, Schmutterer noticed that the entire landscape was defoliated except for the neem trees. Although the insects landed on the neem trees, they quickly flew off without feeding on them. Curious, he began to study neem in an attempt to understand how it worked as a pesticide. His interest in the tree subsequently became the focal point of his career and initiated an era of neem research in the West.

In the years since Schmutterer first observed the neem phenomenon, studies in labs in numerous Western countries confirmed that neem was a tree with vast potential. In 1992, the first comprehensive report on neem available for the lay person in the United States was published by an ad hoc panel of the Board on Science and Technology for International Development, a division of the National Research Council. In an effort to promote neem's potential, the publication was designed not for specialists in the field, but for government officials, voluntary organizations, entrepreneurs and others who could play a role in developing or promoting the tree's myriad uses. Authors said they hoped the reports would help overcome ignorance of the tree in the West. Noel Vietmeyer, director of the study, said that the biggest obstacle to neem's acceptance in the West was that Western scientists were simply unfamiliar with the tree and were skeptical of extravagant claims about its potential. The report's claims for the neem tree were substantial and confirmed, according to Eugene Schulz, chair of the study.[9] According to the report,

> Probably no other plant yields as many strange and varied products or has as many exploitable by-products as the neem. . . . This plant may usher in a new era in pest control, provide millions with inexpensive medicines, cut down the rate of human population growth, and perhaps even reduce erosion, deforestation, and the excessive temperature of an overheated globe.[10]

Current neem research confirmed that the NRC report's optimistic claims were not exaggerated. Neem is currently the only viable candidate for development of a method to combat Chagas disease, an incapacitating disease caused by a parasite and affecting millions in Latin America. Chagas is transmitted by an insect known as the kissing bug, which acts as a host for the developing parasite. Research teams in Brazil determined that blood treated with neem and fed to parasite-infested kissing bugs caused the parasites to disappear 20 days later. A researcher at the U.S. Department of Agriculture has studied neem as a means of combating the fungus, Aspergillus flavus, which grows on foods and produces highly carcinogenic chemicals called aflatoxins. Aflatoxins pose a serious health hazard, particularly in areas where grain and food storage is difficult due to weather conditions. But while neem's many potential uses are compelling, it is its effectiveness as a pesticide that continues to motivate much of Western research on the tree.

The NRC report concluded that in field tests neem proved as effective as pesticides such as malathion, with one notable advantage. Unlike chemical pesticides that could be harsh on the environment, neem's method of operation was compatible with the increasingly popular concept of integrated pest management (IPM). Integrated pest management emphasizes working within the environment to combat pests rather than relying on highly toxic chemical pesticides to control them. In IPM, every pest problem is monitored and then linked with the least toxic method possible to control it. Within the context of an idea like IPM, using neem as a pesticide is a natural and efficient way to deal with the problem: "To employ neem in pest control is to take advantage of the plant kingdom's 400 million years of experience at trying to frustrate the animal kingdom."[11] IPM has attracted interest primarily because of concerns about two major problems facing the agriculture industry: synthetic pesticide toxicity to other animals, including humans, and insects' capability to develop resistance to synthetic insecticides. The World Health Organization rates the former problem a serious one, estimating that synthetic pesticides fatally poison 20,000 people per year.[12] Most chemical pesticides attack insects' central nervous systems, killing them outright. Neem's compounds work against them indirectly, but ultimately provide the same result. Neem contains several compounds that have both behavioral and physiological effects on pest insects. Instead of killing pest insects on contact, neem either deters them from feeding on plants they would normally eat or disrupts their maturation process so that they eventually die. This capability allows neem to both destroy pests and leave non-pests unharmed.

The compound within neem primarily responsible for these ideal effects is azadirachtin, one of the most potent substances found in neem. It is the most active of a class of chemical compounds found in neem that are both anti-feedants and growth regulators. Many leaf-chewing pests that would normally defoliate plants will starve to death rather than eat a plant that has been treated with an azadirachtin solution. Derived from the oil that is extracted from neem seeds, azadirachtin is structurally similar to insect hormones that control the process of metamorphosis. Azadirachtin replicates the work of ecdysones in insects, but imperfectly, so that the process of metamorphosis is disrupted. It blocks the insect's production and release of hormones vital to metamorphosis, thus preventing it from molting and ultimately killing it.

Pest insects seem unable to develop resistance to neem-based pesticides because of the complex workings of compounds like azadirachtin. It is for this reason that neem is one of the few pesticides currently available with any effect on the "superbug" which has devastated crops in California and proven resistant to standard synthetic pesticides.

The azadirachtin molecule, however, has one drawback. It is inherently unstable, breaking down easily in sunlight and heat, and it can degrade in a solution within days.

For farmers in India who produced only enough solution to apply to their crops at any given time, this instability was not a major obstacle, but for individuals or companies trying to produce sufficient amounts to sell, the problem was significant. Several scientists, including some from India, have asserted that the instability of the azadirachtin molecule has been the biggest obstacle to widespread neem use.

NEEM DEVELOPMENT AT GRACE

James Walter, one of Grace's primary neem researchers and a member of the NRC report panel, described development of neem-based pesticides at Grace as "a relatively short story, owing to the great amount of work already accomplished by researchers throughout the world."[13] In 1988, Grace Horticultural Products, a unit of Grace Specialty Chemicals (USA), acquired the rights to a neem pesticide, Margosan-O, through a purchase agreement with Vikwood Botanicals of Sheboygan, WI. Robert Larson of Vikwood, a timber-importing firm, had been interested in Neem's numerous beneficial properties since he had first heard about them on a trip to India in 1973. He began importing neem seeds and testing them. But while he was able to develop a neem-based pesticide, have it patented, and gain EPA registration, he ultimately faced the major stumbling block of azadirachtin's instability.

In order to produce commercial quantities of a neem pesticide he needed a much more stable solution than he was able to produce in his own laboratories. After a failed attempt to contract out the production to another firm, Larson began to look elsewhere. He approached Grace, which he knew to be looking for a viable pesticide that was not harmful to the environment. Grace purchased the rights to the formulation and process for producing Margosan-O and then also began work on a neem pesticide that would be even more storage-stable, a process that ultimately led to the development of Neemix. In March 1994, the EPA registered Neemix as the first neem product cleared in the United States for use on food crops.[14] Walter described the development of neem-based pesticides as an important step to dealing with the problem of pesticide toxicity: "This is a real significant advance in insecticides . . . with all the characteristics you want and none you don't want. I don't see a down side to it."

THE PATENT

Finally, the Neemix researchers were ready to apply for a patent. According to United States patent laws, an invention has to meet three criteria in order to be patented: it has to be novel with respect to "prior art," a legal term referring to previous knowledge about a particular subject matter; it has to be non-obvious from the "prior art" to someone possessing ordinary skill in the art at the time the invention was made; and it has to be useful. The second constraint narrows the first one. Even if the subject matter of a sought patent is different from what is known from prior art, a patent can be denied if the differences are not significant enough to prevent them from being obvious to someone having an ordinary level of knowledge in that subject area. U.S. patent regulations further specify that in order to qualify for a patent, an invention cannot have been known or used in the United States, or patented or described in a printed publication in the United States or elsewhere prior to its invention; nor can the invention have been described in print in the United States or elsewhere more than a year prior to the application of a patent for the invention. The law also mandates that a patent cannot be granted on a naturally occurring substance unless it has been modified in some way: "Patent law requires something more than just the discovery of a naturally occurring product: a legally significant amount of human innovation must have been involved."[15] Grace submitted an application to patent their process for making a neem pesticide with a shelf life of up to 2 years. The patent application stated that the purpose of the invention was "to provide a non-toxic, natural pesticide formulation based on an extract from neem seeds with improved storage stability." The application was filed on October 31, 1990, and on June 23, 1992, the patent was granted. At that point Grace became one of 22 companies, including three in India, to hold approximately 40 patents on neem-based products.

THE PROTEST

On September 14, 1995, the Foundation on Economic Trends (FET), led by its president, Jeremy Rifkin, filed its request for reexamination of the Neemix patent with the U.S. Patent and Trademark Office (PTO). More than 200 organizations from 35 countries joined the FET as petitioners, primary among them, The Research Foundation for Science, Technology, and Natural Resource Policy in Dehra Dun, India, headed by Dr. Vandana Shiva, a scientist and outspoken advocate for indigenous peoples in India, and an Indian farmers organization. In lodging the protest, The FET and its allies challenged the Neemix patent on two levels: they took issue with the granting of the patent within the confines of U.S. patent law and also raised the question of whether the existing patent system could fairly compensate indigenous people.

The coalition challenged the patent on grounds that two of the three criteria necessary for patent granting, novelty with respect to prior art, and obviousness, were absent in the Neemix patent application and that the patent should therefore never have been granted. The groups included in the protest claimed that the patent was invalid because the body of traditional knowledge about neem, including its use as a pesticide, qualified as prior art and therefore should have negated Grace's application with respect to novelty. "Whatever little incremental change W. R. Grace put on this is small compared to the native knowledge that has been accumulated generation after generation on the use of this tree," Rifkin said.[16] More specifically, the protest documents asserted that the patent should be overturned because "the company's method of extracting stable compounds has been widely used prior to the patent's issuance and because the extraction methods have been previously described in printed publications." The protest claimed that Indian researchers had published descriptions of neem seed effectiveness as a pesticide as early as 1928, and cited the studies of neem in India in the 1960s and research conducted at the Indian Agricultural Research Institute on neem's potential as an insecticide and insect repellant, saying they had all preceded Larson and Grace's efforts by a decade. The protesters also asserted that it was unfair to expect any other records of prior knowledge about neem to exist in print because "the accumulated knowledge is the result of many anonymous and individual efforts carried out over hundreds of years. By citing a lack of formal publications as proof of non-obviousness, the company holds the villagers to a standard that is clearly unobtainable."[17] In reference to the obviousness of Grace's formulation, Rifkin asserted that "any chemist worth his salt could have come up with it."[18] The coalition also argued that the Indian farmers who had traditionally used neem could not have been expected to file for a patent themselves because of pragmatic and legal constraints against it: "The fact that Indian researchers failed to obtain patent protection on stabilization techniques is attributable to India's cultural and legal opposition to such patenting. Not only does Indian law prohibit the patenting of agricultural products, but many Indian citizens are ethically opposed to the patenting and ownership of nature. These feelings are especially strong in regard to the neem tree because the tree has played such an important role within Indian culture and religion."[19]

In addition to filing a formal petition with the PTO, the FET and its supporters claimed that, technicalities of patent law aside, patents like the one Grace held on neemix should not be allowed to exist because they represented appropriation of indigenous knowledge without compensation to the people who generated it. "What many Americans have not realized is that the anger, frustration and resentment in the developing countries against what they regard as piracy of their heritage is every bit as intense as the outrage that has been drummed up by the United States over the violation of our intellectual copyrights in the developing world," Rifkin said. He called Grace's patent "the first case of genetic colonialism," and said the neem tree was symbolic of a larger debate over how developing countries and indigenous peoples should be compensated when commercial products based on traditional knowledge were developed.

One of the FET's supporters, Vandana Shiva, a vocal critic of the development of resources indigenous to third-world countries by more technologically advanced nations, argued that the Grace patent presented a serious economic threat to Indian farmers who used neem. The Persian name for neem means "free tree of India," and Shiva argued that patents of any kind on any neem-based product would prevent the tree tree from being just that—financially accessible to the Indian farmers who have used it for centuries. She claimed that Grace's demand for the seeds would drive the price up beyond the reach of poor farmers and would ultimately cause a general shortage of the seeds. She also expressed concern that under the requirements of the World Trade Organization, successor agreement to the General Agreement on Tariffs and Trade, India as a member nation would have to move to align its patent requirements with the West's, and indigenous users of neem would end up having to pay Grace for using it as a pesticide.

THE REBUTTAL

As soon as the FET announced its intention to file the petition for reexamination, Grace issued a statement calling the FET's accusations "incorrect and without merit." Grace's reaction to the petition was one of surprise. The patent had been held for three years when the FET decided to file its protest, and company officials described themselves as flabbergasted by the controversy now surrounding it. Many protesters claimed that Grace had taken out a patent on the neem tree. The company emphatically denied that their patent was in any sense a patent on neem itself, since patenting of naturally occurring substances without any human modification or improvement was against U.S. patent law. Grace acknowledged that there was "nothing Buck Rogers" about their stabilizing formulation, but noted that they had spent approximately $10 million assessing previous ineffective preservation processes and as a result had come up with a procedure that worked. In response to accusations that the patent would prevent Indian farmers who relied on neem as a pesticide from getting access to it, Grace said that U.S. patent law did not restrict Indians from accessing neem seeds in any way and the company had no intention of seeking a patent in India. Further, Grace maintained that they did not apply for a patent on any extraction procedure and their patent was also restricted to the liquid form of the successful process. Grace pointed out that they purchased the neem seeds on the open market and that since the Neemix patent had been granted, they had purchased less than 3 percent of the harvested neem crop. The company works with an Indian company, J. P. Margo, near Bangalor, India, to process the neem seeds, and they said they believe that the company's efforts had contributed positively both to India's exports and to new employment there. "I think we deserve an award," a company spokesman said.

What had begun as an effort to provide a product for consumers interested in protecting both their crops and the environment had culminated in a struggle to defend that product against accusations that it was doing far more harm than good. It was clear that each side felt its own position to be more persuasive. Grace's strongest detractors saw the Neemix patent as representative of illegal, immoral corporate behavior. Even some who supported Grace's legal right to the patent wondered whether such patents could not be more fairly granted under another kind of system, proposing instead that regulation of intellectual property protection take place under the International Convention on Biological Diversity (CBD) rather than the WTO. Unlike the CBD, the WTO did not stipulate that the country of origin of a species or body of knowledge be acknowledged or that those contributing pertinent knowledge to a sought patent be compensated for their contribution. Highlighting both the promise and problems raised by the patenting of neem-based products, Eugene Schultz, the director of the NRC study, said: "You've got a classic case of an ethical dilemma. . . . You can certainly devise new uses that will benefit at least one segment of humankind: those who can afford it. But in the rush to exploit a new profit opportunity, the peasant is often the last person in the world to be considered."[20]

Notes

1. Ralph T. King, "Grace's Patent on a Pesticide Enrages Indians," *Wall Street Journal*, September 13, 1995, B1.
2. Information in this section taken from "Conglomerates: W. R. Grace & Company," in *International Directory of Company Histories*, Thomas Derdak, ed., St. James Press, 1988 pp. 547-550; and from "W. R. Grace & Co." in Hoovers Handbook, Bloomberg.
3. Richard Stone, "A Biopesticidal Tree Begins to Blossom," *Science*, Vol. 255, February 28, 1992 p. 1071.
4. Sy Montgomery, "Scientists Shop in Living 'Drugstore,'" *The Boston Globe*, August 10, 1992, p. 31.
5. National Research Council, *Neem: A Tree For Solving Global Problems* (Washington, DC: National Academy Press, 1992) p. 1.
6. Vithal Nadkarni, "New Roles for Old Neem," *The Times of India* (online version), (27 June, 1993) p. 1.
7. *Ibid.*, 32.
8. National Research Council, p. 32.
9. "Pesticide Tea," *Discover*, 14, July 1992 p. 14.
10. National Research Council, p. v.
11. *Ibid.* p. v.

12. Montgomery, p. 31.
13. *Ibid.*, p. vi.
14. *Science*, Vol. 269, September 15, 1995.
15. Richard H. Kjeldgaard and David R. Marsh, "A Biotech Battle Brewing," *Legal Times*, December 11, 1995, p. 16.
16. Mara Bovsun, "FET Challenges U. S. Patent on India's Natural Pesticide," *Biotechnology Newswatch*, September 18, 1995, p. 1.
17. "More than 200 Organisations from 35 Nations Challenge U.S. Patent on Neem," Third World Network (online newsletter) www.twnside.org.sg
18. "Biodiversity: Groups to Sue to Invalidate Pesticide Patent," *Greenwire*, September 13, 1995.
19. Third World Network, p. 4.
20. "Legal Battle Takes Root Over 'Miracle Tree,'" *USA Today*, October 18, 1995, 8a.

25

W. R. GRACE & CO.
AND THE NEEMIX PATENT
(B)

In the spring of 1996, six months after the FET and its supporting organizations filed a petition to reexamine the Neemix patent in hopes of having it revoked, the PTO rejected the petition. The PTO gave as one reason for its rejection the fact that the petition was backed only by oral proof of neem's use as a traditional herbicide.

Later that spring, WRG sold the division that produced Neemix. On May 14, Thermo Ecotek Corporation announced that it had acquired the assets of the WRG business unit specializing in botanical extracts and microbial products used for pest control. Thermo Ecotek specializes in a variety of environmentally friendly technologies and products, including agricultural pesticides. They said they hoped to use the newly acquired neem-based products to target a $550 million portion of the pesticides market, primarily for protection of citrus groves and crops such as cotton and vegetables. The new business unit was named Thermo Trilogy Corporation.

In August 1996, the neem case once again made news when a similar plan to overturn a patent on medicinal uses of turmeric, a popular spice frequently used to heal wounds in India, was initiated by India's Council of Industrial Research. One activist involved in the turmeric patent controversy cited the neem case as a caveat. She advocated arguing the case not in front of the PTO or under the rubric of the technical

This case was prepared by Kristi Severance and revised by Lisa Spiro under the supervision of Patricia H. Werhane. This case was written as a basis for discussion rather than to illustrate effective or ineffective handling of an administrative situation. Copyright © 1997 by the University of Virginia Darden School Foundation, Charlottesville, VA. All rights reserved.

definition of patentability but rather at the CBD and the WTO, calling into question the idea of indigenous property rights.

A recent United Nations Development Program Report titled "Conserving Indigenous Knowledge-Integrating Two Systems of Innovation" concluded that, while piracy by developing countries of chemical and pharmaceutical patents more than likely costs industrialized countries about $2.7 billion per year, developing countries and indigenous people lose about twice that per year in revenues they would have received if multinational corporations paid royalties for plants and traditional knowledge they use to produce and patent products.

26

BHOPAL (A):
CHOOSING A SAFE PLANT
LOCATION AND DESIGN

In the late 1970s, Union Carbide India [UCIL] brought together a team to analyze whether the company should upgrade its pesticide plant in Bhopal, India. UCIL, a subsidiary of the multinational chemical company, Union Carbide Corporation, had entered the pesticide industry in the early 1960s, just as the market had begun to boom. But after a brief period of economic growth, the market for pesticides had decreased even as competitors grew more plentiful. To maintain their growth and gain share of this decreasing market, UCIL was looking to "backwards integrate," or manufacture the raw materials and intermediate products for pesticides in the hopes of selling them to other manufacturers.[1] The company reasoned that this backwards integration plan would not only help sales but also satisfy the Indian central government, which had been pushing UCIL to make all of the ingredients for its pesticides locally. Indian government policy favored domestic manufacture since it theoretically improved employment ratings and the import-export balance. Yet complete manufacture of Union Carbide's Sevin and Temik brand pesticides meant that UCIL would be producing and storing highly reactive chemicals, such as methyl isocyanate [MIC] and phosgene, which had been used as chemical weapons in World War I.

Prepared by Susan Lacefield and Sarah E. Diersen under the supervision of Michael E. Gorman and Patricia H. Werhane. Partial support for this project was supplied by a grant from the Ethics and Values in Science program of the National Science Foundation and the Olsson Center for Applied Ethics at the Darden School. Copyright © 1999 by the University of Virginia Darden School Foundation. All rights reserved.

COMPANY BACKGROUND AND HISTORY

In the late 1970s and early 1980s, Union Carbide Corporation called itself a "global powerhouse" with subsidiaries and joint ventures in 34 countries. The company had a long and respected history within India since 1934, first as a private company named Ever Ready Company India Limited and then as the public company Union Carbide India Limited. Union Carbide Eastern, Inc., a wholly owned subsidiary of Union Carbide that ran its Asian operations, owned 50.9 percent of UCIL, while the remaining 49.1 percent was owned by Indian investors. Although UCIL had some ties to the Union Carbide Corporation headquarters in Danbury, CT, all the day-to-day operations of the company lay in the subsidiary's hands.

UCIL, known in India primarily for Eveready batteries, began to expand into other markets, such as agricultural products, in the late 1950s and early 1960s. The parent corporation supported and encouraged UCIL's expansion into other markets. The corporation was trying to expand its position overseas, and India, with its large number of scientists, technicians, and environmental protection institutions, seemed better equipped to handle the technology transfer than other developing countries.

When UCIL had expressed interest in expanding into pesticides in the 1960s, the Indian government had welcomed a plant in Bhopal with open arms and low property prices. For many centuries, the problem of famine had ranked at the top of India's list of concerns. In the 1960s and 1970s, the government of India believed the "Green Revolution" would be won with modern technology: high-yielding hybrid grain crops, automated farm equipment, better roads, and pesticides. The government knew that pesticides caused 500,000 deaths each year in developing countries alone and that a third of those deaths occurred in India itself.[2] However, the millions more who could be fed seemed worth the price. The central government was particularly delighted to have the plant in Bhopal.

The government trusted Union Carbide to run a safe plant. The company was a benchmark leader in safety in the chemical industry, which itself was a leader in industrial safety. The chemical industry only had 2.34 lost workday incidents per 100 full time workers in 1983 compared to an industry average of 6.84.[3] Union Carbide was known for being particularly "meticulous" in developing countries.[4] Environmentalist Karim Ahmed, research director of Natural Resources Defense Council, acknowledged on the *McNeil-Lehrer News Hour* that Union Carbide had one of the best records of any U.S. company in those regions.[5]

The Bhopal plant opened in 1969 and only "formulated" pesticides, a process limited to the mixing of several stable substances to create the final product. Then in 1974 UCIL obtained a license from the central government of India to manufacture, rather than simply "formulate," pesticides, requiring the handling of many potentially dangerous chemicals such as MIC. Although the company now was producing more sophisticated pesticides, it still was importing component ingredients, including MIC, from a Union Carbide plant in Institute, West Virginia. UCIL and Union Carbide believed importing MIC was cheaper and safer, since MIC was a highly reactive chemical. Unfortunately, growth in the pesticide market proved short-lived. Poor crops and the eradication of malaria in the late 1970s to early 1980s caused demand to plummet, leading UCIL to reconsider its strategy to manufacture five pesticide components, including MIC.[6]

LOCATION

In determining what to do with the Bhopal plant, the team needed to consider a number of peripheral factors. Despite the fact that the Bhopal plant continued to be a chronic money-loser, it provided important support for Union Carbide's Research and Development Center, located just south of Bhopal. This center was created to allow discovery and testing of pesticides under tropical conditions. The Bhopal plant's existence and its safety was important to the Center. As one scientist put it,

> The advantage of having the plant was that we were constantly forced to think in commercial terms. We were in constant touch with the production people there. Without it, we may be reduced to mere academics like numerous government research institutions-doing work without thought to applicability.[7]

In addition, UCIL had to consider the potential development of a new population around any plant that was built in India. According to one Union Carbide official: "In India, land is scarce and the population often gravitates toward areas that contain manufacturing facilities."[8] Proportionally more money and attention in India was applied to urban industrialization than to rural development. As a result, urban areas had to cope with mass migrations as people heard about possible new jobs. As more people migrated to the city, slums and shanty-towns cropped up, often close to industrial plants. In fact the two neighborhoods of temporary huts and shelters built across the street from the Bhopal plant were not zoned for residential use. Therefore, by choosing this site—a site that would inevitably be surrounded by people—UCIL needed to place even greater importance on the development of safety systems that could be trusted at all times.

If UCIL decided to produce the new chemical, MIC, the company needed to reevaluate whether the city of Bhopal itself was a good location for such a high tech plant.

The Pros for Bhopal

During the assessment, numerous benefits associated with the Bhopal plant location were identified. Bhopal was much better prepared to handle a chemical plant than anywhere else in the Madhya Pradesh province and most other places in India. The local technical institutions produced a large pool of skilled labor which would require only basic maintenance training sessions, should the company choose to invest a portion of its budget into such training.

Also, by staying at its current site, UCIL would save on construction costs. Instead of building a new plant, they could simply revamp the old one. Although some city zoning officials objected, the central government seemed willing to allow the plant to remain on the north side of town.

The Cons against Bhopal

On the other hand, if UCIL did decide to produce MIC instead of importing it, there were many reasons that the Bhopal plant technically should have relocated to the northeastern edge of the city. The 1975 Bhopal Development Plan had zoned the northeastern area for hazardous and "obnoxious" industries. This "greenbelt zone" was downwind from the rest of the city and away from major settlements. But at its current site, UCIL would be producing extremely toxic chemicals within a 3 km radius of 125,000 people,[9] within 2 km of the railroad,[10] and upwind from the center of the city.

PRODUCTION OF SEVIN

Which production method should be used? In spite of Union Carbide's 30 years of experience with MIC, much about the chemical remained unknown. Since MIC was so dangerous and volatile, researchers in general had been reluctant to work with it, and consequently very little was known about the toxicological effects of the chemical.[11] *Chemical and Engineering News* writer Michael Heylin maintained that "high reactivity and high volatility combine with high toxicity to make MIC a far from easy chemical to handle."[12] For this reason, other companies that manufactured MIC, such as the German company Bayer, tried to use as little MIC as possible, and they reduced the amount of time it was in storage.[13]

The original production method involved the production of Sevin without using MIC by combining phosgene, alpha-napthol and methylamine. The use of this method was discontinued in 1978 since it was not cost-effective and it produced a significantly greater amount of waste when compared to the MIC-based methods. So the company had to choose between two methods for the production of Sevin; both methods had been approved by the Indian government.

- The first choice, an alternative method similar to Bayer's, required the production of MIC. However, this method utilized dimethylurea and diphenylcarbonate instead of phosgene to create MIC. This method was moderately cost-effective.[14]
- The second choice was a newer production method that required the use of phosgene and methylamine to make MIC, and then combined MIC and alpha-napthol to produce Sevin. This newer method cost less and produced less waste than the above method. However, this method required the most handling of MIC and its equally dangerous ingredient, phosgene.

If MIC is used, how much MIC should the Bhopal plant produce? Just as arguments arose about the production method for the pesticides, disagreements began to occur between UCIL and its parent company over specific design issues, such as the holding tanks for MIC. The subsidiary argued for small tanks able to hold just enough MIC to be produced as needed. The smaller tanks would be more economical and safer since MIC was a volatile chemical, capable of reacting with water, other substances, and even itself. In addition, the safety devices that were designed to neutralize leaks could only accommodate relatively small amounts of MIC.

One of these safety methods involved the fire brigade spraying water to neutralize the escaping gas before it reached the surrounding populations; therefore, the amount of MIC produced was a critical consideration.[15] Furthermore, the scrubber, which "scrubbed" escaping gas with caustic soda, could only "scrub" about seven tons of gas.[16] This was significantly less than the forty-ton tank size that Union Carbide was encouraging, since the company hoped that the Bhopal Plant eventually would sell excess MIC to other pesticide producers. They also believed that if the plant stored more MIC, Sevin pesticide production would never be interrupted while the plant waited for MIC to be produced. However, some MIC experts believed that storing MIC for long periods was risky, and some countries even banned the practice.[17]

UCIL and Union Carbide did not think that they would ever have to store MIC for a long period of time. Instead, they expected the plant to run at its full 5,000-ton capacity. The parent company argued that its subsidiary should trust their decision; after all, the corporation was recognized as the world expert in MIC production and had been producing the chemical for almost 30 years. This decision placed even greater pressure on the engineers who were assigned the task of designing the new safety systems.

PLANT DESIGN

If the company chose to stay at the old plant location, UCIL needed to redesign the existing plant to handle MIC processing. In redesigning the plant, UCIL could draw from the plans for Union Carbide's existing MIC production plant in Institute, West Virginia. Working against this were a number of factors: UCIL was working on a very limited budget in India; it also had to consider the new environment; and government regulations of industrial plants in India were far less stringent than in the United States. In India, industrial polluters, for example, received only a small fine. Without the government requiring certain safety devices and precautions, Union Carbide had to make this decision on its own.

Automated Safety Systems

The Indian government was pressuring the company both to design a labor-intensive plant that would require the hiring of more Indian workers and to use locally produced equipment when possible. The Institute plant design, however, relied more on computerized or electronic back-up systems and less on manual labor. The Institute design called for an electronically controlled four-stage back-up safety system, a computerized early warning system and data logger, an automatic scrubber system and 24 shutdown devices for the MIC unit alone.[18] Although automatic and computerized systems tended to be more reliable and safer than manual control, the erratic electricity supply in Bhopal might have made relying on computers impractical. If an automated alarm system was not implemented, was it appropriate to rely on the only other option—requiring workers to detect leaks with their eyes and noses?[19]

Training and Maintenance

If safety was to depend on the workers, then the new plant design would also need to include a training program that would focus on the operating and maintenance procedures for the MIC tanks. Such a program would require a significant investment of employee work hours; therefore, the company needed to determine which employees, if any, should be trained to maintain the new plant.

Temperature and Pressure Gauges

The current tanks that would be storing the MIC were each equipped with only one temperature and one pressure gauge. These gauges monitored temperatures that were within the acceptable range and slightly above. The pressure gauges measured up to 55 psig while 25 psig was the highest acceptable pressure. Because a low temperature had to be maintained within the tanks, the temperature gauges only measured a maximum temperature of 77° F. The Institute plant storage tanks each had two to three gauges, capable of measuring a much higher range of conditions. Did storage vessels require two or three pressure and temperature gauges or would one per tank work just as well?[20]

Flare Tower

In the case of an extreme emergency, the plant had a flare tower that could ignite the escaping gas and safely burn it off. In order to route a gas leak from the MIC tanks to the flare tower, connector pipes were required for each tank. The current pipes were old and corroded; thus, the design team needed to decide whether or not the connections needed to be replaced.

SAFETY SYSTEM COSTS

Since the company was required to redesign the safety systems of the Bhopal plant within the smallest possible budget, the cost of each system was a significant consideration. The following table represents the estimated cost associated with each safety measure.[21]

Safety System	Cost[22]
Automated Control System[23]	$50,000
Training[24]	$2,500
Temperature Gauges (2 more/tank)[25]	$12,510
Pressure Gauges (2 more/tank)[26]	$9,667
Flare Tower Connector Pipes[27]	$6,599
Total Cost	$81,276

Demand for Sevin and other products of the Bhopal plant had plummeted. Jagannathan Mukund, the manager of the Bhopal plant, had to keep costs to an absolute minimum while storing increasing amounts of MIC. He faced a hard decision. What safety equipment and procedures were absolutely essential?

Notes

1. Paul Shrivastava, *Bhopal: Anatomy of a Crisis* (Cambridge, MA: Ballinger Publishing Company, 1987) 41.
2. Dan Kurzman, *A Killing Wind* (New York: McGraw-Hill Book Co., 1987), 21.
3. B. Bowander, Jeanne X. Kasperson, and Roger E. Kasperson, "Avoiding Future Bhopals," *Environment*, Vol. 27, No. 7 1985: 6.
4. Richard I. Kirkland Jr., "Union Carbide Coping with Catastrophe," *Fortune* (Jan. 7, 1985): 53.
5. Kirkland, 53.
6. Shrivastava, 41.
7. Jimmy Anklesaria, "Bhopal: The Union Carbide Corporation in India," *The Wall Street Journal*, Monday, Dec. 31, 1984, 419.
8. Bowander, 7.
9. Amrita Basu, "Bhopal Revisited: The View from Below," *Bulletin of Concerned Asian Scholars* (1994): 5.
10. Ward Morehouse and M. Arun Subramaniam, *The Bhopal Tragedy: What Really Happened and What It Means for American Workers and Communities at Risk* (New York: Council on International and Public Affairs, 1986) 3.
11. Rogene A. Buchholz, *Management Responses to Public Issues: Concepts and Cases in Strategy Formulation,* 3rd ed. (Upper Saddle River, NJ: Prentice Hall, 1994).
12. Michael Heylin, "Bhopal," *Chemical and Engineering News* (Feb. 11, 1985): 14.
13. Shrivastava, 54.
14. Kurzman, 22.
15. Kurzman, 50.
16. Kurzman, 51-52.
17. Nath Brojendra and Banerjee, *Bhopal Gas Tragedy: Accident or Experiment?* (New Delhi: Paribus Publishers, 1986) 158.
18. Shrivastava, 54, and Kurzman, 46.
19. Martin and Schinzinger, 258.
20. William Bogard, *The Bhopal Tragedy: Language, Logic and Politics in the Production of a Hazard* (Boulder, CO: Westview Press, 1989) 15.
21. Cecil H. Chilton, *Cost Engineering in Process Industries*, (New York: McGraw Hill Book Company, Inc., 1960).
22. All costs are adjusted with 1960 CPI (29.6) and 1984 CPI (103.9). Each 1960 cost was adjusted with a factor of 3.5034 (1960 CPI/1984 CPI). (Source: www.nnfr.org/econ/cpit.htm).
23. Cost Estimate obtained from Safer Systems (www.safersystems.com) This cost is an *estimate* that represents a system that has the ability to identify a leak, its location, and the magnitude of impact on the surrounding areas. This system does not automatically activate safety systems; therefore, training is required for employees to react to the leak and its location.
24. The cost of training estimate is based on the wages of workers with an average salary of $250/month (Shrivastava, 36). Assuming training would be required for at least 20 workers, minimum cost would be $5,000.
25. The temperature gauge cost is based upon the product cost ($360/gauge) plus the accessory cost (30% base cost) plus the installation cost (35% base cost). Calculation assuming six gauges purchased (two per tank). (Chilton, 238)
26. The pressure gauge cost is based upon product cost ($270/gauge) plus the accessory cost (30% base cost) plus the installation cost (40% base cost). Calculation assuming six gauges purchased (two per tank). (Chilton, 238).
27. The piping cost was based on the average cost of industrial piping for chemical plants ($38/foot) and the average cost of valves required ($750/valve). The cost is based on an estimated 100 feet of piping and two valves (Chilton, 212).

27

BHOPAL (B):
RECIPE FOR A TOXIC MIST

S

Summan Dey arrived at the gate to the Bhopal Union Carbide plant at 10:40 PM on December 2, 1984. He was a 26-year-old shift engineer earning 1400 rupees (about $117) a month. He hoped eventually to win promotion to a supervisory level. Dey had been trained to work with MIC four years ago when he was hired at the Bhopal plant. But huge financial losses had forced the plant to shorten his training period from a year to four months.

Dey was the senior operator in the control room that night. The plant was not producing at that point, and the only pending job was to finish water-washing some pipes that carried filtered MIC to the storage tanks. Any impurities could turn the liquid poison into a toxic gas.

The only possible point of concern was tank 610, which contained 41 tons of liquid MIC. Tank 610 was one of three underground holding tanks measuring 40 feet long and eight feet in diameter with a capacity of 15,000 gallons.[1] When the plant wanted to produce Sevin, it moved MIC out of these storage tanks by adding high-purity nitrogen gas, which increased the pressure in the tank. The gas then passed through a safety

This case was prepared by Sarah E. Diersen under the supervision of Michael E. Gorman and Patricia H. Werhane. Partial support for this project was supplied by a grant from the Ethics and Values in Science program of the National Science Foundation and the Olsson Center for Applied Ethics at the Darden School. This case was written as a basis for class discussion rather than to illustrate effective or ineffective handling of an administrative situation. Copyright © 1999 by the University of Virginia Darden School Foundation. All rights reserved.

valve into a pipe called the relief vent header. This pipe, or line, transferred the gas into the production reaction unit, where the Sevin was made. Another pipe then took the contaminated MIC to the vent gas scrubber, where it was neutralized.

Yet recently, this process had not run so smoothly for tank 610. Dey remembered that a week earlier the nitrogen valve for tank 610 had leaked and the shift was unable to transfer the MIC out of the tank. After the failed production attempt, Dey did not know whether maintenance had inspected the nitrogen valve. The plant's recent worker cutbacks had hit the maintenance crews particularly hard. Management had halved their numbers and eliminated their night supervisor position. Dey doubted maintenance had inspected the tank yet. Instead the tank's nitrogen valve had remained unfixed, possibly allowing small quantities of contaminants, such as metallic impurities, to enter the tank.[2] For a highly reactive gas like MIC, even small amounts of impurities could act as catalysts to run-away reactions.

At 11 PM, Dey noted that the pressure gauge on 610 registered 10 pounds per square inch (psi). The log noted that a half-hour before, it had registered 2 psi. But the gauges were notoriously unreliable, and the pressure was still within safe limits. This problem was not worth reporting to his supervisor, Shakil Qureshi.

At 11:30 PM, several other shift workers smelled MIC.[3]But minor leaks were a routine occurrence at the rupee-pinching plant, and the men searched for the source of the leak almost casually. Qureshi couldn't justify making the men skip their midnight tea break in order to check out what appeared to be minor, everyday problems. At 12:15 AM, in response to concerns, Dey checked the pressure gauge; it was still steady.[4]

But when the men headed to the canteen for their break, they began to cough and choke. The smell of MIC was overpowering. Dey glanced at the indicators for tank 610 and saw that the temperature was now 108 degrees Fahrenheit, almost double its maximum limit, and the pressure had shot past 45 psi and was rising.[5]

He immediately ran to the MIC storage unit where the venting safety valve was screeching as gas escaped into the air. He clambered up onto the concrete slab, which covered the storage tank below and heard a great boiling noise beneath him. Then the concrete began to quiver, buckle, and crack. Dey realized that a runaway reaction was occurring just below him where 50,000 pounds of MIC lay. Somehow water, and possibly some other catalyst such as iron, had leaked into the tank and created a rumbling reaction.[6] When water and MIC mix, a hydrolysis reaction occurs, creating heat-generating polymerizations, additions, and degradations. The pressure from this reaction burst the tank's rupture disk and pressure valve. Once the safety valve finally popped, a cloud of gas began to rise up the vent line.

At about 1:00 AM, Dey set off a siren designed to warn plant personnel and neighboring inhabitants. However, the siren lasted only a few minutes. Qureshi quickly turned to emergency leak measures. First, he called out the fire brigade. They tried to spray the hot vent line with water. Water breaks MIC vapor down into the comparatively safe dimethyl urea and trimethyl biuret.[7] The water curtain, however, only reached 100 feet, while the vent line was releasing gas at a height of 120 feet.[8]

Next he ordered Dey to start the vent scrubber, a rocket-shaped instrument that neutralized the escaping gas with caustic soda. Dey turned on the pump, but the caustic soda indicator did not move. Was the meter defective? Or the pump? Or was there not enough caustic soda? He wasn't sure. In any case, the scrubber was designed to neutralize gas with temperatures up to 158 degrees Fahrenheit, and the gas was now gushing out at 250 degrees.

An operator suggested transferring the contents of tank 610 into the back-up tank 619, designated for handling MIC overflow problems. But Qureshi remembered that tank 619—although it should be kept empty—still had liquid MIC in it. If the two tanks' contents mixed, the result might be even more gas.[9]

The operators knew that if they could cool the gas, they might be able to slow the reaction and gain time to dispose of it safely. Although corporate manuals stated that MIC should be refrigerated, the Bhopal Plant found it safe enough to keep the chemical at room temperature. So five months earlier, plant managers ordered the refrigeration shut off to save on power, and the Freon 22 from the unit removed for use elsewhere in the plant. Workers could not reinstall the unit in time to slow the reaction.

The only safety measure left was to light the flare tower which would burn the toxic gas away. This was a ninety-foot-high pipe that burned the toxic gases before they could get into the atmosphere. It had a pilot flame that was supposed to be kept lit 24 hours a day. But part of the piping that led to the tower was corroded and being repaired. No one knew whether the pilot would light. Dey set out to try, but ran into a cloud of toxic gas. Even if he got through to the tower, igniting it might cause a giant explosion.[10]

Dey, Qureshi, and the other workers were now caught in a deadly mist. Dey had a gas mask, but most of the workers had none, and Qureshi's had been stolen. Qureshi fled the plant, climbed over a fence, fell—nearly breaking his leg—and crawled under a sprinkler, which probably saved his life. Dey stayed in the plant. He believed that MIC was only an irritant, not a killer, but as his air ran out, he wondered.

Jagannathan Mukund[11] apprehensively peered through his windshield at the thick yellowish fog enveloping his car. The fog was alive with a crowd of people running straight toward him, stumbling, jostling to get ahead of one another. In spite of it being well past midnight on a cold December night, people clogged the streets of the northern sections of Bhopal, India. They appeared to be trying to outrun the fog itself. For this was no ordinary fog. This fog made them cough, splutter and vomit as they ran. "Go back! Go back!" the crowd gasped as it streaked past his car. But, unlike the fleeing crowd, Mukund couldn't turn back. As plant manager of Union Carbide India Limited's (UCIL) pesticide plant in Bhopal, he knew exactly what the fog was.

As Dec. 2, 1984 eased into Dec. 3, a 1 AM phone call roused Mukund from pleasant dreams and plunked him into the heart of a nightmare. He should come to the plant, a UCIL security guard said, a leak had occurred and the plant had released a 40-ton cloud of methyl isocynate (MIC) into the night air. In the first bleary moments of waking, Mukund experienced a moment of denial. He refused to believe what the guard was telling him. "The gas leak just can't be from my plant," he thought, "the plant is shut down. Our technology just can't go wrong, we just can't have such leaks."[12]

Yet now there was no denying it. This yellowish fog gave off the distinctive odor and sensation of MIC, a main ingredient in Union Carbide's Sevin brand pesticide. His eyes stinging, his throat burning and his lungs gasping, Mukund wiped his eyes with a damp cool cloth as he slowly made his way toward his plant. Mukund tried to reassure himself with what the company doctor had told him: MIC—although a dangerous, highly reactive chemical—was not lethal. But although Mukund told himself this, he could not help but see people all around him collapse, either unconscious or dead. This time, the doctor and the company's reassurances would prove wrong; thousands would die from exposure to this toxic chemical in the worst industrial accident to date.[13]

Mukund took nearly an hour and a half to crawl against the flow of the crowd to the gates of his plant. The Bhopal plant was only one of 13 plants owned by Union Carbide India Limited [UCIL], a subsidiary of the multinational chemical company, Union Carbide Corporation.[14] To the untrained eye, the Bhopal process plant looked like a wild collage of storage tanks, hoppers, reactors, and pumps all connected by pipes, valves and vent lines. Yet the collage produced a careful series of reactions, which created carbaryl-based herbicides and pesticides under the brand names Temik and Sevin.

By the time Mukund arrived at the plant all the safety measures had failed. Nothing else could be done except sound the alarm and alert the city. As the alarm wailed, Mukund sat, shocked by Dey's narrative. Mukund had trusted his technology and his company. The design for the plant came from Union Carbide Corporation, the world expert in MIC technology with 20 years of experience handling the harmful chemical.[15] His engineers were among the scientific elite of India. Most of them were better trained than even their American counterparts. Indeed, no one had anticipated this worst case scenario. As industrial sociologist William Bogard wrote: "No one seemed to seriously believe that all the crucial safety mechanisms at the facility could fail simultaneously."[16]

When Mukund came aboard in 1981, the plant was a major money loser. Almost as soon as the Bhopal plant had opened, the bottom fell out of the pesticide market. By 1981 the plant was running only at one-fifth of its 5,000-ton capacity. UCIL executives had pulled Mukund from the company's battery division to turn this financially struggling plant into a profit-gainer. When Mukund had arrived in the position, Union Carbide executives were discussing the cost of dismantling the plant and shipping it piece by piece to Mexico or Indonesia. But Mukund was determined to save his plant. So he began trimming off the fat and streamlining plant operations. Why have 12 operators working per shift when six would do? Why replace leaky pipes when a patch job would work? In spite of his economy plan, by 1984 the plant had lost $4 million. Still, Mukund thought he had done his best in a difficult situation. He never thought that he sacrificed safety for the bottom line.

Instead, Mukund had been proud of his safety record. The sign in front of his plant proclaimed that "Safety is everybody's business," and Mukund believed his plant had lived up to that motto. After all, his plant, according to Mukund, had the best safety record in India.[17] The plant had racked up 2 million safe hours, impressive for an American plant, let alone one in the less stringent Indian manufacturing world. In 1983, the plant even received a safety award from Union Carbide Corporation for this feat.

But underneath its reputation for safety and responsibility, a more worrisome picture of the Bhopal plant emerged. Six accidents had occurred at the plant from 1981 to 1984, three involving a release of MIC or phosgene, another toxic chemical used in the production of MIC.[18] A phosgene leak in 1981 had even killed one worker.[19] According to Daniel Kurzman, author of *A Killing Wind: Inside Union Carbide and the Bhopal Catastrophe:*

While Mukund and other plant managers thought the equipment and working conditions were adequate, as the personnel rolls were drastically cut, the workers remembered the orders to speed up their work even if that meant working without gloves; they remembered the patchwork job done on leaking pipes, the equipment that failed to function properly. Nobody told them that they might die, that thousands might die.[20]

For a supposed safety leader, the plant expended little focus or emphasis on safety itself. In the past couple of years, pressure to wear safety gear had decreased and department safety meetings were held only half as often.[21] Although the plant had stringent safety guidelines and standard operating procedures (SOPs), these were often not followed. For example, water might have gotten into tank 610 on the night of the disaster because workers did not follow SOP. When vent lines are washed out, workers are supposed to use a slip bind, a disc-shaped barrier, to isolate the lines from the storage tank. On the night of December 2, workers did not use the slip bind. As a result, the Indian government's investigation team believes that water then entered tank 610 through a leaky valve. The plant also eased back on the amount of training workers received. When the plant first opened, UCIL sent its workers to the Institute Plant (West Virginia) for training. Instead of maintaining this training regimen, the more experienced workers at the Bhopal Plant were supposed to train the new employees. Unfortunately, due to high worker turnover, Dan Kurzman writes that: "With each new cycle, according to the workers, the quality of instruction progressively diminished as employees with simple science degrees and little training themselves imparted to reluctant recruits less and less of their own limited knowledge."[22]

At the same time that the plant eased back on safety requirements, it also cut the number of employees. A smaller workforce meant that instruments were being monitored and maintained only half as often as they used to be. These cutbacks were significant since, unlike its sister plant in Institute, West Virginia, the Bhopal Plant had few automatic alarms or interlock systems. Nor did the plant have any electrical or electronic back-ups to pneumatically operated pressure gauges. Yet the answer to preventing the Bhopal disaster was not as simple as installing a few backup safety systems. Only nine months after Bhopal, the Institute plant would have its own leak, a discharge of methylene chloride and aldicarb oxime that sent 135 people to the hospital. The leak occurred in spite of back-up systems, in spite of $5 million in upgrades that were supposed to make a "safe plant safer," and in spite of heightened awareness.[23] Bogard even suggests that, "The reliance on complex backups may also give rise to unwarranted feelings of security that divert attention from the most immediate form of the hazard, viz., the production of hazardous chemicals itself."[24]

As Bogard intimates, the hazards of MIC were not completely known. Even the Bhopal plant doctor knew about the effects of MIC on the human body only in very general terms, although the company had specifically hired him to treat employees exposed to the chemical.[25] UCC officials had assured the doctor when they hired him that no one had ever died from MIC exposure. The doctor had interpreted that statement to mean the chemical was not lethal. So even though the OSHA permissible exposure limit was 0.02 PPM over an eight-hour period—one hundred times smaller than the odor threshold—the plant used employees' sense of smell to detect small leaks. Due to this cavalier attitude, operators and even managers failed to properly appreciate the dangers of MIC. Most believed it to be just an eye irritant and few received extensive training about it.[26]

Yet not all safety problems remained a mystery. The company, the Indian government and the people of Bhopal had all been previously warned of the safety hazards at the UCIL plant. In May 1982, a Union Carbide safety audit team listed ten major deficiencies in safety features at the Bhopal Plant including—but not limited to—no automated controls on MIC feeder tanks, the unreliability of gauges and valves, insufficient training, lack of preventive maintenance, and the high employee turnover. At the same time, "The team declared it had been impressed with the operating and maintenance procedures at Bhopal."[27] UCIL maintained that they corrected all except one problem, but the auditors never returned to double-check. Then on September 18, 1984, an inspection team of five experts from the Indian government warned of several safety problems that in three months would prove triggers to the disaster. Finally, local journalist Rajukman Keswani published several articles and put up posters warning the city about the potential for disaster at the plant. But at the time, most locals dismissed the articles and posters as sensationalism.

In spite of the warnings, little communication occurred between the plant and the community about what to do if a major accident happened. Two separate safety inspection teams, one in 1979 and one in 1980, had suggested the plant draw up coherent safety procedures that involved the community.[28] Yet no such dialogue had ever taken place. Lacking a detailed safety procedure to follow, plant officials made no effort to inform community leaders about the accident on December 3. Instead, plant workers either ignored concerned calls from the police and other community members or informed them that everything was under control. Even if they had known the release was MIC, local police and doctors would not have known how to treat exposure to it because the company never informed them of the proper treatment. MIC first affects the respiratory system and eyes. These effects can be decreased simply by covering the face with a damp cloth because water hydrolyzes MIC into the less dangerous methylamine and carbon dioxide.[29] On December 3, however, the uninformed police advised panicked crowds to run. This advice only increased people's inhalation and exposure to the gas and thus increased the number of deaths. Mukund had refrained from educating the public because he saw it as a lost cause. The shantytowns that cropped up around the Bhopal plant contained some of the poorest people in Bhopal. Mukund doubted whether they had enough education to rationally understand the risks and complexities of a chemical plant. Telling people to cover their mouths and noses with a wet cloth if a release occurs would have only incited suspicion and panic, Mukund believed.

Even the safety procedures that were in place proved ineffective. The plant did have an alarm siren and buses for evacuation purposes. But on the night of the release, the plant did not sound the siren until two hours after the leak occurred, and the buses remained idle as fleeing employees ran right by them. Even when the siren did sound, most of the citizens ignored it since test sirens went off about 30 times in a typical week.[30]

All these factors compounded to create the Bhopal disaster, which left somewhere between 2,000 and 10,000 dead on the first night alone.[31] Most of those initial deaths occurred almost immediately as MIC affected people's vision and respiratory system.

They died unable to see or breathe, their bodies trembling from the effects of inhaling the gas.

Thousands more continued to die or suffer debilitating illness for many years after the release. In total, approximately 500,000 people (or half the population of Bhopal) were exposed to MIC and 95 percent of those exposed suffered from it.[32] Survivors continued to experience chronic coughs, emphysema, asthma-like conditions, and concentration problems. According to the Council report, one in 14 people in the worst-affected areas suffered from tuberculosis.[33] Many could only work a couple of hours before they became breathless and fatigued. In a survey of 6,000 survivors, 97 percent said they suffered from eye complaints, such as cataracts.[34] Additionally, the gas damaged the central nervous and immune systems of many of the victims. Finally, the effect of the release threatened to continue into the future, since the gas had damaged the reproductive system of many women in neighborhoods surrounding the plant. Four out of five women had pelvic disease problems. They suffered from infection of the uterus, fallopian tubes and accepting tissues. Half of these women have had excessive menstrual bleeding, and 70 percent have had cervical erosion. Stillbirths doubled and spontaneous abortions increased.[35]

The continuing horrors of a MIC release would have been impossible for Mukund to even imagine in the months proceeding December 1984. Now he knew—and there were still thirty tons of MIC left in tanks at the plant. Furthermore, the government had placed him under arrest and told him he had to remain at the plant until it was all neutralized. A team of outside experts did arrive to help, and Dey was called back to assist as well. They had three main options:

1. They could repair the scrubber and the flare tower and run the gas through those safety systems. But what would happen if there were a problem with these safety systems again? Could they handle the volume of MIC remaining in the tank?
2. They could pack the gas in drums and ship it away. But where would they ship it? What if it leaked?
3. They could run the plant again, making the gas into Sevin and selling it, for an estimated 2.5 million rupees ($200,000). Local politicians and citizens were horrified by this option. Why let Union Carbide make more money off its poisons—and put Bhopal at risk again?

Notes

1. Ward Morehouse. *The Bhopal Tragedy*. New York:Council on International and Public Affairs, 1986 p. 3.
2. Paul Shrivastava, *Bhopal: Anatomy of a Crisis*. Cambridge, MA: Ballinger Publishing Co., 1987 p. 54.
3. Dey's account of the disaster has been culled from the following sources: Dan Kurzman, *A Killing Wind*, New York: McGraw-Hill Book Co., 1987 pp. 39-54, and Steven Casey, "Business in Bhopal," in *Set Phasers on Stun*, Santa Barbara, CA: Aegan, 1993 pp. 71-88.
4. Union Carbide claims that Dey and other workers were aware of the possibility of sabotage in the plant at this point, and therefore were tense. Dey and others deny this.
5. Kurzman, 49.
6. The Indian government, Bhopal plant workers and other investigators hypothesized that the water had leaked into the storage tank while shift workers washed out built-up residue in the system's pipes. Union Carbide argues, however, that the runaway reaction resulted from a sabotage attempt either by a disgruntled worker or the Sikh terrorist group.

7. B. Bowander, Jeanne X. Kasperson and Roger E. Kasperson. "Avoiding Future Bhopals," *Environment*, Vol. 27, no. 7 1985: 31.

8. Kurzman, 50.

9. Kurzman, 52.

10. Even if the main safety devices—the scrubber and the flare tower—had been operational, the plant still would have failed to stave off the disaster. Neither the flare tower nor the vent gas scrubber could handle such a large release of gas at such a high temperature and pressure. Union Carbide engineers had designed the safety devices to process small amounts of gas routinely vented off the storage tanks to maintain the proper pressure. No one envisioned them having to handle the contents of the entire tank.

11. Mukund's account is largely based on passages from Kurzman, *A Killing Wind*.

12. William Bogard, *The Bhopal Tragedy: Language, Logic, and Politics in the Production of a Hazard.* Boulder, CO: Westview Press, 1989 p. 14.

13. Two years after the Bhopal incident, the government would say that 2,500 victims died while all the evidence indicates that this figure should be estimated near 8,000. (Kurzman, 130)

14. Shrivastava, 38.

15. Bowander, 6-7.

16. Bogard, 23.

17. Kurzman, 24.

18. Bowander, 8.

19. Phosgene is itself highly toxic. In World War I, phosgene had been used as a primary chemical warfare agent.

20. Kurzman, 167.

21. Kurzman, 42, 91.

22. Kurzman, 41.

23. Roger E. Kasperson and Jeanne X. Kasperson, "Is Safer Safe Enough?" *Environment*, September 1985: 10.

24. Bogard, 15.

25. Kurzman, 81.

26. Bogard, 13.

27. Arthur Sharplin, "Union Carbide India Limited The Bhopal Incident," North American Case Research Association, New York: McGraw-Hill, Inc., 1993 p. 300.

28. Kurzman, 26.

29. Ron Dagani, "Data on MIC's Toxicity Are Scant, Leave Much to Be Learned," *Chemical and Engineering News.* Feb. 11, 1985: 39.

30. Bogard, 4.

31. The Indian government estimates that at least 2,000 people died in the first night alone. Others believe the number to be much higher. For instance, Dan Kurzman—who based his numbers on data from crematorium and cemetery officials—estimates the number of dead to be at least 8,000. (Kurzman, 130-131). Because the neighborhoods most severely affected by the release were some of the poorest in the city, arriving at an exact number of deaths has proved impossible.

32. Kurzman, 130.

33. Pearce, 25A.

34. Kurzman, 146.

35. Kurzman, 146.

28

ESKOM AND THE SOUTH AFRICAN ELECTRIFICATION PROGRAM (A)

THE BEGINNING OF THE ELECTRIFICATION PROGRAM

The year was 1994 and Tienz[1] sat at his desk contemplating the enormous scope of the job that was in front of him. Electricity had always been an integral part of the developmental processes of the South African nation[2] as a whole; in fact, Kimberley, South Africa was electrified while London was still using gas lamps to light its streets. Because of this history of helping to shape the formation of the South African nation,[3] Eskom now saw itself as a necessary participant in the reconstruction process that the new ANC[4] government[5] was outlining in an effort to rebuild the country from its Apartheid past. The company even had a past history of not only participation but also in the creation of upliftment programs[6] under Apartheid. For example, in the late 1980s the company had implemented an Affirmative Action policy in order to recruit black South Africans into management positions and created programs to improve the school systems within black South African communities.[7] However, the present situation was a bit more complicated than Eskom's past initiatives because in 1994 the new government

Prepared by Brian D. Cunningham, graduate student, Systems Engineering and Division of Technology, Culture, and Communications at the University of Virginia, under the supervision of Michael E. Gorman and Patricia H. Werhane. Partial support for this project was supplied by a grant from the Ethics and Values in Science program of the National Science Foundation and the Olsson Center for Applied Ethics at the Darden School. Copyright © 1999 by the University of Virginia Darden School Foundation. All rights reserved.

had specifically mentioned that electrical access to all citizens was essential to the Reconstruction and Development Program (RDP), which was an outlining of initiatives that would help the country rebuild itself from its Apartheid Past.[8] Accordingly, management had informed Tienz that the company had made the decision to aid the new government in its reconstruction process and implement a country-wide electrification program, which was a far cry from simply extending the grid a few kilometers from urban centers.

The scope and scale of the proposed electrification program seemed overwhelming to Tienz. How was he going to develop a system to provide electrical connections to approximately 1.75 million homes (approximately 9 million people) by the year 2000 in a cost effective manner? Not only would new transmission lines have to be constructed, but safe and reliable distribution meters had to be designed to meet the unique conditions that existed in black South African townships, squatter camps,[9] and villages. Not only would the project be demanding from a technological standpoint but one look at the situation made the possibility of recapturing the capital costs involved seem impossible. For the consumer market that Eskom was going to be electrifying not only had grown accustomed to using coal, wood, and paraffin for all of its energy purposes but also had dramatically low and inconsistent monthly incomes. So how was Tienz supposed to develop a pricing structure for these new connections given the depressed economic situation that existed in the areas that the company was going to be electrifying?

In fact, it was easy for Tienz to see the economic differences that Apartheid had helped to engrain between white and black South Africans on his drive into work each morning. The highway was lined with hundreds of shacks that people had built out of spare wood, tin, and even cardboard in order to have a home closer to the city and the economic activity close to its borders, which seems bizarre for a country that has a standard of living comparable to that of anywhere in the world. The average monthly income for a black South African was R294,[10] which was even further reduced by the fact that the average monthly expenditures for food and housing for this individual were R28 and R251 respectively,[11] and half of all black South Africans live below the poverty line. Moreover, approximately 41 percent of the black South African population was unemployed, and those that were employed had jobs that were either seasonal in nature or inequitable in salary structure. For example, black South Africans make up about 75 percent of South Africa's population, but they earn only 28 percent of the country's total income; whereas, white South Africans make up only 13 percent of the population, but they earn 61 percent of the country's income.

The electrification program was seen as a "basic need" by the ANC government because although black South Africans made up 75 percent of the country's total population, only 20 percent of them had access to electricity in 1994. Housing and water were identified as the two other basic needs, both of which are dependent upon electricity, because one-fourth of all blacks either have no housing or live in shacks and 40 percent do not have access to clean water. These basic needs were identified because of the wide discrepancies between white and black South Africans, which were not only economic. For example, a typical black South African's life expectancy is 57 years of age as compared to 73 years of age for a white South African, and infant mortality is 57 per 1000 live births for blacks as compared to 13 per 1,000 live births for whites.

An electricity program was also seen as a viable option because the country already had an electrical grid in place to supply both the residential areas and industry with electricity; therefore, the infrastructure was already in place to electrify the black population. In fact, there were approximately 240,000 km of lines currently employed in the country to transmit and distribute electricity. However, extensions to the existing electrical grid would undoubtedly be capital intensive; for example a one kilometer extension of low voltage, medium voltage, and high voltage lines would cost Eskom R40,000, R100,000, and R1,000,000, respectively. Although the line extensions in the electrification process would use mostly low voltage line extensions, some medium and high voltage extensions would be necessary to carry the needed electrical capacity to the areas being electrified. Although Eskom was operating at about 10 megawatts in excess capacity, the newly electrified customers would demand more electricity from the system and lower this excess in generation capacity. Therefore, the company could possibly find itself in the position of having to build more generation facilities,[12] and incur the associated capital expenditures in order to meet the new demand that it was in essence creating.

The cost of the program had been estimated at R1.2 billion annually. However, Eskom's revenues were R15,417 million and its operating expenditure was R11,864 million, which left the company a total operating income of R3,553 million at its disposal.[13] The latter meant that Eskom needed to fund the program with approximately 35 percent of its operating income annually, which would be an enormous expenditure for the company to make on a project that had an uncertain future. But three factors made the RDP's goals achievable by Eskom:

1. *The fact that its policies were determined by the Electricity Council, which was linked so closely to the government executive and the finance ministry.*
2. *The fact that it had much experience with generating revenue by issuing bonds on financial markets.*
3. *The fact that Eskom had reserve generation capacity, which meant that capital expenditures for electrification exclude generation equipment, which reduce total expenditures significantly.*

Given the size of the capital expenditures that Eskom was going to undertake in the electrification program, the company needed to develop a program that would be affordable, add value to the lives of the people that it was electrifying, and contribute to South Africa's reconstruction process.

How to Deliver Service

Because of the possibility of not receiving a sufficient return on its investment,[14] Eskom considered several options for the delivery of electricity. Of these options, two surfaced as being the most viable alternatives; (1) a pre-payment metering system or (2) fixed cost connections. In the former case, people pay for electricity before they actually use it, and in the latter, people pay a monthly fixed fee for unlimited use at a fixed current level. Option (1) would allow Eskom the opportunity to offset the risk of people defaulting on their bills and the costs associated with recovering money owed, and option (2) would allow people to use as much electricity as they needed for growth at a fixed low monthly fee.

Fixed-rate connections had already been used in other countries for similar electrification projects because of the lowered capital expenditures associated with being able to distribute electricity with low voltage lines and not having to supply meters with each connection, which also offsets additional maintenance costs. However, would it be possible for Eskom to set an affordable fixed monthly fee that consumers, who have variable monthly incomes at best, would be willing to pay each and every month? Again, the people being connected are struggling with a tremendously high unemployment rate and have sporadic monthly incomes. Given the fact that employment was variable at best, would the average person be able to afford the service that was being provided? If it would be possible to develop an affordable monthly fee that people would agree to have billed to them each month, would these people be willing to switch to a usage based fee in the future if their electrical demands surpassed the amount of electricity that was available under a fixed-rate option? On the other hand, pre-paid meters would cost more than fixed-rate connections, and even more than traditional meters; thereby raising the capital costs associated with the electrification program. However, the advantage of the pre-paid metering system was in the fact that the consumers could stop using electricity and not pay whenever they did not have sufficient income or even a job.

Tienz now needed to decide which option would be better for the electrification program and why. He had to figure out how to finance such a capital intensive program. The program was projected to need approximately R20 billion to complete. So how was Eskom to raise the capital that was necessary for a program that would take R1.2 billion annually? How was Eskom to develop sustainable communities who could use the electricity that was being supplied to them?

APPENDIX A
EARLY SOUTH AFRICAN BEGINNINGS

In 1652 an expedition by the Dutch East India Company landed in what is now South Africa, for the purposes of establishing a garrison to supply East India ships with fresh water and food. Soon the garrison grew into a colony and in 1657 the first settlers built their homes on the grazing land of the local indigenous people,[15] which inevitably sparked conflict between these two groups of people in southern Africa. In 1660, after winning a number of conflicts with these tribes, the Dutch settlers planted a thorn hedge across 6000 acres of the Cape in order to separate the colony from the tribe.[16] This hedge and its use to separate the races serves as an early symbolic representation of the Apartheid doctrine that was yet to come.

Although these periods of clashes between the white and black South Africans were frequent, there was a fair degree of trading and social interaction between the two groups.[17] Soon, however, further measures were placed into effect in order to regulate black and white interaction. For example, in 1829 a pass system was implemented in order to monitor and control the flow of black South Africans into white areas. Moreover, as more European settlers came to the country, stern competition arose between the two groups for the limited amount of land and water in the country which led to more frequent and serious conflicts. This competition for land started when 70 percent of the white population in the mid-1850s were forced into black controlled lands because of the limited land available in white controlled areas and the resulting competition with other white farmers for land rights.[18] Because of the white invasion into the tribal lands and the ensuing conflicts with the indigenous tribes, the white population learned to survive in these areas by dominating and controlling the black populations. This domination by the white population, on both the battleground and in farming, was felt by both populations as a feeling of white superiority. Therefore, a master-servant relationship came into effect with black indigenous people doing manual work for the white population in southern Africa.

The agricultural economy of southern Africa soon turned into one centered upon mining when in 1867 diamonds were discovered. The master-servant relationship between the black and white populations was thereby further instilled when the white owned mines recruited cheap black labor. Moreover, this recruitment of black labor led to a huge influx of blacks into the white controlled lands, and since this was going against the measures that had been put in place by the whites to control race interaction, the Native Land Act was placed into effect in order to control the incoming black population. This Act granted blacks temporary status to live and work within South Africa and a portion of land was even set aside far from white areas for the incoming black population to inhabit. However, white control went even further than controlling black populations in the white areas of South Africa. In the early 1900s, the white government went further in its control over the black populations in its midst by placing mandates on black mobility, education, and housing.

APPENDIX B
BEGINNING OF ELECTRICITY SUPPLY

It's hard to imagine that one of the far corners of the world was where electricity was first utilized, but given that "necessity is the mother of invention," South Africa's mining industry inevitably called for the use of electricity in the mid-1880s.[19] In fact, when the streets of London were still being lit by gas lamps, Kimberley, South Africa was using electric street lights in 1882. Mining companies installed their own electrical reticulation systems in order to supply electricity to the mines for illumination and power for equipment. These systems soon grew to the point of supplying the nearby cities with electricity, and it was soon recognized that large centralized power stations would supply more reliable and cheaper power than smaller dedicated mining power stations. This eventually led to the formation of the Rand Central Electric Works[20] and the Victoria Falls Power Company in 1906.

Eventually, the Electric Supply Commission (Escom) was established in 1923 in order to supply electricity more cheaply and efficiently to industry and local authorities. In 1937, Escom's headquarters was the tallest building in South Africa (21 stories tall), which indicates the growth that Escom underwent in order to meet the growing needs of the mining industry as new gold reserves were discovered. During the booming years after WWII, electrical demand was soaring and Escom was faced with the challenge of meeting these demands effectively. However, although South Africa was blessed with a wealth of natural resources, [21] the country did not have an adequate water supply, so Escom recognized that it had to effectively utilize the huge coal reserves to produce electricity. In fact, the coal seams in the country were abundant, thick, shallow, and unfaulted, which meant that extraction costs would be minimal and that these lowered costs could be passed on in the form of cheaper electricity prices.

During the 1960s more coal fired generation facilities were constructed and Escom successfully designed dry cooling towers for burning the lower quality coal that was abundant in South Africa. In the 1970s, future electrical demand and load growth were expected to increase even more, so new facilities (one nuclear plant and several pumped storage plants) were built. However, load growth did not increase as planned and Eskom[22] was left with a surplus of generation capability at its disposal, which would ultimately lead to Eskom being able to supply even cheaper electricity in the 1990s.

At the end of 1997, Eskom was one of the five largest utilities in the world with total assets equaling R96,894 million, total revenue equaling R20,448, and approximately 40,000 employees.[23] The company supplies more than 98 percent of the electricity used in South Africa, which constituted approximately 60 percent of the electricity used on the entire continent of Africa. The electricity is generated by 20 power stations with a 39,154 total megawatt capacity. The power is distributed by way of more than 26,065 km of high voltage power lines within South Africa. Because of the overanticipated electrical demand in the 1980s and the additional generation sites that were constructed as a result, Eskom is currently operating at a surplus capacity of approximately 10,000 megawatts. Moreover, estimates have shown that Eskom's surplus capacity will not be exceeded until the year 2007, even with the electrification project and growth in demand for industrial power.[24]

APPENDIX C
THE "NEW" SOUTH AFRICA

After winning the seat of government in the first open elections[25] in South Africa by receiving 62.5 percent of the vote and obtaining 252 of 400 seats in the legislature, the African National Congress (ANC) thus needed to implement a plan to make a better life for all.[26] For it was recognized that a period of development must be undertaken in order to offset the past hindrances of Apartheid. Therefore, the Reconstruction and Development Program (RDP) was developed in order to guide the post-Apartheid state in South Africa. It is a socio-economic policy that seeks to mobilize all of South Africa's people and resources to eradicate the lingerings of Apartheid and build a non-racial, democratic future. The program consisted of six basic principles and five key programs.

The six principles were:

1. Maintain an integrated and sustainable program.
2. Center on a people-driven process.
3. Ensure peace and security for all.
4. Embark on nation building.
5. Link reconstruction and development.
6. Democratize the nation.

The principles were set to be achieved by the five programs:

1. Meeting basic needs.
2. Developing human resources.
3. Building the economy.
4. Democratizing the state and society.
5. Implementing the RDP.[27]

However, as the statistics in Tables 1 and 2 illustrate, the task would not be easy.

Table 1   Income Statistics for Different Ethnic Groups[28]

	Asians	Colored	Whites	Blacks
Percent of Population (out of 42 million)	3	8	16	73
Percent Unemployment	17.1	23.3	6.4	41.1
Avg. monthly personal income	R1,304	R711	R2,875	R294
Avg. spent monthly on food/housing	R871/R640	R521/R275	R1,072/R827	R251/R28

Table 2   South African Statistical Indicators[29]

GDP	R433 billion
GDP/capita	$3,004
Unemployment	32.6%
Inflation	12.5%
Interest Rate	18.4%

APPENDIX D
EARLY SOCIAL INVESTMENT BY ESKOM

During the Apartheid era, before the electrification program, it is estimated that 98 percent of all white households had electricity, whereas 80 percent of black households lacked it. [30] In addition, the power that was sold to blacks was subjected to highly arbitrary rates. Eskom acted as a wholesaler of electricity to approximately 450 different municipalities, which were typically white-controlled under the Apartheid system. Because of the number of municipalities involved, over 2000 different rate structures were constructed. In some areas, such as in Soweto on the border of Johannesburg, black residents were paying double the rates of nearby whites within Johannesburg proper. Moreover, it could be argued that the electrical service for the blacks' areas was of much lower quality than for white customers: "If the power went out, you could wait a week, a month or even longer for a crew to show up."[31] Thus, Eskom's history of corporate social investment (CSI) is, not surprisingly, racially directed.

However, anticipating the likely changes in the Apartheid regime, [32] Eskom committed to cultural change in 1985. It created an affirmative action program to create contact between the races, which by the 1990s resulted in the recruitment of talented black personnel into executive positions. In 1988 it launched its "New South African" program, a CSI program initially funded with R4 million. About two thirds of this budget was initially spent on electrifying 10 schools per year in Soweto. The rest of the budget was largely spent on funding education-oriented, non-government organizations which sought to improve the educational conditions in poor, black regions. [33]

Moving to alleviate further some of the problems associated with the Apartheid system, Eskom's investments in electrification accelerated and expanded beyond schools to an "Electricity for All" program. At the end of 1990 it launched this program with the philosophy that economic development within South Africa's black communities would not occur until they had access to electricity. However, there were no accurate statistics representing the proportion of the South African population that lacked electricity; in fact, there was no accurate database of housing at all in South Africa at that time. Accordingly, Eskom's first task was to compile housing statistics in order to determine the extent of electrification in South Africa's urban and rural areas, and it revealed that out of 7.2 million homes in South Africa, only 3 million had access to electricity. [34] This translated into approximately 23 million people, just over half of the population of South Africa at the time, without electricity.[35] Almost all of these homes were in black impoverished urban, township, and rural regions.

Eskom piloted the first electrification program, and by the end of 1991 Eskom succeeded in connecting 31,000 residences to the electrical grid. Eskom worked with local government councils and offered incentives to regions if they could electrify homes in their areas. Viewed as a success, the program was continued, with a connection of an additional 159,000 homes in 1992 with an average cost per connection of R2600. At the end of 1992, approximately 1 million black South Africans had been connected to the grid and over 260 electrification projects were underway. Eskom recognized that mere connections were not all that the poorer people in South Africa needed in order to have access to electricity. The company made it its goal to reduce the "real price"[36] of electricity in order to stimulate economic growth and provide an affordable service to the people that it was electrifying. Therefore, Eskom had achieved substantial momentum in electrification just at the time when political power was changing hands in South Africa.

APPENDIX E
ESKOM'S COMMITMENT TO THE RDP

John Maree[37] wrote in Eskom's 1992 Annual Report:

> As the new South Africa becomes a reality, large organizations will need to have relevance to our society and demonstrate that, through the conduct of their business, they bring value, not only to their own stakeholders but also to the wider society. Their products and services will have to meet the emerging consumer needs and contribute to the well-being and progress of the community and particularly the disadvantaged.

Moreover, access to electricity was identified as one of the top two needs of the citizens of the country. Therefore, Eskom's early electrification efforts were embraced by the new government, and the electrification of homes was identified as one of the most important aspects of the "Meeting basic needs" program. An accelerated and sustainable electrification program was planned to provide access to electricity for an additional 2.5 million households by the year 2000, thereby, increasing the level of access to electricity to about 72 percent of all South African households, which would be double the 1992 number of households with access to electricity. Accordingly, Eskom would play a major role in meeting the goals set out by the RDP and these goals became central to Eskom's electrification goals. Eskom's 1995 stated goals based on the RDP were:

1. Further reduce the real price of electricity by 15 percent, so as to become the world's lowest cost supplier of electricity.
2. Electrify an additional 1,750,000 homes, improving the lives of 11 million South Africans.
3. Change the staffing profile so that 50 percent of management, professional and supervisory staff are black South Africans.
4. Educate, train and upgrade sufficient numbers of people to meet Eskom's future managerial, technical and other professional staff needs by employing 370 black trainees and bursars per year, and enabling all Eskom employees to become literate.
5. Maintain transparency and worker consultation in decision making.
6. Contribute R50 million per year to electrification of schools and clinics, and other community development activities, particularly in rural areas.
7. Enable all Eskom employees to own a home.
8. Encourage small and medium enterprise development, through Eskom's buying policies and giving managerial support.
9. Protect the environment.
10. Finance the above from Eskom's own resources and from overseas development funding.

Because the company believed that electricity was a vital part of modern life and that it would encourage economic growth within the newly electrified areas, Eskom committed to the RDP goals of electrifying approximately 2.5 million of the 4.2 million homes (60 percent of the people without electricity) through both grid and non-grid (solar) connections. The remaining number "would be difficult to electrify due to either structure of the dwelling, the distance from the existing grid, access to alternative energy sources, or simply as a matter of affordability." Other reasons why Eskom proclaimed commitment were that the standard of living improved through access to hot water, stoves, and TV; that gender specific roles could be revamped (e.g., time previously spent on collecting firewood could be used for other goals); that educational standards improved by access to lighting; and that health standards improved through access to refrigeration, since food and medicines could be kept handy and since smoke from cooking fires could be eliminated.[38] The company cited Japan, Taiwan and Korea as "winning nations," and stated "economic growth could not reach impressive figures before the overwhelming number of homes in the country had electricity."[39] In addition to electrifying 300,000 homes per year until the year 2000, Eskom also made a pledge to reduce the price of electricity in real terms by 15 percent by the year 2000 in order to provide the newly connected homes with an affordable service. The latter is in keeping with Eskom's overall vision of offering the lowest electricity rates in the world.[40] All such goals stem from Eskom's belief that little economic growth can occur without the widespread use of electricity.

In 1994 it was estimated that the electrification program would cost around R12 billion (approx. US$3.5 billion), with annual investments peaking at around R2 billion.[41] How would it be possible to implement such a large social investment project in a viable manner? Although Eskom was producing the lowest priced electricity in the world at the time and was operating at an excess capacity, the capital expenditures that would be incurred would be astronomical. Moreover, given the history of Apartheid, the people that it was going to electrify had become dependent on other sources of energy[42] for their daily needs. Was there a guarantee that these people would use the electricity when it was supplied to them? The unemployment rate in South Africa also lingered at approximately 45 percent and there was a history of "non-payment" among the black population,[43] so how was Eskom going to implement a system in which it was lowering the risk on return for its investment?

Notes

1. Fictitious Afrikaans name for the decision maker for this case.
2. For a brief historical perspective of South Africa see Appendix A.
3. For a historical description of Eskom's background see Appendix B.
4. The African National Congress which took control in 1994 during the first racially open elections in South Africa. For a description of the 1994 elections and the Reconstruction process that was outlined see Appendix C.
5. For a description of Eskom's corporate initiatives and policies under Apartheid see Appendix D.
6. Programs that were used to narrow the discriminatory gap between the white and black South Africans.
7. For a description of Eskom's stated commitment to the South African reconstruction process see Appendix E.
8. African National Congress. *The Reconstruction and Development Programme.* Johannesburg, South Africa. 1994.
9. People could settle on municipal lands under new South African law, which meant that thousands of people were constructing make-shift structures for houses in areas that were not designed for residential development (e.g. areas beside freeways and even airport runways).
10. The South African Rand has fluctuated against the U.S. Dollar in the range of 3:1 in 1994 to 6:1 in 1998.
11. Reconstructed from *SA to Z: The Decision Maker's Encyclopedia of the South Africa Market.* 1996.
12. One generation facility would cost approximately R16 billion and take several years to build.
13. From Eskom's 1994 Annual Report.
14. Again because of the low monthly wages and the high unemployment rates in South Africa.
15. The Khoikhoi (aka the Hottentots).
16. Louw, L., Kendall, F. *South Africa: The Solution.* Ciskei, South Africa: Amagi Publications, 1986.

17. Ibid.
18. Orpen. *Productivity.*
19. The mining shafts were going deeper into the ground and needed to be ventilated.
20. The first commercially supplied electricity in South Africa.
21. South Africa has 91% of the world's manganese reserves, 82% of its platinum group metals, 58% of its chrome, 53% of its gold. As a result, South African mines are deeper than those of any other country in the world, at depths of almost 4 kilometers in places (e.g., Western Deep Levels Mine).
22. Escom was renamed Eskom in 1987.
23. Eskom's 1997 Annual Report.
24. "South Africa: Large Energy Economy Enjoyed by Few," *African Economic Digest*, July 31, 1995. Although this fact is not emphasized in Eskom's literature, it is likely that this excess capacity may be one of the main reasons why Eskom began electrifying schools and homes as early as 1988 and the early electrification programs in 1990.
25. April 26-28 of 1994
26. "South Africa," *Hilfe Country Report*, July 1996.
27. The Conference Board, 4.
28. Table constructed from data from *SA to Z: The Decision Maker's Encyclopedia of the South African Consumer Market*. (1996).
29. Table constructed from data from *SA to Z: The Decision Maker's Encyclopedia of the South African Consumer Market*. (1996).
30. "South Africa: Large Energy Economy Enjoyed by Few," *African Economic Digest*, July 31, 1995.
31. Peter Adams, Eskom spokesman, as quoted in Drogin, A1.
32. For details on the political changes of this period, see Elling Njal Tjonneland, *Pax Pretoriana: The Fall of Apartheid and the Politics of Regional Destabilization*, Uppsala: Scandanavian Institute of African Studies, 1989.
33. Myra Alperson, *Foundations for a New Democracy: Corporate Social Investment in South Africa*, Johannesburg: Ravan Press, 1995, p. 70.
34. Eskom, "Bringing Power to the People." Video prepared for the Edison Electric Institute, 1996.
35. Bob Drogin, "S. Africa Bringing Power to the People," *Los Angeles Times*, January 31, 1996, A1.
36. Eskom's goal was to produce and distribute the cheapest electricity in the world.
37. Chairman of the Electricity Council.
38. Eskom, *Eskom Corporate Profile*, 1995.
39. Eskom, *Eskom Corporate Profile*, 1995.
40. Rob Stephan, "Challenges and Innovations Facing Eskom," *Transmission & Distribution World*, January 1996, 30.
41. African National Congress, *The Reconstruction and Development Programme. A Policy Framework*, Johannesburg: ANC, 1994, p. 31.
42. Paraffin, coal, candles, dung, and wood.
43. Used as a protest against the Apartheid government. See Eskom Case B.

29

Eskom and the South African Electrification Program (B)

A CULTURE OF NON-PAYMENT

During the Apartheid years there was a great deal of conflict between the black South Africans opposing the established government and the military and police of South Africa. The conflicts ranged from covert ANC bombings to public demonstrations. One of the most commonly used forms of protest against the Apartheid state was consumer boycotts. In essence, the latter was when non-payment was used as a form of protest against the government. The idea behind non-payment was to not support the infra-structure that the Apartheid government had forced upon the black South Africans. Rent, electricity, and consumables were boycotted from being paid by black South Africans.

Non-payment started during Apartheid as a method supported by the ANC to undermine the South African Government. It spread widely through the poor population that was eager to avoid paying for anything out of their scarce incomes. The problem of non-payment went further in that local authorities would typically respond by cutting off services to the areas boycotting payment. The residents of these areas naturally adapted to pirating the services (tampering with the electrical grid and water system) that were being denied to them in order to function.[1] As a result, many of the problems

This case was prepared by Brian D. Cunningham under the supervision of Michael E. Gorman and Patricia H. Werhane. Partial support for this project was supplied by grants from the Ethics and Values in Science Program of the National Science foundation and the Darden School. Copyright © 1999 Darden School Foundation. All rights reserved.

that the current South African government is facing are a result of the past boycotts that it helped to support.

In fact, ANC members of government, who had anticipated the use of non-payment to stop as soon as power was democratically held in the country, openly called for a end to the boycott when the lack of payments was threatening the supply of services on a national scale. However, a culture of non-payment had permeated throughout the country, and it threatened the development of the new South African government and the RDP campaigns, and it also inhibited foreign investment when companies from abroad recognized a risk of negative returns on investments.[2] Therefore, the government was enacting extensive educational reforms in order to help the citizens recognize the need of payment for services.

Mr. van Rooyen was assigned the task of determining what to do about the fact that Eskom was owed a total of R1.5 billion by black municipalities that had not paid for service during Apartheid, and the fact that further non-payment would hinder the electrification program.[3] Although Mr. van Rooyen remembered that the company had historically approached the problem of non-payment with the threat of cutting off the power to municipalities, he soon decided that this policy was not viable for a number of reasons. First of all, there was a question of equity and fair treatment of the people living within those communities who are paying their bills. Would it be fair to remove access to a service for which these people had in fact paid for? Secondly, the effects of the Apartheid regime were now more noticeable and the company was committed to helping these people develop. Past action by municipal authorities against non-payment had led to riots and violence. Mr. van Rooyen was torn between having to earn a return on the company's investments and contributing to the quality of life of the citizens of South Africa.

Notes

1. R. W. Johnson. *Riots and Bulldozers Return to Townships.* The Times Overseas News. August 9, 1997.
2. *Part 5 Africa and Latin America: Weekly Economic Report.* The British Broadcasting Corporation. March 21, 1995.
3. Kevin Morgan, legal adviser to the South African National Electricity Regulator, in an interview with Africa News. August 9, 1996. *Pay-back Time for South African Electric Users.* Tebello Radebe.

30

ESKOM AND THE SOUTH AFRICAN ELECTRIFICATION PROGRAM (C)

RESIDENTIAL TAMPERING

Muenda,[1] one of Eskom's top managers, looked at the figures and couldn't believe what he was seeing. On average, as much as 40 percent of Eskom's pre-paid connections had been tampered with and this has led to a loss in revenue in as much as R300 million annually.[2] This wasn't surprising to him considering that even children in the sixth grade had the knowledge to pull electricity illegally off of the electrical grid. In fact, they can even demonstrate how the recoil[3] will knock a person down if a mistake happens while tampering with the grid, and many others have been electrocuted to death while tampering. During Apartheid, people in these communities learned that in addition to not paying for services,[4] they could further undermine the local white authority by tapping into the electrical grid and drawing service for free.

As a result, Muenda looked more closely at the numbers and determined that it would be cheaper for the company to connect people to electricity and not charge for usage.[5] The cost per connection averages R3000 and Eskom performs 1000 connections on a daily basis, which equates to approximately R1.095 billion annually. However, Muenda decided to calculate the present value of this venture and determine the pay-

This case was prepared by Brian D. Cunningham under the supervision of Michael E. Gorman and Patricia H. Werhane. Partial support for this project was supplied by grants from the Ethics and Values in Science Program of the National Science foundation and the Darden School. Copyright © 1999 Darden School Foundation. All rights reserved.

back period, which would be a bit more complicated than simply looking at the overall costs and revenues associated with the program. In order to offset illegal draws from the grid, Eskom has to go through additional expenditures of having its employees inspect the grid. Not only does Eskom have to pay for the man-hours and expenses associated with inspection, many times these employees are attacked or have their cars hijacked when in the areas that they are inspecting, which is and of itself a valid argument for supplying fixed-rate connections because of the concern over employee safety. Upon examining the figures, Muenda unearthed the fact that although the total annual sales per electrified customer was R96, the total annual operating costs per customer was R104. Therefore, due to the excess costs associated with collection, maintenance, and inspection from non-payment and tampering, Eskom had a negative return per customer of R8. In other words, Eskom was not only absorbing the initial capital expenditure of R3000 per customer to connect people to electricity, the company was also incurring a R8 fee annually for each customer connected to the electrical grid under the electrification program.

What was Muenda to do? According to his figures the program was not providing the company with a return on its investment, even several years after the project began. In fact, Muenda determined that it would simply be more cost effective for the company to give electricity away for free, and thereby lower the costs associated with billing, maintenance, and metering equipment. But the company had not only committed to the RDP goal of electrifying 1.75 million households by the year 2000, but it was also attempting to foster a responsible culture of payment within the consumer base.[6] Should he recommend that the company stop the electrification program until his group could plan a way to generate adequate revenue from the consumer base? Although the costs of the program were increasing because some of the residents were tampering with their connections, there were people who were managing their connections responsibly within the communities. These people had been paying their bills, not tampering with their meters, and not drawing electricity from illegal connections to the electrical grid. Would it be fair to the latter type of consumer to stop the electrification program because of the people who were being irresponsible? Should these people be denied access because of what others are doing in the community? From a theoretical perspective, it was easy to determine that it would not be fair to deny future responsible consumers from electrical connections because of the past irresponsible behavior of customers. But what was Muenda to do when he found hundreds of illegal connections coming off of the grid in a community? The question of who was responsible, the individual or the community at large, became very difficult to answer in such a situation. Should Eskom disconnect the entire community in such a case?

Notes

1. Fictitious Zulu name used for case example.
2. Robyn Chalmers. *Meter Tampering Costs Eskom R300m*. Africa News. May 21, 1998.
3. Keller, Bill. "Township Gets Electricity (and It's Free, Too)," *The New York Times*. September 1, 1993.
4. Boycotting payment for service as a protest of the Apartheid government.
5. Interview with Paul Maree (current Eskom manager for the electrification program).
6. See Eskom Case A.

31

ESKOM AND THE SOUTH AFRICAN ELECTRIFICATION PROGRAM (D)

TRAINING TO TAMPER

Mr. Withers[1] was reading the paper and he noticed the headline that said that the unemployment rate for black South Africans currently hovers at 41.1 percent of the total population in South Africa.[2] He remembered the issue of poverty being addressed by the African National Congress in the following way:

> Poverty is the single greatest burden of South Africa's people, and is the direct result of the Apartheid system and the grossly skewed nature of business and industrial development which accompanied it. Poverty affects millions of people, the majority of whom live in the rural areas and are women. It is estimated that there are at least 17 million people surviving below the Minimum Living Level in South Africa, and of these at least 11 million live in the rural areas. For those intent of fermenting violence, these conditions provide fertile ground.[3]

In order to improve the quality of life for all South Africans, the RDP stresses that poorer citizens must be empowered to take control over their own lives.[4] Part of the government's strategy to promote empowerment is to improve living conditions, boost production and household income through job creation, and create opportunities for all

---

This case was prepared by Brian D. Cunningham under the supervision of Michael E. Gorman and Patricia H. Werhane. Partial support for this project was supplied by grants from the Ethics and Values in Science Program of the National Science foundation and the Darden School. Copyright © 1999 Darden School Foundation. All rights reserved.

citizens to sustain themselves. In fact, job creation is specifically linked with public works projects and projects aimed at meeting people's basic needs[5] in the RDP. In these ways, job creation was a primary focus of the ANC government, and Mr. Withers, a manager at Eskom, recognized the role that Eskom could play in the RDP.

Therefore, Mr. Withers recommended that Eskom use local labor as part of the electrification process. By taking people and providing them with basic electricity skills, he was attempting to meet the problem of unemployment in South Africa. The plan was that the people trained in basic electricity would be paid for assisting in the electrification process of the surrounding areas. Although they will not be full-time employees with Eskom, because others will be trained to assist with the electrification process in their respective areas, these people would have a marketable skill to use when attempting to procure jobs. Electrical skills would be marketable to industry and these skills would also provide a means for people to start small businesses within their communities. For as load growth and electrical demand increase in newly electrified areas, people will start to use more electrical appliances. Therefore, a market would arise for the repair and resale of these appliances, which would fall into the hands of the people being trained by Eskom.

Mr. Withers was astonished to learn that although illegal connections had been discouraged, electricity was being consumed by areas in which people were not purchasing tokens for their pre-paid meters. In order to examine what was going on, Mr. Withers chose pilot sites and placed meters on the connections going into the communities to determine how much electricity was going into the community for a given time period. He then looked at their electricity sales for that community for the same time period and compared the amount of electricity going in to the sales of electricity. It was determined that tampering was prevalent in almost all of the communities that had been electrified, and even as high as 80 percent in some areas.[6] After investigating the matter, it came to Mr. Withers' attention that the people who had been trained and paid to assist in the electrification process had actually been stealing electricity from Eskom. In other words, he had inadvertently trained people to steal from the company. These people would approach their neighbors and by-pass pre-paid meters for small fees, thereby providing free electricity to the people who would pay for such illegal connections.

This situation only compounded the problem that Mr. Withers had encountered with residential tampering. If the company decided to continue with the electrification program, what type of message would the company be sending the residents when Eskom employees themselves were aiding in illegal tamperings? The purpose of training local laborers in the electrification process was an attempt to help curb the high unemployment rate for black South Africans. So what should he recommend the company do? Should it continue to train, pay, and use local labor in the electrification process, even though the company already has approximately 40,000 employees operating in a country that is only a little more than twice the size of Texas,[7] which means that it has the existing infrastructure to perform the electrification process on its own, without training and employing local labor? In fact, it even costs Eskom an additional amount on top of the electrification process to train these people at all. But now they are helping to steal from the company. Obviously, this type of employee behavior is driving the costs of operation even higher. But what is more important, providing people with a marketable skill and curbing the unemployment rate or lowering the costs involved? How could Mr. Withers' group achieve both?

Notes

1. Fictitious name used for case example.
2. *SA to Z: The Decision Maker's Encyclopedia of the South African Consumer Market.*
3. Section 2.1.1 of The Reconstruction and Development Programme. African National Congress. 1994.
4. Ibid. Section 2.2.3.
5. Ibid. Section 2.3.2.
6. Soweto, South Africa.
7. Total area of 471,000 square miles as compared to 270,000 square miles.

32

ESKOM AND THE SOUTH AFRICAN
ELECTRIFICATION PROGRAM
(E)

ELECTRICAL DEVELOPMENT VERSUS THE ENVIRONMENT

Mr. Ndlovu, a new hire at Eskom,[1] read Eskom's corporate slogan which was "To provide the lowest priced electricity in the world in order to promote growth and development," and he knew that the utility was, in fact, in yearly competition with other countries for producing the lowest priced electricity in the world.[2] One factor influencing the low price of Eskom's electricity is the lowering finance charge that the company has experienced. The finance charge has mainly decreased as a result of the enormous capital expenditures, which the company incurred in the 1970s and '80s[3] in building excess generation facilities, finally reaching a break-even point and because of a temporary moratorium placed upon Eskom from acquiring new debt in 1985.[4] As a result, the finance charge has decreased by 62 percent since 1987, which has led to the reduction of the total price of electricity by 61 percent.[5] Moreover, because of the reduction of investment programs, the company has been able to finance many of its expenditures from its own treasury[6] and lower its debt to 40 percent of its 1985 level.[7]

Mr. Ndlovu also knew that Eskom's low price was influenced by the improvement of internal management practices and the gain in operational performance that resulted

---

This case was prepared by Brian D. Cunningham under the supervision of Michael E. Gorman and Patricia H. Werhane. Partial support for this project was supplied by grants from the Ethics and Values in Science Program of the National Science foundation and the Darden School. Copyright © 1999 Darden School Foundation. All rights reserved.

from such practices. For example, although typical coal generation facilities are considered efficient for remaining on-line 31 to 33 percent of the time, Eskom was able to achieve a 96 percent measure of availability in 1997. In other words, Eskom was able to meet unanticipated peak demand with plants already on-line providing electricity to the grid, instead of having to keep excess plants in reserve in order to meet the risk of peak load demand. Accordingly, this improvement of availability, and the offset costs of keeping excess plants in reserve, was transferred to the customer in the form of lower electricity prices. When these cost saving practices are added to the fact that electrical sales have increased by as much as 50 percent or more from the 1985 levels,[8] it becomes easier to understand how Eskom is able to provide some of the lowest electricity prices in the world. Other factors influencing the lowered cost of Eskom's electricity were the lowering of labor costs due to the downsizing of Eskom from 66,000 in 1985 to 40,000 in 1998 and the depreciation of coal costs by as much as 30 percent since the mid-1980's. All in all, Mr. Ndlovu knew that the electrification program, and its increasing costs, was possible because of Eskom's over-investment in the 1970s and '80s. For the excess generation capability that was built into Eskom's infrastructure during that period of time has allowed the company to meet new demands and growth with marginal capital expenditure.

However, Mr. Ndlovu couldn't ignore the fact that the price of South Africa's coal was an eighth the price of other countries and 46 percent the price of U.S. coal. He also realized that South Africa relies upon coal for 72 percent of its energy needs, and although the country accounts for .8 percent of the world's population, it contributes 1.6 percent of the world's greenhouse gas emissions.[9] In fact, the coal fired facilities require approximately 90 million tons of coal[10] annually to produce electricity, which means that the environment is being adversely affected from the mining that is necessary to extract such large amounts of coal. Moreover, Mr. Ndlovu had just discovered that the burning of this coal in generating electricity produces approximately 1300 kilotons of Sulfur Dioxide, 600 kilotons of Nitrogen Oxide, 170 kilotons of Carbon Dioxide, and 10 kg/Mwh of fine particulate emissions[11] annually.[12] Therefore, Eskom was averaging a daily contribution of 40ppb[13] of Sulfur Dioxide and Nitrogen Oxide, both greenhouse gases, to the atmosphere. But the company was within South African operating guidelines because the Department of Environmental Affairs and Tourism had placed the allowable limit of Sulfur Dioxide and Nitrogen Oxide at 100ppb and 400ppb, respectively, which meant that Eskom was currently emitting approximately 40 percent (~40ppb) of the allowable Sulfur Dioxide limit and 10 percent (~40pbb) of the allowable Nitrogen Oxide limit.[14] However, these South African standards may not be as strict as the standards imposed in more developed countries. For example, the World Bank's guideline for Sulfur Dioxide emissions is no more than 500 tons of emission per day regardless of generation capacity, which meant that the company was emitting 1117.5 kilotons of excess Sulfur Dioxide than allowed.

Mr. Ndlovu's dilemma derived from the fact that the low price of Eskom's electricity was not only related to the price of coal but also to the fact that the company has not retrofitted the generation facilities with SOx or NOx emission controls. The company did not place these environmental measures on its facilities. The costs associated with the retrofits are not justified because they are already operating well below the set environmental guidelines.[15] In fact, recent studies had also shown that the current levels of SO_2 and NO_2 would have only negligible effect on the vegetation of South Africa. [16] Moreover, the money that would be used to retrofit the plants with emission controls could be used to provide the people of South Africa with access to electricity instead.[17] Also the retrofitting of the plants with filters would raise the price of electricity by 30-50 percent, which would impede Eskom from providing the lowest priced electricity in the world to its customers. The costs associated with electrifying the people of the country would be cheaper, wealth generating, and also improve the environmental impact by supplying electricity to people who would otherwise be burning coal for residential energy needs. In 1990, Andre van Heerden said:

> Our dilemma lies in where we should be spending our money. For the price of R6 billion (R2 billion less than fitting desulphurisation filters on the eight largest plants), the townships can be electrified. At present much of the atmospheric pollution is caused by the townships with coal fires. (The pollution levels are 2/6 times higher than where the power stations are based.) The coal that the household stoves burn is low-grade heavy pollutant. Eskom burns the coal more efficiently than an individual ever could.[18]

However, the problem was not as simply stated. For when Mr. Ndlovu decided to look into the situation he discovered that wood is the primary domestic energy source[19] for half of all South Africans, which translates to 11 million tons annually. In fact, eight million tons of wood are cut from natural woodlands annually, which is roughly equivalent to the natural production rate. [20] The latter is obviously an unsustainable situation and would soon lead to the deforestation of South African woodlands. Moreover, the burning of this wood in homes accounts for the majority of carbon monoxide and methane emissions in South Africa, which is higher than that released by Eskom's generation facilities. As a result of this discovery, Mr. Ndlovu commissioned a study in order to determine where emissions were originating. The study[21] found that although coal-fired stations were contributing more greenhouse gases to the atmosphere than residential burning of biomass, the facilities were only accounting for 11 percent of particulate emissions; whereas approximately 41 percent of the particulate emissions were coming from residential use. Although this finding did not initially seem significant when compared with such things as greenhouse gases and global warming, Mr. Ndlovu soon discovered that people were being exposed to 65 times the U.S. Environmental Protection Agency's guideline[22] for particulate emissions and double the WHO's guidelines for carbon monoxide. These levels were shocking for Mr. Ndlovu because similar levels of exposure had been linked to illnesses and deaths from respiratory disease, cardiac arrest, and lung cancer. [23] This air pollution from residential use seemed to be the obvious cause of the fact that respiratory infections were the second highest cause of infant mortality in the country, which were 270 times higher than the Western rate.

Mr. Ndlovu couldn't help but think that these types of situations could be avoided by providing people with electricity, for they would then have a safer source of energy for cooking and heating and not have to rely upon wood or coal. Although Mr. Ndlovu did not like the fact that the generation facilities were contributing to a global greenhouse gas situation, they were currently operating well below the set South African guidelines and also producing the lowest priced electricity in the world, which is exactly what the people in these communities needed given the high rate of unemployment and variable incomes. Therefore, Mr. Ndlovu was struggling with the question of what was presently more important: the environment or development? What should he do? Should he recommend that the company incur the capital expenditures to make the retrofits and operate at lower emission levels, but offset the costs associated with retrofits by either raising the price of electricity or slowing the electrification program?

Notes

1. Fictitious Zulu name used for case example.
2. Eskom's price per kWh in 1997 was 1/2 the U.S. price.
3. See Appendix B of Case A for Eskom's history.
4. De Villiers Commission of 1985.
5. Davis, M. *Household Electrification. How and Why in South Africa*. EDRC, UCT. Cape Town, South Africa, 1997.
6. In 1994 Eskom's treasury was given a credit rating equal to the South African's government by the international community.
7. van Horen, C. *Eskom, Its Finances and the National Electrification Programme*. Development Southern Africa. 189-204.
8. Due to the electrification program.
9. Wells, R. B. *Air Pollution and Its Impacts on the South African Highveld: Global Issues*. Environmental Scientific Association. Cleveland, South Africa. 1996.
10. Eskom's 1997 Environmental Report.
11. Coal ash in the atmosphere.
12. Eskom's 1997 Environmental Report.
13. Parts per billion.
14. Eskom's 1997 Environmental Report.
15. The result of the coal having a low sulfur content.
16. Walmsley, R. *Air Pollution and Its Impacts on the South African Highveld:Impacts*. Environmental Scientific Association. Cleveland, South Africa. 1996.
17. The Electrification Program.
18. Euromoney Supplement. September 12, 1990 p. 7.
19. Cooking and space/water heating.
20. Helas, G. and Pienaar, J. *Air Pollution and Its Impacts on the South African Highveld: Biomass Burning Emissions*. Environmental Scientific Association. Cleveland, South Africa. 1996.
21. Ammegarn, H. et al. *Air Pollution and its Impacts on the South African Highveld: Residential Air Pollution*. Environmental Scientific Association. Cleveland, South Africa. 1996.
22. The EPA's *Revised Particulate Matter Standard* sets the health limit at 65 micrograms per cubic meter in a 24 hour period; however, the South African example is being exposed to 2367 micrograms per cubic meter in a 24 hour period.
23. van Horen, C. *Energy and Environment Policy in South Africa: Assessing the Priorities After Apartheid*. EDRC. Cape Town, South Africa. 1995.

33

THE VOLTA RIVER PROJECT

In 1998, Ghana needed to consider new alternatives of electricity to counteract the recurring problem of power shortages due to droughts. Guided by lessons from the past, any new alternatives would need to be practical, affordable, and sustainable choices for electricity in Ghana. The options included (1) thermal energy, (2) importing electricity, (3) construction of additional hydroelectric dams, and (4) other options such as nuclear energy, solar energy, and other fossil fuel powered plants and generators.

INTRODUCTION

March 6, 1997 marked the fortieth anniversary of Ghana's independence from British colonial rule. During the early years, Kwame Nkrumah (see Exhibit 1, Some Key Terms), Ghana's first elected president, was keen on establishing Ghana's economic independence. In conjunction with multinational interests, his government oversaw the construction of Akosombo Dam on the Volta River. Akosombo would become the primary power source for the nation. Nkrumah believed that industrialization was dependent on ample and affordable electricity. Forty years later, the "miracle dam" was not able to supply enough power to meet energy needs in Ghana.

Prepared by John Riverson, graduate student in Civil Engineering at the University of Virginia, under the direction of Michael E. Gorman and Patricia H. Werhane. The conclusions are the responsibilities of the authors and do not reflect the views of the organizations. Copyright ©1999 by the School of Engineering and Applied Science of the University of Virginia and the University of Virginia Darden School Foundation. All rights reserved.

The Volta River Project was the name given to the association of the Volta River Authority (VRA), Ghana's statutory power provider, and the Volta Aluminum Corporation (Valco) whose power intensive aluminum smelting operations justified the construction of the dam. Valco, which is 100% owned by U.S. interests, lobbied heavily with the Ghanaian government and other contributors to see the speedy completion of the dam between 1963 and 1966. Although Akosombo Dam was a tremendous engineering feat which became a symbol of national pride, the effects of dam construction, the consequences of contractual negotiations and agreements with Valco, and Ghana's dependence on hydroelectric power continually resurfaced as Ghanaian policy makers faced the challenges of meeting a growing power demand. During the worst droughts, water levels were not sufficient to generate enough power to meet Ghana's energy needs. Although other energy alternatives were considered and some implemented, Ghana's power infrastructure was dependent on the rise and fall of the water level in the Akosombo reservoir. Ghana's power infrastructure needed to change.

HISTORY OF GHANA BEFORE THE VOLTA RIVER PROJECT

During the 1400s, the Portuguese were the first Europeans to arrive in what is known today as Ghana. Their primary objective was gold exploration. The Portuguese gave the name "Gold Coast" to the territory because of its wealth of gold and other natural resources. In 1482, they constructed Elmina Castle near Cape Coast; this castle would later become the last stopover for thousands of slaves before they were shipped to the new world. Between 1471 and 1957, several other European kingdoms explored the Gold Coast. Among these were Denmark, Holland, England, Prussia, and Sweden. They constructed elaborate castles and forts to establish and protect their presence in the territory. When the British merchants arrived in mass during the 1700s, they sought to capitalize on natural and human resources: gold and slaves. Slave trade continued until the late 1800s when it was abolished in the western nations. It was the British who finally colonized the territory in 1874. British colonial rule continued from 1874 until 1957, when the Gold Coast gained independence and became the Republic of Ghana.

In 1914, Sir Albert Kitson, director of the Gold Coast Geological Survey, discovered bauxite deposits near Mpraeso. Bauxite is a mineral ore containing aluminum oxide or hydroxides with several impurities. When refined, bauxite becomes alumina, the principal ingredient for aluminum production. The following year, while engaged in a rapid canoe voyage down the Volta, Kitson observed that the river flowed through a gorge surrounded by a large range of hills near Akosombo. He was the first person recorded to envision a dam at that location. Kitson's infrastructure proposals were not limited to Akosombo. He also identified Bui, on the Black Volta, as a second feasible site for a dam. He felt that a dam at that location, near the mid-western border of Ghana, would serve to electrify a future railway to the north (Moxon, 51).

A Yorkshireman by the name of Duncan Rose would later carry Kitson's dream closer to reality. After graduating from Cambridge in 1930, Rose emigrated to South Africa to pursue his fascination with aluminum. He thought aluminum could be the metal of the century (Moxon, 52). When he came across Kitson's bulletin in the public library at Johannesburg, Rose planned an exploratory trip to the Gold Coast. Working with his financing partner, T.W. Charles, Rose acquired the support of the Anglo-

Transvaal Consolidated Investment Co., a leading South African mining finance house. Together, they formed the African Aluminum Syndicate, which would later be joined by a South African engineer by the name of Christopher St. John Bird. By 1939, St. John Bird was in the Gold Coast preparing preliminary reports while Rose was negotiating concessions for dam construction with the Gold Coast government.

World War II caused the Syndicate to suspend its physical operations in the Gold Coast. Rose left for duty in England to manage a munitions factory; however while in England, he vigorously lobbied for support of the Gold Coast aluminum scheme in both government and business circles. Among his investor targets was British Unilever. After the war, momentum for the dam continued to build in the Gold Coast. Rose formed the West African Aluminum Ltd (Wafal), which replaced the pre-war African Aluminum Syndicate. One indication of the growing success of the proposal was that in March 1946, Unilever, through its subsidiary the United Africa Company, acquired financial interest in Wafal.

MORE ON COLONIAL INTERESTS

In 1949, Christopher St. John Bird and Duncan Rose were compiling proposals for the aluminum-hydroelectric dam. They reasoned that since the land on the banks of the Volta River was of "low value," the dam, which was then estimated to cause about 5180 square kilometers (2000 square miles) of flooding, would not have a significant negative impact on the country. As retribution, St. John Bird suggested that a sum of £1 million be given to the Gold Coast government (Hart, 34).

St. John Bird was a partner in an engineering consulting firm in South Africa before coming to the Gold Coast. His proposals were basically "apartheid" in nature (Hart, 35). In his plans for the Akosombo village, the European executives and senior workers would have their homes constructed on a ridge where they would enjoy a cool breeze. Their living area would include tennis courts, a swimming pool, and a dance hall among other recreational amenities. The African workers would live in the valley within a mile of the humid riverbanks, where they would be closer to the work site. St. John Bird suggested constructing aluminum houses for the African laborers because those houses "would prove palatial in comparison with the local product" (Hart, 35). The Europeans would be paid 14 to 25 times the salary of the African workers. The African laborers would be paid according to their skills and technical worth to the project. In his original proposals, no concessions were made for hiring Ghanaian managers or technical experts. St. John Bird anticipated that only a few Ghanaians would hold low-level management positions.

The White Paper Cmd 8702 of November 1952 illustrated the U.K.'s mental model for the association between aluminum and hydroelectric power in Ghana. This document, bearing the title "The Volta River Aluminum Scheme," strongly suggested that hydroelectric generation was more for the purpose of cheap electricity for aluminum production than for Ghana electrification. The preliminary plans presented in this document involved the production of 564 MegaWatts (MW) of power, of which 514 MW would go to the smelter and 50 MW to other users in Ghana (Hart, 36). As a part of the "scheme," the smelter would be obligated for 30 years to sell at least 75% of the metal produced to buyers in the U.K.

The White Paper concluded that:

> Her Majesty's Government in the U.K. [is] favorable in principle to participation in the scheme, which would further their policy of encouraging the development of the resources of the [Gold Coast] as well as contributing to the raw material needs in the U.K. They believe, on the basis of the information so far available, that it is soundly conceived that its successful completion would bring substantial benefits to the two countries (Hart, 37).

Back in Ghana, the British Aluminum group (Wafal) and Aluminum Ltd. of Canada (Alcan) were actively compiling final reports from site investigations. During the preparation of these reports, African rights activist Kwame Nkrumah was released from prison. Nkrumah had been sentenced to two years for demonstrations surrounding his Political Action Campaign, in which some demonstrators had died. Before the Gold Coast government could approve the Wafal-Alcan reports, the political climate changed.

NKRUMAH AND THE VOLTA RIVER PROJECT

In 1951, soon after his release from prison, Kwame Nkrumah's Convention People's Party (CPP) swept the polls at the February general election. He was appointed Governor-General (a post that later became Prime Minister) of the Gold Coast under the Queen of England. The CPP became the first African-majority government to hold power in colonial Africa.

Nkrumah had started his career as a teacher before leaving for ten years to continue his education in the United States at Lincoln University and at the University of Pennsylvania. He had also attended the London School of Economics. Dr. Nkrumah soon found his way among the intellectual elite of Ghana. He believed that the key to securing African solidarity and independence from colonial rule was a unified Africa. Together with other African leaders, some of their more revolutionary ideas included forming a confederation of African nations and adopting Swahili as a continental language to unify all African peoples. In 1963 the Organization of African Unity (OAU) was formed. Some believe that Nkrumah wanted a more powerful centralized structure where he could dominate continental politics. Much of his ideas were based on socialist theory and represented a unique blend of Christian and Marxist ideas (Hart, 6).

Nkrumah maintained working relations with the Soviet Union and Red China as well as the West while he solicited foreign investment to boost the economy of the newly independent Ghana. Nkrumah's government was overthrown in 1966. The coup occurred after the commissioning of Akosombo, while Nkrumah was visiting Peking. Suspicion of American involvement was verified when *The New York Times* published that "the CIA advised and supported the Ghanaian Army and Police officers who took over the Government" (Moxon 270). Before the coup, many Ghanaians criticized Nkrumah for focusing too much on foreign policy and not enough on the needs of his own country, while others believed that these allegations were disseminated in CIA propaganda (Moxon 270). Nevertheless, African leaders were disappointed after his overthrow because Nkrumah's efforts for the cause of pan-African unity brought about economic, social, and political benefits to the entire continent. Ever since Nkrumah had led

Ghana to independence nearly ten years before his overthrow, many other African colonies had taken steps toward achieving their own independence.

While president, Nkrumah emphasized the importance of diverse foreign investment in Ghana and national electrification as necessary precursors for development. He had embraced Kitson's vision of a dam at Akosombo in hopes of developing Ghana's bauxite reserves, among other interests. Nkrumah knew that involving an aluminum smelter was the only way to secure finances for the construction of Akosombo Dam.

ALUMINUM AND HYDROELECTRIC POWER

Refining aluminum from bauxite ore is an energy intensive process. Bauxite is a mineral ore containing aluminum oxide or hydroxides with several impurities. Bauxite must be treated at a high enough temperature (around the melting point of aluminum: 660°C/ 1220°F) to burn away all the impurities and leave behind the resulting alumina powder. When molten alumina is processed into marketable aluminum, it must be cooled at a slow rate to increase ductility and prevent a brittle product. Generating one six pack of aluminum cans requires the same amount of electricity as running a 21-inch color TV for more than 11 hours (Gitlitz, 1993). By 1998, the annual hydroelectric power used worldwide in aluminum production nearly equaled the annual power demand of Australia, or of about 35 million US residents. On average, electricity accounted for about 20-30% of the total cost of aluminum production.

Electrical energy, rather than direct heat (*i.e.* from burning fossil fuels), is the best form of energy for aluminum processing. Aluminum is a poor current conductor. The structure of aluminum is such that instead of easily passing through it, a current is trapped and converted to heat energy. High electrical currents are required to perform the smelting operations.

Because of the high power costs associated with making aluminum, manufacturers usually seek the least expensive sources of power. During the sixties and seventies, world energy costs increased by 500%, while serious doubt arose about the safety of nuclear power, which had once been a cheap and reliable power alternative for the aluminum industry worldwide (Graham, 88). Hydroelectric power was soon regarded as the next cheapest alternative for generating electricity. Throughout history, aluminum smelters have frequently been established in conjunction with new dams (Gitlitz, 1993).

VOLTA ALUMINUM COMPANY (VALCO)

Valco was the name of the aluminum company associated with the Akosombo Dam. During preliminary negotiations in Ghana in the early 1960s, Valco representative Edgar Kaiser expressed that Ghana's rich bauxite resources were part of the reason for their interest in Ghana (Tsikata, 4). President Nkrumah saw the link between aluminum and hydroelectric power as the best way to bolster the Ghanaian economy. Furthermore, the presence of an aluminum smelter justified the construction of a hydroelectric dam to the foreign investors.

Kitson's vision for developing Ghana's aluminum industry was the framework around which Valco was established. A more wealthy country was invited to provide loans for the power infrastructure, establish a bauxite refinery and an aluminum smelter, and develop the local bauxite. It was a mutually benefiting design with very good intentions toward the host country. A host country that did not have the necessary infrastructure could cash in on an undeveloped natural resource, while a percentage of the production sales helped the foreign aluminum company liquidate their investments. It was envisioned that after an agreed period of time, the contract would expire and the entire operation would be turned over to the host country. Valco opted not to construct the bauxite refinery, because Kaiser's economists found that for the time remaining on their contract, it was more profitable to continue importing alumina powder from Jamaica and Guinea than to invest high initial capital on a bauxite refinery in Ghana. Valco tests concluded that because of the impurities in Ghana bauxite, the same amount of energy would yield less alumina than bauxite refined elsewhere. The forgone bauxite factory left the Volta River Project vision incomplete, and Ghana's bauxite reserves untapped.

Valco would be 100% owned by foreign interests, both of which were among the six most powerful corporations in the aluminum industry. One was Kaiser Aluminum Corporation (Kaiser, NYSE: KLU) of Houston Texas. Kaiser, which would become one of the world's leading producers of alumina, primary aluminum, and fabricated aluminum products, owned 90% of Valco. Kaiser would later be supported by MAXXAM Inc. (ASE: MXM), which directly and indirectly held about 78% of the common stock. Kaiser's remaining 12% belonged to other private interests. Reynolds Metal Company owned the other 10% of Valco. The Valco smelting operation was designed as a service facility or a tolling station because it actually would not own any of the alumina or aluminum that it processed. Imported alumina was passed through the plant, processed at a fee, and exported for sale.

Valco would become the single largest consumer of electricity in Ghana. During the 1970s Valco consumed some 60% of Ghana's electricity to produce 200,000 tons of aluminum annually (Ghana, 176). In July 1982, when a second smaller dam (Kpong Dam) was built downstream on the Volta River at Akuse, VRA's maximum electricity generating capacity increased by 20% to a total of about 1100 MW. By 1993, Valco consumed about 45% of VRA's power production. Valco hired about 2% of the Ghanaian private sector labor force (Sims, 16).

NEGOTIATING A DAM

Nkrumah needed President Kennedy's support in 1961 in order to bring international financial investors to the negotiating table. Beyond the financial needs for the Volta River Project, Nkrumah wanted to attract foreign investors to Ghana and establish a foundation for future development of other infrastructure, such as the Bui Dam. While the West was involved in building Akosombo Dam, the Soviet Union, after performing extensive investigations, was prepared to undertake construction of the Bui Dam. James Moxon, an Englishman who joined Ghana's Information Service in 1948 and worked closely with Volta River Project participants, suggests that Nkrumah used the Bui dam to maintain "some kind of political balance between the West and the East" (p. 245). In 1961, Nkrumah successfully completed a two month visit to Khrushchev and Mao Tse-tung, became the Kennedy family's first visiting head of state at the White House, and hosted Queen Elizabeth and Prince Philip in Accra (Moxon, 269). With the support of President Kennedy, negotiations for the Volta River Project began.

In February 1962, over twenty agreements were signed concerning the financing, construction, and operation of Akosombo Dam. The parties represented in the negotiations included (1) the Ghana government and its agencies, (2) Valco and shareholders, (3) the International Bank of Reconstruction and Development (IBRD/ World Bank), (4) the U.K. Government, and (5) some U.S. government institutions which insured U.S. corporations operating outside the United States.

Ghana's budget provided £35 million in cash ($98 million in 1962 dollars), which was half of the building costs for Akosombo Dam; the remaining finances consisted of loans from the World Bank, USAID, US Export-Import Bank (EXIM), and the UK Bond of Trade (Tsikata, 2). Valco shareholders gave $32 million for the building of the smelter, and another $20 million came as loans for other initial capital expenses required to establish aluminum operations in Ghana (See Exhibit 3: *Principal Agreements*).

The Ghana government and VRA agreed to a 30 year fixed rate of 2.625 mills (0.2625 cents) for every kilowatt-hr of energy supplied to Valco starting April 25, 1967 (Tsikata, 2). This rate remained a controversial matter for various policy makers over the decades. The Master Agreement is the document that resulted from the proceedings between VRA and Valco. As part of the agreement, Valco could demand power for an additional 20 years on the same terms after the initial 30 years had passed, extending contractual agreements until the year 2017. This rate, however, was 40% lower than that originally advised by the World Bank and other consultants to the Ghana government at the time. Under pressure from the World Bank and from Kaiser to commence the building project, the Ghana government agreed upon the lower rate. To Ghana, Kaiser would provide a long-term demand to generate revenue needed to amortize the dam. It was also reasoned that since the hydroelectric plant would produce a surplus of electricity, the benefits of building the dam would jumpstart the economy and pay off in the long run. Akosombo began operations in January 1966 and the smelter in April 1967. After completion of the Volta River Project, Ghana would receive 99% of its power from hydroelectric power for the next thirty years.

At the ground-breaking ceremony of the Valco Smelter in 1964, Kwame Nkrumah and Edgar Kaiser stood cordially side by side. In previous months, the Volta River Project operations had triggered mixed emotions from the Ghanaian citizens and the international participants. These had taken the form of anti-American demonstrations in the streets of Accra to months of heavy repairs near the foundation at Akosombo dam caused by flooding. During the rainy season in 1963 (and specifically in July), rains produced floods reaching 15,800 cubic meters per second (557,970 cubic feet per second) a level never recorded in the previous 25 years of records for the Volta River's natural cycles (Impregilo, 1982). Furthermore, the assassination of President Kennedy and an assassination attempt on President Nkrumah less than six weeks later both cast a dark shadow on the fate of the Volta River Project. While still balancing delicate political relations with the West and the Communist nations, the ongoing Volta River Project reassured Nkrumah of at least one great victory for Ghana. At the ceremony, the words of the late President Kennedy were quoted, when he said of "the new states whom we welcome to the land of the free . . . we shall not always expect to find them supporting our view. But we shall always hope to find them strongly supporting their own freedom" (Moxon, 270).

"TAMING" THE VOLTA

The catchment area of the Volta basin is about 390,000 square kilometers, of which 42% (which contains the highest water volume) lies within Ghana. The Volta begins as a small stream in the Kong Mountains of Burkina Faso (Upper Volta). After flowing northeast, then due south for some 515 kilometers (320 miles), it enters Ghana as the Black Volta. It then travels along the western border between Ghana and Ivory Coast before turning through a narrow gorge at Bui near the border. The river then meanders northeast until it joins the White Volta (which also finds its source in Burkina Faso). Together, they combine to flow the remaining 483 kilometers (300 miles) to the sea. The Volta River basin is also fed by the Oti and the Afram Rivers (See Exhibit 2: *Map of Ghana*).

In 1963, construction of Akosombo Dam was commenced under the management of Impregilo, an Italian contractor. As the world's fifth largest dam at the time, Akosombo stood 134 meters high, and approximately 700 meters long (440 by 2250 feet), with a power rating capacity of 912 MW (Impregilo, 1982). Because of the high surplus of electricity in Ghana at that time, many viewed Akosombo as a permanent solution to electricity provision in Ghana for many years to come. In due course, one of the first programs abandoned by the government following Nkrumah's overthrow was the Bui Dam.

Lake Volta, which is the world's largest artificial lake (in terms of surface area), now lies behind Akosombo Dam. The damming of the Volta River resulted in 8502 square kilometers (3275 square miles) of flooded riverbanks. In comparison, the combined surface area of two U.S. states, Delaware and Rhode Island, is 8466 square kilometers (3270 square miles). About 80,000 people (more than 1% of Ghana's population at the time) had to be resettled from the area. In addition to the resettlement of the river communities, damming affected local health, agriculture, fishing, and navigation. To this day, treetops can be seen above the waters of Lake Volta at various locations.

Effects on Resettled Communities

The spreading lake behind Akosombo Dam forced 739 villages along the banks to be moved. However, this was not the first time that Ghana had resettled citizens. In 1956, members of the Frafra people in the Northern Region first had their homes relocated because of overpopulation. They were settled in a less populated and more fertile land at Damongo. Despite the generous provisions, houses, bullocks, and plows, the people had a hard time departing from their traditional lands. For many years, they would send their dead to be buried back home in Frafra, which was over 200 miles away. The second resettlement was the Tema Manhean Project (1959), which resulted from the construction of the Tema Harbor seaport. Some small fishing villages along the coast were moved about three miles from their original location to a modern village, where each house was replaced on a room for room basis.

The Volta Resettlement Scheme, Ghana's third of its kind, carried a budget of $9.8 million (£3.5 million). Before 80,000 people could be displaced, economic, social, physical, political, and psychological factors had to be addressed. Since resettlement would drastically affect the lifestyles of the people, it was essential to make the transition as smooth as possible while preserving sacred traditions and rituals of life. Furthermore, there was a prevailing sentiment among the people that the government "owed them something." Many of the people needed to regain a sense of worth and reestablish their contribution to society. Everyone was given the option of either monetary compensation or resettlement into one of the 52 specially constructed townships. Over 70,000 people chose resettlement over monetary compensation.

Before Akosombo, many of the people along the Volta lived in tiny scattered villages. The average village house was constructed with swish (soil-based) walls and thatch roofs. Subsistence farming, animal grazing, and river fishing were the most common practices in the area; and these traditions were passed down from generation to generation. According to 1956 preparatory studies, only about 6% of the land covered by the lake was "used productively," while the rest was "unsuitable for agriculture or unoccupied" (Hart, 77). The resettlement scheme offered a unique opportunity to consolidate the scattered villages into more organized communities and provide them with schools, improved sanitary facilities, and increased revenue potential through mechanized farming techniques and organized livestock breeding. Furthermore, this consolidation would facilitate future electrification of the area.

A resettlement house was constructed with landcrete walls (landcrete is concrete made with local soil) and an aluminum roof. In terms of the *sturdiness* and *durability* of the building materials used, a resettlement house was superior to the average village house. The layouts of these houses were modeled after the traditional living quarters, which consisted of a central compound surrounded by several rooms. Because of time and cost constraints, VRA constructed the foundations, built the "core" one bedroom house, and provided building materials (which would have the cost to the tenant spread over a five year period) and training so that the resettled citizens themselves could finish the additional rooms. They aimed to cut down on labor costs, give the citizens a sense of ownership, and provide them something to do during the first few months of transition since many had lost their occupations underneath the lake. Although each family was given a "core" house, overcrowding was common because previously, every household built as many rooms as they needed. Also, many of the houses were never completed. In many of the resettlement villages, it was common to see the traditional swish houses constructed alongside the resettlement houses. During the cooler months of the year, many complained that their new houses were too cold. The landcrete walls and aluminum roofs could not insulate as well as the swish and thatch they had been using for hundreds of years.

The resettlement project also aimed to replace the common practice of subsistence farming with "cash crop" farming. In doing so, each farmer would be taught new farming techniques to produce enough for his family and some extra crops to sell for income. In order to support crop rotation, virgin forests were cleared for farmlands; but this was not always done without resistance (the government often clashed with traditional chiefs over who owned the land). As a subsidy, the government also provided chicks, piglets, and other young livestock to the people to rear on the new livestock farms and later, to sell for profit. After many of the animals began to die prematurely from disease and malnutrition (usually from improper care), the government stopped giving out the young livestock at no cost to the farmer.

Many agree that the Volta Resettlement project improved the physical environment for the average rural Volta citizen; however, the debate continues as to whether or not there were social and psychological improvements. VRA tried as much as possible to settle people of the same ethnic group into a village. But sometimes, there were cultural conflicts because a Fanti would not want to be governed by an Ewe chief, for example. Other problems arose from lifestyle issues. Some who were seasoned fishermen did not want to become cash crop farmers. Many left their resettlement homes and constructed wooden shacks along the lakeside so that they could be closer to their best-known source of income. As more people encroached on the lakeside and the communities diversified their activities, illegal clearing and farming along the banks led to increased sediment deposit into the lake. With the receding perimeter of the lake due to the drought in 1998, the government made efforts to replant trees along the lakeside to control erosion.

Effects on Health

The dam virtually halted the rate of flow in the Volta River, increasing stagnant water conditions and consequently, creating ideal breeding grounds for carriers of waterborne diseases. Before Akosombo and Kpong Dams, malaria (from mosquitoes) was not much of a problem along the swift-flowing Volta River, but after it became a stagnant lake, malaria became a greater public health concern in lakeside villages. Likewise, only 1-5% of the population suffered from schistosomiasis (a disease transmitted by snails) before the dam was constructed. By 1979, urinary schistosomiasis had grown to become the most prevalent disease in the area, affecting some 75% of lakeside residents (comment from Gitlitz, 1993).

Humans are infected by urinary schistomiasis through water that contains the larvae (cercariae) of the parasitic worm. When ingested, the larvae travel into the blood stream, where they may become lodged in the liver, lungs, or heart. Inside the human host, the cercariae mature into the parasitic worm. The worms may also travel through the blood stream, where they can sometimes clog arteries and veins, leading to cardiac failure. The worms lay eggs that leave the body through the urine. The eggs hatch on contact with water, releasing miracidia. The miracidia quickly find new hosts in certain species of stagnant water snails, whose numbers increased in the lake environment. Inside the snails, the miracidia mature into cercariae, which return back to the water, completing the cycle. Symptoms include skin complaints, fever, inflammation and coughing. In more advanced stages, one may notice blood in the urine. Schistosomiasis leads to death through cardiac failure, fibrosis of the lungs, an enlarged spleen, or secondary bacterial infection of the urinary tract.

During the construction of Kpong Dam in the early 1980s, flooding provided some health benefits. The dam was sighted a few kilometers downstream from Kpong town, so that the backwaters would flood the Kpong Rapids. This area was the largest breeding ground for the tsetse fly in Ghana. Sleeping sickness, carried by the tsetse fly, was a major problem to the British colonists, foreigners, and other people who did not have acquired biological defenses. Tsetse flies breed in the dense bush bordering bodies of water, and are most prevalent in the lower part of the Brong Ahafo Region, the Ashanti Region, and parts of the Eastern Region into the Volta Region. Sleeping sickness may linger quietly in a person for many years, causing a loss of energy and reduced immunity to other diseases. Full-blown sleeping sickness leads to quick death.

Effects on Agriculture

Long before Akosombo was constructed, the fertile banks along the Volta River were some of Ghana's richest agricultural land. Archeological finds show that the Volta Basin was once well populated (comments from Kaplan et. al., 17). Much of the natural vegetation was burned down for agriculture over a period of more than a thousand years, which led to the eventual drying and erosion of the land. However, the floodplains along the raging Volta River provided a constant source of fertile agricultural land for local farmers.

Before Akosombo Dam, local farming along the Volta was structured around the rise and fall of the river. The damming put an end to natural cycles, which deposited nutrient-laden silts along the flood plains. The river ecosystem was transformed into a lake ecosystem. Damming led to a drastic curtailment in subsistence agricultural production and animal grazing. Farming communities downstream continually petitioned VRA to coordinate its spillage with the traditional flooding cycles to simulate the natural flood cycles necessary for agricultural stability. Unfortunately, demands for electricity could not always be synchronized with the traditional flooding seasons. Furthermore, the reduced flow into the Gulf of Guinea resulted in saltwater intrusion at the Volta River delta and estuary. Salt water destroyed clam beds and lowered drinking water quality. Many of the stream and clam fishermen downstream moved north to the lake, where they hoped to restore their careers.

The Volta River Project also included plans for an irrigation network in the Afram Plains, which was considered Ghana's agricultural breadbasket. However, these plans were pushed down the agenda for various economic, social, and political reasons. The sudden change in government in 1966 led to budget restructuring during the first year of Akosombo's operation, which affected many of the original project initiatives, including the irrigation network and the resettlement scheme. Teaching new farming techniques was expensive, and there was no guarantee that the traditional farmers would embrace them. In 1998, only 2000 hectares of irrigated land existed in Ghana.

Effects on Fishing Industry

Although it was created primarily as a hydroelectric reservoir, Akosombo created a lake environment suitable for fish breeding. Lake Volta soon grew to become a highly productive fishing area yielding around 40,000 tons annually.

Before dam construction began, St. John Bird wanted to remove the trees in the floodplains of the Volta River so that broken limbs would not damage the turbines. Only a few trees in the river section closest to the turbine intakes were removed. Those upstream were never removed. Further tree removal would have been good for fishermen. Submerged growth in the lake entangled and destroyed fishing nets. Mobile nets (winch nets) typically catch more fish than stationary nets. Not only would tree removal safeguard the turbines, but also, local fishermen could use winch nets to increase their fish catch, and consequently, increase their earning potential.

Stationary fishing methods such as gill nets, traps, long lines, cast nets, and spears would remain the most widely used methods. Although fish were more available, fishing was difficult for some fishermen because (1) finding an open area without too much submerged growth was difficult, (2) those open areas, which were only accessible by boat, were typically located along the main channel, (3) those areas were often overfished by winch fishermen, (4) fishing nets entangled in submerged trees required lots of time and energy to free, and (5) mending or replacing damaged nets was expensive in terms of time and money. Many fishermen in lakeside communities also engaged in complementary economic activities such as farming and livestock rearing (Agyenim-Boateng, 48).

Life in lakeside communities is characterized by hardship. In 1998, policy makers of the Atebubu district in the Brong Ahafo Region, were hesitant to build schools for the children of fishing communities located along the lake. Many of the fishermen and their families migrated with the fish, and those who were stationary chose not to send their children to school because they served as valuable labor hands. Many of these villages were also located within restricted lakeside areas reserved for farming. Most parents could not afford to send their children to better schools outside of the region; instead, their children were sent to earn money as menial labor hands for local fishermen. The wealthier fishermen, who would send their own children to better schools in the cities, overworked their neighbors' children. These children were usually between eight and eleven years old. They could be found placing and retrieving bamboo traps and fishnets in the lake (Ghana Focus: May 19, 1998). Not only were they subjected to deplorable working conditions, but also, these children were deprived of education during critical years of social and mental development.

The growth of the fishing industry led to the migration of various people groups to the lakeside settlements. Survey data indicate that 80% of the fishing villages near Yeji were inhabited by more than one tribe, and 50% include two or three tribes (Agyenim-Boateng, 56). Cultural differences were expressed in their inter-tribal relationships. Ewe fishermen, who principally used stationary nets, clashed with Adangbe and Adas over their use of winch nets. Ewes and Adangbes with established homes and livelihoods in the area complained of Fantis and Adas, who came during prime fishing seasons to make money and go home. Territorial clashes arose over who has the right to fish where.

Over time, the use of larger fishing boats and winch fishing nets in some parts of the lake proved quite profitable for those fishermen, some of which had migrated from the coastal areas to Lake Volta. In 1998, the threat of over-fishing in the lake became an issue of national concern, and the use of certain nets was prohibited. By request of the Ghana Fisheries Department, the Navy began monitoring fishing operations at Yeji. Fishermen who were suspected of using unauthorized nets had them confiscated. This exercise enforced fishery regulations regarding the use of nets, with mesh sizes of less than 2 inches, as a means of preventing over-fishing in the lake.

Effects on Aquatic Navigation

Between the time of Kitson's original vision (1915) and the actual construction of Akosombo (1963), several proposals were drafted concerning the size and capacity of the dam. Each time, the conceptual size increased to generate more power capacity and a larger lake that would theoretically make navigation to the bauxite deposits easier (although Valco opted not to developed Ghana's bauxite resources). Before the dam, east-west routes were the most common mode of river navigation. Villagers could easily row across the river to trade goods and communicate with other villages. Most villages spoke the same language and exhibited similar lifestyles since they were separated by a relatively narrow Volta River that was hardly suitable for large scale north-south navigation.

With the construction of the dam, the immense lake consumed riparian land and increased east-west rowing distances an average of 24 kilometers (15 miles). After dam construction, a shipyard was constructed at Akosombo, and ferries began navigation along Lake Volta between Akosombo and Yeji. The lake provided a 400 kilometers (250 mile) north-south navigational corridor for an inland shipping route. Together, the Volta, Ankobra, and Tano Rivers provided 168 km of perennial navigation for launches and lighters; Lake Volta provided 1,125 km of arterial and feeder waterways (CIA, 1995).

WHEN POWER FADES

During the 1970s, when oil prices reached record high prices worldwide, energy prices in Ghana increased by 900% from their 1962 levels, making the Valco contractual agreements far less representative of the current state of affairs (Tsikata, 2). In 1972, 1973, and 1977, Valco agreed to some adjustments to the rate, but VRA and its lenders regarded the changes as unsatisfactory. By 1982, the power rate had been increased from the original 2.265 mills per kW/h to 5 mills per kW/h, an increase of 100% over a time period during which energy prices had generally increased by 900% (Sawyerr, 62).

In 1982, Ghana called Valco into negotiations. The first question that arose was whether Ghana had the legal right to call for renegotiations of previously agreed contractual terms. If Valco was not willing to renegotiate, Ghana could take unilateral action under certain codes of international law. This right of a host country to pass sanctions against or regulate the activities of a foreign investor who was viewed as exploiting natural resources with its jurisdiction was a controversial matter in international law.

Various resolutions of the United Nations General Assembly's *Charter on the Economic Rights and Duties of States* say that a host country is free to "exercise full permanent sovereignty including possession, use, and disposal over all its wealth, natural resources, and economic activities." At the same time, Article 12 of the *Harvard Draft Convention on International Responsibility of States for Injuries to Aliens* also says that "the violation through arbitrary action of the state of a contract or concession to which the central government of that state and alien are parties is wrongful." Furthermore, under the Hickenlooper amendment to protect US investors in foreign countries, the US government is obligated to cut off all aid to any country that nationalizes the property or activities of any US investor "without adequate compensation." Many considered it a bold move for Ghana to call Valco into renegotiations, but at the same time, Ghana's reasons were being heard internationally, and Valco needed to respond.

Between 1982 and 1985, Ghana and Valco were engaged in renegotiations. Ghana's primary concern about the invalidity of the previous terms was that power production was calculated by average power. Valco was entitled to a percentage of VRA's average generating potential. In a country where there is a diversified, relatively stable power infrastructure, average power is an appropriate measure of available power. Ghana argued that due to the variable nature of hydroelectric power, the terms should have been assessed on a firm power basis, that is, by the actual generating potential at a given time. If the system faced a drought, with power generation being far less than average, Ghana argued that they would be unfairly obligated to provide power that would not be attainable for the system. Not only did the renegotiations succeed in rewriting the contracts in terms of firm power, but also, Ghana's relations with the US were preserved.

Under the Master Agreement, Valco was allowed to mine bauxite from about 40 square miles of land within Ghana without paying duties on mining or processing. However, the Agreement (under Article 20) also allowed Valco to import "all raw materials" from other countries duty-free as long as such materials were not locally available in quality, quantity, or at competitive prices. Since aluminum was Valco's primary resource, an exception was permitted to exclude it from Article 20. Valco was free to import alumina *duty-free* from wherever it pleased, even if comparable alumina was available in Ghana. Consequently, Ghana lost the import duty on alumina as a levying weapon against increases in electricity production costs. As of 1998, Valco imported 100% of its alumina from Jamaica, which was processed in Ghana at a low electricity price rate. Only 10% of the finished product remained in the country and 90% was exported to Europe (Ghana Independent, June 11, 1998).

In 1977 and 1978, "wildcat strike action" resulted from rebellious struggles against the Ghana government (Tsikata, 3). As a result of sabotage, power to Valco was interrupted without notice. Valco demanded compensation of $55 million from the government for repair costs and lost profits, sighting the Master Agreement (Article 7(D)). The clause stated that the government must "make good to Valco all losses, damages, costs, expenses, incurred by Valco by reason of any default on the part of VRA in the fulfillment of its obligations" (Tsikata, 3). It was determined that the government was not directly liable for the interruptions since the forces were beyond the control of VRA. To avoid litigation, the Ghana government paid Valco $10 million.

The "wildcat strike action" against the government may have been attributed to unrest between the military regime and labor unions. From the time of Nkrumah's overthrow well into the 1980s, the government's political climate was characterized by coups and passive military rule. Each successive government assumed power with both its supporters and rivals close at hand. Meanwhile, many believe that the rights of the people were often overlooked in the crossfire. At the time of the strike, labor unions made up of doctors, lawyers, and other professionals were in vocal disagreement with the government over unfair treatment and inadequate salary compensation. Some believe that the reason the government paid Valco $10 million was also to draw eyes away from the civil unrest within the country and put the government in favorable standing with investors.

In 1983, when a severe drought significantly reduced the water level in the dam, VRA began to question the sustainability of hydroelectric power as a sufficient source of electricity for Ghana's future. By August of 1984, the cumulative inflow into Lake Volta reached a 50 year record low, resulting in a water level of 73 meters (239.5 feet), well below VRA's 75.5 meter (248 feet) minimum level of generating power without risk of damaging the turbines. Some critics blamed the power shortages on VRA's poor management of the reservoir, accusing them of "guesswork rather than science" in predicting water levels and spillage quantities (Gitlitz, 1993). The annual flooding cycles are between the months of July and November. The final level after this time often determines the power generating capacity for the following year. In 1992, the water level reached its highest level of 84 meters (275 feet) since the 1982 drought. In June of 1997, VRA predicted satisfactory rainfall. But by the beginning of November 1997, the lake level still lingered around a meager 74 meters (242 feet). After some rains in the northern region, the end of the flooding cycle saw water levels reach only 78 meters (256 feet). Akosombo Dam operated at or below 50% capacity throughout the first half of 1998.

GHANA POWER CRISIS: 1997–1998

Meteorologists attributed the Volta River droughts and the subsequent 1997-1998 Ghana power crisis to El Niño, the worldwide weather phenomenon responsible for climate fluctuations, storms, natural disasters, floods, and droughts around the globe (Aggrey, 1998). Although past droughts have affected power production, the 1997-1998 drought is arguably the worst in Ghana history because of its long duration.

March 23, 1998 marked the eve of the first visit to Ghana by a U.S. President. Bill Clinton arrived to witness the institution of the largest electricity rationing schedule in Ghana history. Under the new plan, electricity would be supplied for 12 out of every 24 hours. Households would be cut to 50 percent of normal power while businesses and industries received between 50 percent and 70 percent (LCG, March 23, 1998).

Effects on the Household

Because of the power crisis, households were forced to look for alternative sources of light energy such as candles, lanterns, rechargeable and battery powered flashlights. A market survey conducted by the Ghana News Agency on the prices of some of these commodities in Accra, Ghana's capital, showed that increased demand for them has led to price hikes and shortages (Aggrey, 1998). Some of the more affluent Ghanaians have purchased private generators for their homes. Demand for generators has increased, but market competition has kept the prices stable. Generators with capacities ranging between 1.4-3.0 KVA range in price between $2300 and $7000 (Aggrey, 1998).

Ghanaian cost of living increased as a result of the power shortage. The shortages have affected demand for imported household electrical appliances such as televisions, stereos, refrigerators, and blenders. Similarly, the prices of Ghanaian manufactured goods and household food items have increased. Even the price of ice has doubled, increasing soda and beer prices at local drink bars. Many factories have been forced to reduce their labor force to avoid economic losses.

Effects on Industry and Exports

As part of the electricity rationing schedule, industries were supplied with slightly more electricity than households were. They received electricity up to 70 percent of the time (LCG, March 23 1998). According to Mr. Emmanuel K. K. Hayford, of Ghana Customs, Excise and Preventive Services (CEPS), who has been watching the effects of the power crisis on industry, these provisions seem to be working well for them. A more difficult endeavor is to estimate the real impact of the power curtailment on export and on the economy as a whole. Because of the special arrangements, most of the industries work round the clock to make up for lost time. Many companies have also purchased heavy-duty generators to supplement the electricity supplied by VRA.

Mr. Hayford commented that because of improper city planning, some of the industries have established themselves within residential zones and vice-versa. Those industries situated in residential zones are relatively small in size and their levels of production are relatively low compared to those located within industrial zones. Their small size, combined with their unfortunate location within residential zones, which receive electricity for 12 hours of the day, greatly reduces their productivity.

Since much of the power curtailment has negative effects only on smaller industries situated in residential zones, and since larger industries have intensified their work schedules to suit their power supply arrangements, one is "tempted to assume that this problem has not affected exports much," says Mr. Hayford. The effect of power curtailment on export quantities is negligible. However, its effects are reflected in increased production cost, since many industries have purchased diesel generators to supplement the power supply. This may raise the price of exports from Ghana (in the case of industrially manufactured goods).

WHAT LIES AHEAD FOR GHANA?

Thermal Energy

The Ghana Generation Planning Study of 1985 identified Combustion Turbines as the most attractive power supplement to the existing hydroelectric system. A Thermal Combustion plant could be powered by Light Crude Oil (LCO) or natural gas. Given the high availability and relatively cheaper cost of fuel, a thermal combustion plant would prove to be both economical and a constant source of power since droughts could not affect generating capacity. A site was identified near Takoradi for the construction of a thermal generating plant at an estimated cost of $400 million.

In 1992, Acres International Ltd. of Canada recommended the construction of a 400 MW generating facility by 1997. The proposed plant was composed of a 300 MW combined cycle plant and a 100 MW simple cycle combustion turbine with associated transmission line expansion to tie it into the existing national grid. Following further analysis and June/July 1993 negotiations with the World Bank, which was the major funding agency, the project was re-dimensioned to 300 MW. The new proposed plant was composed of two 100 MW combustion turbines, each with a 50 MW heat recovery steam generator.

A detailed environmental assessment was performed to ensure that the project met the environmental requirements of the funding agencies. A detailed pre- and post-construction program covered the terestrial ecology of the site and transmission corridor, ambient site air quality, noise "pollution" levels, and biological characteristics of the local marine environment. For example, the cooling water used by the turbines had to be within 2°C of the receiving water temperature before it could be returned to the ocean.

Accelerated by the power crisis and the need for electricity, the first 100 MW combustion turbine was completed and synchronized into the national grid in November of 1997, and the second 100 MW turbine on January 8, 1998. The turbines were online before the rest of the facility was constructed. On March 16, an explosion in the lower chamber of the turbine chimney took one of the 100 MW units out of service. It was quickly repaired and running in order to lessen the effects on the public. Much suspicion surrounded this explosion. Some blamed the accelerated nature of the construction and others blamed the US contractor of using second-grade General Electric components to build the turbines, but VRA attests that new parts were used by their contractor to construct the turbines.

Thermal Power has supplemented the energy grid in Ghana, and many believe that it remains a viable option for future expansion and development. Although the plant was constructed with a 300 MW capacity, the design is adaptable for future expansion to 600 or 900 MW. In February of 1998, CMS Energy Corporation (NYSE:CMS) of Dearborn, Michigan announced it has reached an agreement with the Government of Ghana VRA for the acquisition and expansion of the Takoradi Thermal Power Plant (TTPP) and development of further energy infrastructure projects in Ghana. It would become a 50% partner in ownership and operation of the plant, and also assist to double the capacity of the plant in an accelerated timetable. In 1997 and 1998, the Thermal Plant burned LCO, but the turbine design allowed for a clean switch to cheaper and cleaner-burning natural gas if and when it became more readily available.

Importing Electricity

At June 1998 meetings of West African energy experts in Abidjan, the commercial capital of Ivory Coast, several alternatives were examined to deal with the power crisis which had then spread to Ghana's eastern neighbors, Benin and Togo.

Earlier in March of 1998, Benin Prime Minister Adrien Houngbedji and his Togo counterpart Kwassi Klutse met in Abidjan with officials from Compagnie Ivoirienne d'Electricite (CIE), Ivory Coast's national utility, asking for energy to supplement cutbacks from Ghanaian power exports to their countries. Ivory Coast imported electricity from Ghana for many years until natural gas reserves were discovered off their sea coast. The natural gas reserves, combined with modern, more efficient power plants, transformed Ivory Coast from an importer into an exporter of electricity. As power became more available, the distribution grid within the Ivory Coast developed, and the power demand increased, limiting its export potential. Ivorian sources warned that satisfying the power demands in Benin and Togo could result in shortages in Ivory Coast.

In order to ensure against future West African crises, Ghana had to cooperate with its West African neighbors to establish a secure power network. At the 1998 gold award symposium for the Economic Community of West African States (ECOWAS) in Lagos, Nigeria, Executive Secretary Lansana Kouyate, announced plans to begin construction on the $260 million West African Gas Pipeline by the end of calendar year 1998.

For many years, the vast natural gas reserves trapped in the air above Nigeria's oil reserves were flared away to waste. During the 1998 power crisis, they were viewed as a viable solution and a potential safety buffer against future power shortages. The gas pipeline project followed a World Bank study showing that Nigeria's surplus gas could meet the energy needs of the West African sub-region if well harnessed. According to Kouyate, the goal of the West African Pipeline was to ensure that energy generation in the sub-region would be from gas by the year 2000 (Ikeh, 1998).

According to the plans, the underwater pipeline would extend from Nigeria along the West African coastline to supply natural gas to Ghana, Benin, and Togo. The gas pipeline project is expected to pipe 50 million cubic feet per day of Nigeria's natural gas to the three countries over 20 years, starting from 1999. According to project plans, the volume of gas piped to the countries will rise to 160 million cubic feet per day by the year 2018 (Ikeh, 1998). The West African pipeline could eventually supply natural gas to the Thermal Plant at Takoradi, reducing energy costs (from burning LCO) by more than 50%.

Hydroelectric Power

Other sites for potential hydroelectric plants have been suggested along the Pra, Tao, White Volta, and Ankroba rivers. However, a dam (with an estimated capacity of 400 MW) at Bui, along the Black Volta River in the Brong Ahafo region, is under serious consideration. Future hydroelectric power would require substantial investment, but at the same time, provide a relatively clean source of power.

In a press release early in 1998, Ghana Minister of Mines and Energy, Fred Ohene-Kena, said that depending on the feasibility and designs, Bui may generate between 100 to 200 or 400 MW (Joy 99.7 FM, May 23, 1998). If a 400 MW-producing dam is constructed, the backwaters will inundate parts of the Bui National Park. In 1998, Bui National Park was a protected area of guinea savannah extending about 1800 km^2. International environmentalists noted the Bole Game Reserve and nearby Bui National park as one of the last remaining, highly diverse West African rainforests.

The Volta River Authority performed extensive site studies of the area encompassed within the Bui National Park. It was realized that the boundaries of the park were poorly defined, and not well secured. Poachers, illegal farmers and fishermen entered the land at will to take advantage of the available resources. About 383 km^2 of land (20% of the National Park) would be flooded if the Bui Dam were constructed. As compensation, VRA proposed to secure the Game Reserve by establishing protected boundaries, and hiring rangers to monitor the up keep and preservation of the entire area. With the construction of the Bui Dam would also come the establishment of a defined and protected National Park, and secured buffer zones surrounding the boundaries. The objective of these buffer zones was to better involve the local population in the protection of the park by developing activities (such as tourism, controlled hunting, and fishing) which would generate profit for the people in harmony with the protection of the park.

For the long-term plan of the Bui hydro project, the Swedish-American Company, SKANSA, expressed interest to build on a turnkey basis. SKANSA, which had a lot of interests in Southern and Eastern Africa, had also shown interest in toll roads construction in Ghana and even had plans to start feasibility studies on the projects. In 1998, SKANSA was actively building pipelines for water from Kpong to Accra and also expressed interest in the Kotoka International airport improvement project and the Ambassador Hotel rehabilitation program in Accra. It established a Ghana office, which was also responsible for projects in Burkina Faso, Cote d'Ivoire and Nigeria (Joy 99.7 FM, May 23, 1998).

Some Other Options

In late 1994, a research nuclear reactor was nearing completion at Kwabenyan, near Accra. At that time, the Ghana Atomic Energy Commission (GAEC) also recommended the construction of another nuclear physics center in Kumasi at the University of Science and Technology. They believe that if properly researched and implemented, nuclear energy could provide a lasting source of emission-free power to meet all of Ghana's energy needs. But critics say that Ghana does not have the proper infrastructure to deal with the possibility of a nuclear disaster resulting from an accident at a nuclear generating station. By 1998 VRA had not actively entertained the possibility of adding nuclear power to its power options. The push for nuclear power also suffers from growing sentiment against the construction of new plants.

Solar energy has been used on an experimental basis. It was viewed as a possible way of electrifying rural regions outside of the power grid. Due to high capital costs, solar power has not surfaced as a viable option for wide-scale integration in Ghana

Small, localized, and relatively cheap fossil fuel plants have been constructed at some locations in Ghana to supplement power demand. For example, VRA had a 30 MW capacity diesel plant at Tema, which operates during the peak hours of 1700 GMT to 2200 GMT (Panafrican, 1997). Although these plants provide a temporary solution to localized problems, the challenges of ensuring future national power viability outshadow prospects of further localized plants.

In the heat of the 1998 power crisis, Ghana faced important decisions to safeguard its future economic viability. In 1994, 1997, and 1998, water levels were not sufficient to power hydroelectric generators to meet Ghana's growing energy demands. This led to a nationwide electricity rationing schedule, reduction in exported electricity to Togo and Benin, and extensive negotiations and monetary compensation to Valco.

Decision makers (a few of whom include the Ghana Department of Mines and Energy, VRA, and the Ghana Electricity Supply Company), must make practical, affordable, and sustainable choices for electricity in Ghana. The options include: (1) thermal energy (2) importing electricity, (3) construction of additional hydroelectric dam(s), and (4) other options such as nuclear energy, solar energy, and other fossil fuel powered plants and generators. If you were a consultant to the Ghana Department of Mines and Energy, what would you recommend?

President Clinton's 1998 visit to Ghana brought new spirit to U.S. and multinational interest in Ghana. Many Ghanaians regard the flood of companies coming to Ghana for power generation, among other reasons, as a benefit to Ghana. How will the lessons from Ghana's history and past experiences affect Ghana's dealings with these multinational interests? What steps must be taken to ensure that future agreements and projects are economically and environmentally sustainable?

Acknowledgments

Special thanks to Mr. R.O. Ankrah, Engineer and Executive Director, Takoradi Thermal Power Plant Project, and family for their loving hospitality and assistance; Frank Ashon, Systems Administrator VRA information networks; Agyenim-Boateng, Manager Engineering Personnel, Fisheries Expert and Historian; Emmanuel Antwi-Darkwa and Theophilus Sackey, Civil Engineers VRA Akuse; Owura K. Sarfo, Manager VRA Engineering Department in Akuse; Erik N. Yankah, VRA Executive Director of Personnel, member 1982-1985 VRA-Valco Negotiations Team; Ricky Evans-Appiah and J. Amissah-Arthur, Administrator and Director VRA Engineering and Design Department Akuse; K. K. Hayford, Ghana Customs Excise and Preventive Services; Esther Riverson, Ph.D., Ghana Ressettlement Project Specialist; John Riverson, World Bank; Albert Wright, World Bank, and former Professor, University of Ghana.

Sources

Aggrey, Emily (May 25, 1998). "El Niño Causes High Energy Prices." Panafrican News Agency, http://www.africanews.org/west/ghana/stories/19980525_feat2.html.

Central Intelligence Agency, U.S. (1995). *The World Factbook.* September 07, 1995.

Ghana: A Country Study (1995). ed. LaVerle Berry. Federal Research Division, Library of Congress: Washington, D.C.

Ghana Focus (May 19, 1998). "Rich fishermen exploiting children." Africa News Online. http://www.africanews.org/west/ghana/stories/19980519_feat1.html.

Gitlitz, Jennifer (August 1993). "The Relationship Between Primary Aluminum Production and the Damming of the World's Rivers." International Rivers Network (IRN) Working Paper #2.

Graham, Ronald. "Structural Problems in the World Economy: A Case Study of the Ghana-Valco Renegotiations." Published in *Essays from Ghana-Valco Renegotiations,* ed. Fui S. Tsikata. VRA: Accra, 1986 (pp. 87-111).

Hart, David (1980). *The Volta River Project.* Edinburgh University Press: Edinburgh, UK.

Ikeh, Goddy (June 2, 1998). "West African Gas Pipeline Takes Off 1998." Panafrican News Agency, http://www.africanews.org/west/stories/19980602_feat3.html.

Impregilo (1982). *1956/1981: Twenty-Five Years of Worldwide Activity.* Impregilo: Milan, Italy.

Joy 99.7 FM (May 23, 1998). "No More Power Outages for Industries by July," http://www.joy997fm.com.gh/news2.htm#This Week's Stories.

Kaiser (November 14, 1997). "Kaiser Aluminum Smelter in Ghana Receives Notice of Reduced Power Allocations for 1998." Company Press Release, http://f2.yahoo.com/bw/97114/Kaiser_aluminum_1.html.

Kaplan, Irving et al. (1971). *Area Handbook for Ghana.* Library of Congress: Washington D.C.

LCG Consulting (March 23, 1998). "Ghana Power Crisis Spreads Along Gold Coast." EnergyOnline, http://www.energyonline.com/Restructuring/news_reports/news/c23afr.html.

Moore, James (1989). *Balancing the Needs of Water Use.* Springer-Verlag: New York.

Moxon, James (1984). *Volta, Man's Greatest Lake.* Deutsch: London.

Panafrican News Agency (August 23, 1997). "Ghanaians Told to Conserve Power." Africa News Online, http://www.africanews.org/west/ghana/stories/19970823_feat1.html.

Sawyerr, Akilagpa. "Some Legal Issues Arising from the Valco Agreement." Published in *Essays from Ghana-Valco Renegotiations*, ed. Fui S. Tsikata. VRA: Accra, 1986 (pp. 60-86).

Sims, Rod and Louis Casely-Hayford. "Renegotiating the Price and Availability of Energy." Published in *Essays from Ghana-Valco Renegotiations*, ed. Fui S. Tsikata. VRA: Accra, 1986 (pp. 15-50).

Tsikata, Fui. "Dealing with a Transnational Corporation." Published in *Essays from Ghana-Valco Renegotiations*, ed. Fui S. Tsikata. VRA: Accra, 1986 (pp. 1-14).

EXHIBIT 1
SOME KEY WORDS

Alumina A powder of refined bauxite that is smelted at high temperatures to form aluminum products.

Bauxite A mineral ore containing aluminum oxide or hydroxides with several impurities.

Bui A town in western Ghana. Potential site for a hydroelectric dam.

Burkina Faso Ghana's northern neighbor. Previously called Upper Volta.

Gold Coast Name given by first Portugese explorers to the territory that is now Ghana. Became the Republic of Ghana after independence from Great Britain in 1957.

Impregilo Italian contractor who constructed Akosombo and Kpong Dams.

Kaiser, Edgar American owner and founder of Kaiser Aluminum Corporation.

Kitson, Albert (*later* Sir) Director of the Gold Coast Geological Survey, discovered bauxite deposits near Mpraeso in 1914 and first proposed a dam at Akosombo.

Kpong Dam A smaller hydroelectric plant, downstream from Akosombo Dam, on the Volta River.

Master Agreement The document outlining the negotiations and the terms governing the relationship between VALCO and VRA.

Nkrumah, Kwame African rights activist and Ghana's first elected president.

Rose, Duncan English engineer who had a keen interest in aluminum production.

St. John Bird, Christopher South African Engineer who worked with Duncan Rose to spur international interest for aluminum production in Ghana.

Takoradi Thermal Power Plant. VRA Light Crude Oil/Natural Gas power plant constructed to supplement hydroelectric power from Akosombo and Kpong.

Volta Aluminum Corporation (VALCO). A consortium of American aluminum companies including Kaiser (78%), Reynolds (10%).

Volta River Authority (VRA). Ghana's statuary power provider.

Volta River Project. The name given to the association of the Volta River Authority (VRA), and the Volta Aluminum Corporation (VALCO).

EXHIBIT 2
MAP OF GHANA

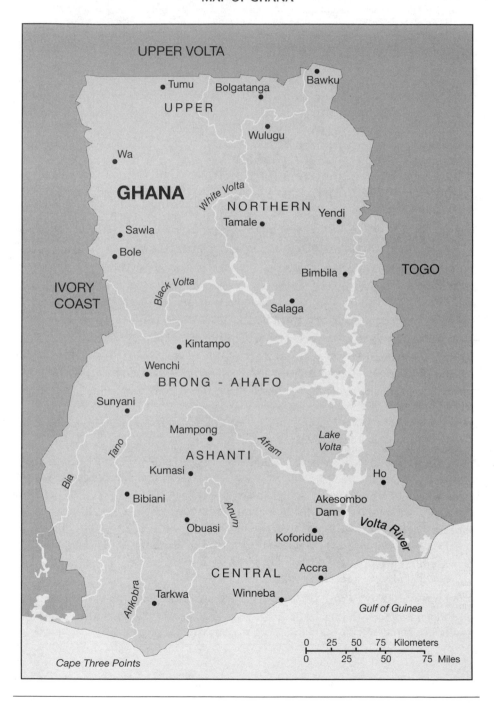

EXHIBIT 3
PRINCIPAL AGREEMENTS

Schematic diagram of financing participants and principal agreements for the Volta River Project, executed on February 8, 1962 (Hart, 31)

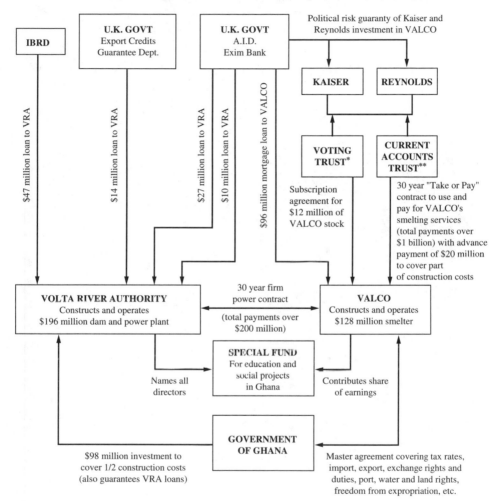

*Morgan Guaranty Trust Co., Voting Trustee. . . if VALCO fails to build smelter, voting trustee replaces management until construction completed.
**First National City Bank of New York, Trustee . . . Handles all payments by Kaiser and Reynolds to VALCO, payment of VALCO expenses and taxes, and retains balance in New York.